Palgrave Studies in the History of Social Movements

Series Editors
Stefan Berger
Institute for Social Movements
Ruhr University Bochum
Bochum, Germany

Holger Nehring
Contemporary European History
University of Stirling
Stirling, UK

Around the world, social movements have become legitimate, yet contested, actors in local, national and global politics and civil society, yet we still know relatively little about their longer histories and the trajectories of their development. This series seeks to promote innovative historical research on the history of social movements in the modern period since around 1750. We bring together conceptually-informed studies that analyse labour movements, new social movements and other forms of protest from early modernity to the present. We conceive of 'social movements' in the broadest possible sense, encompassing social formations that lie between formal organisations and mere protest events. We also offer a home for studies that systematically explore the political, social, economic and cultural conditions in which social movements can emerge. We are especially interested in transnational and global perspectives on the history of social movements, and in studies that engage critically and creatively with political, social and sociological theories in order to make historically grounded arguments about social movements. This new series seeks to offer innovative historical work on social movements, while also helping to historicise the concept of 'social movement'. It hopes to revitalise the conversation between historians and historical sociologists in analysing what Charles Tilly has called the 'dynamics of contention'.

More information about this series at
http://www.palgrave.com/gp/series/14580

Stefan Berger · Alexandra Przyrembel
Editors

Moralizing Capitalism

Agents, Discourses and Practices of Capitalism
and Anti-Capitalism in the Modern Age

Editors
Stefan Berger
Institute for Social Movements
Ruhr University Bochum
Bochum, Germany

Alexandra Przyrembel
Modern European History
University of Hagen
Hagen, Germany

Palgrave Studies in the History of Social Movements
ISBN 978-3-030-20564-5   ISBN 978-3-030-20565-2   (eBook)
https://doi.org/10.1007/978-3-030-20565-2

This Palgrave Macmillan imprint is published by the registered company Springer Nature Switzerland AG
The registered company address is: Gewerbestrasse 11, 6330 Cham, Switzerland

Series Editors' Preface

Around the world, social movements have become legitimate, yet contested, actors in local, national and global politics and civil society, yet we still know relatively less about their longer histories and the trajectories of their development. Our series reacts to what can be described as a recent boom in the history of social movements. We can observe a development from the crisis of labour history in the 1980s to the boom in research on social movements in the 2000s. The rise of historical interests in the development of civil society and the role of strong civil societies as well as non-governmental organisations in stabilizing democratically constituted polities has strengthened the interest in social movements as a constituent element of civil societies.

In different parts of the world, social movements continue to have a strong influence on contemporary politics. In Latin America, trade unions, labour parties and various left-of-centre civil society organisations have succeeded in supporting left-of-centre governments. In Europe, peace movements, ecological movements and alliances intent on campaigning against poverty and racial discrimination and discrimination on the basis of gender and sexual orientation have been able to set important political agendas for decades. In other parts of the world, including Africa, India and South East Asia, social movements have played a significant role in various forms of community building and community politics. The contemporary political relevance of social movements has undoubtedly contributed to a growing historical interest in the topic.

Contemporary historians are not only beginning to historicise these relatively recent political developments; they are also trying to relate them to a longer history of social movements, including traditional labour organisations, such as working-class parties and trade unions. In the longue durée, we recognise that social movements are by no means a recent phenomenon and are not even an exclusively modern phenomenon, although we realise that the onset of modernity emanating from Europe and North America across the wider world from the eighteenth century onwards marks an important departure point for the development of civil societies and social movements.

In the nineteenth and twentieth centuries the dominance of national history over all other forms of history writing led to a thorough nationalisation of the historical sciences. Hence social movements have been examined traditionally within the framework of the nation state. Only during the last two decades have historians begun to question the validity of such methodological nationalism and to explore the development of social movements in comparative, connective and transnational perspective taking into account processes of transfer, reception and adaptation. Whilst our book series does not preclude work that is still being carried out within national frameworks (for, clearly, there is a place for such studies, given the historical importance of the nation state in history), it hopes to encourage comparative and transnational histories on social movements.

At the same time as historians have begun to research the history of those movements, a range of social theorists, from Jürgen Habermas to Pierre Bourdieu and from Slavoj Žižek to Alain Badiou as well as Ernesto Laclau and Chantal Mouffe to Miguel Abensour, to name but a few, have attempted to provide philosophical-cum-theoretical frameworks in which to place and contextualise the development of social movements. History has arguably been the most empirical of all the social and human sciences, but it will be necessary for historians to explore further to what extent these social theories can be helpful in guiding and framing the empirical work of the historian in making sense of the historical development of social movements. Hence the current series is also hoping to make a contribution to the ongoing dialogue between social theory and the history of social movements.

This series seeks to promote innovative historical research on the history of social movements in the modern period since around 1750. We bring together conceptually-informed studies that analyse labour movements, new social movements and other forms of protest from early modernity to the present. With this series, we seek to revive, within the context of historiographical developments since the 1970s, a conversation between historians on the one hand and sociologists, anthropologists and political scientists on the other.

Unlike most of the concepts and theories developed by social scientists, we do not see social movements as directly linked, a priori, to processes of social and cultural change and therefore do not adhere to a view that distinguishes between old (labour) and new (middle-class) social movements. Instead, we want to establish the concept 'social movement' as a heuristic device that allows historians of the nineteenth and twentieth centuries to investigate social and political protests in novel settings. Our aim is to historicise notions of social and political activism in order to highlight different notions of political and social protest on both left and right.

Hence, we conceive of 'social movements' in the broadest possible sense, encompassing social formations that lie between formal organisations and mere protest events. But we also include processes of social and cultural change more generally in our understanding of social movements: this goes back to nineteenth-century understandings of 'social movement' as processes of social and cultural change more generally. We also offer a home for studies that systematically explore the political, social, economic and cultural conditions in which social movements can emerge. We are especially interested in transnational and global perspectives on the history of social movements, and in studies that engage critically and creatively with political, social and sociological theories in order to make historically grounded arguments about social movements. In short, this series seeks to offer innovative historical work on social movements, while also helping to historicise the concept of 'social movement'. It also hopes to revitalise the conversation between historians and historical sociologists in analysing what Charles Tilly has called the 'dynamics of contention'.

A European Youth Revolt is asking the question whether the diverse urban protest movements of the 1980s can be summed up under the label of a youth revolt. Highlighting the internationalism of these networks of social movements in the 1980s, this volume edited by Andresen and Steen is seeking to identify a number of characteristics that united a set of highly diverse movements which were nevertheless often seen, also by contemporary observers, as belonging together and forming one movement. Thus, these social movements were often characterised by an emphasis on subjectivity ('the personal is the political') and a desire to act within local contexts. Dismissive of formal politics and political parties, the movements sought to create autonomous political spaces of their own. Certain movements within the movement especially the house occupation movement obtained a prominent place and sometimes became the public face of the movement which was, however, always broader than squatting. Overall, the volume is underlining the European-wide repercussions of these protest movements that even found echoes behind the iron curtain.

The diverse contributions in this volume are united by their desire to highlight how ideas and practices transgressed national boundaries and how transnational protest networks emerged in the 1980s. Uniting the fields of culture and politics, the volume puts a spotlight on protest politics that was often strongly intertwined with youth politics and frequently had the hallmarks of a new youth movement. Europe, youth, revolt and the 1980s are the four pillars in this book that uphold an edifice of scholarly investigation that is tantalisingly fresh and demonstrates the vitality of transdisciplinary research between social science and contemporary history. It is an edifice with many rooms, many of which are designed quite differently. There is sometimes little unity in the phenomena that all find a place in this house and the overview of its many inhabitants is sometimes quite kaleidoscopic. Nevertheless the editors have been successful in assembling a volume that has an inner unity and showcases 1980s social and political protest as having common roots, strategies and self-understandings.

Moralizing Capitalism: Agents, Discourses and Practices of Capitalism and Anti-Capitalism in the Modern Age introduces questions of morality to the booming field of the history of capitalism. In many studies capitalism still appears predominantly as an economic system that has to be analysed, above all, with the toolbox of the economic historian using economic benchmarks. Within the framework of political economy, political processes influencing economic decision-making has also been analysed in great detail. However, the contributions assembled in this volume analyse capitalism through the lens of cultural and intellectual history asking about moral values and their impact on the development of capitalism and its critics. The articles deal predominantly with ideas and cultural practices and their influence on economic, social and political processes. The agency of diverse actors, who were either opposed to capitalism or defended it are being put centre-stage.

The editors have divided the book into four parts. The first one examines capitalism as knowledge system that can be taught and evaluated on the basis of specific moral criteria. Thus, criticisms of wealth accumulation stand next to moral and religious justifications of capitalism. The second part of the book examines aspects of political economy and the impact of questions of morality on this field. Here we encounter notions of fair taxation, ideas of combining capitalist practice with humanistic endeavour, and thoughts about turning multinational companies into morally responsible citizens. The third part of this volume investigates the ethics of capitalists, in particular those working for the stock exchange and merchants confronted with bankruptcy. Finally, the book also takes an in-depth view at social movements and their problematisation of capitalist practices. Here issues of morality were very much to the fore. Thus we encounter Catholic critiques of economic justice in the US, ideas about 'shameful profiteering' underpinning anti-capitalist movements, attempts to achieve fairer systems of trade, and changing ideas of morality associated with the boom years of capitalism after the Second World War. Overall, this volume provides tantalising glimpses of a history of capitalism that takes seriously the toolbox of the new cultural history that has also increasingly influenced traditional forms of history writing, including economic, social and political history. In this sense the volume makes a contribution to a reconceptualised history of capitalism that takes as starting point an understanding of capitalism as a cultural system that, like an octopus, expanded into all spheres of life and cannot be reduced to economics alone.

Bochum, Germany   Stefan Berger
Stirling, UK   Holger Nehring

ACKNOWLEDGEMENTS

The history of capitalism is booming. This was also reflected in the reactions we received to our call for papers. In March 2016 we organized the conference "Moralizing Capitalism: Agents, Discourses and Practices of Capitalism and its Opponents in the Modern Age". Our aim was to link economic historical perspectives with cultural questions. In particular we wanted to explore to what extent morality mattered in criticism and justifications of capitalism. In the course of the three days, a variety of different topics were discussed: from the history of slavery, one of the classic themes of the history of capitalism, to theoretical approaches to case studies on waste disposal or labor relations in India. We thank all the participants of the conference for the lively exchange at the conference. Special thanks go to Prof. Dr. Jürgen Kocka (Berlin), who set central impulses with his opening remarks on the history of capitalism. We wish to thank our authors for their patience in going through several rounds of revisions in the aftermath of the conference to arrive at what we hope to be a coherent volume.

We also have to thank our research assistants Stefan Braun, Alexander Dufft and Claudia Scheel for helping us to organize the conference. Furthermore a special thank you goes to the team of the study center Berlin (FernUniversität in Hagen) where the conference took place. The FernUniversität in Hagen also supported the conference financially. All in all, the three days in Berlin turned out to be both intellectually stimulating and enjoyable.

Many colleagues were involved in making this book. Especially we have to thank Dr. David Kelly (Western Sydney University, Australia), who proofread the manuscript with patience and sensitivity. Claudia Scheel and Alessandra Exter have been very supportive in helping to finalize the manuscript. At Palgrave Molly Beck, Oliver Dyer and Maeve Sinnott have been, as usual, exemplary editors.

Last but not least, we would like to express our gratitude to the Thyssen Stiftung for its generous financial support of the conference "Moralizing Capitalism" and for the copy-editing of this volume. Without this generous support, it would not have been possible to produce this sustained reflection on the interrelation between capitalism and morality from the nineteenth to the twentieth centuries.

Fritz Thyssen Stiftung
für Wissenschaftsförderung

CONTENTS

Notes on Contributors

Stefan Berger is Professor of Social History and Director of the Institute for Social Movements at Ruhr University Bochum. He is also Executive Chair of the Foundation History of the Ruhr and an Honorary Professor at Cardiff University in the UK. He has published widely on the history of deindustrialization, industrial heritage, memory studies, the history of historiography, nationalism, and labour movement history. His most recent publications are a special issue, co-edited with Steven High, on de-industrialization by the North American journal Labor 19:1 (2019) as well as a special issue on German labour history by the British journal German History 32:2 (2019).

Christian Olaf Christiansen is Associate Professor at Aarhus University, Institute for Culture and Society. Christian is an intellectual historian working with twentieth century economic and political thought in an American and global context. He currently works a comparative intellectual history of two approaches to reducing global poverty during post-war globalization: socio-economic human rights and market/business-based ideas for poverty reduction. Starting in 2019, Christian will be the research leader on the project "An Intellectual History of Global Inequality, 1960–2015", investigating the relationship between geographic location and the intellectual history of inequality. Publications include *Progressive Business: An Intellectual History of the Role of Business in Society* (Oxford University Press, 2015) and *Global Inequality: New Historical Perspectives* (Palgrave, 2019). In 2015, Christian was awarded the Sapere Aude: DFF Young Research Talent grant by the Danish Council for Independent Research, and in 2018 he was awarded the Sapere Aude: DFF Research Leader by the Independent Research Fund Denmark.

Giulia D'Alessio obtained her Ph.D. in Contemporary History from the University of Rome La Sapienza with a dissertation entitled *Holy See and United States during the pontificate of Pius XI: Catholic Social Doctrine, the Great Depression and the New Deal.* She has been Visiting Researcher at the History Department of Georgetown University (Washington, DC), Banca d'Italia Postdoctoral Fellow at FSCIRE (Fondazione per le Scienze Religiose Giovanni XXIII, Bologna), adjunct (Contemporary History) at the University of Rome la Sapienza and collaborated as a book reviewer with "La Civiltà Cattolica". Her main research interests include USA–Vatican relations, Catholic Social Doctrine, American Catholic Social Thought. She has published articles and book chapters on these topics. Among others: 'Stati Uniti, Chiesa cattolica e questione sociale', in *Diplomazia senza eserciti*, eds. Emma Fattorini, Rome, Carocci, 2013; 'Il dialogo fra Stati Uniti e Santa Sede negli anni Trenta. Tre figure di mediazione Cicognani, Pacelli, Spellman', in Pettinaroli Laura (ed.), *Le gouvernement pontifical sous Pie XI. Pratiques romaines et gestion de l'universel*, Rome, Ecole française de Rome, 2013; 'United States and Vatican 1936–1939: from Eugenio Pacelli's visit to the U.S. to Myron Taylor's Mission to the Holy See', in C. R. Gallagher, D. I. Kertzer, A. Melloni (Eds.), *Pius XI and the Americas: Proceedings of the Brown University Conference*, LIT Verlag, Berlin, Münster-Wien-Zurich-London 2012; *Dialogo e rapporti diplomatici fra Stati Uniti e Santa Sede dagli anni Trenta alla seconda guerra mondiale,* "L'Osservatore Romano", pp. 4–5, 15 January, 2011; *Santa Sede, Stati Uniti e cattolicesimo americano negli anni di Pio XI* in A. Guasco, R. Perin (eds.), *Pius XI Keywords*, LIT Verlag, Berlin- Münster- Wien-Zurich-London 2010.

Wim de Jong is a postdoctoral researcher at the Open Universiteit Nederland. He has published on the history of democracy and citizenship education in the Netherlands, the history of freedom of education, history of electoral culture, and the role of social science experts in democratic politics. His most recent publication is on apathy and antipolitics in the post-war Netherlands, 'Partizipationsunterlassung, Antipolitik und Apathie als *repertoires of democracy*: die Niederlande im europäischen Kontext (1945–1990)', in: Theo Jung (ed.), *Zwischen Handeln* *und Nicht-Handeln. Unterlassungspraktiken in der europäischen Moderne* (Frankfurt/New York: Campus 2019) pp. 64–100 and Mapping the Demos: The Scientisation of the Political, Electoral Research and Dutch Political Parties, c. 1900–1980', *Contemporary European History* (2017) nr. 1, pp. 111–138, with Harm Kaal.

Jürgen Finger is head of the Department of contemporary history at the German Historical Institute in Paris. He published on the history of National Socialism, post-war trials, business history, the history of social norms and French social history. His recent publications include articles about life spheres of the rich in Nazi Germany (in: Gajek/Kurr/Seegers, *Reichtum in Deutschland*, Wallstein publisher, 2019, 77–97) and speculative practices of John and Jane Doe on the gray financial market of Belle Époque Paris (Archiv für Sozialgeschichte 56 (2019), 139–168).

Boris Gehlen is Associate Professor ('Privatdozent') of Economic and Social History at Bonn University and Researcher at the Institute for Contemporary History Munich-Berlin. His main research areas are financial and business history. His most recent publications are Corporate Law and Corporate Control in West Germany after 1945 (Business History, published online (http://dx.doi.org/10.1080/00076791.2017.1319939) and a paper on Regulation and admission practices at the Berlin Stock Exchange (*Jahrbuch für Wirtschaftsgeschichte* 2018/1).

Elsbeth Heaman is a professor of history at McGill University in Montreal. The author of several books on the Canadian state, taxation, and exhibitions, she is currently completing a new project on civilization, history, and conservative politics in Canada.

Sibylle Marti is a lecturer in modern European history at the FernUniversität in Hagen, Germany. Her dissertation deals with the history of radiation research and radiation protection in Cold War Switzerland. Recently, she co-edited a volume on the imaginary of the Cold War. Her postdoctoral research project funded by the Swiss National Science Foundation (SNSF) explores the history of informal labour in the twentieth century.

Sandra Maß is Professor of Nineteenth Century Transnational History at Ruhr University Bochum. She is co-editor of "L'Homme. Europäische Zeitschrift für feministische Geschichtswissenschaft". Her recent publications include: Kinderstube des Kapitalismus? Monetäre Erziehung im 18. und 19. Jahrhundert, Berlin/Boston 2018 [Publications of the

German Historical Institute; 75]; Useful knowledge. Monetary educa-
tion of children and the moralization of productivity in the nineteenth
Century, in: Bänziger, Peter-Paul; Suter, Mischa (eds.): *Histories of
Productivity: Genealogical Perspectives on the Body and Modern Economy.*
London: Routledge 2017, pp. 74–91; Ed. with Margareth Lanzinger
and Claudia Opitz, Ökonomien (Economies), special issue of L'Homme.
Europäische Zeitschrift für feministische Geschichtswissenschaft 1, 2016.

Benjamin Möckel is Assistant Professor at the University of Cologne.
Currently, he is a fellow at the Oxford Centre for European History. He
has published on the history of generations, post-war memory in East
and West Germany, consumer history and popular culture in post-war
Europe. His most recent publications include: The Material Culture of
Human Rights. Consumer Products, Boycotts, and the Transformation
of Human Rights Activism in the 1970s and 1980s, in: *International
Journal for History, Culture and Modernity* 6 (2018) 1, S.76–104, and:
Humanitarianism on Stage: Live Aid and the Origins of Humanitarian
Pop Music, in: Joachim Häberlen/Mark Keck-Szajbel/Kate Mahoney
(Hg.), *The Politics of Authenticity. Countercultures and Radical
Movements Across the Iron Curtain, 1968–1989* (Berghahn, 2019).

Nikos Potamianos is an assistant researcher at the Institute for
Mediterranean Studies—Foundation for Research and Technology-Hellas,
based in Rethymno, Greece. He is member of the academic board in the
journal *Ta Istorika*. He has published widely on the contemporary social
and political history of Greece, focusing on labour history, the lower middle class of shopkeepers and artisans, populism and radicalism. His new
book is about the social history of the carnival of Athens in 1800–1940
(Cretan University Press, forthcoming). He is currently working on the
concept of moral economy and its potential for historical research.

Alexandra Przyrembel is Professor of Modern European History in
Hagen. She has published on the history of antisemitism, of sexuality, history of emotions, history of knowledge and most recently on the history
of memory studies. Her most recent publications are a book chapter on
emotions and National Socialism and an edited volume on sites of memory
(Emotions and National Socialism, in: *A Companion to Nazi Germany*,
New York (2018); Erinnerungsorte im Bild, Bielefeld 2019). Most
recently, she also participated in a roundtable on New Directions in the
history of knowledge and postcolonial history (Trajectories 29 (2018)).

Thomas Sokoll is Professor of Early Modern History at the University of Hagen. His research interests include historical demography, historical anthropology, the comparative study of structure and change in pre-modern Europe 700 BC–1850, the social and cultural history of poverty and the industrialisation in Britain. His most recent publications are concerned with Max Weber's theory of modern capitalism and its historical reception.

Abbreviations

A3WH	Aktion Dritte Welt Handel
AFL-CIO	American Federation of Labor and Congress of Industrial Organizations
AG3WL	Arbeitsgemeinschaft Dritte Welt Läden
ASWSP	Archiv für Sozialwissenschaft und Sozialpolitik
CDU	Christian Democratic Union of Germany
CIA	Central Intelligence Agency
CSR	Corporate Social Responsibility
ECA	Economic Cooperation Administration
ECOSOC	United Nations Economic and Social Council
EEC	European Economic Community
EPA	European Productivity Agency
EU	European Union
FAE	Fund for Adult Education
FDR	Franklin Delano Roosevelt
G77	Group of 77
GDR	German Democratic Republic
GEP	Group of Eminent Persons
GEPA	Gesellschaft zur Förderung der Partnerschaft mit der Dritten Welt mbh
NCWC	National Catholic Welfare Council
NGO	Non-governmental organization
NIEO	New International Economic Order
NYSE	New York Stock Exchange
OPEC	Organization of the Petroleum Exporting Countries
PE	Protestant Ethic

RN	*Rerum Novarum*
SPD	Social Democratic Party of Germany
UNCTAD	United Nations Conference on Trade and Development
UNESCO	United Nations Educational, Scientific and Cultural Organization
US(A)	United States (of America)
USSR	Union of Soviet Socialist Republics

LIST OF TABLES

CHAPTER 1

Introduction:
Moralizing Capitalism: Agents, Discourses and Practices of Capitalism and Anti-capitalism in the Modern Age

Stefan Berger and Alexandra Przyrembel

'MORALIZING CAPITALISM'? CONCEPT AND IDEA

The book 'Moralizing Capitalism' ties in with the current research interest in the history of capitalism and chooses a very specific perspective: it is interested in the relationship between morality and capitalism. But what actually are moral sentiments, and how did they change over time? What is to be understood by 'capitalist morality' and what role do moral beliefs play for the implementation and consolidation of capitalism?

S. Berger (✉)
Institute for Social Movements,
Ruhr University Bochum, Bochum, Germany
e-mail: Stefan.Berger@ruhr-uni-bochum.de

A. Przyrembel
Modern European History,
University of Hagen, Hagen, Germany
e-mail: alexandra.przyrembel@fernuni-hagen.de

© The Author(s) 2019
S. Berger and A. Przyrembel (eds.), *Moralizing Capitalism*,
Palgrave Studies in the History of Social Movements,
https://doi.org/10.1007/978-3-030-20565-2_1

1

To what extent did social movements opposed to capitalism establish an independent 'moral economy'? And what moral arguments did entrepreneurs use to legitimize 'morally' their decisions, some of which might have threatened social peace?

While the history of capitalism is flourishing,[1] the interconnections between 'morality' and capitalism have hardly been addressed so far. In 1971 E. P. Thompson used the concept of 'moral economy' to understand the moral values of social groups that revolted against industrialization. In his essay 'The Moral Economy of the English Crowd in the Eighteenth Century', he rejected the assumption of economic historians that in the eighteenth-century uprisings of hunger were caused by deprivation. Instead, Thompson claimed that such revolts were based on 'consistent traditional views of social norms and obligations, of the proper economic functions of several parties within the community, which, taken together, can be said to constitute the moral economy of the poor'.[2] As the author notes ironically in a later essay, in which he responds to his critics, the concept moral economy 'has long forgotten its paternity'.[3] What Thompson alludes to is that the concept of the 'moral economy' wandered from the eighteenth century to modern history to explain various historical phenomena. Since the publication of Thompson's essay historians with different research interests have taken up his concept. William G. Reddy for example understands moral economy as 'a set of values and moral standards that were violated by technical and commercial change'.[4] Recently, anthropologists such as Didier Fassin have applied the concept of 'morality' and 'moral sentiments' to different fields that represent challenges (i.e. migration politics, humanitarian aid, the making of punishment) for contemporary society. Fassin provides a very broad

---

[1] Sven Beckert, *Empire of Cotton: A New History of Global Capitalism* (London: Allen Lane, 2014); Jürgen Kocka and Marcel van der Linden, eds., *Capitalism: The Reemergence of a Historical Concept* (London: Bloomsbury Academic, 2016).

[2] E. P. Thompson, 'The Moral Economy of the English Crowd in the Eighteenth Century', *Past & Present* 50 (1971): 76–136.

[3] E. P. Thompson, *Customs in Common* (London: Merlin Press, 1991), 351.

[4] William M. Reddy, *The Rise of Market Culture: The Textile Trade and French Society, 1750–1900* (Cambridge: Cambridge University Press, 1987), 331–333, for a critical comment, see Thompson, *Customs*, 340f.; Lorraine Daston, 'Moral Economy of Science', *Osiris: Constructing Knowledge in the History of Science* 10 (1995): 2–24.

definition of how morality shapes the social order understanding moral economy as the production of moral feelings, emotions and values, norms and obligations by also considering their impact on social relations.[5]

The concept of morality itself, as well as moral values (e.g. justice, fairness, honour), has changed over time. For example, the idea that morality is used as a concept to explain social order is closely intertwined with the history of knowledge, particularly with the writings of Émile Durkheim.[6] Moral movements have also shaped the understanding of morality and moral values. These organizations covered a broad social spectrum. They operated at both the local and transnational levels.[7] In their *Communist Manifesto* (1848) Karl Marx and Friedrich Engels polemized against those activities fostered by 'economists, philanthropists, humanitarians, improvers of the condition of the working class, organizers of charity, members of societies for the prevention of cruelty to animals, temperance fanatics, hole-and-corner reformers of every imaginable kind'.[8] Many of these associations fought a cultural war to prevent a decline in values. Others, such as the anti-slavery movement which is central to the history of capitalism in the nineteenth century, committed themselves to the universalization of human rights.[9] The exact history of these movements and smaller associations is not of interest here.[10] However, the above mentioned social movements introduced

---

[5] Didier Fassin, 'Les économies morales revisitées', *Annales HSS* 64 (2009): 1237–1266, 1257; see also Didier Fassin, 'Introduction: Toward a Critical Moral Anthropology', in *A Companion to Moral Anthropology*, ed. Didier Fassin (Hoboken, NJ: Wiley-Blackwell, 2012), 1–15.

[6] Émile Durkheim, *The Division of Labour in Society* (New York: Palgrave Macmillan, 1974).

[7] For the transnational interlocking of these movements, see already Francis S. L. Lyons, *Internationalism in Europe, 1815–1914* (Leydon: AW Sythoff, 1963).

[8] Karl Marx and Friedrich Engels, *The Communist Manifesto*, From the English Edition, ed. Friedrich Engels, Downloaded October 16, 2018.

[9] Eric Williams, *Capitalism and Slavery*, 6th ed. (London: Deutsch, 1983 [1944]).

[10] Jessica Piley, Robert Kramm, and Harald Fischer-Tiné, eds., *Global Anti-vice Activism, 1890–1950: Fighting Drinks, Drugs, and 'Immorality'* (Cambridge: Cambridge University Press, 2016). For an overview see also Alexandra Przyrembel, 'From Cultural Wars to the Crisis of Humanity: Moral Movements in the Modern Age', in *The History of Social Movements in Global Perspective: A Survey*, ed. Stefan Berger and Holger Nehring (Palgrave studies in the History of Social Movements, London: Palgrave Macmillan, 2017), 355–383.

moral categories into the public debate and maintained the discussion on moral values in various discursive contexts. Following this observation, we will explore further in this volume how the critique of capitalism was linked with 'moral' arguments and taken up by 'moral' social movements.

Already in 2001, the sociologists Luc Boltanski and Eve Chiapello pointed out that the critique of capitalism is a central, possibly constitutive element of capitalism. In their book *Le nouvel esprit de capitalisme* (2001) they argue that anti-capitalist movements actually legitimize the economic order they seek to undermine.[11] The critique of capitalism has indeed accompanied the implementation of capitalism since the nineteenth century. In his recent essays, Jürgen Kocka underlined the importance of critique as cultural practices in various works since the French socialist Louis Blanc (1811–1882) coined the term 'capitalism' in 1850.[12]

In this book, we want to take up these ideas. We argue that the critique of capitalism in the nineteenth and twentieth century is structured by a set of moral values which is constantly (re)-negotiated by social movements, entrepreneurs and above all the state. The interpretation of capitalism can be seen as 'Promothean event for it at once marked the acme of humanity's command over nature as well as the deluge which then ensued'.[13] If this is correct, then a morally legitimized or framed critique of capitalism moves between two poles: on the one hand, criticism of capitalism is ignited by the success of capitalism, even though it does not 'harm' capitalism as an economic system. On the other hand, it is ignited by experiences of crisis. It is no coincidence that capitalism and its history has been examined again with new ferocity since the global financial and economic crisis of 2007.

---

[11] Luc Boltanski, and Ève Chiapello, *The New Spirit of Capitalism* (London: Verso, 2007 [in French 2001]).

[12] Louis Blanc, *Organisation du Travail*, 9th ed. (Paris, 1850). In earlier editions of the book the concept capitalism cannot be found; see Jürgen Kocka, 'Schöpferische Zerstörung: Joseph Schumpeter über Kapitalismus', *Mittelweg* 36, no. 6 (2017): 45–54, 1. For a broad introduction see Jürgen Kocka, *Capitalism: A Short History* (Princeton: Princeton University Press, 2016).

[13] Michael Zamkin, and Gary J. Konrblith, 'Introduction: An American Revolutionary Tradition', in *Capitalism Takes Command: The Social Transformation of Nineteenth-Century America*, ed. Michael Zakim and Gary J. Kornblith (Chicago: 2012), 1–12, 3.

A New History of Capitalism?

Histories of capitalism have been proliferating ever since the financial crisis starting in 2007. It prompted a renewed critical interest in an economic system that had won the Cold War around 1990, when its 'really existing' alternative, state socialism, collapsed in the Soviet Union and Eastern Europe. After the end of the Cold War, the triumphalism of the capitalist West is best represented by Francis Fukuyama's best-selling *The End of History and the Last Man*, first published in 1992.[14] In the 1990s, the rivalries of two economic systems seemed settled—with little interest in histories of capitalism, and, at best, occasional questions about how to live with capitalism.[15] When this changed, the new histories of capitalism had to relate themselves to a century and a half of research on capitalism.[16]

Some of the new interest was accompanied by new scenarios of decline, where the crisis was seen as the beginning of the end of capitalism.[17] Such predictive histories followed a long tradition of critiques of capitalism. These critiques have historically followed two paths: on the one hand, we have a fundamental critique aimed at transforming capitalism. These critics tended to stress the exploitative and alienating features of capitalist systems. On the other hand, reformist critiques aimed at making capitalism better and improving it.[18] Capitalism transformed itself many times under the impact of diverse forms of critique and its

---

[14] Francis Fukuyama, *The End of History and the Last Man* (London: Penguin, 1992).

[15] Will Hutton and Antony Giddens, eds., *On the Edge: Living with Global Capitalism* (London: Vintage, 2001).

[16] Reviews discussing the recent flurry of publications in the field include Friedrich Lenger, 'Die neue Kapitalismusgeschichte. Ein Forschungsbericht als Einleitung', *Archiv für Sozialgeschichte* 56 (2016): 1–36; Jürgen Kocka and Marcel van der Linden, eds., *Capitalism: The Reemergence of a Historical Concept* (London: Bloomsbury, 2016).

[17] See, for example, Immanuel Wallerstein, Randall Collins, Michael Mann, Georgi Derluguian, and Craig Calhoun, *Does Capitalism Have a Future?* (Oxford: Oxford University Press, 2013); Elmar Altvater, *Das Ende des Kapitalismus, wie wir ihn kennen. Eine radikale Kapitalismuskritik* (Münster: Westfälisches Dampfboot, 2011); and Wolfgang Streeck, 'Wie wird der Kapitalismus enden?', *Blätter für deutsche und internationale Politik* 60, no. 3 (2015): 99–111.

[18] Werner Plumpe, 'Debatten über die Gestaltbarkeit des Kapitalismus, 1900–1938', *Kapitalismus und Zivilgesellschaft, special issue of Forschungsjournal Soziale Bewegungen* 29, no. 3 (2016), ed. Frank Adloff and Jürgen Kocka, 164–181.

ability to change its shape and content as a response to criticism belongs to its most remarkable characteristics. This changeability led to manifold ambiguities and multiplicities of capitalisms which make the phenomenon notoriously difficult to define.[19] Undoubtedly private property has been crucial, as have been markets and competition. Decentralized decision-making over economic processes, the accumulation of capital and the importance of investments have also been vital ingredients of capitalism. But the fact that capitalism is best understood as a process that is changing over time, partly due to critiques of capitalism, makes it difficult to come up with 'one size fits all' definitions.

Another characteristic of the renewed interest in the histories of capitalism is that capitalism is no longer of interest exclusively to economic historians. Political historians, social historians, cultural historians and historians of knowledge and science have all contributed in important ways to debates on the history of capitalism, as capitalism is seen to have impacted not just on the economic, but also the social, cultural and political spheres.[20] Consumption histories and the histories of the 'fiscal-military state' belong centrally to the history of capitalism.[21] Capitalism has arguably been the most important structure giving order to modern societies, not just in the realm of the economy, but also in its cultural, social and political realms. Actors of capitalism, discourses on capitalism and knowledge production in and through capitalism all need to be studied to gain a better understanding of how capitalism as an 'essentially contested concept' has worked over the centuries.[22] With Jens Beckert, it makes sense to understand capitalism as

[19] Peter A. Hall and David Soskice, *Varieties of Capitalism: The Institutional Foundations of Comparative Advantage* (Oxford: Oxford University Press, 2001).

[20] Nancy Fraser, 'Behind Marx's Hidden Abode. For an Expanded Conception of Capitalism', *New Left Review* 86 (2014): 55–72; Hartmut Berghoff and Jakob Vogel, eds., *Wirtschaftsgeschichte als Kulturgeschichte. Dimensionen eines Perspektivenwechsels* (Frankfurt: Campus, 2004).

[21] Peer Vries, *State, Economy and the Great Divergence: Great Britain and China, 1680s–1850s* (London: Bloomsbury, 2015); Jan de Vries, *The Industrious Revolution: Consumer Behaviour and the Household Economy, 1650s to the Present* (Cambridge: Cambridge University Press, 2008); and Christof Dejung, *Die Fäden des globalen Marktes. Eine Sozial- und Kulturgeschichte des Welthandels am Beispiel der Handelsfirma Gebrüder Volkart, 1851–1999* (Cologne: Böhlau, 2013).

[22] On 'essentially contested concepts' see W. B. Gallie, 'Essentially Contested Concepts', *Proceedings of the Aristotelian Society* 56 (1955–1956): 167–198.

a 'system of expectations' that, for some, successfully opened up horizons of a better future time and again in modern history, while for others it was producing the preconditions for its own demise and downfall.[23] Any historicization of capitalism will thus also have to start from its future-orientation.[24]

Furthermore, the renewed interest in the history of capitalism has been accompanied by the rise in popularity of global history. Hence the development of capitalism is increasingly discussed in its global perspectives. If capitalism emerged in Europe and if Europe can, to some extent, be seen as the continent of capitalism, it expanded and became a global phenomenon that only made sense when viewed in its global contexts.[25] Major studies have emphasized the importance of the slave trade for the development of capitalism.[26] Export markets, trade and the ability to import cheap raw materials were all crucial in explaining Britain's comparative advantage vis-à-vis the Netherlands which ultimately led to Britain becoming the first workshop of the world. War and violence have been crucial means of establishing a global capitalism.[27] Commodity chains have almost become a separate research field within studies on capitalism—all focussing on the importance of trade in shaping capitalism.[28]

If the literature on capitalism has been growing almost exponentially over the last ten years and if capitalism is increasingly discussed in its global ramifications, there has been relatively little attention paid to the way in which both criticism and justifications of capitalism have been related to questions of morality. The current volume wants to

---

[23] Jens Beckert, 'Capitalism as a System of Expectations: Towards a Sociological Micro-Foundation of Political Economy', *Politics and Society* 41, no. 3 (2013): 323–350; idem, *Imagined Futures: Fictional Expectations and Capitalist Dynamics* (Cambridge: Cambridge University Press, 2016).

[24] Thomas Welskopp, 'Zukunft bewirtschaften. Überlegungen zu einer praxistheoretisch informierten Historisierung des Kapitalismus', *Praktiken des Kapitalismus, special issue of Mittelweg* 36, no. 1 (2017), ed. Sören Brandes and Malte Zierenberg, 81–97.

[25] Peter Kramper, 'Warum Europa? Konturen einer globalgeschichtlichen Forschungskontroverse', *Neue Politische Literatur* 54 (2009): 9–46.

[26] Joseph E. Inikori, *Africans and the Industrial Revolution in England: A Study in International Trade and Economic Development* (Cambridge: Cambridge University Press, 2002).

[27] Sven Beckert, *Empire of Cotton: A Global History* (New York: Vintage Books, 2014).

[28] Kenneth Pomeranz and Steven Topik, *The World That Trade Created: Society, Culture, and the World Economy, 1400 to the Present*, 4th ed. (London: Routledge, 2017).

make a contribution to filling this gap in the literature by asking how morally loaded the arguments of both the apologists of capitalism and their critics were over the course of the nineteenth and twentieth centuries.[29] Almost from its beginnings, intellectuals and social movements voiced strong scepticism vis-à-vis an economic system that was justified in a positive sense by a wide variety of eighteenth-century Enlightenment thinkers. The criticism focussed on the production of enormous wealth and deepest poverty, on the profit-orientation of capitalists. It was to see many reincarnations from the eighteenth century to the critics of capitalist globalization in the twenty-first century. In the following, we would like to survey the history of modern capitalism with a view to moral critiques and justifications, while in the second part, we will attempt to draw out some of the red lines and common themes of the contributions to this volume.

Histories of Capitalism and Questions of Morality

The most comprehensive and influential nineteenth-century critic of capitalism was Karl Marx. Building on British economists, like Adam Smith and David Ricardo, and on French historians, like Jules Michelet and François Guizot, he arrived at his philosophy of historical materialism. Marx always insisted on the scientificity of his theories and had nothing but disdain for what he described as mere moral critiques of capitalism that he associated with the early socialists that preceded him.[30] And indeed the early socialists, like Wilhelm Weitling, Charles Fourier and Robert Owen, developed profound moral critiques of capitalism. Their respective indictments of capitalism, different as they were, all aimed at avoiding the moral degradation that was allegedly the consequence of capitalist regimes of production.[31] And yet we can also find strong moral

---

[29] It thus continues an exploration first started by Stefan Berger and Alexandra Przyrembel, 'Moral, Kapitalismus und sozialen Bewegungen: Kulturhistorische Annäherungen an einen alten Gegenstand', *Historische Anthropologie* 24, no.1 (2016): 88–107.

[30] Gareth Stedman Jones, *Karl Marx: Greatness and Illusion* (London: Penguin Books, 2016).

[31] Keith Taylor, *The Political Ideas of the Utopian Socialists* (London: Routledge, 1982); Lothar Knatz and Hans-Arthur Marsiske, eds., *Wilhelm Weitling: ein deutscher Arbeiterkommunist* (Hamburg: Ergebnisse Verlag, 1989).

overtones in the works of Karl Marx. Thus Marx argued that capitalist forms of production alienated humans from their natural state as social beings. Every form of work under capitalism has to be forced labour, as it is alienated labour. Human beings are degraded by such forms of labour and held back in developing their full human potential.[32] At the core of Marx's critique of capitalism is his insistence that a different economic system is necessary to allow mankind to become truly humane. Of course, Marx was also a scathing critic of bourgeois morality as a form of ideology that represented the interests of the ruling classes. But this did not prevent him from endorsing a higher morality that aimed at the liberation of humanity through the proletariat.[33] According to Simon Clarke, Marx's writings on political economy betray a 'powerful moral dimension', as it upholds notions of moral human qualities that are depraved by capitalism.[34]

Many of those dealing with the history of capitalism after Marx took their cue from him, to criticize him or to modify him. Marxism became a powerful body of thought with very diverse inflections. Friedrich Engels, himself the son of a wealthy industrialist from Barmen, today Wuppertal, was morally outraged by what he observed in the factories and working-class neighbourhoods of Manchester. His *Condition of the Working Class in England* was not just a precise description of the immiseration and exploitation produced by the factory system, it also amounted to a moral indictment, and a call for revolution.[35] What would rise with socialism, according to Engels, would be a 'truly human morality'.[36]

---

[32] Severin Müller, *Phänomenologie und philosophische Theorie der Arbeit, Bd 1: Lebenswelt – Natur – Sinnlichkeit* (Freiburg i.Br. 1992), especially part 3: 337–493.

[33] Wolfgang Fritz Haug, 'Marx, Ethik und die ideologische Formbestimmtheit von Moral', in http://www.wolfgangfritzhaug.inkrit.de/, 3 December 2015; also Rodney G. Pfeffer, *Marxism, Morality and Social Justice* (Princeton: Princeton University Press, 1990); and Philip J. Kain, *Marx and Ethics* (Oxford: Oxford University Press, 1988).

[34] Simon Clarke, *Marx, Marginalism and Modern Sociology: From Adam Smith to Max Weber*, 2nd ed. (Basingstoke: Macmillan, 1991), 76.

[35] Friedrich Engels, *The Condition of the Working Class in England*, first published in German in 1845 and in English in 1887. See also Steven Marcus, *Engels, Manchester and the Working Class* (New York: Transaction, 2015).

[36] Cf. Eugene Kamenka, *The Ethical Foundations of Marxism* (London: Routledge, 1962), 2; Alexandra Przyrembel, *Verbote und Geheimnisse. Das Tabu und die Genese der europäischen Moderne* (Frankfurt/New York: Campus, 2011), 181–194.

Engels' 'theory of modern society was motivated by an aesthetic and moral revulsion against the entire world of commerce and its consequences'.[37]

Next to Engels, one of the most important interpreters of Marx in the late nineteenth and early twentieth centuries was Karl Kautsky, who insisted on morality playing a major role in strengthening the resistance to the ruling classes. For Kautsky, there was no absolute and universal morality. It was relative to particular cultures, civilizations and to particular times. However, in the class struggle 'the rising classes acquire a moral ideal which becomes bolder and bolder as they gain in strength. ... the boldness of the new moral ideal will be accompanied by increasing enthusiasm for it'.[38] His fellow socialist Franz Mehring, distinguished between 'bourgeois morality' and 'proletarian morality', but questions of ethics were of vital importance to him as well as they were to many Marxist socialists.[39] This is also true for Lenin and the Bolsheviks. For Lenin Communist morality, based on the class struggle, was the precondition for any higher development of humankind.[40] Questions of morality and ethics were even more important to Eduard Bernstein's revisionist modifications of Marx. Influence by neo-Kantian philosophy, Bernstein, alongside other revisionists in the German Social Democratic Party sought to develop moral imperatives on which socialism and the socialist future society were to rest.[41] For one of Bernstein's strongest critics, Rosa Luxemburg, morality had to be based on an analysis of material reality, but moral commitment was also the precondition for any in-depth understanding of those realities.[42] Antonio Gramsci later was to build on those ideas by linking morality to historical materialism. Marxism to him was a 'moral science' as it was in line with scientific

[37] Alfred G. Meyer, 'Engels as a Sociologist', in *Karl Kautsky and the Social Science of Classical Marxism*, ed. John H. Kautsky (Leiden: Brill, 1989), 8.

[38] Karl Kautsky, 'Ethics and the Materialist Conception of History', in *Karl Kautsky: Selected Political Writings*, ed. Patrick Goode (Basingstoke: Macmillan, 1983), 39.

[39] Till Schelz-Brandenburg, ed., *Eduard Bernsteins Briefwechsel mit Karl Kautsky (1891–1895)* (Frankfurt: Campus, 2011), 192.

[40] Nicholas Churchich, *Marxism and Morality: A Critical Examination of Marxist Ethics* (Cambridge: James Clarke & Co., 1994), 38.

[41] Matthias Neumann, *Der deutsche Idealismus im Spiegel seiner Historiker: Genese und Protagonisten* (Würzburg: Königshausen und Neumann, 2008), 229.

[42] Andrea Nye, *Philosophia: The Thought of Rosa Luxemburg, Simone Weil and Hannah Arendt* (London: Routledge, 1994), 51 f.

evidence and powered by the will to struggle for the conditions that would overcome the immoral present.[43]

In the course of the twentieth century the appeal of Communism in the Soviet Union after 1917, and in Eastern Europe and diverse parts of the developing world after 1945 rested to a large extent on the moral condemnation of capitalism, and the upholding of a Communist morality understood as a higher form of morality that underpinned the emancipation of all working people across the globe.[44] Arguably, communism as an ideology had such a strong appeal among third-world liberation movements, as it could speak a powerful moral language, both in condemning imperialism and capitalism in moral terms, and in holding out the promise of a more moral, i.e. more socially just society of the future. Indeed the merger of Communism with Third Worldism gave Communism a new lease of life in much of the developing world in the 1960s and 1970s.[45] Ironically, ideals of Communist morality could appeal to third-world audiences at a time when anti-communism in the West was already attacking the moral bankruptcy of Communist regimes in the Soviet Union and Eastern Europe. Revolutions against communism in East Berlin in 1953, in Budapest in 1956 and in Prague in 1968, all involving strong working class elements, could only be crushed by Soviet military force, and the cleavage between Communist rhetoric and Communist reality was becoming ever more visible, drawing criticisms of a hypocritical and double-faced ideology serving the interests not of the working classes but of a bureaucratic nomenklatura ruling by means of a dictatorship.[46]

If the Communists in countries of 'really existing socialism' found it increasingly difficult to speak a convincing moral language, this was not necessarily the case with Western Marxists, increasingly prone to distance

---

[43]Marco Fonseca, *Gramsci's Critique of Civil Society: Towards a New Concept of Hegemony* (London: Routledge, 2016), 57.

[44]On 'communist morality'and its impact on Khrushchev's Soviet Union see Deborah A. Field, *Private Life and Communist Morality in Khrushchev's Russia* (Bern: Peter Lang, 2007).

[45]Silvio Pons, *The Global Revolution: A History of International Communism, 1917–1991* (Oxford: Oxford University Press, 2014), 255 ff.

[46]Luc van Dongen, Stéphanie Roulin, and Giles Scott-Smith, eds., *Transnational Anticommunism and the Cold War: Agents, Activities and Networks* (Basingstoke: Palgrave Macmillan, 2014).

themselves from Soviet and East European versions of socialism. Here we find a Marxist tradition of critiquing capitalism that has been arguing with much greater moral force than the Marxist tradition under Communism. Already in the interwar period Austro-Marxists, such as Otto Bauer, argued that ethical concerns were vital to strengthening socialism politically. A Kantian moral imperative, according to Bauer, would mobilize support for anti-capitalist resistance in the face of much scepticism vis-à-vis socialist solutions.[47] For Georg Lukacs, the ultimate aim of communist morality was freedom—the freedom of the individual from oppression and alienation.[48] The Marxist historian Richard Tawney, in his *Religion and the Rise of Capitalism*, indicted capitalism morally as a cynically unjust system that had emerged under the guise of Christianity but was ultimately incompatible with true Christian values.[49] In the 1970s E. P. Thompson pointed to the importance of the workers possessing a moral sense of what was right and what was wrong that emerged out of their lived experience and led to moral demands for a more just economic, social and political system.[50] This notion of 'moral economy' has been an inspiration to generations of Marxist and non-Marxist historians alike.[51] Most recently, Ute Frevert has rediscovered the concept for her own research group on the history of emotions.[52]

The New Left, to which Thompson also belonged, was not only intrigued by the impact of moral judgements on historical criticisms of capitalism. They also practiced a strong politics of moral condemnation when it came to imperialism and imperialist warfare, whether it was in Algeria or Vietnam. And their moral outrage was equally strong when it

---

[47] Paul Blackledge, *Marxism and Ethics: Freedom, Desire and Revolution* (Albany: SUNY Press, 2012), 113.

[48] Michael Löwy, *Georg Lucacs: From Romanticism to Bolshevism* (London: New Left Books, 1979), 165.

[49] Richard Tawney, *Religion and the Rise of Capitalism* (New York: Harcourt, Brace and Co., 1926).

[50] E. P. Thompson, 'The Moral Economy of the English Crowd in the Eighteenth Century', *Past and Present* 50 (1971): 76–136.

[51] Katarina Friberg and Norbert Götz, eds., special issue on 'Moral Economy: New Perspectives', *Journal of Global Ethics* 11, no. 2 (2015).

[52] Ute Frevert, *The Moral Economy of Trust: Modern Trajectories* (London: German Historical Institute, 2014).

came to domestic battles, over women's liberation, over racial equality or gay rights.[53] A key opponent of Thompson, when it came to the reception of Althusserian structuralist Marxism, Perry Anderson, nevertheless was adamant that socialist politics required moral imagination.[54] And if we move from the New Left to the thinker who has perhaps become the most important reference point for all those who want to return to a form of tamed capitalism, Karl Polanyi—his notion of an 'embedded' capitalism is based on an ethical, moral understanding of the world that assumes that human beings take responsibility with other human beings for the well-being of humanity.[55]

There has then been a distinguished tradition of thinking morally with Marx on capitalism and critiquing capitalism from a moral standpoint. But our last reference to Polanyi, a life-long critic of Marxism and socialism, also points to an at least equally strong tradition of thinking morally about capitalism in a non-Marxist and often anti-Marxist tradition. One of the most important and profound adversaries of Marx was Max Weber, who is analysed in some depth in this volume by Thomas Sokoll. Weber's idea of the Protestant ethic as motor of capitalist development still finds echoes in today's literature on capitalism.[56] Another key thinker on capitalism was Werner Sombart, who believed, at least around the turn of the century, in the compatibility of capitalism and socialism.[57] Sombart, like Weber and other non-Marxist interpreters of capitalism saw the economic system of capitalism strongly tied to the emergence of modernity. As critics of aspects of that modernity they were also critics of aspects of capitalism, but on the whole they defended capitalism as the most efficient and strongest economic system. The long-term resilience of capitalism and its ability to correct itself and

---

[53]Van Gosse, *Rethinking the New Left: An Interpretative History* (New York: Palgrave Macmillan, 2005).

[54]Paul Blackledge, *Perry Anderson, Marxism and the New Left* (London: Merlin, 2004), 101.

[55]Gregory Baum, *Karl Polanyi: On Ethics and Economics* (Montreal: McGill Queen's University Press, 1996), 23.

[56]See, for example, David Landes, *The Wealth and Poverty of Nations: Why Some Are so Rich and Some so Poor* (New York: Abacus, 1998); Joyce Appleby, *The Relentless Revolution: A History of Capitalism* (New York: W. W. Norton, 2010).

[57]Friedrich Lenger, *Werner Sombart, 1863–1941: eine Biographie* (Munich: C.H. Beck, 1994).

change track in response to criticism was widely seen as one of its greatest strength. Theories of modernization, like the one associated with Talcott Parsons, equate capitalism with development and rationality.[58] A strong defence of capitalism is, however, not just a response to Marx; it can be found before Marx. Thus, for example, Adam Smith was perhaps only the most well-known Enlightenment thinker defending capitalism, which, to him, is the system best incorporating what he perceived as the natural urge of humans to trade in always existing markets. Smith saw this not only as the most efficient but also as the most humane way of organizing the economy; capitalism, for Smith, was thus a moral system in line with human nature.[59] Albert Hirschmann has argued that those eighteenth-century defenders of capitalism thought self-interest morally far superior to the amoral system of destructive passions that it sought to replace.[60] Joseph Schumpeter believed fervently that capitalism was imbued with moral values in the nineteenth century, but by the 1930s, according to his analysis, 'all moral beliefs have gone out of capitalist life'.[61] In his book *Capitalism, Socialism and Democracy*, published in London in 1943, he attributed to capitalism the emergence of modern international morality. Praising the historic achievements of capitalism, he celebrated in this book the 'creative destruction' unleashed by capitalism which, however, would also be the reason for its eventual downfall. Hence, ultimately Schumpeter joins the chorus of those predicting capitalism's demise.[62]

Overall, non-Marxist social theory has almost been obsessed with making capitalism morally acceptable and giving it moral underpinnings. Whereas many Marxist critics of capitalism sought to transform capitalism, non-Marxist critics often attempted to reform capitalism and bring it into line with Christian, social liberal and social democratic ideas of a

[58] Uta Gerhardt, *Talcott Parsons: An Intellectual Biography* (Cambridge: Cambridge University Press, 2002).

[59] Spencer J. Pack, *Capitalism as a Moral System: Adam Smith's Critique of the Free Market Economy* (London: Edward Elgar, 1991).

[60] Albert O. Hirschmann, *The Passions and the Interests: Political Arguments for Capitalism Before Its Triumph* (Princeton: Princeton University Press, 1977).

[61] Joseph Schumpeter, *The Economics and Sociology of Capitalism* (Princeton: Princeton University Press, 1991), 370.

[62] Joseph Schumpeter, *Capitalism, Socialism and Democracy* (London: Routledge, 1943).

capitalism with a human face. The Christian idea of bringing capitalism into line with Christian social teaching is deeply rooted in the nineteenth century, but was reconfirmed shortly after the end of the Cold War, in 1991, with the encyclical *Centesimus Annus* that stated: '... alienation ... is a reality in Western societies ... This happens in consumerism ... Alienation is also found in work, when it is organised so as to ensure maximum returns and profit with no concern, whether the worker, through his own labour, grows or diminishes as a person'.[63] Especially in Britain, a variant of liberal humanism and ethical liberalism remained strong, both inside and outside the Liberal Party, in the nineteenth and twentieth centuries. It sought to combine concern for social equality with classical liberal concerns for freedom.[64] One of the strongest ideas that emerged in the context of making capitalism morally better was the Social Democratic idea of controlling markets through states.[65] After the Second World War, at least from the 1950s to the 1970s, it would appear for a short while as though the Social Democratic idea could be successful in making capitalism work for everyone.[66]

Despite the fact that there is a strong link between capitalism and morality, both in justifications of capitalism and in criticisms of it, there is, to date, at best a subterranean interest in exploring this link. Within communitarian thought, the question of morality and capitalism has at least been considered. Thus Amitai Etzioni has presented us with a vision of a new economy that is governed by moral considerations at the end of a decade that is often seen as the highpoint of a neo-liberal economy of greed.[67] However, more recently the new criticism of capitalism has also re-invigorated interest in the link between capitalism and morality. Axel Honneth has reminded us that in Marx's writings moral evil is woven

---

[63] http://w2.vatican.va/content/john-paul-ii/en/encyclicals/documents/hf_jp-ii_enc_01051991_centesimus-annus.html (accessed 27 September 2018).

[64] Michael Freeden, *Liberalism Divided: A Study in British Political Thought, 1914–1939* (Oxford: Oxford University Press, 1986), especially Chapter 7, 223–292.

[65] Gosta Esping-Andersen, *Politics Against Markets: The Social Democratic Road to Power* (Princeton: Princeton University Press, new ed. 2017 [originally published in 1985]).

[66] Adam Przeworski, *Capitalism and Social Democracy* (Cambridge: Cambridge University Press, 1983).

[67] Amitai Etzioni, *The Moral Dimension: Towards a New Economics* (New York: Free Press, 1988).

through the structure and essence of capitalism.[68] Artur M. Melzer and Steven J. Kautz have edited a collection that deliberately asks: 'Are Markets Moral?', and they provide a wide-ranging exploration of this theme from the Enlightenment to the present day, taking into account both justifications and criticism of capitalism.[69] The volume presented here aims at contributing further towards bringing this interest more out into the open and encouraging others to explore this relationship between morality and capitalism further.

'MORALIZING CAPITALISM': CONCERN AND STRUCTURE OF THIS BOOK

The chapters in this book span a period of more than 150 years. They cover the period from the development of modern economic theory in the early nineteenth century to the 1970s, when the United Nations established its *Centre on Transnational Corporations*—a deliberate attempt to find a new moral 'code of conduct' for multinational companies. Thus we find, in what follows, analyses of intellectual debates about the 'spirit of capitalism' around 1900 as well as US American discussions within Catholicism about post-World War I economic justice or 'politically' and 'morally' correct consumption during the 'boom' in the prosperous 1970s. We have grouped the essays into four thematic sections highlighting the interrelationship between 'morality' and capitalism in, first, the history of knowledge, secondly, in the realm of the political, thirdly, the value system for economic actors, and fourthly, the frameworks of anti-capitalist protest cultures, as they have shaped industrial capitalism since its formation during the nineteenth century.

Looking at the first theme, we can start with the observation that the history of knowledge has become an important category for historians during the last decade.[70] 'Knowledge' is not a neutral category, but is

[68] Axel Honneth, 'Die Moral im "Kapital": Versuch einer Korrektur der Marxschen Ökonomiekritik', in *Nach Marx: Philosophie, Kritik, Praxis*, ed. Rahel Jaeggi and Daniel Loick (Frankfurt: Suhrkamp, 2013), 351 ff.

[69] Arthur M. Melzer and Steven J. Kautz, eds., *Are Markets Moral?* (Philadelphia: University of Pennsylvania Press, 2018).

[70] Philipp Sarasin, 'Was ist Wissensgeschichte?', *Internationales Archiv für Sozialgeschichte der Deutschen Literatur* 36, no. 1 (2011): 159–172, for a general introduction see Peter Burke, *A Social History of Knowledge* (Cambridge: Polity Press, 2000).

closely tied to the implementation of power. This was shown in histories of colonialism and imperialism.[71] The interrelationship between power and morality was also reflected in the production and transformation of economic knowledge in the nineteenth and twentieth century.[72] In her chapter, Sandra Maß turns to an early phase of the subject of political economy, when it gradually became an academic discipline. Based on self-help books as well as academic texts she shows how German and English pedagogues, economists and philosophers tried to connect the world of children with the rising capitalist and consumerist economy in manifold and contested ways. In the early nineteenth century, political economists propagated an ideal image of economic behaviour. This ideal was still strongly oriented towards religious values and also aimed at the control of emotions. At the threshold of the twentieth-century moral expectations towards individual economic behaviour shifted. At the same time Werner Sombart and Max Weber devoted major studies to understand the 'spirit of capitalism'. In those chapters that undertake a critical reading of these writings two different approaches are applied to the question how Sombart's and Weber's concepts of capitalism were morally charged. Thomas Sokoll's chapter argues that Max Weber's Protestant ethics expressed a universal morality of capitalism. He examines both the historical and the moral value of Weber's *Protestant Ethic* in a new light and against a long tradition of previous misconceptions. He contends that modern capitalism arising from an inherently Protestant ethical imperative opposed the worst forms of 'adventure capitalism'. Alexandra Przyrembel's chapter shows how anti-Jewish ideas were reflected in the writings of Werner Sombart. His *Jews and Modern Capitalism* carried on traditional ideas about a specifically 'Jewish' form of economic activity and an alleged Jewish 'aptness' for capitalism. All three chapters in this section thus focus on the production and circulation of economic knowledge and show that 'knowledge' about capitalism is closely intertwined with the political.

[71] Frederick Cooper and Ann L. Stoler, eds., *Tensions of Empire: Colonial Cultures in a Bourgeois World*, Reprint (Berkeley: University of California Press, 2007).

[72] Mary Poovey, *A History of the Modern Fact: Problems of Knowledge in the Sciences of Wealth and Society* (Chicago: University of Chicago Press, 1998); Daniel Speich Chassé, 'Was zählt der Preis? Dogmengeschichte und Wissensgeschichte der Ökonomie', *Berichte zur Wissenschaftsgeschichte* 37, no. 2 (2014): 132–147.

The connection between capitalism and the political is particularly evident in cases where states or supranational organizations appear as political actors who order or regulate capitalism. The chapters in the second thematic section deal with political attempts to regulate capitalism in order to make it comply with moral values. Elsbeth Heaman uses the example of Canada to analyse debates on a 'fair' tax policy at the transition to the twentieth century. She highlights how Canadian governmental tax politics were grounded in moral values. Wim de Jong and Christian Olaf Christiansen focus on different phases of economic history after 1945.[73] De Jong's chapter deals with the reconstruction efforts after World War II focusing on West Germany. After 1945, it was clear to elites in industry and politics that the reconstruction effort in Europe would have to involve efforts to harmonize the interests of corporations and the labour movement. This meant a politics aimed at 'humanizing' capitalism. De Jong shows that American corporate philanthropic organizations like the Ford Foundation fostered the implementation of such a capitalism in the early years of the Cold War. Politics, in association with pro-capitalist philanthropy were led by moral considerations on how to make capitalism more humane.

During the 1970s, economic globalization took up speed; at the same time, the decade saw a surge in human rights activism. Christiansen shows in his chapter that contemporaries developed a human rights-based critique of practices common among transnational corporations. The newly founded *United Nations Centre on Transnational Corporations* was concerned with working out a new 'code of conduct' for multinational corporations in which both actors form the global South and the 'developed' world participated. Its failure shows that attempts to tame multinational companies by applying 'moral' values were limited.

The centre's failure also highlighted the value systems of economic actors that stand in the centre of our third thematic section. Debates on the responsibility of merchant and industrial capitalists for upholding certain moral standards in their economic activities have a long tradition reaching back centuries.[74] In this volume, Boris Gehlen and Jürgen Finger

---

[73] Tony Judt, *Postwar: A History of Europe Since 1945* (New York: Penguin, 2005).

[74] For Early Modern History, see Natalie Zemon Davis, 'Religion and Capitalism Once Again? Jewish Merchant Culture in the Seventeenth Century', *Representations* 59 (1997): 56–84.

explore this question on the basis of two case studies from the nineteenth century. The first case study deals with the stock exchange as place of speculation, while the second case study focuses on bankruptcy as moral failure of the individual capitalist. Both highlight the role of economists in developing concepts of morality that have been applied to economic transactions. Already prior to World War I, stock exchanges were repeatedly blamed for causing crises. Brokers were sometimes referred to as 'a low wretch', 'parasite' or 'a social excrescence'. This reputation did not correspond with their self-images as honourable businessmen. In his chapter, Gehlen shows for the New York Stock Exchange (NYSE) that stockbroker's concept of honour became a functional instrument for organizing markets. Finger shows that bankruptcy posed both an economic and a 'moral' problem in France around 1848. Although bankruptcy was rare and therefore a marginal phenomenon of economic activity, it is suitable for exploring the relationship between individual failure or misconduct and public interest. Socialists like Charles Fourier (1772–1837) interpreted bankruptcy as the 'vice' of merchants. Moral arguments about capitalists were frequently framed using a strongly derogatory language.

Critiques of the moral standards of capitalists and capitalist institutions formed the bases for the evolution of anti-capitalist social movements that are at the centre of attention in our fourth thematic section. During the nineteenth and twentieth centuries, the expression of anti-capitalism has taken different forms. In addition to interventions such as letters, newspaper articles by churches or critical journalists as well open and explicit forms of protest, social movements in particular became the focal point of a sustained critique of capitalism. The chapters in this section deal with central topics that condense a 'moralizing' critique of capitalism: profit and social inequality, work regimes and the history of consumption. Churches and religious associations were often in the vanguard of the most outspoken critics of an allegedly inhuman and amoral capitalism. Christian social doctrine amounted at times to a full-blown attack on capitalism.[75] Giulia d'Alessio analyses in her chapter how the US Catholic Church often displayed an interventionist and critical attitude towards the American 'economic system' and towards the 'errors and distortions' of capitalism during the Great Depression. In

[75] Vincent D. Rougeau, *Christians in the American Empire: Faith and Citizenship in the New World Order* (New York: Oxford University Press, 2008).

the wake of this economic crisis, representatives of the Catholic Church argued that only state intervention could guarantee harmony between capital and labour.

Nikos Potamianos, in his chapter, analyses the discourse against 'shameful profiteering' unfolding in Greece in the early twentieth century. This critique, embraced by labourers, white-collar employees, members of the middle classes and bourgeois politicians alike, relied on the notion of a reciprocal relationship between the idiom of profiteering and the rise of statism. Moral issues, too, were cental to this critique in which the (a)morality of commercial profit was pitted against a producerist work ethic. Echoes of such a critique can be found in the Federal Republic of Germany in the 1970s. Sibylle Marti argues in her chapter that 'work' and 'work regimes' were negotiated in moral terms and categories. In particular, the changing work values and the increasing precarity of employment were often discussed as examples of an alleged immorality of capitalism.

In her book *Irresistible empire*, Victoria de Grazia demonstrates how the United States became during the twentieth century 'a great imperium with the outlook of a great emporium'.[76] Above all, mass consumption led to the economic dominance of the United States.[77] Mass consumption also provoked resistance. Intellectuals like Habermas criticized the 'commodification of emotional life during the "economic miracle"'.[78] In his chapter, Benjamin Möckel shows that from the 1960s onwards, modern consumerism became a key topic through which a moral and emotional critique of capitalism was connected to collectively shared emotional regimes and practices of everyday life. The emerging fair trade market of the 1970s and 1980s is an instructive example for the everyday implications as well as the dialectics of a critique of consumerism. The 'moralization' of capitalism in the context of fair trade unfolds at two levels: On the one hand, the product itself becomes a symbol of a 'counterculture' that represents the critique of existing

---

[76] Victoria de Grazia, *Irresistible Empire: America's Advance Through Twentieth-Century Europe* (Cambridge, MA: Belknap Press of Harvard University Press, 2005), 3.

[77] Lizabeth Cohen, *A Consumers' Republic: The Politics of Mass Consumption in Postwar America*, 1st ed. (New York: Alfred A. Knopf; Distributed by Random House, 2003); Heinz-Gerhard Haupt, and Claudius Torp, eds., *Die Konsumgesellschaft in Deutschland 1890–1990: Ein Handbuch* (Frankfurt: Campus, 2009).

[78] See Jan-Werner Müller, *Another Country: German Intellectuals, Unification and National Identity* (New Haven: Yale University Press, 2000), 39.

forms of capitalism. On the other hand, fair trade products must assert themselves on capitalist markets. Against this background, fair trade is experimenting with more 'humane' forms of capitalism that guarantee adequate pay for wage labour.

All four thematic perspectives need further research. In the last part of this introduction we will outline some ideas on how the interconnectedness of 'morality' and capitalism can be explored in greater depth in years to come. In addition to the four themes outlined above, i.e. history of knowledge, the realm of the political, ideas of ethics among economic actors, and anti-capitalist protest culture, it would be crucial to integrate a fifth theme, namely the public sphere.

'Moralizing Capitalism': A Research Programme

Experiences of crisis in the wake of financial turmoil in 2007 have led to critical interventions by social scientists and historians: David Graeber's *Debt* (2011), Thomas Piketty's *Capital in the 21st Century* (2013) and finally Adam Tooze's *Crashed: How a Decade of Financial Crises Changed the World* (2018) analyse the experience of crises and review the struggle for answers. At the same time, they show that the public controversy over consequences of capitalism meets with the interest of the book market.[79] In the nineteenth and twentieth centuries, the critique of capitalism and experiences of crisis have often been closely intertwined. The concept of 'moralizing capitalism' offers a productive framework for discussing the symbiotic relationship between critics of capitalism and their adversaries involving at least five different sub-fields of historical writing.

First, the discussion of capitalism in terms of its morality is an important aspect of the history of knowledge which has been gaining momentum for a number of years now.[80] The 'moral' implications of key texts on the history of capitalism by Max Weber and Werner Sombart have already been mentioned. An entangled history of 'morality' and

---

[79] Thomas Piketty, *Capital in the Twenty-First Century* (Cambridge, MA: Belknap Press of Harvard University Press, 2014); David Graeber, *Debt: The First 5,000 Years* (Brooklyn, NY: Melville House, 2011); and Adam J. Tooze, *Crashed: How a Decade of Financial Crises Changed the World* (New York: Viking, 2018).

[80] See for instance the activities of the Center 'History of Knowledge' in Zürich, https://www.zgw.ethz.ch/en/home.html which also focusses on questions of economic knowledge; Christof Dejung, Monika Dommann, and Daniel S. Chassé, eds., *Auf der Suche nach der Ökonomie: Historische Annäherungen* (Tübingen: Mohr Siebeck, 2014).

'knowledge' would find rich research fields in statistics on the one hand, and in consumption on the other. The development and professionalization of statistics was an important thread in the knowledge history of capitalism. In the early nineteenth-century statistical surveys were closely linked to surveys of social topography, which reproduced social inequality.[81] With the institutionalization of economic numeric methods by statistical offices operating on local and national levels, experts emerged who increasingly categorized wealth and poverty with the help of figures. In particular, the invention of the 'gross national product' represented a new standard for linking inequality to political action on a global scale.[82] Thus development aid workers defined social relations in the 'global South' along hierarchical categories such as 'above' and 'below' based on statistical knowledge.[83]

Werner Sombart interpreted a specific form of consumption as one of the central driving forces of capitalism: the indulgence of luxurious objects.[84] During the eighteenth century, statesman and intellectuals were preoccupied by 'a shifting divide between need and desire, necessities and luxuries'.[85] The emerging academic discipline of political economy advocated increasingly fragile concepts in regard to the moral rejection of luxury. Adam Smith, John Stuart Mill, and David Hume increasingly promoted in their writings a 'demoralization' of luxury that can drive people to new forms of (economic) progress. However, in the early twentieth century the sociologist Thorstein Veblen has condemned 'conspicuous consumption' as social practice of an elite.[86] However, the

[81] Eileen Janes Yeo, *The Contest for Social Science: Relations and Representations of Gender and Class* (London: Rivers Oram 1996), see also Chapter 5 in this volume.

[82] Daniel Speich Chassé, *Die Erfindung des Bruttosozialprodukts. Globale Ungleichheit in der Wissensgeschichte der Ökonomie* (Göttingen, 2013; Kritische Studien zur Geschichtswissenschaft, 212), 21.

[83] David C. Engerman, *The Price of Aid: The Economic Cold War in India* (Cambridge, MA and London: Harvard University Press, 2018).

[84] Werner Sombart, *Luxury and Capitalism*, trans. W. R. Dittmar, first published in 1913 (Ann Arbor: University of Michigan Press, 1967).

[85] Maxine Berg, and Elizabeth Eger, 'The Rise and Fall of the Luxury Debates', in *Luxury in the Eighteenth Century: Debates, Desires and Delectable Goods*, ed. Maxine Berg and Elizabeth Eger, first published in paperback (Basingstoke: Palgrave Macmillan, 2007), 7–27.

[86] On the history of knowledge of luxury: Dominik Schrage, 'Vom Luxuskonsum zum Standardpaket: Der Überfluss und seine Zähmung als Thema der Soziologie' in *Luxus: Die Ambivalenz des Überflüssigen in der Moderne*, ed. Christine Weder and Maximilian

debates on luxury from the eighteenth to the twentieth century show that the boundaries between the 'necessary' and the 'superfluous' have proven to be politically and morally contested.[87]

Secondly, different political cultures have been pre-occupied with moral critiques of capitalism. Thus democratic political cultures have often held capitalism responsible of preventing democratic and transparent structures and instead promoting secretive and conspiratorial backstage channels of power that undermine and threaten democracies.[88] The institutional structures of capitalism, its critics argue, are incompatible with democratic norms and values. They have long maintained that capitalism is compatible with democracy only in periods of overall economic growth and political stability. When the going gets tough, capitalism and capitalist interests revert to authoritarian political solutions.[89] Yet it is not only the spurious attachment of capitalism to liberal democracy that comes in for a good deal of criticism, it is also its ability within liberal democracies to influence unduly political decision-making processes in the interest of capital. In more authoritarian and dictatorial political cultures, the interests of capital are often seen as being inextricably linked with those holding political power. For some, 'really existing socialism' in the USSR after 1917 and across Eastern Europe after 1945 has only been a form of state capitalism, in which a corrupt party nomenklatura organized a form of state capitalism in their own interest.[90]

Bergengruen, 1st ed. (Göttingen: Wallstein Verlag GmbH, 2012), 58–72; Thorstein Veblen, *The Theory of the Leisure Class: An Economic Study of Institutions*, New ed. (New York: Macmillan, 1912). An overview is provided by John Sekora, *Luxury: The Concept in Western Thought, Eden to Smolett* (Baltimore: John Hopkins University Press, 1977).

[87] Ute Tellmann, 'Figuren des Überflüssigen und die politisch-moralischen Grenzziehungen in der Ökonomie: luxuriöse Dinge, Menschenmassen und Parasiten', in *Luxus: Die Ambivalenz des Überflüssigen in der Moderne*, ed. Christine Weder and Maximilian Bergengruen, 1st ed. (Göttingen: Wallstein Verlag GmbH, 2012), 73–89, 73.

[88] Stefan Berger and Dimitrij Owetschkin, eds., *Contested Transparencies Between Promise and Peril* (Basingstoke: Palgrave, 2019).

[89] Left-wing theories of fascism have often upheld this alleged link between fascism and the interests of capital. See Sebastian Voigt, 'Fascism, Capitalism and Democracy', *Journal of Contemporary European History* (2020, forthcoming).

[90] Stephen A. Resnick and Richard D. Wolff, *Class Theory and History: Capitalism and Communism in the USSR* (London: Routledge, 2002), especially part 2 on 'state capitalism'.

Thirdly, a morally informed criticism of capitalism has directly addressed its key agents, such as bankers and stock market speculators. The personalization of moral critique was hugely important for producing a strong emotional response to capitalism that tends to measure its failure in terms of its tendency to produce huge social inequalities, endanger social cohesion and enrich the few to the detriment of the many.[91] Corruption scandals regularly have provoked debates about the ethical behaviour of managers.[92] The immorality of individual representatives of capitalism was not so much seen as the result of individual failures, but as the outcome of structural shortcomings to do with the character of capitalism itself.

Fourthly the mobilization of anti-capitalist protest cultures depended vitally on those moral criticisms of individual and systemic failure. Nineteenth-century labour movements thrived on scandalizing forms of luxury and wealth that stood in marked contrast to the poverty and deprivation of industrial workers. Trade unions demanded a greater share of the spoils of profiteering for their members. Producer and consumer cooperatives sought to organize production chains without the parasitic middlemen who were again seen as amoral agents of a capitalism that rewarded unproductive labour to the detriment of producers and consumers. Working-class political parties sought to extend the democratic sphere by extending the franchise regardless of property and education.[93] Whether working-class politics sought to reform or abolish capitalism, it was always about imagining a politics that would be morally better than the one that was seen as being in the service of capitalism. In the course of the twentieth century a whole array of social movements, from the environmental movement to the women's movement and further to the peace movement, to mention just some of the most prominent, combined their emancipatory agendas with an explicit moral critique of capitalism.[94] Was not capitalist greed responsible for the gradual

[91] For the Germany after 1945 see Hans-Ulrich Wehler, *Die neue Umverteilung. Soziale Ungleichheit in Deutschland* (München: Beck'sche Reihe 6096, 2013).

[92] Jens Ivo Engels, *Krumme Touren in der Wirtschaft. Zur Geschichte ethischen Fehlverhaltens und seiner Bekämpfung* (Köln/Wien: Böhlau, 2015).

[93] Geoff Eley, *Forging Democracy: The History of the Left in Europe, 1850–2000* (Oxford: Oxford University Press, 2002).

[94] Donatella della Porta and Mario Diani, eds., *The Oxford Handbook of Social Movements* (Oxford: Oxford University Press, 2015).

destruction of the planet? Were women not held back by the gendered logic of male-dominated capitalist systems, which allocated the reproductive sphere to women? Was not the military-industrial complex responsible for many of the wars that had accompanied the history of capitalism? And had capitalism itself not emerged in the context of a war capitalism that mobilized the armies of imperial states in order to divide the world among the most powerful capitalist nations? Anti-capitalist protest cultures time and again challenged capitalism through their moral critiques and led to those in defence of capitalist structures seeking to adjust capitalism in ways that would accommodate those criticisms.[95]

Finally, those anti-capitalist protest cultures depended on gaining a space of the public sphere in which they could operate. As we indicated above, this is a important field of research that we have not systematically explored in this volume although it is implicit in some chapters. The debate on social inequality or 'unfair' working conditions became the subject of mass media coverage that is explored in the chapters of Alexandra Przyrembel and Sibylle Marti.[96] In the 1960s, for example, the Yellow press reported extensively on the wealthy at a time when class conflict was prominently discussed in the public sphere.[97] Future research will have to explore in much greater depth to what extent the social imagination of 'the rich' was constructing the wealthy as amoral profiteers of capitalism. Similarly one could ask about the 'winners' and 'losers' of capitalism and their representation in the press, which was frequently interwoven with contradictory emotions such as greed, envy, but also trust in the respectability of entrepreneurs.[98] Especially the history of emotions can be used for a productive examination of the 'moral history' of capitalism.[99] Moral indignation also played an important role in the artistic and cultural engagement with capitalism in literature, film

---

[95] Donatella della Porta, *Social Movements in Times of Austerity: Bringing Capitalism Back into Protest Analysis* (Cambridge: Polity Press, 2015).

[96] See Chapters 5 and 10.

[97] Peter Brügge, 'Die Reichen in Deutschland', *Der Spiegel*, 1966. This series had five parts.

[98] Eva M. Gajek and Christoph Lorke, eds., *Soziale Ungleichheit im Visier: Wahrnehmung und Deutung von Armut und Reichtum seit 1945* (Frankfurt: Campus, 2016).

[99] Nicole Eustace, Eugenia Lean, Julia Livingstone, Jan Plamper, and Willam M. Reddy, Barbara H. Rosenwein, 'AHR Conversation: The Historical Study of Emotions', *American Historical Review* 117, no. 5 (2012): 1487–1531.

and theatre.[100] Overall it seems clear that the current volume is barely scratching the surface of a topic, the moral critique of capitalism, that deserves much fuller attention in future.

[100] See the article Melena Ryzik, 'A Bare Market Lasts One Morning', *New York Times*, 1 August 2011, https://www.nytimes.com/2011/08/02/arts/design/zefrey-throwells-ocularpation-wall-street.html; see also the the exhibition 'Constructing the World: Art and Economy 1919–1939, and 2008–2018', Kunsthalle Mannheim, 10 December 2018–2 March 2019.

PART I

History of Knowledge

CHAPTER 2

Teaching Capitalism: The Popularization of Economic Knowledge in Britain and Germany (1800–1850)

Sandra Maß

History has yet to record the existence of a way of structuring and running an economy that dispenses with notions of good order, of right
and wrong. The history of economic ideas is unimaginable without
ethics and morals to give direction, set limits, and provide legitimation
to people's actions within economic systems. That said, it was Bernard
Mandeville's *Fable of the Bees* (1705/1710) that marked the starting point of intensified debate on the rules and modes of action governing economic life. In writing the *Fable*, its Dutch author created an
idea of human actions and motivations that drew severe criticism from
his contemporaries due to its claim that unscrupulous dealings were the
only possible source of wealth and the virtuous man was fated to remain
impoverished.[1] From this point onward, people as economic actors

---

[1] Lisa Herzog, 'Einleitung: Die Verteidigung des Marktes vom 18. Jahrhundert bis
zur Gegenwart', in *Der Wert des Marktes. Ein ökonomisch-philosophischer Diskurs vom 18.*

S. Maß (✉)
Ruhr University Bochum, Bochum, Germany
e-mail: sandra.mass@ruhr-uni-bochum.de

© The Author(s) 2019
S. Berger and A. Przyrembel (eds.), *Moralizing Capitalism*,
Palgrave Studies in the History of Social Movements,
https://doi.org/10.1007/978-3-030-20565-2_2

29

occupied a central place in economic discourses, with their behaviour, values and emotions key factors in the description of economic orders or in calls for their reform.

Discussions around economic education, conducted by econo-mists,[2] moral philosophers, educators and clerics, emerged at the time of the Enlightenment.[3] The education of young people in schools and within the family was a significant vehicle for the contemporary popu-larization of economic knowledge. A consistent theme of the latter was the dangers of the new capitalist order said to be posed by the repudi-ation of Christian temperance and the proliferation of selfishness and greed, and which education sought to contain and divert into appropri-ate channels. The political economists of the first half of the nineteenth century were no exception to this general picture. It is certainly the case that their publications pursued the primary aims of disseminating their designs for an economic order, spreading up-to-date economic knowl-edge, explaining changes in processes of production, and constituting economics as a science and a learned field. Nevertheless, they too, either in their own publications or in the popular versions of their writings produced by other authors, linked matters of the economic order with appropriate behaviours, role models and morals in general. British polit-ical economists in particular urged the integration of relevant teachings

Jahrhundert bis zur Gegenwart, ed. L. Herzog and Axel Honneth (Frankfurt am Main: Suhrkamp, 2016), 14 f.

[2] The term 'economist' did not find popular use until the academic discipline of eco-nomics became professionalized and institutionalized in the nineteenth century. Before this, economic matters had been the province of theologians, political scientists, special-ists in public finance (cameralists) and moral philosophers. On the history of the term 'economist', see Klaus Lichtblau, 'Ökonomie, politische', in *Historisches Wörterbuch der Philosophie*, vol. 6 (Darmstadt: Wissenschaftliche Buchgesellschaft, 1984), columns 1163–1173.

[3] The *homo oeconomicus* evolved at this time into a central and controversial literary fig-ure. See Manuel Bauer, *Ökonomische Menschen. Literarische Wirtschaftsanthropologie des 19. Jahrhunderts* (Göttingen: V&R unipress, 2016); Laurenz Volkmann, *Homo oeconomi-cus. Studien zur Modellierung eines neuen Menschenbilds in der englischen Literatur vom Mittelalter bis zum 18. Jahrhundert* (Heidelberg: Universitätsverlag Winter, 2003); Thomas Rommel, *Das Selbstinteresse von Mandeville bis Smith. Ökonomisches Denken in ausgewählten Schriften des 18. Jahrhunderts* (Heidelberg: Universitätsverlag Winter, 2006); Joseph Vogl, *Kalkül und Leidenschaft. Poetik des ökonomischen Menschen* (Munich: Sequenzia, 2002); and Eva Ritthaler, *Ökonomische Bildung. Wirtschaft in deutschen Entwicklungsromanen von Goethe bis Heinrich Mann* (Würzburg: Königshausen & Neumann, 2017).

into curricula for elementary education.[4] Their German counterparts did likewise, although their focus on these questions was as a rule not accompanied by specific calls for economic education in schools providing basic instruction.

Although the fields of political economy and, to use the German terms, *Nationalökonomie* and *Staatswissenschaften*, produced limited numbers of popular publications and book series[5] when compared with the natural sciences, there were certainly books on the market that sought to explain to children and young people actions in the economic sphere, the handling of money, and the teachings of the discipline of political economy. While doing so, they used examples of morally questionable behaviour to strengthen the idea that economic behaviour was bound to the control of emotions and to Christian values, thus creating a set of ideas that could be called capitalist morality avant la lettre.

In Great Britain in particular, popular works written by men and women alike and aimed at a broad audience complemented the canonical writings of the discipline. Such publications explicitly addressed women, children and workers as target audiences.[6] There is a relatively

---

[4]W. D. Sockwell, *Popularizing Classical Economics: Henry Brougham and William Ellis* (New York: St. Martin's Press, 1994), 115; cf. Geoffrey R. Searle, *Morality and the Market in Victorian Britain* (Oxford: Clarendon Press, 1998).

[5]This said, Massimo M. Augello and Marco E. L. Guidi, in a European perspective, demonstrate the contemporary existence of an impressive number of publications popularising political economy. See Massimo M. Augello and Marco E. L. Guidi, 'The Making of an Economic Reader: The Dissemination of Economics Through Textbooks', in *The Economic Reader: Textbooks, Manuals and the Dissemination of the Economic Sciences During the 19th and Early 20th Centuries*, ed. Massimo M. Augello and Marco E. L. Guidi (London and New York: Routledge, 2012), 22f. Cf., on the history of the popularisation of the sciences, Carsten Kretschmann, ed., *Wissenspopularisierung. Konzepte der Wissensverbreitung im Wandel* (Berlin: Akademie-Verlag, 2003); Aileen Fyfe, ed., *Science and Salvation: Evangelicals and Popular Science Publishing in Victorian Britain* (Chicago: Univrsity of Chicago Press, 2004); Aileen Fyfe and Bernard V. Lightman, eds., *Science in the Marketplace: Nineteenth-Century Sites and Experiences* (Chicago and London: University of Chicago Press, 2007); Angela Schwarz, *Der Schlüssel zur modernen Welt. Wissenschaftspopularisierung in Großbritannien und Deutschland im Übergang zur Moderne* (ca. 1870–1914) (Stuttgart: Franz Steiner Verlag, 1999); and Andreas W. Daum, *Wissenschaftspopularisierung im 19. Jahrhundert. Bürgerliche Kultur, naturwissenschaftliche Bildung und die deutsche Öffentlichkeit* (Munich: R. Oldenbourg Verlag, 1998).

[6]Cf. Greg Myers, 'Science for Women and Children: The Dialogue of Popular Science in the Nineteenth Century', in *Nature Transfigured: Science and Literature, 1700–1900*, ed.

substantial body of research in existence on British efforts to popularize political economy.[7] By contrast, studies of the popularization of the economic discipline in German-speaking territories are, with few exceptions, notable by their absence.[8] This chapter will therefore commence by discussing British initiatives of the first half of the nineteenth century for the promotion of economic education and the integration of political economy into school-based education, before going on to explore German publications in this field and the similarities and differences between them and their British counterparts. We proceed from the hypothesis that it would be reductive to describe the tradition of German economics as it emerged in this period as simply a belated, hesitant and passive response to political economy in Britain and France.[9] Instead, German-speaking territories developed their own hybrid discipline consisting of perspectives drawn from *Staatswissenschaften* and cameralistics on the one hand and liberal ideas on the other, as is evident in the writings of Gottlieb Hufeland, Johann Heinrich von Thünen and Friedrich Benedict Wilhelm von Hermann.[10] Departing from the ostensibly sound and secure paths of the reconstruction of national ways of thinking

John Christie and Sally Shuttleworth (Manchester and New York: Manchester University Press, 1989), 171–200.

[7] We might point here particularly to the works of Willie Henderson: *Economics as Literature*; 'Harriet Martineau or "When Political Economy Was Popular"', *History of Education* 21, no. 4 (1992): 383–403, Further, Brian P. Cooper, *Family Fictions and Family Facts: Harriet Martineau, Adolphe Quetelet and the Population Question in England, 1798–1859* (New York: Routledge, 2007). For general discussion of the popularization of political economy from socialist quarters, see Noel W. Thompson, *The People's Science: The Popular Political Economy of Exploitation and Crisis 1816–1834* (Cambridge: Cambridge University Press, 1984); and Sockwell, *Popularizing Classical Economics*.

[8] Harald Hagemann and Matthias Rösch, 'Economic Textbooks in the German Language Area', in *Economic Reader*, ed. Augello and Guidi, 96–123. The authors focus on textbooks for universities and do not include school textbooks in their study.

[9] Thomas Nipperdey, *Deutsche Geschichte 1800–1866. Bürgerwelt und starker Staat* (Munich: C.H. Beck, 1998), 520.

[10] Karl Pribram, *Geschichte des ökonomischen Denkens*, vol. 1 (Frankfurt am Main: Suhrkamp, 1998), 387. Further examples of early responses to Smith's writings among German philosophers, political scientists and theoreticians of political economy can be found in Birger Priddat, 'Deutsche Bedenken an Adam Smith. Feder, Sartorius und der notwendige Staat', in *Produktive Kraft, sittliche Ordnung und geistige Macht. Denkstile der deutschen Nationalökonomie im 18. und 19. Jahrhundert*, ed. Priddat (Marburg: Metropolis, 1998), 111–132.

within the context of a history of ideas will enable us to recognize that, although British and German publications in this area carried different labels, the one calling its self-produced discipline 'political economy' and the other *Staatswissenschaften*, *Volkswirtschaft* or *Nationalökonomie*, their divergences resulted essentially from the weightings they gave to various positions within a spectrum of essentially identical issues and questions.[11] This evident continuum is equally valid for the treatment of matters of education in writings from the discipline of economics. The present chapter, basing its exploration of the field on British and German economics books published for schools, universities and domestic use, will seek to demonstrate the close interconnections and interdependency between the economic teachings of the time, the economists' ideas of humanity, and the moral principles they espoused. Morally acceptable behaviour was to be learned and framed from early years onwards as new forms of knowledge arose and the capitalist economy gathered pace.

EDUCATION AND ECONOMY

The discussions that took place around the economic education of children and adolescents in the first half of the nineteenth century were inextricably linked to the emergent field of economy as an independent domain of knowledge. However, unlike philosophy or law, economy, or, as it came to be known, economics, was yet to successfully establish itself as such in terms of its institutions, discourses and array of experts. Mary Poovey has retraced this process principally from the overlaps in the meanings of economic terms apparent in the phase of transition to modernity which Reinhart Koselleck has termed the *Sattelzeit*. The terminology of the mercantile and cameralistic age, as well as the term *economy* itself in the sense of the deployment and administration of resources, were as clearly in evidence as the language of the emerging disciplines of political economy and *Nationalökonomie*.[12] It

[11] Frank Trentmann and Martin Daunton, 'Worlds of Political Economy: Knowledge, Practices and Contestation', in *Worlds of Political Economy: Knowledge and Power in the Nineteenth and Twentieth Century*, ed. Frank Trentmann and Martin Daunton (Houndsmill: Palgrave Macmillan, 2004), 1–23.

[12] Mary Poovey, *Making a Social Body: British Cultural Formation, 1830–1864* (Chicago and London: University of Chicago Press, 1995), 7. The economic historian Lars Magnusson likewise emphasizes the fact that Britain saw phases of transition in this regard,

is impossible to pin a precise date on the process by which economics transitioned to a professional discipline, due to the differing speeds at which the semantic systems, institutions and media that structured and carried the field developed.[13] In the first half of the nineteenth century, the self-descriptions made by the authors of these publications still varied considerably. At the century's dawn, male authors called themselves not economists, but philosophers, cameral officials, *Staatswissenschaftler* or experts in the law.[14] Only a handful of the authors we will discuss in what follows held positions as economists at a university during the first half of the nineteenth century; two among them were Richard Whately in Oxford and Karl Heinrich Rau in Heidelberg.[15] Women writing in this field called themselves simply writers, where they gave themselves an explicit label at all. As a general rule, all authors active in this field set themselves the objective of enabling their audiences to actively grasp and form an idea of a world in which 'the economy' was generating expanding fields of knowledge; their belief was that the successful negotiation of

although he argues in the opposite direction as regards historical development, asserting that as early as the seventeenth century, the mercantilists had regarded 'the economy' as a system within which people acted on markets with prices, wages, and rates of interest. See Lars Magnusson, *Mercantilism: The Shaping of an Economic Language* (London and New York: Routledge, 2002), 11. Cf. the detailed discussion of the historical development of the division between politics and 'economy' in Stefan Scholl, *Begrenzte Abhängigkeit. 'Wirtschaft' und 'Politik' im 20. Jahrhundert* (Frankfurt am Main and New York: Campus, 2015).

[13]On the emergence of 'economy', or economics, as a science in the final third of the nineteenth century, see Trentmann and Daunton, *Worlds of Political Economy*, 4f.; Mary Poovey, *Genres of the Credit Economy: Mediating Value in Eighteenth- and Nineteenth-Century Britain* (Chicago and London: University of Chicago Press, 2008), 229. Cf. also Massimo M. Augello and Marco E. L. Guidi, eds., *The Spread of Political Economy and the Professionalisation of Economists: Economic Societies in Europe, America and Japan in the Nineteenth Century* (London: Routledge, 2001); and Marion Fourcade, *Economists and Societies: Discipline and Profession in the United States, Britain, and France, 1890s to 1990s* (Princeton: Princeton University Press, 2004).

[14]Daunton and Trentmann, *Worlds of Political Economy*, 4.

[15]Deborah A. Redman, *The Rise of Political Economy as a Science: Methodology and the Classical Economists* (Cambridge, MA: MIT Press, 1997), 136. In 1727, the Prussian king ordered the establishment of chairs in '*Oeconomie, Policey und Cammersachen*' ('economy, policy and cameral affairs') at the universities of Halle and Frankfurt an der Oder. As of 1798, 36 German universities offered courses of study in cameralistics. See Keith Tribe, *Governing Economy: The Reformation of German Economic Thought, 1750–1840* (Cambridge: Cambridge University Press, 1988), 116.

this world called for detailed awareness of the way money worked in the economic space and the moral and practical dangers involved in navigating this space. It was a view of the world in which moral and economic matters were intrinsically linked.[16]

Until this point, authors had primarily approached this relationship between the economic and the moral in the context of the inculcation of a work ethic into the lower orders. Under the influence of the educational and Enlightenment ideas which had come to prominence in the eighteenth century, they considered improvements in schooling to be crucial to ensuring the whole of society progressed.[17] Economic aspects were at the heart of this mission, with those writing in the field advancing the view that it would be cheaper for the state to implement a minimum of education than to deal with the costs generated by the numbers of criminals that were sure to rise in the absence of such provisions.[18] Many economists created schemes for education revolving around utility. They hailed the teachings of Smith, Say, Malthus and Ricardo as a contribution to the solution of the social question with its ever-mounting urgency and as an instrument for the social control of the increasing masses of the impoverished in Britain as in the German states. The notion that the poor needed to be trained to work and acquire a work ethic further found broad support in philanthropic, charitable and administrative circles. In the face of spiraling poverty, educators, politicians and economists were forced to consider the matter of the large numbers of children growing up in poverty and their future prospects. In both Britain and the German lands, these efforts gave rise to state-led regulatory measures and legislative initiatives targeting pauper children, orphans and children of no fixed abode. The middle classes had a particularly marked tendency to apply socio-moralistic categories to these issues, attempting to impress upon the lower orders that labour was worthy and idleness sinful in an effort to reduce the cost of welfare and eliminating public mendicancy. It was at this time that the first provident savings banks came into being; one such institution was Hamburg's Ersparungskasse, founded in 1778, which enabled workers to pay small

---

[16]Cf., on the long history of the relationship between capitalism and morality, Herzog and Honneth, *Der Wert des Marktes*.

[17]Redman, *Political Economy*, 139.

[18]Cf. E. G. West (1975) *Education and the Industrial Revolution* (London and Sydney: Barnes & Noble).

sums into an account. These philanthropic initiatives were launched with the hope that the condition of the lower social strata might improve if these were to alter their financial attitudes and behaviours on an individual level.[19]

Karl Heinrich Rau, professor of Nationalökonomie at Heidelberg, emphasized in his influential *Lehrbuch der politischen Ökonomie* of 1828 that the expansion of elementary education in schools raised the 'moral and intellectual condition of a people' and aided the populace in comprehending the world of trade and the 'order of families' households'.[20] Education, he continued, acted as a preventative to poverty and exerted a long-term effect in favour of the 'dominion of steady reason over the passions', particularly when it came to early marriage and procreation.[21] Rau's ideas of good social order were in no way drawn from the notion of a dichotomy between public and private. His conception of political economy assumed close links between the household, the family and the state; in his view, improved education provided the basis for an overarching societal moral compass as well as well-ordered individual lives. Orphans and children in particularly dire poverty were to be educated in pauper or 'ragged' schools.[22] Rau's ideas chimed with those behind the industrial schools which had arisen in the late eighteenth century and whose purpose was to provide basic education alongside the teaching of skills required for trades. The children attending these institutions were taken from their parents, who were deemed unfit, and placed under the supervision of the school's head. Rau considered that regular daily routines, training in frugality, the inculcation of a work ethic and of techniques of manual labour, and religious instruction would serve to instil self-discipline in the pupils and provide them with the potential to join

---

[19] Eckhard Wandel, *Banken und Versicherungen im 19 und 20. Jahrhundert* (Munich: Oldenbourg, 1998), 3f.

[20] Karl Heinrich Rau, *Grundsätze der Volkswirthschaftspflege mit anhaltender Rücksicht auf bestehende Staatseinrichtungen (Lehrbuch der politischen Ökonomie, Bd. 2)* (Heidelberg: Winter, 1828), 24.

[21] Rau further cites the utility of saving money and of taking 'joy in money saved' (*Freude an Ersparnissen*) as measures for the prevention of poverty. Rau, *Grundsätze*, 379f.

[22] Cf. Wolfgang Dreßen, *Die pädagogische Maschine. Zur Geschichte des industrialisierten Bewusstseins in Preußen und Deutschland* (Frankfurt am Main and elsewhere: Ullstein, 1982), 280–283.

the labour force: 'The good education of such children will thus win for society a number of assiduous and morally upstanding citizens in place of the same number of feral idlers'.[23] The elementary education planned for these orders of society was in no way intended to raise them to a status approaching that of the middle classes; instead, its purpose was to fit the people thus educated, in line with their social class, to do their work and refrain from acquiring ideas above their station.

POLITICAL ECONOMY IN SCHOOLS

The access of wider societal groups, beyond those to be targeted by such instruction, to education in economic matters presupposed the availability of versions of key economic works that were comprehensible to children and non-specialists. Such popular writings supplied economics in general and political economy in particular with a broader readership than the little-read, in parts extremely complex works of Thomas Robert Malthus, Jean-Baptiste Say and David Ricardo could achieve. The authors of these popular publications addressed their writings to women, children and adolescents, alongside increasing attempts to appeal to the working class, mass appeal variants of the great economic works also attracted considerable male readerships. Additionally, almost every professor of economy, cameralistics, political economy, *Nationalökonomie* or *Volkswirtschaftslehre* issued a textbook consisting of the contents of his lectures compiled for students.[24] Additionally, political economy textbooks attained transnational reach, circulating among European states and undergoing multiple processes of copying and translation.[25] These efforts toward popularizing economic knowledge

---

[23] Rau, *Grundsätze*, 412. The original German is as follows: 'Die unter die genannten Classen gehörenden Kinder würden, wenn man sie ihrem Schicksale überließe, größtentheils zu arbeitsscheuen, unwissenden und sittenlosen Menschen werden, welche nur im Betteln oder in andern noch verderblicheren Ernährungsarten ihr Fortkommen suchten und fänden. Die gute Erziehung solcher Kinder gewinnt daher der Gesellschaft eine Anzahl fleißiger und gesitteter Bürger an der Stelle von ebensovieln verwilderten Müßiggängern [*sic*]'.

[24] Hagemann and Rösch, 'Economic Textbooks', 96.

[25] Augello and Guidi, *The Making of an Economic Reader*, 33.

in schools and universities acted to undermine concurrent attempts to define 'economy', especially political economy, as an exact science, as they transcended the division between economy and matters of morals, the education of the young or incapable (or those deemed to be so) and religion.[26] John Stuart Mill, for example, although he took great care over his narrow definition of political economy as a science, was well aware that that definition effectively invalidated itself as soon as the term appeared in publications aimed at a wider audience: 'the didactic writer on the subject will naturally combine in his exposition, with the truths of the pure science, as many of the practical modifications as will, in his estimation, be most conducive to the usefulness of his work'.[27]

The popularization of the discipline of political economy was not only an attempt to improve the economic awareness of the population at large, exercise social control and combat pauperism, but also an example of the extent to which the boundaries between what would later emerge as academic disciplines were at this point designed to allow transgression and flexibility. All those in the field were aware of this permeability and welcomed its perceived potential to help spread the salutary ideas of the new science. In the foreword of the 1820 German edition of Jane Marcet's *Conversations on Political Economy*, the translator emphasizes the relevance of political economy as a science to those of all stations in life: 'a science […] which is of close concern to the resident of civilized society, of sufficient interest to warrant familiarization as early as possible with its central principles'.[28] Further, citing a French review of the work's English edition, the translator pointed to the close interrelationship between political economy and the fields of *Staats- und Sittenlehre*: 'and so the desire for it [political economy] to be included among

---

[26] Claudia Klaver, *A/moral Economics: Classical Political Economy and Cultural Authority in Nineteenth Century Britain* (Athens, GA: Ohio State University Press, 2003), XVf.

[27] John Stuart Mill, 'On the Definition of Political Economy; and the Method of Investigation Proper to It', in *Essays on Some Unsettled Questions of Political Economy*, ed. Mill (London: John W. Parker, 1844), 120–164, 140f.

[28] Translator's preface, in Jane Marcet, *Unterhaltungen über die National-Oekonomie, worinn die Grundsätze dieser Wissenschaft vertraulich erklärt werden* (Ulm: Ebner, 1820), IV: 'eine Wissenschaft als welche den in der civilisirten Gesellschaft lebenden Menschen so nahe angeht, interessant genug, um sich so frühe als möglich mit ihren Hauptgrundsätzen bekannt zu machen […]'.

the matters taught to young people and become a substantial part of liberal education is entirely natural'.[29]

Malthus was one of the first, around the turn of the nineteenth century, to call for the incorporation of the teachings of political economy into textbooks for schools. Should instruction for the common people on this topic not be achievable, Malthus opined in 1803, political economy should at least be taught at universities, so as to familiarize the clergy and the political elite with the world of economic thought: 'It is of the very utmost importance that the gentlemen of the country, and particularly the clergy, should not, from ignorance, aggravate the evils of scarcity every time that it unfortunately occurs'.[30] Over 20 years later, he added, in a new edition of *On the Principle of Population*, a remark professing his satisfaction with the inclusion of political economy at establishments of higher education, noting that the discipline was on the advance through the educational institutions.[31]

The proposal, arising in turn-of-the-century England, to teach children and young people the tenets of political economy was an idea ahead of its time, yet it did begin to find acceptance among educators and in governmental circles in the 1830s.[32] Material on economics to be included in the textbooks and readers used by parish schools was sourced from the popular economics books

---

[29] Marcet, *Unterhaltungen*, III. The translator is quoting a French review of the English-language edition of 1816.

[30] Thomas Robert Malthus, *On the Principle of Population; Or, A View of Its Past and Present Effects on Human Happiness* (London: John Murray, 1803), 554.

[31] 'This note was written in 1803; and it is particularly gratifying to me, at the end of the year 1825, to see that what I stated as so desirable twenty-two years ago, seems to be now on the eve of its accomplishment. The increasing attention which in the interval has been paid generally to the science of political economy; the lectures which have been given at Cambridge, London, and Liverpool; the chair which has lately been established at Oxford; the projected University in the Metropolis; and, above all, the Mechanics Institution, open the fairest prospect that, within a moderate period of time, the fundamental principles of political economy will, to a very useful extent, be known to the higher, middle, and a most important portion of the working classes of society in England.' Thomas Robert Malthus, *On the Principle of Population, or, A View of Its Past and Present Effects on Human Happiness* (*Bd. 2*), 6th ed. (London, 1826), 354f.

[32] For a general view, cf. David Layton, *Science for the People: The Origins of the School Science Curriculum in England* (London: Allen & Unwin, 1973).

Conversations on Political Economy (1816) by Jane Marcet, James Mill's *Elements of Political Economy* (1821), Richard Whately's *Introductory Lectures of Political Economy* (1831), and two works by the American writer John McVickar, *Easy Lessons on Money Matters: For the Use of Young People* (1837) and *First Lessons of Political Economy for the Use of Elementary Schools* (1837).[33] The authors of these works read, and copied from, one another on a large scale and adapted the content of their publications to specific national needs. McVickar for example emphasized the importance of Whately's publication to his own work, commenting that he had first considered reprinting the latter before reflecting on the specific conditions in place in the US and restricting himself to copying the chapter on money.[34]

Many of these authors operated inside a social context that placed matters economic within a religious or political framework. Both Italian Catholics and Dutch Calvinists were among those who placed particular emphasis on the proximity of religious values to the laws governing the economy.[35] Before British textbooks and readers were reformed, their content was dominated by the idea of a rural world strongly influenced by the divine, in which inequality between rich and poor was cushioned by charity, and nobody left their predetermined station in life.[36] This content diversified with the shift to a more secular education, one aligned more closely with the tenets of economic thought. Differences in social status were now no longer regarded as outworkings of the divine will, but rather as the results of economic laws in action.[37] Although these changes called into question the reading of the Bible and of prayer books that had predominated in this area of education thus far, all religious denominations supported the shift and produced

[33] Jeffrey H. Marsh, 'Economics Education in Schools in the Nineteenth Century: Social Control', *Economics: The Journal of the Economics Association* 13 (1977): 116–118; Sockwell, *Popularizing Classical Economics*, 116.

[34] John McVickar, *First Lessons of Political Economy: For the Use of Primary and Common Schools* (Albany: Common School Depository, 1837).

[35] Cf. the examples in Augello and Guidi, *The Making of an Economic Reader*, 30.

[36] J. M. Goldstrom, *The Social Content of Education, 1808–1870: A Study of the Working Class School Reader in England and Ireland* (Shannon: Irish University Press, 1972), 34f.

[37] Goldstrom, *Social Content*, 71.

their own series of readers.[38] The *Daily Lesson Books* (1840–1842) issued by the Dissenters, the *Reading Books* (1851–1860) that the Society for Promoting Christian Knowledge published, the Congregationalists' *Training School Reader* (1851), and the *Catholic Reading Book Series* (1862) were only some of the publications appearing in the spectrum of English-language religious readers of this time. Alongside exemplary stories and moral tales, these books gave very practical pointers regarding money management and supplied explanations on matters pertaining to political economy. In one of the most significant English-language publications in the field, *The Training System* (1848), the author called for children to be encouraged to play shopkeeper so that they might learn the various forms of bookkeeping through practice.[39]

WOMEN, CHILDREN AND THE ECONOMY

Both the supply of and demand for economic knowledge had seen a marked increase by the beginning of the nineteenth century. There was public debate around the extent to which this new knowledge, set within the framework of the liberal economic order, was also relevant to children and women, and whether women should be permitted to teach it. The books and stories written by women in this

---

[38] In 1803, there were 7125 Sunday schools in Britain. Thomas W. Laqueur, *Religion and Respectability: Sunday Schools and Working Class Culture 1780–1850* (New Haven: Yale University Press, 1976); Goldstrom, *Social Content*, 9.

[39] David Stow, *The Training System of Education, for the Moral and Intellectual Elevation of Youth, Especially in Large Towns and Manufacturing Villages* (Edinburgh and London: Blackie and Son, 1846), 228. Stow further remarked that money could serve to test pupils' honesty; Stow, *Training System*, 403f. In later years, Millicent Garrett Fawcett called in *Political Economy for Beginners* (1870), a work that came into being through her collaboration with her blind husband, the economist Henry Fawcett, for political economy to be taught in the context of basic schooling. This publication proved an eminently successful seller. Fawcett felt herself to be very much in the tradition of predecessor works on economy composed by women such as Jane Marcet and Harriet Martineau. Willie Henderson, 'Millicent Garrett Fawcett's Political Economy for Beginners: An Evaluation', *Paedagogica Historica* 40, no. 4 (2004): 435–453 (435). A further publication of Fawcett's was *Tales in Political Economy* (1874), in whose authorial preface she references the influence on her of the tales written by Harriet Martineau. Millicent Garrett Fawcett, *Tales in Political Economy* (London: Macmillan, 1874).

area received mixed reactions. A reviewer writing in *Tait's Edinburgh Magazine* in 1832 was evidently surprised at his own observation that '[t]he ladies seem determined to make the science of Political Economy peculiarly their own'.[40] One of the earliest and most significant books to emerge in this context was Jane Marcet's *Conversations on Political Economy*,[41] published in London in 1816, whose intended audience was young middle-class people of both sexes.[42] An emphatic success, the book saw at least 14 English-language editions and was translated into Dutch and Spanish as well as German and French.[43] Jane Marcet, born Haldimand (1769–1858), was the eldest of ten children of a wealthy Protestant banking family from Geneva, living in London.[44] Upon her father's death in 1817, she inherited a substantial portion of his wealth, which enabled her to write independently. Her activities as a doyenne of London society brought her into frequent and lively contact with political and economic reformers living and working in the city; among the luminaries she hosted at her home were Henry Brougham, founder of the Society for the Diffusion of Useful Knowledge, Thomas Malthus, David Ricardo and James Mill. Her origins, her wealth and her salon combined to make her stand out as a woman on the London scene.[45] Marcet's initial success in publishing came through her book *Conversations on Chemistry, Intended More Especially for the Female Sex* (1806), which was translated into several languages, copied widely, and adapted as a basis for school textbooks. She regarded the dissemination of new insights and knowledge in the sciences and economics as her mission. In 1816, in a letter to Pierre Provost, she wrote, 'I can assure you that the greatest pleasure I derive from success is the hope of doing good by the propagation of useful truths amongst a class of people,

[40] 'Miss Martineau's Illustrations of Political Economy', in: Tait's Edinburgh Magazine, August 1832', in *Harriet Martineau, Illustrations of Political Economy: Selected Tales*, ed. Deborah Anna Logan (Toronto, 2014), 416–418, 416.

[41] Jane Marcet, *Conversations on Political Economy; In Which the Elements of That Science Are Familiarly Explained* (London: Longman, Hurst, Rees, Orme and Brown, 1816).

[42] Marcet, *Conversations*, VI.

[43] The US edition in particular is referred to as the first 'textbook in economics education'; Henderson, 'Economics as Literature', 44.

[44] One of her brothers later became director of the Bank of England.

[45] Evelyn L. Forget, introduction to Jane Marcet, *Conversations on the Nature of Political Economy*, ed. Evelyn L. Forget (New Brunswick: Transaction, 2009), VII–XXXVI.

who, excepting in a popular familiar form, would never have become acquainted with them'.[46] As an author, she felt she had the 'sole object of diffusing useful truths'.[47] Her further publications, *John Hopkins's Notions on Political Economy* (1833), intended to be read by working people, and *Rich and Poor* (1851), met with lesser success.[48] The latter was a compilation of 13 lessons she had written to explain to children the state of social harmony between the poorer and wealthier classes.[49]

Turning to the contested terrain of definition of the new discipline, Marcet described political economy as a science whose popularization and incorporation into education was imperative: 'Political Economy, though so immediately connected with the happiness and improvement of mankind, and the object of so much controversy and speculation among men of knowledge, is not yet a popular science, and is not generally considered as a study essential to early education'.[50] Children and 'savages'—observed Marcet, using an analogy quite in the tenor of her age—lived as a rule in the present, and there only; yet education could allow them to entertain ideas of a future and a past, which were prerequisites for actions in the economic field aimed at increasing individual and general wealth. Marcet's focus here was not exclusively the instruction of children, but also the education of the working classes. In her view, working people who pledged themselves to the values of assiduity, frugality and moderation could be freed from their misery and formed into individuals with well-tempered emotions: 'Education gives rise to prudence, not only by enlarging our understandings, but by softening our feelings, by humanizing the heart, and promoting amiable affections'.[51]

The *Conversations* comprise a collection of 22 dialogues between the mature teacher Mrs. B. and her younger pupil Caroline on the key terms of political economy: property, capital, population, money, value, credit

[46] Cited in introduction to Marcet, *Conversations*, XVII.

[47] Marcet, *Conversations*, VIII.

[48] Keith Tribe, 'Economic Manuals and Textbooks in Great Britain and the British Empire 1797–1938', in *Economic Reader*, ed. Augello and Guidi, 43–75 (48).

[49] Jane Marcet, *Rich and Poor: Dialogues on a Few of the First Principles of Political Economy* (London; Longman, Brown, Green, and Longmans, 1851).

[50] Marcet, *Conversations*, V–VI.

[51] Marcet, *Conversations*, 158.

and interest. Marcet had employed the dialogic style in her successful book on chemistry and, as she sets out in the *Conversations'* preface, deemed it likewise appropriate for the subject of economy: '[…] because it gave her an opportunity of introducing objections, and placing in various points of view, questions and answers as they had actually occurred to her own mind […]'.[52] It was a format not unusual for works of the time; originating from a rhetorical technique used in classical antiquity and reminiscent of the Socratic method of dialogue aiming at discovery, and employed for educational purposes in the eighteenth century in particular. The format of the dialogic teaching of knowledge was not reserved for the popular presentation of complex content, nor was it limited to the education of women and children, although the advancing nineteenth century assigned it exactly this purpose.[53]

Marcet regarded education as a component of societal progress, a belief she illustrates at the *Conversations'* outset by having the figure of the pupil reject the topic at hand: 'I confess that I have a sort of antipathy to political economy'. Continuing, Caroline explains that, while the matter was the subject of much discussion at home, it appeared to her as 'the most uninteresting of all subjects',[54] causing her to yawn openly and lapse into boredom and despair at the constant lionization and deification of Adam Smith in light of the incomprehensible language in which he expressed himself. At this point, Marcet counters with an initial exposition of the utility of the discipline, which Caroline's teacher maintains has closer ties to daily life than one might commonly imagine, and the knowledge of whose laws might prevent the misjudgements which so often befell the poets.[55] Here, Marcet suggests the superiority of the new liberal economic ideas over the presumedly archaic assumptions of moral economy, still defended only by poets and other enthusiasts not much troubled by reality.[56]

---

[52] Marcet, *Conversations,* VIII–IX.

[53] Myers, 'Science', 174 Michèle Cohen, 'The Pedagogy of Conversation in the Home: "Familiar Conversation" as a Pedagogical tool in Eighteenth- and Nineteenth-Century England', *Oxford Review of Education* 41 (2015): 447–463.

[54] Marcet, *Conversations,* 5.

[55] Marcet, *Conversations,* 8–10.

[56] Marcet, *Conversations,* 10.

This introductory dialogue on the uses of political economy initiates the education of the young Caroline on these matters. She proceeds to learn that wealth is not measured in money alone, but in all objects and goods that can be converted to a monetary value. She discovers that the differences in the valuation of labour in evidence among 'savages' and the 'civilized' arise from the former group's lack of a clear idea of the future and from its wish for comfort and ease. To her great joy, she is apprised of the dependence of the general wealth on the existence of the idea of private property and of settled life, and of the fact that the division of labour brought with it an enormous increase in the production of goods. At this point, Marcet has her Caroline exclaim delightedly, 'These effects of the division of labour are really wonderful!'[57] The final dialogue, 'On Expenditure', revolves around the hazards attaching to money, taking in the legitimacy of luxury and appropriate consumption and touching on the dangers encountered by working-class people who come into money suddenly.

The dialogues are dramatized as a process of continuous progress in the attainment of knowledge.[58] Almost at their end, the author, speaking with the voice of the now-converted Caroline, paints a picture of divine harmony among the classes, a symbiosis of rich and poor, of capitalists and workers; a harmony emerging from the fact that only capital employed productively can increase. By securing the capitalist, runs the message, capital simultaneously assures the livelihood of the working classes: 'The more I hear on this subject, and the better I understand it, the greater is my admiration of that wise and beneficent arrangement which has so closely interwoven the interests of all classes of men!'[59] The voice of the teacher adds to the symphony of praise, remarking that providence is not only present in nature but also in moral life and in the order of the economic world, and that it would be wrong for political interference to disturb this quasi-divine balance and order.[60]

Marcet's publication popularized an economic order based on the division of labour and the formation of capital. It is an order within

[57] Marcet, *Conversations*, 73.

[58] Marcet, *Conversations*, 44f.

[59] Marcet, *Conversations*, 428.

[60] Marcet, *Conversations*, 428f.

which progress takes place through an awareness of temporality and the investment of capital with an eye to the future; these attitudes and actions are represented as enabling both those social classes in possession of capital and those without to attain higher standards of living. In thus advocating this order of things, Marcet emphatically took the side of those who no longer regarded capital formation and profit as contradictory to the Christian values which had deemed them legitimate only where they were accompanied by corresponding acts of charity and generosity. Indeed, Marcet's delineation of the benefits of this economic order for all classes and of the harmony thus emerging was an attempt to depict the investment of capital itself as a bountiful act.

CAPITALISM AS PROVIDENCE

Some years after Marcet's success with the *Conversations*, a further popular outline of political economy and its principles aroused lively interest and found entry into teaching materials on the topic for schools. *Easy Lessons on Money Matters: for the Use of Young People* was published in 1837 and aimed toward children aged eight and above. Its author, Richard Whately, joined many of his contemporaries in emphasizing the necessity of commencing education in economic and money matters in childhood: 'Many, even of what are called the educated classes, grow up with indistinct, or erroneous, and practically mischievous views on these subjects […]'.[61] Far from being a third-rate author of now-forgotten penny literature for children, Whately, the archbishop of Dublin and professor of political economy at Oxford, had a professional interest in the mission of schooling young minds in matters economic. Indeed, it was a topic worth a book of its own—which would be partially serialized in the *Saturday Magazine* prior to its publication—to Whately, who had made a vocal contribution to the political controversies around the Irish Poor Laws and the education system. The work enjoyed great success and considerable influence, enduringly bolstered by its author's position as Irish Commissioner of National Education. Around the middle of the century, there was barely a school reader in the British Isles which did not feature extracts from the *Easy Lessons*.[62]

---

[61] Richard Whately, *Easy Lessons on Money Matters: For the Use of Young People* (London: J. W. Parker, 1837), VI.

[62] Sockwell, *Popularizing Classical Economics*, 102; Cooper, *Family Fictions*, 93.

The book consisted of sections revolving, *inter alia*, around money, trade, coins, value, wages, poverty and wealth, capital and taxes. Basing his sketches of the subject on everyday objects and substances such as sugar, Whately argued that children and young people needed to understand the way in which individual goods were tied into the global routes of trade.[63] His work presented a mixture of information on the global economy and explication of the divine order of things on which his discussion was predicated. This link between matters moral and economic manifests particularly clearly in the illustration appearing in conjunction with the first lesson, on 'Money'. The image shows a charitable gesture by a young boy whose hand is held by an adult woman. The boy bends down to a figure sitting outside a simple dwelling who is holding out a hat to beg for alms, and throws in a coin. The text that follows discusses the act of benefaction as a virtue desired and prized by the divine will,[64] although it then proceeds, somewhat in contrast to this allusion to Christian ethics, to offer the rather unbiblical observation: 'What a useful thing is money!'[65]

Unlike other authors, who joined with Thomas Carlyle in critically regarding and mistrusting money as an epitome of modern life, Whately combined his liberal ideas of economics with the presumption of a civilization born through money and presided over by divine providence. In his further rationale for the division of responsibilities within society, however, Whately left the terrain of the divine order and predicated his argument upon the necessity of the existence of wealth. Wealthy people, he claimed, secured a living for the poor by means of the opportunities for labour they provided. This classic narrative of contemporary political economy served Whately well in his legitimization of the cleft between rich and poor.[66] Although, as Whately admitted, rich men were indeed selfish, nevertheless in making every effort to increase their level of wealth their utility to the common good was impossible to overlook.[67] Whately's paean to the productive effects of money extended beyond the prospect of intergenerational upward social mobility secured

[63] Whately, *Easy Lessons*, XII.

[64] Whately, *Easy Lessons*, 3.

[65] Whately, *Easy Lessons*, 1.

[66] Whately, *Easy Lessons*, 28. 'The more Capital there is in a country, the better for the labourers [...].' Whately, *Easy Lessons*, 38.

[67] Whately, *Easy Lessons*, 30.

through the wise education of one's children. He held out the promise that people might see benefits in their own lifetimes; although he warned that wealth would not increase by frugal hoarding alone.[68] He went on to explain that a sum of money only begins to increase when its owner lends it, against the assurance of its return and for a charge called interest.[69] In presenting this explanation, Whately clearly refuted the criticism of interest from religious quarters. His approving description of the process of lending money against interest, in a publication aimed at children and adolescents, was unusual indeed; there was generally little mention of this particular mechanism of capital formation in the materials used for the instruction of children in the first half of the nineteenth century.

Whately's *Easy Lessons on Money Matters* made a link between the communication of economic knowledge and the providence of the divine Father who had created the world in such a way as to assure its continuous improvement through self-regulation. This mechanism, which Adam Smith had termed the 'invisible hand', finds explicit depiction as divine providence in Whately's work:

> It is curious to observe how, through the wise and beneficent arrangement of Providence, men thus do the greatest service to the public, when they are thinking of nothing but their own gain. And this happens, not only in the case of corn-dealers, but generally. When men are left quite free to employ their Capital as each thinks best for his own advantage, he will almost always benefit the public, though he may have no such design or thought.[70]

According to this argument, monetary self-interest leads to the increase of the general wealth. This rejection of specific religiously founded doubts about the processes of capital formation and pursuance of profit

---

[68]Whately, *Easy Lessons*, 37.

[69]Whately, *Easy Lessons*.

[70]Whately, *Easy Lessons*, 42f. Moritz Carl Ernst von Prittwitz is likewise in accord with Adam Smith when he writes that the pursuit of self-interest positively affects the welfare of the whole of society. Moritz Carl Ernst von Prittwitz, *Die Kunst reich zu werden, oder gemeinfaßliche Darstellung der Volkswirthschaft. Ein Handbuch für Beamte, Studirende, Gemeindevorsteher, Fabrikanten, Kaufleute, Landwirthe und überhaupt jeden Gebildeten* (Mannheim: 1840), VI.

was characteristic of the period, as Boyd Hilton has likewise observed.[71] Whately was one of the few authors who did not baulk at communicating this notion to children.

Economic Knowledge in School Instruction in Germany

The contemporaneous situation in the German states stood in contrast to the periodic inclusion in British textbooks of economic questions in general and elements of political economy specifically. In Prussia, education legislation introduced in 1819 mandated the expansion of elementary schooling (*Volksschulen*) and provided for stricter application of the requirement for children aged six and above to attend school. At this time, education officials drew up schemes for the instruction of these children which were by no means aimed at utility alone. With this, the Prussian government responded to these neo-humanistic designs for a comprehensive reform of education not focused solely on schooling for a specific purpose, be it vocational or oriented toward enabling pupils to take their place in a specific stratum of society. Their intention was for a general education of the whole person, transcending social class, to form the basis for all further education and to banish 'fixations and pedagogical biases' (*Fixierungen sowie pädagogische Einseitigkeiten*).[72] This theoretical design initially came up against de facto limits, as the *Volksschulen* remained institutions for the lower social classes. In practice, until the mid-nineteenth century, the teaching delivered in the *Volksschulen* in both rural and urban areas was dependent on regional particularities, the teachers and the resources available to each school. Generally, priority was given to literacy education and religious instruction, the latter driven by constant study of the Bible.[73] There was relatively little instruction in

---

[71] Boyd Hilton, *The Age of Atonement: The Influence of Evangelicalism on Social and Economic Thought* (Oxford; Clarendon Press, 2008).

[72] Karl-Ernst Jeismann, *Das preußische Gymnasium in Staat und Gesellschaft*, vol. 1 (Stuttgart: Klett-Cotta, 1996), 349; cf. also Dietrich Benner, *Wilhelm von Humboldts Bildungstheorie. Eine problemgeschichtliche Studie zum Begründungszusammenhang neuzeitlicher Bildungsreform* (Weinheim: Juventa, 1990).

[73] Gerd Friedrich, 'Das niedere Schulwesen', in *Handbuch der deutschen Bildungsgeschichte, Bd. III: 1800–1870*, ed. Karl-Ernst Jeismann and Peter Lundgreen (Munich: C.H. Beck, 1987), 123–152, 132f.; Frank-Michael Kuhlemann, *Modernisierung*

arithmetic, although intermediate classes did sums using coins and more advanced pupils were taught to calculate discounts and interest.[74]

Meanwhile, German political scientists and economists did not need to be convinced of the economic importance of education and the utility of instruction in economic tenets. As early as the opening years of the nineteenth century, they called for education on matters economic. One of the authors to do so was the German government adviser and writer Friedrich Julius Heinrich von Soden (1754–1831), whose work *Die Nazional-Oekonomie*, published in several volumes from 1805 onward, emphasized the need for Germany to create for itself a concept of '*Nazional-Bildung*', providing an economic rationale: 'These educational establishments are a truly national-economic effort of the state. The education of the citizens of the state boosts production; this boost increases the national wealth, and thus returns the investment many times over'.[75] He emphasized the economic significance of reforms to school-based education with a particular eye to higher establishments of learning, and proposed comprehensive reforms to the existing school system so it could serve the 'national need' (*Nazional-Bedürfniß*) better.[76] In his view, it was incumbent upon academies, establishments for advanced schooling and universities to put a stop to the proliferation of 'unfruitful, speculative studies that are not conducive to national wealth',[77] and education in languages at academic secondary schools should be reduced to make room for more 'scientific instruction in all aspects of national production'.[78] Soden was not alone in his views, which were shared by various German contemporaries including the legally trained national economist Johann F. E. Lotz (1771–1838), who called for education to be evaluated according to its economic utility and directed toward training pupils to negotiate the world of economic goods:

---

und Disziplinierung. Sozialgeschichte des preußischen Volksschulwesens, 1794–1872 (Göttingen: Vandenhoeck & Ruprecht, 1992), 237.

[74] Friedrich, 'Schulwesen', 134–138.

[75] Friedrich Julius Heinrich von Soden, *Die Nazional-Oekonomie. Ein philosophischer Versuch über die Quellen des Nazional-Reichthums und über die Mittel zu dessen Beförderung 9 Bde*, vol. 5 (Leipzig: J. A. Barth, 1811), 194.

[76] Soden, *Die Nazional-Oekonomie*, 192.

[77] Soden, *Die Nazional-Oekonomie*, 189.

[78] Soden, *Die Nazional-Oekonomie*, 192.

A person's intellectual education is what enables him to recognize rightly his relationship to the world of goods; it is what makes him industrious and hard-working, and, finally, it is what teaches him to use goods everywhere in a manner truly conducive to the human desire and aspiration to be better and become better.[79]

Some authors aimed their textbooks and writings toward older audiences, particularly their students in the universities. In the preface (*Vorerinnerungen*) to his *Lehrbuch der politischen Oekonomie* (1813), the German cameralist Friedrich Benedict Weber (1774–1848) recounted how strongly he had felt the need of such a book for his lectures.[80] Albeit still owing much in his work to the '*Staats-* [and] *Polizey-Wissenschaften*', Weber stressed the necessity of the new economic sciences, maintaining that political economy could and should be learned in university lectures, in self-study, by attending academies, while travelling, through familiarizing oneself with the principles of public administration, and through personal acquaintances and practical activity.[81]

In the German states, these ideas came up against an education system whose elementary stage, in the mid-nineteenth century, largely rested on work with readers. These publications increasingly formed the basis of the instruction delivered at German *Volksschulen*; concomitant developments were the relegation of Bible study as *Realienkunde* emerged and nature, geography, the nation (*Vaterländische Gesinnung*) and morality became dominant themes.[82] Thus, the reader became not solely a source of literacy instruction, but also the central instrument within the school setting for the communication of models of desirable moral behaviour such as charity, frugality and the repudiation of greed.[83] A brief depiction

[79] Johann Friedrich Eusebius Lotz, *Handbuch der Staatswirthschaftslehre*, vol. 1 (Erlangen: Palm und Enke, 1821), 208f.

[80] Friedrich Benedict Weber, 'Vorerinnerung', in *Lehrbuch der politischen Ökonomie* (Breslau, 1813).

[81] Weber, *Lehrbuch*, 23f.

[82] See Swantje Ehlers, 'Der literarische Kanon im Volksschullesebuch Mitte des 19. Jahrhunderts', in *Das Lesebuch 1800–1945. Ein Medium zwischen literarischer Kultur und pädagogischem Diskurs*, ed. Hermann Korte and Ilonka Zimmer (Frankfurt am Main: Peter Lang, 2006), 103–121.

[83] Peter Lundgreen, 'Analyse preußischer Schulbücher als Zugang zum Thema "Schulbildung und Industrialisierung"', *International Review of Social History* 15 (1970): 85–121, 108, 111.

in narrative form, as a fable or short tale, of specific instances of desired money management behaviour was used to illustrate to children a morally acceptable relationship with money. The story 'Wealth' (*Der Reichthum*) in the widely disseminated reader *Preußischer Kinderfreund* saw the desire of a pupil to possess greater amounts of money challenged and confronted by the rejoinder of his former teacher that the important things in life, such as health and nature, surpassed money in significance.[84] Other stories in the collection, like 'The Horse and the Purse' (*Das Pferd und der Geldbeutel*) and 'The Little Stock-Trader' (*Der kleine Börsenhändler*), made reference to the charitable deeds of the rich toward the poor, or, as in 'The Voice of Conscience' (*Die Stimme des Gewissens*), to the deleterious consequences of a lack of charity.[85] The Catholic reader issued by the cleric Christoph von Schmid likewise included a considerable number of short stories, such as 'The Purse' (*Der Geldbeutel*), in which rich characters reward poor ones for honesty.[86] This content was no different in nature from that of Protestant readers.

Textbooks, arithmetic and reading primers frequently located processes of learning both in school and in the family; the authors of many of them therefore aimed them at a hybrid readership. Albert Gerth, a teacher at the Königliches Pädagogium on the Baltic island of Rügen, was no exception; his *Accounting for Children* (*Buchhaltung für Kinder*, 1839) was directed not so much toward the 'children' referenced in the book's title but toward adolescent boys who were preparing to leave home to study or enter vocational training. He underlined the importance of keeping order in small things for the functionality of the state

---

[84] Jäger, 'Der Reichthum', in *Preußischer Kinderfreund. Ein Lesebuch für Volksschulen, zusammengestellt von A.E. Preuß und J.A. Vetter* (Königsberg, 1839), 39–40. Cf. also the story '*Kindesdank*' (Gratitude of a Child), in *Kinderfreund*, 103–104.

[85] *Kinderfreund*, 68–69, 91–92, 119–120. Cf. also the rhyme: 'Mark well, the way to gain the pound Is by the penny, I declare; For he who fails to watch the pennies Never shall in riches share' ('Weißt wo der Weg zum Thaler ist? Dem Pfennig nach; merk' dir die Lehr'! Denn wer nicht auf den Pfennig sieht, Der kommt zum Thaler nimmermehr.'); *Kinderfreund*, 188. An appendix to the narrative part of the book gives an overview of coins, currencies and conversion rates.

[86] 'Der Geldbeutel', in Christoph von Schmid, *Lehrreiche kleine Erzählungen für Kinder. Ein Lesebüchlein für Volksschulen* (Rotweil: Herder, 1833), 75–77.

economy, and called for the teaching of economic knowledge to begin during schooling, so that young people might be assured of smooth development into 'men and citizens':

> And if school is intended to prepare the boy, and its rules and admonitions to raise him, morally and intellectually, to be a future man and citizen, why does it not also give him direct instruction on how he is to manage the material affairs of the life of citizenship he is to enter? Why does it not send him into the world equipped with particular rules of economy and frugality?[87]

The rationale in evidence here for providing economic education for boys and young men from the middle classes was their future professional careers.[88] Continuing, Gerth asserted that teaching boys in these aspects was also of importance due to the fact that most disciplinary incidents with which he had to deal could be traced back to profligacy with pocket money: 'Never will such a boy, led astray into disarray, extravagance and hedonism, do well in school, and much less does he promise [to meet] the requirements of a future respectable position in the system of the State'.[89] It was not so much the new ideas of the discipline of political economy that served to legitimate this author's ideas, but rather the civic order of the state, which he perceived as resting on the economic rationality of men.

While pupils at German schools were thus familiarized with the moral dimension of matters economic, the German political economist and statistician Otto Hübner (1818–1877) published *Der kleine Volkswirth. Ein Büchlein für den Elementarunterricht* (The Little Economist: A Little Book for Elementary Instruction, 1852), a book for *Volksschule*

---

[87] Albert Gerth, *Buchhaltung für Kinder oder Anweisung zur Ordnung und Sparsamkeit in Geldsachen für den Selbstunterricht und Gebrauch in Schulen* (Stralsund: Löffler, 1839), V–VI.

[88] In his preface, the author made use of anti-Semitic semantics to defend himself against the anticipated accusation of materialism, and demonstratively took up the pose of a passionate pedagogue who sought only to act in his pupils' best interests, denying that he was a merchant or a Jew, 'after booty like a creeping Israelite' (*auf Beute aus wie ein kriechender Israelit*). Gerth, *Buchhaltung*, VI–VII.

[89] Gerth, *Buchhaltung*, VIII, IX–X.

aimed at teachers and decidedly economic in emphasis and tone.[90] His
self-declared aim was to 'present the fundaments of the moral economy
in a manner comprehensible to children'. In the course of the second
half of the nineteenth century, *Der kleine Volkswirth* was translated into
French, Spanish, Dutch, Turkish and Portuguese, adapted each time to
the specificities of the national readership.[91] In 13 lessons, the author,
who had made his name as a statistician, discussed topics including
labour and its division, money, the various professions and trades, property, capital, and interest; the work concluded with a look at poverty and
wealth. Each lesson was structured in the same way. It commenced with
an outline of the topics involved for young people, with no further rec-
ommendation as to appropriate age. Then followed tasks for teachers to
set their pupils, in question form; thus in the lesson on labour, 'What do
we call work? […] Why do you work? […] What are the consequences of
idleness? How would things look if everybody refused to do any work?'[92]
Hübner was unambiguous about the objective of his book on economic
education to see off any tendencies toward socialism:

> Socialism is making such great strides because popular education has thus
> far failed to cultivate in children's minds the fields upon which the virtues
> and passions of adults act and has left it to chance to shape their idea[s] of
> what is mine and what is yours, of property and purchase, of the value of
> goods and of people.[93]

Hübner wished the factual instruction his book provided in the terminology of the economic world to be accompanied by the teaching of
virtues such as respect, hard work, abstinence, and integrity, which he
regarded as requiring presentation not only as 'sacrifices pleasing to God'

[90] Otto Hübner, *Der kleine Volkswirth. Ein Büchlein für den Elementarunterricht*
(Leipzig: Mayer, 1852). Hübner published a number of writings on political economy
and statistics, including *Die Banken* (1854), and had been editor of the *Jahrbuch für
Volkswirthschaft und Statistik* since 1852. Hübner, *Der kleine Volkswirth*, IV.

[91] Augello and Guidi, *The Making of an Economic Reader*, 19f.; Deniz T. Kilinçoğlu,
Economics and Capitalism in the Ottoman Empire (Routledge Studies in the History of
Economics; London and New York: Routledge, 2015), 31.

[92] Hübner, *Volkswirth*, 13.

[93] Hübner, *Volkswirth*, III–IV.

but as characteristics advantageous to the individual.[94] He drew an analogy between teachers of economy and factory owners: 'As he who runs a factory transforms a block of iron into useful tools, so does the teacher transform the ignorant boy into a man of use in the world'.[95]

Its orientation toward global trade set *Der kleine Volkswirth* apart from other contemporary popularizations of economics. The book is a vivid delineation of the advantages to economic progress wrought by property, the division of labour, and money, factors Hübner regarded as fundamental to the emergence and simplification of global relations of trade. A further legitimation supplied by Hübner for the consumption of products and the global exchange of goods was a religious one; he deemed these to be 'one of those great arrangements of divine wisdom' whose plan involved the human contact and communication which had enabled Christianity to 'spread across the whole world'.[96] God, Hübner continued, had also 'arranged' (*angeordnet*, a term also meaning 'ordered' in the further sense of the issuance of a command) the division of labour between the people of each country as well as between the 'various zones of the earth'. Thus, Hübner concluded, a lack of global exchange and communication was in contradiction to the will of God.[97] Hübner's chapter about money likewise emphasizes the necessity of trading worldwide, observing that money made it easier to 'exchange across great distances'.[98] He explained that the increasing complexity of markets made it impossible to remain on the level of simple barter of goods desired by each party to the transaction. A baker, for instance, would not give bread in exchange to a shoemaker if he did not need shoes at that point in time. Money, by contrast, simplified the exchange of goods due to its enabling of decisions regarding consumption which could be made independently of the products each party had at their disposal.

Hübner's book also differed from others of its kind in its treatment of capital and interest. The author is clear in his defence of the practice of charging interest on monies lent. Anticipating the objection that

---

[94] Hübner, *Volkswirth*, V–VI.

[95] Hübner, *Volkswirth*, 50.

[96] Hübner, *Volkswirth*, 24.

[97] Hübner, *Volkswirth*, 28.

[98] Hübner, *Volkswirth*, 33.

'the capitalist' received interest 'without working for it' (*ohne dafür zu arbeiten*),[99] he rebutted it by observing that capital itself contained previously performed labour which needed to be paid for when that capital was lent and that interest was a form of 'compensation' (*Entschädigung*) for its use.[100] In the book's final lesson, on 'rich and poor', Hübner stressed the necessity of wealth; while admitting that it was 'certainly a Christian desire' to reduce the gap between the wealthy and the impoverished,[101] he argued that a redistribution of wealth would not have the desired effect and was incapable of lifting the lower classes out of their penury, and that the wealth of the few likewise provided an advantage for the poor.[102]

Despite the calls from German authors for education in matters economic and for instruction suited to the situation of the contemporary economy, Otto Hübner is the only author of this time who explicitly declared his wish list for *Volksschule* teachers to include the teaching of political economy. Apart from the handful of exceptions discussed above, the material for economic instruction in the German states was dominated by readers primarily presenting economic activity as it related to religion and morality and providing factual information on currencies and types of money. We may therefore conclude that, while the figures in the German states who supplied ideas about economics and how to teach it had intentions not dissimilar to those seen in Britain, the instruction given in Prussia's *Volksschulen* was not comparable to the British approach to education in economics, not least due to the fundamental differences in practical implementation. This said, Deborah Redman's history of political economy points out that even in Britain economic instruction did not enjoy long-term success. The decline and fall of *laissez-faire* thought, the increasing critique to which the idea of political economy was subjected, and eventually the end of the reign of classic political economy itself, sealed the disappearance at the outset of the twentieth century of the books which had specifically made instruction

[99] Hübner, *Volkswirth*, 71.

[100] Hübner, *Volkswirth*, 70.

[101] Hübner, *Volkswirth*, 75.

[102] Hübner, *Volkswirth*, 78.

in the discipline their mission.[103] The hybrid genre of popularization of and simultaneous instruction in economic matters gave way to educational series produced by publishers for the classroom, containing topics relating to the economy alongside geography, history and literature. As Augello and Guidi's incisive European analysis shows, the specific genre of popularizing educational books in this manner thus met its end.[104]

Independent of the national background of their authors, all publications aiming to popularize economic knowledge explicated it in the context of morality, visions for the future, and notions of utility that should be enhanced in school and family education. Religious references were prominent across the board, either pointing to God as the father of the economic global order or arguing for the mitigation of dangerous passions like greed. Well into the nineteenth century's second half, *homo oeconomicus* remained an active subject with emotions to be controlled, knowledge to be gained, and a predestined position within the society and divine order within which s/he moved. It was not until the twentieth century that economic theory made its attempt to reduce the human individual to a model in order to make reliable predictions regarding trends in economic development.

Translated by Dr. Katherine Ebisch-Burton

---

[103] Redman, *Political Economy*, 142; Marsh, *Economics Education*, is an earlier, very brief, exploration of the topic.

[104] Augello and Guidi, *The Making of an Economic Reader*, 22, 33.

CHAPTER 3

Moralizing Wealth: German Debates About Capitalism and Jews in the Early Twentieth Century

Alexandra Przyrembel

INTRODUCTION

After many years of neglect, the history of capitalism is now being inten-sively discussed. But while interest in capitalism has been reignited, the supposed and actual beneficiaries of capitalism are still disregarded by historians. The history of the wealthy as the profiteers of capitalism has remained largely unexplored. In his recent best-selling book *Capital in the Twenty-first Century*, the French economist Thomas Piketty addresses the global flourishing of capital in its entanglement with increased social inequality.[1] Despite the criticism it aroused on both sides of the Atlantic, Piketty's social critique of wealth's uneven distribution—according to Paul Krugman, a columnist for the *New York Times* and winner of the

---

[1] Thomas Piketty, *Capital in the Twenty-First Century* (Cambridge, MA: The Belknap Press of Harvard University Press, 2014).

A. Przyrembel (✉)
Modern European History, University of Hagen, Hagen, Germany
e-mail: alexandra.przyrembel@fernuni-hagen.de

© The Author(s) 2019
S. Berger and A. Przyrembel (eds.), *Moralizing Capitalism*,
Palgrave Studies in the History of Social Movements,
https://doi.org/10.1007/978-3-030-20565-2_3

Nobel Prize—has changed the current debate on the winners and losers of capitalism: 'We'll never talk about wealth and inequality the same way we used to'.[2] In a similar vein, a German scholar summarizes the impact of Piketty's book on social sciences as a 'plea for repoliticization' and 'remoralization'.[3]

The topic of increasing social inequality caused by an 'untamed' capitalism has shaped the debates about wealth since the first formulation of a critique of capitalism in the early nineteenth century. Karl Marx, the famous author of *Capital*, underlined in dramatic terms the injustices of capitalism, which according to his interpretation are based mainly on the exploitation of labour, most visible in children's labour 'And the first birthright of capital is equal exploitation of labour-power by all capitalists […] The children [employed in the silk mills] were slaughtered out-and-out for the sake of their delicate fingers'.[4] Already these two observations written more than 150 years apart indicate that the core of the critique of capitalism is an imputation of injustice.[5] In this article, I will argue that the construction of Jews as profiteers of capitalism permeates the critique of capitalism well into the twentieth century.

In his lucid essay on the challenges of writing a history of capitalism, the German social historian Jürgen Kocka emphasizes that the history of capitalism is inevitably entangled with the history of its criticism.[6] According to his argument, the very concept of capitalism emerges during the nineteenth century from the perspective of comparison with other political regimes, particularly socialism. Debates on capitalism

---

[2] Paul Krugman, 'Why we're in a New Gilded Age', *New York Times*, 6 May 2014.

[3] Gisela Hürlimann, 'Review-Symposium Piketty 'Das Kapital im 21. Jahrhundert'', *H-Soz-u-Kult*, 5 March 2015.

[4] Karl Marx, Capital: A Critique of Political Economy, trans. Samual Moore and Edward Aveling, ed. Frederick Engels, English Edition First published in 1887; Volume I, 192, 193.

[5] Gareth Stedman Jones, *Karl Marx: Greatness and Illusion* (First Harvard University Press edition. Cambridge, MA: The Belknap Press of Harvard University Press, 2016); Edmund Silberner, *Sozialisten zur Judenfrage: Aus dem Englischen übersetzt von Arthur Mandel* (Berlin: Colloquium Verl, 1962).

[6] Jürgen Kocka, 'Durch die Brille der Kritik: Wie man Kapitalismusgeschichte auch schreiben kann' *Journal of Modern European History* 15, no. 4 (2017): 480–489; Jürgen Kocka and Jeremiah Riemer, *Capitalism: A Short History* (Princeton: Princeton University Press, 2016).

and those on wealth do not necessarily overlap. However, parallel to the emergence of key works on capitalism at the beginning of the twentieth century, debates about wealth spread. Werner Sombart's book *Der moderne Kapitalismus* was particularly instrumental in causing the concept of capitalism to circulate in the German-speaking world.[7] Werner Sombart (1863–1941) was one of the most influential German social scientists of his time. He held the chair in economics at universities in Wrocław (Breslau) and Berlin. As with the output of Max Weber, Sombart's critical analysis of capitalism was deeply grounded in the German academic tradition of social sciences, and particularly Nationalökonomie.[8] Another contributor to the critique was Rudolf Martin (1867–1939), author of *Jahrbuch des Vermögens und Einkommens der Millionäre* (Yearbook of the assets and income of millionaires). In contrast to Sombart's academic influence and international reputation, Martin was a former bureaucrat and would remain an outsider to the academic world. However, his Yearbooks significantly influenced the debate on wealth in Wilhelminian Germany. Publishing 20 volumes under this unassuming title, Martin provided a thorough study of wealth in the German Empire in the form of an overview of its wealthiest members, from major cities like Berlin and Hamburg to those in German states large and small.[9]

This chapter draws on these two authors and their work to focus on narratives on wealth in the early twentieth century.[10] Both of them attracted great public attention that was independent of their capacity to provoke—as Martin certainly did—a public scandal. Recent contributions to the history of wealth have emphasized that debates about wealth

---

[7] See Werner Sombart, *Der moderne Kapitalismus* (Leipzig, 1902); The first two volumes of *Der moderne Kapitalismus* were published in 1902: Vol. 1: *Die Genesis des Kapitalismus*, Vol. 2: *Die Theorie der kapitalistischen Entwicklung*. Several revisions followed. Sombart's work *Der moderne Kapitalismus* has not been translated into English. Werner Sombart, 'Quintessence of Capitalism: A Study of the History and Psychology of the Modern Business Man' *Der Bourgeois*, trans. and ed. M. Epstein (London, 1915), Friedrich Lenger, Werner Sombart, 1863–1941: *Eine Biographie* (Müchen: C. H. Beck, 1994).

[8] Birger P. Priddat, *Produktive Kraft, sittliche Ordnung und geistige Macht: Denkstile der deutschen Nationalökonomie im 18. und 19. Jahrhundert* (Beiträge zur Geschichte der deutschsprachigen Ökonomie 13, Marburg: Metropolis-Verl., 1998).

[9] Rudolf Martin, ed., *Jahrbuch des Vermögens und Einkommens der Millionäre im Königreich Sachsen* 1 (Berlin, 1912).

[10] Eva M. Gajek, 'Sichtbarmachung von Reichtum: Das Jahrbuch des Vermögens und Einkommens der Millionäre in Preußen', *Archiv für Sozialgeschichte* 54 (2014): 79–108; Friedrich Lenger, *Werner Sombart, 1863–1941: Eine Biographie* (München: C.H. Beck, 1994).

were significantly characterized by the assumption that wealth remains hidden from the public sphere.[11] The chapter shows that in addition to accusations of inhuman working conditions, the criticism of unfair distribution of capitalism's benefits is one of the central aspects of debates about capitalism. The debate on the 'super-rich' as profiteers of capitalism is linked with the 'moral' assumption that the 'rich' embody capitalism's injustices. I argue that regardless of a presumed (in)visibility of wealth in the public sphere, the image of the 'rich' Jew circulated in a variety of genres. The following deals with the question of how statistics as a specific technique 'moralizes' social inequality.

MORALIZING WEALTH AROUND 1900: STATISTICS AND THE PUBLIC

More than three decades ago, the British social historian William Rubinstein claimed that the phenomenon of 'wealth' was 'virtually untouched' by historians.[12] He nominates two reasons to explain this lack of interest. In methodological terms it seems difficult to explore wealth, as the rich do not represent a coherent social group, nor does it seems possible to compare their assets. In addition, Rubinstein explains this lack of interest of social historians in wealth as historical phenomenon as due to their focus on social inequality.[13] Since Rubinstein's critical inquiry historians have taken up some of those issues by focussing on the wealthy as representative of a social elite, rooted in the economic bourgeoisie.[14] More recently, younger scholars have suggested approaching wealth as a culturally produced category which changes over time.[15]

[11] Eva M. Gajek and Christoph Lorke, eds., *Soziale Ungleichheit im Visier: Wahrnehmung und Deutung von Armut und Reichtum seit 1945* (Frankfurt/Main, 2016).

[12] William D. Rubinstein, 'Introduction', in *Wealth and the Wealthy in the Modern World*, ed. William D. Rubinstein (London: Croom Helm, 1980), 9–45, 10; Hartmut Berghoff, 'British Businessmen as Wealth-Holders 1870–1914: A Closer Look', *Business History* 33, no. 2 (1991): 222.

[13] Rubinstein, 'Introduction', 11.

[14] For an early overview see David Blackbourn, 'The German Bourgeoisie: An Introduction', in *The German Bourgeoisie: Essays on the Social History of the German Middle Class from the Late Eighteenth to the Early Twentieth Century*, ed. David Blackbourn and Richard Evans (London [u.a.]: Routledge, 1991), 1–45.

[15] Winfried Süß, '"Gold ist Trumpf und weiter nichts": Reichtumskonflikte im langen 19. Jahrhundert', *Werkstatt Geschichte* 73 (2016): 31–49.

Such an open concept allows wealth to be used as a lens to understand the forging of social relations.[16] Wealth is often contrasted with social misery. However, the interest in wealth in the late nineteenth century was based on the experience of growing social division. The 'rich man' as social figure plays a visible role in the social fabric of the German state of Prussia. From 1854 to 1913 the assets of the richest 5 percent of income earners increased significantly: There is an increase of the income which is shown by the statistics. It grew from one-fifth to one-third of all declared income.[17]

In following the idea of an open concept of wealth, I am interested in the narrative Martin's yearbooks produced about wealth in the early twentieth century. What kind of narrative is it? Rudolf Martin, a trained lawyer, served in the Prussian administration from 1897. Following the appearance of a couple of controversial publications by him in which he criticized the German government, Martin faced disciplinary measures and was finally dismissed from his position.[18] Rumours that Martin had removed confidential information during his time as a tax official could not be proven.[19] His reasons for undertaking the project remain in the end unclear.[20] On the one hand, as in his other publications Martin assumed the role of 'enfant terrible' and provocateur. On the other hand, he was responding to the increasing accumulation of capital, something that the general public remained unaware of: 'The power of the media protects today's tycoons'. He pursued the task of drawing a detailed image of the '*beati possidentes*' in Prussia, which he maintained was the 'enormous cultural work' needed in order to be able to grasp the meaning of statistics on wealth.[21] Martin's project can also be explained with reference to the growing importance of, and reliance on, statistics,

---

[16] Simone Derix, *Die Thyssens: Familie und Vermögen. Familie - Unternehmen - Öffentlichkeit* (Paderborn, 2016).

[17] Winfried, 'Gold ist Trumpf', 33.

[18] Gajek, 'Sichtbarmachung von Reichtum', 81.

[19] Rudolf Martin, *Die Zukunft Rußlands und Japans: die deutschen Milliarden in Gefahr* (Berlin: Heymann, 1905); Rudolf Martin, *Deutsche Machthaber*, 13th ed. (Berlin and Leipzig: Schuster & Loeffler, 1910).

[20] Gajek's essay on Martin is based on archival material in the Geheimes Staatsarchiv Preußischer Kulturbesitz (Gajek, 'Sichtbarmachung von Reichtum').

[21] Rudolf Martin, ed., *Jahrbuch des Vermögens und Einkommens der Millionäre in Preußen* (Berlin, 1912), VIII, VI.

demonstrated by the foundation of government institutions at the national level like the Imperial Statistical Office (Kaiserliches Statistisches Amt), founded in 1872. Their surveys served as the basis of national tax policy (on e.g. inheritance taxes).[22]

Between 1911 and 1913 Martin published 20 volumes listing the rich in all corners of Germany. Ultimately, he published a ranking of the richest. Earlier attempts to gather information about the very rich had failed due to a lack of cooperation.[23] Martin's rankings included professions, addresses and religious affiliation, as well as extended family relationships and networks. Altogether, his volumes came up with around ten thousand names of German millionaires. On the one hand, his yearbooks pursue the attempt to objectify wealth by using tax records. On the other hand, they expose the 'super-rich' by classifying the material according to social rankings.[24] This voyeuristic approach to wealth remains a typical way to take an interest in it today. Thus, for example, Forbes regularly lists 'The world's billionaires'. On its website, the US magazine even invites its readers to a virtual meeting with the most well-to-do and announces daily the winners and losers in the market according to the day's trading.[25]

As might be expected, the publication of Martin's Yearbooks triggered a political debate about issues of transparency. Prussia's Minister of Finance conducted an investigation against Martin on the basis of a suspected violation of tax secrecy.[26] The press too gave wide coverage to the publication of the Yearbooks. A popular magazine (*Kladderadatsch*) made fun of those super-rich who complained about the debate on

[22] J. A. Tooze, *Statistics and the German State, 1900–1945: The Making of Modern Economic Knowledge* (Cambridge Studies in Modern Economic History 9, Cambridge, UK and New York: Cambridge University Press, 2001); Daniel Speich Chassé, *Die Erfindung des Bruttosozialprodukts: Globale Ungleichheit in der Wissensgeschichte der Ökonomie* (Kritische Studien zur Geschichtswissenschaft Band 212. Göttingen: Vandenhoeck & Ruprecht, 2013); and Gajek, 'Sichtbarmachung von Reichtum', 88.

[23] Hermann Blenhard, *Die 'Gerissenen' oder 'Woher haben Sie Ihren Reichtum?': Zehn Antworten von Millionären, die mit nichts angefangen haben*, [Neuer Abdr] (Berlin: Boil & Pickardt, 1907).

[24] See the ad: Martin Rudolf, ed., *Jahrbuch des Vermögens und Einkommens der Millionäre in Westfalen* 13 (Berlin, 1913), 1.

[25] In March 2018, the US Magazine listed 321 Billionaires: https://www.forbes.com/billionaires/list/#version:static.

[26] Gajek, 'Sichtbarmachung von Reichtum', 91.

affluence.[27] Some years after the first publication of the Yearbooks, in 1914, there was a controversy over fair taxation in the Prussian Parliament. Referring to Martin's Yearbooks, the Social Democratic Party argued for tax reform. One member complained, for example, that above all it was the nobility that managed to accumulate capital, which remained untaxed.[28] Throughout, Martin himself acted with considerable aplomb; he was well aware of the implications of what he had done. He described the 'excitement' when his Yearbooks were announced by the publisher.[29] In advance of the first volume's appearance the publisher wrote to those presumably most affected to advise them that information regarding their assets was about to be made public. Not surprisingly, this courtesy provoked some nervousness.[30] Underlining not only the special marketing value of his Yearbooks, Martin claimed that this large-scale project would have a 'lasting effect' on the general perception of wealth. In his introduction he referred to the comprehensiveness of his data. 'For the first time a complete list of the top ten thousand' richest people in Prussia was being made accessible to the public.[31] In one of his advertisements for the Yearbooks he also claimed that his Yearbooks are read by the very richest people. Overcoming the 'ignorance and superstition of the Middle Ages', he wrote, his project contributed to 'enlightenment' on the topic of wealth in Wilhelminian Germany.[32]

Like Piketty a hundred years later, Martin legitimized his project by claiming the need for transparency regarding the distribution of wealth.[33] Aside from his explicit goal to stigmatize wealth, Martin provided comprehensive data about the regional

[27] See the front page of *Kladderadatsch*, 26 March 1911, reprinted in Gajek, 'Sichtbarmachung von Reichtum', 93.

[28] 58. Session of the Prussian Parliament (Preußisches Abgeordnetenhaus), 3 March 1914, quoted in Gajek, 'Sichtbarmachung von Reichtum', 90.

[29] Martin Rudolf, ed., *Jahrbuch des Vermögens und Einkommens der Millionäre im Königreich Sachsen* 1 (Berlin, 1912), III.

[30] For the correspondence regarding Martin's yearbook see Gajek, 'Sichtbarmachung von Reichtum', 86.

[31] Martin Rudolf, ed., *Jahrbuch des Vermögens und Einkommens der Millionäre in Westfalen* 13 (Berlin, 1913), n.p.

[32] Martin Rudolf, ed. *Jahrbuch des Vermögens und Einkommens der Millionäre im Königreich Sachsen* 1 Berlin, 1912, III.

[33] Dolores L. Augustine, *Patricians and Parvenus: Wealth and High Society in Wilhelmine Germany* (Oxford: Berg, 1994).

distribution of wealth in the German Empire. His statistical data have been extensively evaluated by social historians studying bourgeois elites, particularly entrepreneurs and financial elites.[34] Due to the material density and, above all, the broad regional scope of his Yearbooks, Martin succeeded in making possible a comprehensive knowledge of wealth throughout Germany.

The use of statistical data to classify social relations is based on a long tradition. Since the emergence of statistical societies in the 1830s, the collection of statistical data was pursued as a valid approach to understanding social phenomena.[35] In the 1830s, the Manchester Statistical Society carried out surveys interviewing more than half of the city's population, particularly focussing on the poorest areas. The interviewers collected data on a broad variety of questions such as religion, actual living conditions, rental costs. These surveys sought to understand early industrialization's impact on social relations. The work of the Manchester Statistical Society gained a wide reputation; Friedrich Engels referred extensively to their studies in his classic *The Condition of the Working Class in England*.[36]

A substantial literature on the statistical movement has highlighted the way that surveys by statistical societies introduced the concept of 'objectification' of working-class conditions while at the same time assigning moral categories to the different social classes.[37] In the multivolumed *Life and Labour in London (1886–1903)* this correlation between quantification and moral topography becomes quite evident. At the end of the nineteenth century, the entrepreneur and social reformer Charles Booth hired a team of social scientists to examine the poverty line of the London population. This survey led to his famous collection

[34] His yearbooks were consulted frequently by social historians in the 1980s. See among others, Augustine, *Patricians and Parvenus*.

[35] Report of a Committee of the Manchester Statistical Society on the condition of the working classes in an extensive manufacturing district, in 1834, 1835, and 1836. Read at the Statistical Section of the British Association for the Advancement of Science, Liverpool September 13th, 1837, London 1838.

[36] Friedrich Engels, *The Condition of the Working-Class in England in 1844* (London, 1892).

[37] Eileen Janes Yeo, *The Contest for Social Science: Relations and Representations of Gender and Class* (London: Rivers Oram Press, 1996).

including interviews as well as maps of London's 'poverty' areas. These maps were colour-coded, allowing them to be read as a moral topography of London's population. Using seven colours—from black (identified as 'Lowest Class, vicious, semi-criminal') to yellow ('Upper-middle and upper classes')—he and his team linked the social value of the urban population to its relative income.[38]

Another social reformer, the socialist Beatrice Webb, who worked for Booth's survey on London, penned a detailed description of the social mobility of Jewish immigrants. In it, she concluded: 'In short, he has become a law-abiding and self-respecting citizen of our great metropolis, and feels himself the equal of a Montefiore or a Rothschild'.[39] Reservations towards 'rich' Jews thus also circulated in this context.[40]

In contrast to such social surveys and moral topographies, Martin did not bring social scientific principles to bear in his studies, nor did he personally interview the rich of Germany. Rather, his volumes are exclusively based on tax documents that he must have collected over years. However, his publications stigmatized wealth through his repeated comments on the 'moral dimensions' of being rich. He adopted a number of analytical and discursive strategies. By comparing and ranking the rich and assuming that they are driven by competition among themselves, he depoliticized the phenomenon of wealth as a signifier of social inequality. In addition, he drew critical attention to the ways that particularly wealthy individuals were amassing their riches. For example, he pointed out that the assets of Bertha Krupp von Bohlen und Halbach increased in a linear fashion.[41] He was able to demonstrate that neither

---

[38] See Charles Booth, ed., *Labour and Life of the People in London* (London, 1889).

[39] Beatrice Potter, 'The Jewish Community', in *Labour and Life of the People in London*, ed. Charles Booth (London, 1889), 564–590, 583, quoted from Tobias Metzler, 'Werner Sombart im Ausland - Die Juden und das Wirtschaftsleben in England, Amerika und Fraunkreich', in *Kapitalismusdebatten um 1900: Über antisemitisierende Semantiken des Jüdischen*, ed. Nicolas Berg (Leipziger Beiträge zur Jüdischen Geschichte und Kultur 6, 2008, Leipzig: Leipziger Universitätsverl., 2011), 255–292, 265.

[40] See also Joseph Jacobs, *Studies in Jewish Statistics, Social, Vital, and Anthropometric* (London, 1891), 10. He rejects the conviction that Jews are particularly rich: 'Led by a fallacy akin to the old mercantile theory that all wealth is money, the peoples of Europe appear to have argued that because some Jews deal in Money'.

[41] Martin, *Jahrbuch des Vermögens und Einkommens der Millionäre in den drei Hansestädten* (Hamburg, Bremen, Lübeck), III–XI.

the emperor nor the 'old nobility' commanded the German Empire's greatest wealth, which was held instead by industrialists and bankers such as the Frankfurt Rothschild families;[42] an assumption that a few privileged persons accumulate the wealth of a society runs through all his Yearbooks.[43] Although Martin does not directly deal with the overall economic system, i.e. capitalism, his case studies illustrate the emergence of a new class of the rich associated with 'mobile capital', who he said frequently strove to avoid public attention. Compared with former times when wealth consisted of property, largely land and cattle, Martin held that today's wealth remains invisible. Taking the port city Hamburg as an example, he maintained that within the last 50 years a new class of super-rich had emerged which could be assumed to own more than appeared in the statistics alone.[44]

Before publishing the Yearbooks, Martin also had addressed the question of wealth in his book *Unter dem Scheinwerfer* (In the Spotlight), published in 1910, written specifically to attack Germany's former political leader, Chancellor Bernhard von Bülow. Some of its chapters describe wealth in more detail. In this book, he attempted to capture the milieu of the rich rather than focussing on statistics. In the chapter on Berlin's millionaires, for example, he commented ironically on 'class differences' among the wealthiest in the Germany capital.[45] Here he criticized the decadence which he observed among the very rich. In the case of Friedrich Friedlaender Fuld (1858–1917), who gained considerable wealth from coal and the manufacture of coke, Martin highlighted his indulgence in excessive luxury, which exceeded 'anything Berlin had ever seen'.[46] This excessive luxury manifested itself in a private tennis court, frequent balls and trips to Monte Carlo, but above all in the privilege to move within the Empire's courtly elite. Martin saw Fritz Friedlaender

[42] Martin, ed. *Jahrbuch des Vermögens und Einkommens der Millionäre im Königreich Sachsen* 1 (Berlin, 1912), III.

[43] Martin, ed., *Jahrbuch des Vermögens und Einkommens der Millionäre im Königreich Sachsen* 1 (Berlin, 1912), III.

[44] Martin, *Jahrbuch des Vermögens und Einkommens der Millionäre in den drei Hansestädten* (Hamburg, Bremen, Lübeck), VIII.

[45] Martin Rudolf, *Unter dem Scheinwerfer*, 14th ed. (Berlin [u.a.]: Schuster & Loeffler, 1910).

[46] See Martin, *Unter dem Scheinwerfer*, 183; see also the chapter on Friedlaender: Martin Rudolf, *Deutsche Machthaber*, 13th ed. (Berlin & Leipzig: Schuster & Loeffler, 1910), 242–249.

Fuld as an 'American phenomenon in modern Germany'.[47] Due to his contacts with the political establishment, in this case the imperial court, and
his economic success, Friedlaender Fuld represented, at least in Martin's
eyes, the 'big capitalists'.[48] Expressing his reservations about Jewish con-
verts, he reflected on Friedlaender Fuld's assumed Catholicism.[49] He
extrapolated from this individual to comment generally on the increasing influence of Jews on the Kaiser, maintaining that the German public had not yet realized the impact on society of 'our great Jews' as a
social class.[50] Perhaps responding to these anti-Semitic undertones, one
reader pencilled an annotation in the margin alongside the economic success story of another case, the Hamburg shipowner Albert Ballin (1857–
1918): 'typical Jewish'.[51]

The demand for transparency of wealth is a central topic within
the history of capitalism in the West. Criticism of capitalism and criticism of benefiting from capitalism meet in the figure of the 'rich Jew'.
The representation of Jews as capitalism's profiteers re-emerged around
1900. Martin's Yearbooks use implicitly anti-Semitic stereotypes, but he
generally constructs the rich as emblematic figures of a modern society
associated with increasing prosperity and social inequality. In contrast
to Martin's ambivalent perception of Jews, the social scientist Werner
Sombart draws a direct connection between capitalism, wealth and the
Jews.

MORALIZING WEALTH: JEWS
AS CAPITALISM'S PROFITEERS AROUND 1900

In 1925, the Munich branch of the Centralverein deutscher Staatsbürger
jüdischen Glaubens (Central Association of German Citizens of the
Jewish Faith) published the pamphlet 'The Jews are to blame for
everything'.[52] It was an Association whose local branches tended to

---

[47] Martin, *Deutsche Machthaber*, 240.

[48] Martin, *Deutsche Machthaber*, 240.

[49] Martin, *Deutsche Machthaber*, 241.

[50] Martin, *Deutsche Machthaber*, 242.

[51] Martin, *Unter dem Scheinwerfer*, 57.

[52] Local Branch Munich, Flyer of the *Centralvereins deutscher Staatsangehöriger jüdischen
Glaubens*, 1925, Deutsches Historisches Museum (https://commons.wikimedia.org/wiki/
File:CV_Flugblatt.jpg), downloaded on 8 December 2017.

attract particularly liberal Jews.[53] The pamphlet dismantles the perception of Jews as 'the scapegoat for everything'. As well as addressing a number of stereotypes, the pamphlet refers to assumptions about the ambivalent role of Jews in the context of capitalism. According to the authors, Jews are perceived as being responsible for all the 'evils of capitalism' while at the same time being blamed for the 'sufferings' caused by a (Bolshevik) revolution which 'wishes to eliminate' such evils.[54] Around the same year, the Association published its regularly updated volume 'Anti-Anti Facts about the Jewish Question' in which the authors provide an overview of central anti-Semitic stereotypes. A separate entry is dedicated to the topic of wealth. This section sharply criticizes the 'fairy tale' of Jewish wealth: Jews do not control the banks, nor do they possess 90% of mobile capital. In fact, Jews were particularly affected by the crisis years during the Weimar Republic.[55] For those reasons, so the argument went, the question of Jewish poverty is more pressing than that of Jewish wealth.[56] The image from the Middle Ages of Jews as moneylenders lived on long into the twentieth century. These images were epitomized in certain figures like Shylock or the German court Jew Joseph Süß Oppenheimer.[57] Since the early nineteenth century, prominent voices in the socialist left frequently targeted Jews as profiteers and specific agents of capitalism. In his writings, the French socialist Charles Fourier (1772–1837) polemicized against Jewish merchants.[58] Historians like Edmund Silberner, or more recently Jerry Z. Muller, have critically examined this facet of socialist history.[59]

[53] Avraham Barkai, 'Wehr dich!': Der Centralverein deutscher Staatsbürger jüdischen Glaubens (C.V.) 1893–1938 (München: Beck, 2002).

[54] Barkai, 'Wehr dich!'.

[55] Centralverein Deutscher Staatsbürger Jüd. Glaubens, ed., Anti-anti: Tatsachen zur Judenfrage, 6. Rev. ed. (Berlin: Philo-Verl. 1932).

[56] Ibid., 62b.

[57] Alexandra Przyrembel and Jörg Schönert, eds., 'Jud Süß': Hofjude, literarische Figur, antisemitisches Zerrbild (Frankfurt am Main [u.a.]: Campus Verl., 2006); Edna Nahson and Michael Shapiro, eds., Wrestling with Shylock: Jewish Responses to the Merchant of Venice (Cambridge, UK: Cambridge University Press, 2017).

[58] See also Finger's chapter in this volume.

[59] Edmund Silberner, Sozialisten zur Judenfrage, Aus dem Englischen übersetzt von Arthur Mandel (Berlin: Colloquium Verl., 1962); Edmund Silberner, Western European Socialism and the Jewish problem, 1800–1918: A selected Bibliography (Jerusalem, 1955);

The following deals with one of Sombart's most controversial books, *Die Juden und das Wirtschaftsleben* (1911), which was soon published in English under the revised title *Jews and Modern Capitalism*.[60] His works gained international acknowledgement. In 1896, Sombart had published the book *Sozialismus und soziale Bewegung*, which introduced Marx to a broader public.[61] His main work *Der moderne Kapitalismus*, which went through multiple revisions, similarly introduced the term capitalism.[62] Sombart also became known to an international audience. The *New York Times* published an obituary on the occasion of his death in 1941.[63]

Jews and Modern Capitalism analyzes why Jews are particularly pre-destined to capitalism. In the first of three parts, 'The contribution of the Jews to Modern Economic Life', Sombart argues a connection between the expulsion of Jews from Spain and the emergence of capitalism in the fifteenth century. Sombart asserts a 'striking parallelism between the wanderings of Jews and the economic development of nations'.[64] The role of Jews as central actors in capitalism began taking shape from the moment of their expulsion. Jews, despite being minorities and outsiders in society, were the ones who designed the economic system of colonialism as well as the modern state thanks to their special role in establishing a system of finance capital.[65] The second part, 'Aptitude of the Jews for Modern Capitalism', examines the entanglement of Jews with the emergence of capitalism. Sombart identifies some key factors such as the special social status of Jews, their religion, and general Jewish 'characteristics'. A subchapter applies those characteristics to the structure of capitalism: 'In all relations between sellers and buyers,

Jerry Z. Muller, *Capitalism and the Jews* (Princeton, NJ: Princeton University Press, 2010); and Avraham Barkai, 'Der Kapitalist', in *Antisemitismus. Vorurteile und Mythen*, ed. Julius Schoeps and Joachim Schlör (München/Zürich, 1995), 265–272.

[60] Werner Sombart, *The Jews and Modern Capitalism*, trans. M. Epstein (New York, 1915). In his preface the translator explains that he slightly revised the book and chopped some of Sombart's remarks on race. Werner Sombart, *Die Juden und das Wirtschaftsleben* (Leipzig, 1911).

[61] Werner Sombart, *Socialism and the Social Movement* (New York, 1968).

[62] See footnote 7.

[63] 'Werner Sombart, Berlin Economist: Prolific Writer on Economic and Social Problems Dies at 78', *New York Times*, 20 March 1941.

[64] Sombart, 'Table of Contents', VI.

[65] See Chapter 4, The Foundation of Modern Colonies and Chapter 5, The foundation of the modern state, in: Sombart, *Jews and Capitalism*, 28–48, 50–60.

and between employers and employees, [the Jew] reduces everything to a legal and purely business basis'.[66] The third part, 'The Origin of the Jewish Genius', finally turns to race theory to explain the putative specifics of the Jewish 'character'.[67]

The framing of Sombart's ideas within contemporary discourses on race and sexuality shows clearly in some of his remarks. Sombart explains Jewish affinity for capitalism by referring to sexual stereotypes. In *Jews and Capitalism* Sombart argues that sexual restrictions due to strict regulation of marriage divert energy into capitalist agency. Sombart advises his readers, 'We can see that a good deal of the capitalist capacity which Jews possessed was due in large measure to the sexual restraint put upon them by their religious teachers'.[68] In his later book *Luxury and Capitalism*, first published in 1922 and translated into English in the 1930s, Sombart perceives luxury as a product of (particularly female) sexual desires, using psychoanalytic arguments: 'All personal luxury springs from purely sensuous pleasure. Anything that charms the eye, the ear, the nose, the palate, or the touch, tends to find an ever more perfect expression in objects of daily use. And it is precisely the outlay [of money] for such objects that constitutes luxury. In the last analysis, it is our sexual life that lies at the root of the desire to refine and multiply the means of stimulating our senses, for sensuous pleasure and erotic pleasure are essentially the same. Indubitably the primary cause of the development of any kind of luxury is most often to be sought in consciously or unconsciously operative sex impulses'.[69]

Jews and Capitalism provoked widespread attention among Jewish and non-Jewish authors. In the United States the book also triggered a controversy, which the *New York Times* alluded to in its headline 'German Professor's Book stirs Jewish Circles here'.[70] The article labelled a couple of Sombart's assumptions about Jewish influence in the

[66] See Jewish Characteristics as applied to Capitalism, in Sombart, *Jews and Capitalism*, 273–278, here 277.

[67] See Part III, The Origin of the Jewish Genius, in Sombart, *Jews and Capitalism*, 281–354.

[68] Sombart, *Jews and Capitalism*, 237.

[69] Werner Sombart, *Luxus und Kapitalismus* (München/Leipzig, 1922); Werner Sombart, *Luxury and Capitalism,* intro. Philip Siegelman (Ann Arbor, 1967), 60f.

[70] *New York Times,* 3 March 1912.

economic world as untenable, including that 'The Jews are the fathers of the modern capitalist system and of modern commerce'.[71] Many years after the publication of *Jews and Capitalism*, in 1927, the German publisher in one of its promotions described the book as a great success. By linking the prominent role of Jews within capitalism to their dispersion across the world, their close ties and networks, and particularly their wealth, the publisher revived the book's anti-Jewish prejudices. It also referred to racial stereotypes resulting from the 'problem of the Jewish character'.[72] The disturbing effect of Sombart's book is also illustrated by a dissertation submitted two years later that devoted itself exclusively to the many responses directed towards it.[73]

Why did *Jews and Capitalism* provoke so many diverse responses? On the one hand, Sombart wrote almost lyrically about Jewish economic history from the Middle Ages to the early twentieth century in what was a well-written narrative. On the other hand, he exposed the success story of Jews in capitalism to various anti-Semitic prejudices. Reactions to his book varied vastly. While Zionist reviewers could identify with Sombart's interpretation of the Jewish impact on the modern state and capitalism, liberal-minded Jews instead emphasized his anti-Semitism.[74] However, *Jews and Capitalism* is deeply entangled in arguments for which Shulamit Volkov coined the expression 'anti-Semitism as cultural code'.[75]

---

[71] Ibid.

[72] Note of the publishing company on the occasion of the re-edition in 1927, quoted from Nicolas Berg, 'Juden und Kapitalismus in der Nationalökonomie: Zu Ideologie und Ressentiments in der Wissenschaft', in *Juden. Geld. Eine Vorstellung: Eine Ausstellung des Jüdischen Museums Frankfurt am Main, 25. April bis 6. Oktober 2013*, ed. Fritz Backhaus, Raphael Gross and Liliane Weissberg (Frankfurt am Main: Campus-Verl., 2013), 284–307, 292.

[73] Alfred Philipp, 'Die Juden und das Wirtschaftsleben: eine antikritisch-bibliographische Studie zu Werner Sombart: Die Juden und das Wirtschaftsleben' (Inaugural-Diss., Philosophischen Fakultät der Friedrich-Wilhelms-Universität zu Berlin, Straßburg: Heitz, 1929).

[74] Arno Herzig, 'Zur Problematik deutsch-jüdischer Geschichtsschreibung', *Menora* I (1990): 209–234.

[75] Shulamit Volkov, 'Readjusting Cultural Codes: Reflections on Anti- Semitism and Anti-Zionism', *The Journal of Israeli History* 25 (2006): 51–62; first published under the title 'Antisemitism as a Cultural Code: Reflections on the History and Historiography of Antisemitism in Imperial Germany', *The Leo Baeck Institute Yearbook* 23, no. 1 (1978): 25–46.

More than four decades ago Volkov very convincingly demonstrated that anti-Semitism was deeply embedded in Wilhemian Germany, especially in the academic world.[76]

All in all, in *Jews and Capitalism* Sombart refers to a broad range of anti-Semitic stereotypes. His premise is that Jews show a specific affinity with capitalism due to their capacity for abstract thinking, which the economist traces back to Jewish religion. It was Sombart's understanding of Jewish religion in particular that Julius Guttmann, one of the leading Jewish scholars and philosophers of religion in Germany, addressed in detail in his response written in 1913.[77] Guttmann was especially critical of the book's one-sided interpretation of Jewish ethics. He rejects Sombart's assumption of a Jewish 'friendliness towards wealth' (*Reichtumsfreundlichkeit*).[78] This presumed affinity with wealth, explains Guttmann, is specifically not justified by Jewish ethics, which in contrast supports the concept of benevolence. According to the German philosopher, Sombart also underestimates the moral, i.e. virtuous, interpretation of work in the Talmud.[79]

In her early essay 'Religion and Capitalism Once Again', the historian Natalie Zemon Davis turns to the question of whether Sombart was 'an Anti-Semite' in his book *Jews and Capitalism*, 'a Nazi before the letter?'[80] How much Sombart's book addressed pressing questions regarding Jewish economic history becomes most evident in the seminar 'The Jews in Economic Life', conducted in Lyon in 1941. This seminar was

[76] For a thorough reading of his anti-semitism see also Nicolas Berg, 'Juden und Kapitalismus in der Nationalökonomie: Zu Ideologie und Ressentiments in der Wissenschaft', in *Juden. Geld. Eine Vorstellung: Eine Ausstellung des Jüdischen Museums Frankfurt am Main, 25. April bis 6. Oktober 2013*, Fritz Backhaus, Raphael Gross and Liliane Weissberg, eds. (Frankfurt am Main: Campus-Verl., 2013), 284–307.

[77] Julius Guttmann, 'Die Juden und das Wirtschaftsleben', *Archiv für Sozialwissenschaft und Sozialpolitik* 36 (1913): 149–202. Thomas Meyer interprets Guttmann's reading of Sombart as a convincing example of 'Jewish obstinacy': Thomas Meyer, 'Zur jüdischen Rezeption von Werner Sombart - Julius Guttmanns Antwort', in *Kapitalismusdebatten um 1900: Über antisemitisierende Semantiken des Jüdischen*, ed. Nicolas Berg (Leipziger Beiträge zur Jüdischen Geschichte und Kultur 6, 2008, Leipzig: Leipziger Universitätsverl., 2011), 293–318.

[78] Guttmann, 'Die Juden und das Wirtschaftsleben', 193.

[79] Guttmann, 'Die Juden und das Wirtschaftsleben', 198.

[80] Natalie Z. Davis, 'Religion and Capitalism Once Again? Jewish Merchant Culture in the Seventeenth Century', *Representations* 59 (1997): 56–84.

part of a study project of the Central Consistory of France for scholars excluded from their posts by the Vichy Statut des Juifs of October 1941. Led by the French economist Louis Rosenstock-Franck, the seminar analyzed Sombart's text 'to study and … to unmask the first important effort at systematizing the influence of the Jews on economic life'.[81] Davis herself takes Sombart's *Jews and Capitalism* as starting point to reflect on economic action as a cultural practice. On the basis of the autobiography of Glikl bas Judah Leib (1645–1724), a German businesswoman who lived in Hamburg, Davis critically examines Sombart's remarks on Jewish capitalism. Sombart reads Glikl's life as presented in the merchant's 'splendid book' as evidence of the 'predominating interest of money among Jews in those days'. 'In very truth', Sombart adds, 'money is the be-all and end-all with her, as with all the other people of whom she has anything to say'.[82] In contrast to notions of the 'supremacy of gain' which Sombart finds there, Natalie Zemon Davis emphasizes a 'deep ambivalence about the unending pursuit of gain' in Glikl's autobiography. Likewise Glikl insisted that 'honor counted as much as riches in a good life'.[83] On the basis of Glikl's autobiography, Davis illustrates how intangible ideas such as conceptions of honour and family networks shape economic practices, whether there is a Jewish background or not.

CONSTRUCTING WEALTH AROUND 1900

Around 1900 a new interest in theories of capitalism emerged, significantly associated with Werner Sombart and Max Weber. Both intellectuals connect the power of modern capitalism with a specific driving force. In the case of Sombart, this new capitalist spirit is best represented in 'Jewish' aspiration for economic success as well as their handling of money. According to him, these attributes make Jews predestined for the new order of capitalism. In contrast, Weber explains the success of capitalism as rising out of the power of self-restraint. He noted the words of Benjamin Franklin in this vein: 'nothing contributes more to the raising

---

[81] Louis Rosenstock-Franck, *Les Juifs et la vie économique* (seminar presentations, Lyon, 1941), quoted from Davis, 'Religion and Capitalism', 60.

[82] Sombart, *The Jews and Modern Capitalism*, 131.

[83] Davis, 'Religion and Capitalism', 69.

of the young man in the world than punctuality and justice in all his dealings'.[84]

Parallel to this academic interest in the theories of modern capitalism, social reformers, journalists and entrepreneurs had discovered the social groups most affected by economic transformation: the poor and the rich. In the early nineteenth century statistical societies like the Manchester Statistical Society compiled surveys on poverty. However, comparable surveys on the rich as profiteers of the new order emerged much later. Rudolf Martin's Yearbooks gave an in-depth overview of wealth in the German states, attacking the 'invisibility' of wealth in the public sphere, explicitly demanding more transparency in relation to the accumulation of wealth. At the same time, critics of capitalism often referred to Jews as the profiteers of capitalism, irrespective of their political positioning on the left or right. This contempt for Jews as the exploiters of a new economic order encompassed different genres. Sombart's *Jews and Capitalism* evoked strong reactions as he offered a teleological narrative around Jews as the driving force of capitalism. The book met with a broad response outside the academic world. How much the response of Sombart's book had touched a nerve is shown by the many reviews. Two of his own publications which appeared in the following year addressed the question of Jewish identity: *The Future of Jews* and his short essay 'The Baptism of Jews' (*Judentaufen*).[85] Both deal with Jewish conversion to Christianity, which Sombart interprets as evidence for Jewish adaptiveness to capitalism. In both texts, Sombart responded to the criticism that he avoided taking a position on concrete policies towards Jews.[86] Suggesting the benefits of Jewish emancipation, he at the same time demands that Jews should not take advantage of this political privilege.[87]

[84] Max Weber, *The Protestant Ethic and the Spirit of Capitalism*, trans. Talcott Parons, with a foreword by R. H. Tawney (1930); reprinted 1958, 49–50, quoted from Davis, 'Religion and Capitalism', 57. See Sokoll's chapter The moral foundation of modern capitalism: towards a historical reconsideration Max Weber's 'Protestant Ethic' in this volume.

[85] Sombart, Werner. *Die Zukunft der Juden* (Verlag von Duncker & Humblot, 1912).

[86] Sombart, *Die Zukunft der Juden*, 7.

[87] Sombart, *Die Zukunft der Juden*, 87.

In these texts Sombart intermingles both philosemitic and anti-Semitic stereotypes.[88] With respect to capitalism, he describes the role of Jews as temporary, arguing that their influence vanishes in countries which have already implemented high-capitalist structures.[89]

The late nineteenth century forms a constitutive phase for the understanding of modern capitalism as an economic and social system. This master narrative was significantly influenced by Werner Sombart's writings. Remarkably, his son Nicolaus (1923–2008), bohemian, author and EU official, wrote a short radio piece on the 'Apologies of wealth'. In contrast to his father, who offered a genealogical understanding of modern capitalism, Nicolaus Sombart describes his interest in wealth during the 1950s and 1960s as follows: 'It's about the definition of the sublime sphere, that is to say, the place where the misery of the world is not discerned'.[90] A section of his essay deals with the 'difficulties to praise wealth'.[91] With a certain sense of irony, Sombart Jr. included in his collection of newspaper clippings articles on modern snobbery and advertisements for shoes made of crocodile leather.

The history of wealth in the twentieth century is closely linked to the (moral) debate on social inequality. In order to critically examine this master narrative, it appears necessary to analyze wealth as political and social institution beyond its moral implications.[92] At the same time, however, debates about social inequality are inherently bound to the political: in the case of Sombart's *Jews and Capitalism*, to the battle for political emancipation of Jews in Germany.

[88] Sombart, *Die Zukunf der Juden*, 37: 'We do not want to loose their deep sad eyes' as a cause of assimilation.

[89] Sombart, 'Judentaufen', 7.

[90] Staatsbibliothek zu Berlin, Nachlass Nicolaus Sombart (405), Akte 354, Apologie des Reichtums, 55.

[91] Ibid., 96.

[92] Digby E. Baltzell, *Philadelphia Gentlemen: The Making of a National Upper Class* (New York, 1958), 5.

CHAPTER 4

The Moral Foundation of Modern Capitalism: Towards a Historical Reconsideration of Max Weber's 'Protestant Ethic'

Thomas Sokoll

Current debates about the economy have again brought capitalism in from the cold, or more precisely the issue of moral justice within capitalism. Both in the political arena and within scholarly discourse, this marks a sharp contrast to previous habits. While 'capitalism' had been a derogatory label during the cold war, when economists (other than Marxist ones) preferred less threatening terms like 'market economy', the collapse of the Soviet Union and the euphoric frenzy around deregulation and globalization saw the renaissance of capitalism as a self-congratulatory keyword epitomizing the victory of the free world of the Western type. But with the global financial crisis starting in 2008, the moral predicament of an unfettered market system has come back

T. Sokoll (✉)
Early Modern History, University of Hagen, Hagen, Germany
e-mail: thomas.sokoll@fernuni-hagen.de

© The Author(s) 2019
S. Berger and A. Przyrembel (eds.), *Moralizing Capitalism*,
Palgrave Studies in the History of Social Movements,
https://doi.org/10.1007/978-3-030-20565-2_4

to the fore. Critical voices like those of Tony Atkinson and Thomas Piketty are now acclaimed for having raised the issue of increasing social inequality and injustice, questioning the traditional belief that economic growth and prosperity would automatically lead to social equity.[1]

There has also been a growing interest in the history of capitalism which now extends to scholars of various political inclinations (whereas, again, in the old days this was more of a Marxist affair).[2] As much as this may be welcomed, it is no less obvious that there is no agreement as to what the history of capitalism is about, or capitalism in itself for that matter. For example, Jürgen Kocka has opted for a pretty strict ideal-type definition of capitalism as a modern economic system based on private enterprise, market system and capital accumulation.[3] By contrast, several contributions to the highly praised *Cambridge History of Capitalism* simply identify capitalism with modern economic growth, while those concerned with pre-industrial economies tend to include anything to do with money exchange, market relationships or trade routes under 'capitalism', thus extending the semantic range of the term to the point of historical (and theoretical) meaninglessness.[4] Similarly, Joyce Appleby sees no need to distinguish between merchant adventures and industrial enterprises, but assumes a single continuing story of capitalism, an escape

[1] Thomas Piketty, *Capital in the Twenty-First Century* (Cambridge, MA: Harvard University Press, 2014); Anthony B. Atkinson, *Inequality: What Can Be Done?* (Cambridge, MA: Harvard University Press, 2015). Their collaborative works include Anthony B. Atkinson and Thomas Piketty, eds., *Top Incomes over the Twentieth Century: A Contrast Between European and English-Speaking Countries* (Oxford: Oxford University Press, 2007); *Top Incomes: A Global Perspective* (Oxford: Oxford University Press, 2010); Anthony B. Atkinson, Thomas Piketty, and Emmanuel Saez, 'Top Incomes in the Long Run of History', ibid., 684–779.

[2] The outstanding example (still full of valuable insights) is Maurice Dobb, *Studies in the Development of Capitalism* (London: Routledge, 1946; rev. ed. 1963). For an influential anti-Marxist counterexample, arguing that most historians had got it all wrong, see F. A. von Hayek, ed., *Capitalism and the Historians* (Chicago: University of Chicago Press, 1954).

[3] Jürgen Kocka, *Geschichte des Kapitalismus* (Munich: Beck, 2013), Chap. 1 (esp. 20–22), drawing on Marx, Weber and Schumpeter.

[4] Larry Neal and Jeffrey G. Williamson, eds., *The Cambridge History of Capitalism*, vol. 1: *The Rise of Capitalism: From Ancient Origins to 1848*, vol. 2: *The Spread of Capitalism: From 1848 to the Present* (Cambridge: Cambridge University Press, 2014). See also the review by Jürgen Kocka, *Vierteljahrschrift für Sozial- und Wirtschaftsgeschichte* 103 (2016), 585–589.

from traditional society beginning in the seventeenth century and running to the present day.[5]

Interests and Objectives

It is against that background of an increasingly vague understanding of capitalism that the present paper is devoted to the historical reconsideration of Max Weber's most famous text, *The Protestant Ethic and the 'Spirit' of Capitalism* (henceforth 'the PE'). My argument rests on the assumption that the PE, despite all the critical objections it has aroused, is still a convincing and promising agenda for the theory of modern capitalism in general and of the moral issues involved in its historical record in particular.[6] More specifically, I contend that there are three reasons why we should have another go at that text (and its complicated reception). First, the PE suggests, on the basis of the Marxian model, a particularly strict notion of modern capitalism which remains a powerful tool for clarification. Second, it discusses the moral containment of modern capitalism from within the system itself, thus rendering a theoretical platform based on an ethic of responsibility, as opposed to the traditional attitude following an ethic of conviction. Third, recent research into the textual history of the PE, both in itself and in relation to Weber's other works, has opened new perspectives for the appreciation of the PE, its reception and its continuing analytical potential.

While the interests and objectives of the following exercise should be clear enough, then, it nevertheless needs emphasizing that any attempt at reconsidering the PE from the vantage point of the (early modern) historian is by necessity at once a delicate and cumbersome matter. It requires no less than the recovery of the original argument in the PE *against* the long tradition of its historical misunderstandings, which means that we need to go back as far as to the text of the PE itself (in *both* versions:

[5] Joyce Appleby, *The Relentless Revolution: A History of Capitalism* (New York: W. W. Norton, 2011). For an illuminating contrast to her elusive discussion of capitalism (ibid., 3–26), see the clear exposition by Dobb, *Studies*, 1–32.

[6] For the current interest in the history of capitalism, see also Friedrich Lenger, 'Die neue Kapitalismusgeschichte. Ein Forschungsbericht als Einleitung', *Archiv für Sozialgeschichte* 56 (2016), 1–38. For the moral issues, Stefan Berger and Alexandra Przyrembel, 'Moral, Kapitalismus und soziale Bewegungen. Kulturhistorische Annäherungen an einen "alten" Gegenstand', *Historische Anthropologie* 24 (2016), 88–107.

1904–1905 and 1920) and also address some of the issues involved in the process of its subsequent misrepresentation. This is not to indulge in Weberian antiquarianism or historiographical complacency. It is necessary in order to catch up with the most advanced achievements in recent research on the PE, both in itself and as part of the wider 'biography' of Weber's work.

THE COMPOSITION OF THE PE: A BRIEF OVERVIEW

Weber's PE is a special text. The core of it, a historical investigation of moral discourse concerned with the ethics of work in early modern Protestantism, is complex, both in substantive and methodological terms. In its weight of erudition, depth of knowledge and scale of learning, it is overwhelming. At the same time, it bears an open, experimental character, raising lots of questions which are not pursued further let alone answered conclusively. The PE is an essay in the true sense of the word, an attempt at discussing a complex historical question (which is why some scholars have said that the argument in the PE is 'overcomplex'). Nevertheless, the composition of the text and the overall structure of the argument are fairly simple (numbers refer to the sections as given in the text; see also Table 4.1).[7]

[7] Unless otherwise stated, I refer to the second edition of the PE (1920) in the new English translation by Kalberg: Max Weber, *The Protestant Ethic and the Spirit of Capitalism with Other Writings on the Rise of the West*, trans. and intro. Stephen Kalberg (Oxford: Oxford University Press, 2009), 59–159 (text), 458–551 (notes), cited as Weber, *PE* (Kalberg). Kalberg has also included related texts by Weber written between 1905 and 1920, such as the essay on 'Protestant Sects' (1920), various pieces scattered across *Economy and Society* (1909–1912, 1912–1914, 1919–1920), the (posthumous) *General Economic History* (1923), and, of course, the famous 'Prefatory Remarks' (1920) to the 'Collected Essays on the Sociology of Religion' (in which the PE features as the first piece). I also give cross-references to the 1930 translation of the PE by Parsons since this is the most widely quoted and still the most accessible one (and occasionally better than Kalberg's): Max Weber, *The Protestant Ethic and the Spirit of Capitalism*, trans. Talcott Parsons and intro. Anthony Giddens (London and New York: Routledge, 2002), cited as Weber, *PE* (Parsons). For an English translation of the first version of the PE (1904–1905), including Weber's papers (1907–1910) in his dispute with Fischer and Rachfahl (though not their papers), see Max Weber, *The Protestant Ethic and the 'Spirit' of Capitalism and Other Writings*, trans. Peter Baehr and Gordon C. Wells (London: Penguin Classics, 2002), cited as Weber, *PE* (Baehr/Wells). The definitive critical edition of the German texts of the PE (1904–1905, 1920) is now available in two volumes within the Max Weber Gesamtausgabe (MWG): Max Weber, *Asketischer Protestantismus und Kapitalismus*.

Table 4.1 Weber's PE: Composition of text/structure of argument (1904–1905/1920)

Text PE (1904–1905)[a]	Timescale	Sources	Themes, topics, concepts	Contraindications
I. Problem				
1. Denomination and social stratification	c. 19/20	Offenbacher (official statistics)	Protestant predominance: capital, entrepreneurs, workers (school/training)	
2. 'Spirit' of capitalism [1920: Spirit; *modern cap.*]	c. 18	Franklin	vocational duty = ethical maxim of conduct of life [1920: psychological premium]	Fugger: merchant adventurer (ethically indifferent)
3. Luther's concept of calling	c. 16	*Luther Prot. Bible transl.*	occupation (*Beruf*) = calling, vocation fulfilment of innerworldly duties (meritocratic proof *in* this world)	monastic asceticism (calling) (flight *from* this world)
II. Idea of calling in ascetic Protestantism [1920: vocational ethic]				
1. Religious foundations of innerworldly asceticism				
[a] Calvinism (Puritanism)	c. 16/17	*Calvin*	inner isolation of individual (predestination)	salvation through good works monastic asceticism (= method. self-discipline)
		Calvinist synods Baxter, Bunyan	restless work/systematic *self-control methodical conduct of life* = sign of election *innerworldly asceticism*	
[b] Pietism	c. 17/18	Spener, Francke	awakening/mission conversion/rebirth	institutionalized church (Lutheran + Catholic)
[c] Methodism	c. 18	Wesley	individ. revelation, relig. community	church discipline = external drive
[d] Baptist movement (Quakers)	c. 17/18		ascetic religiosity = internal drive [1920: sect]	
			asceticism, performance/achievement, rationalization	

(continued)

Table 4.1 (continued)

Text PE (1904–1905)[a]	Timescale	Sources	Themes, topics, concepts	Contraindications
2. Asceticism and capitalism [e] Puritanism	c. 17	*Baxter*	general duty to work (God's command > Old Test.)	> Jews (minority)
			(increased) efficiency (division of labour)	class-specific tasks
			capital formation through ascetic compulsion to save	greed
				luxury
		[1920: Petty]	bourgeoisie/middle classes = social carrier of PE	wholesaler/adventurer
(Summary and prospect)	(c. 4–19)		Christian *asceticism* → idea of *calling rational* (= *middle class*) *conduct* occupational specialization as doom of modernity	

[a]Alterations in 1920 edn in square brackets; main sources and key concepts italicized

I. 1/I. 2. For the opening, statistical data are given to illustrate that capital owners, entrepreneurs and skilled workers were predominantly Protestant in the manufacturing industries of late nineteenth-century Baden. However, the figures are no sooner quoted than cast aside as superficial, extrinsic evidence, inappropriate for any deeper appreciation of the intrinsic psychological forces within modern capitalism. Likewise, the explication of the 'historical individual' of the 'spirit of capitalism' in the writings of Benjamin Franklin is subsequently dropped as inappropriate (too late, wrong place) even though those writings are held to point (back) into the right direction in that they address habits like conscientiousness, honesty, reliability, strictness and self-discipline as entrepreneurial virtues.

I. 3. The real historical investigation begins with the analysis of Luther's concept of the 'calling' (*Beruf*), which is said to have paved the way to a radically new appreciation of work. For Luther, the true praise of God was not that you would flee from this world, as in monastic asceticism, but to prove yourself in your business *in* this world.

II. 1. The religious foundations of this new attitude of inner-worldly asceticism are to be found in the four main types of ascetic Protestantism. Calvinism (including Puritanism), Pietism, Methodism and the Baptist movement (esp. Quakers). Calvinism is said to be the most important. Calvin's notion of predestination led to the inner loneliness of the individual, who could never know whether he belonged to the favoured few or the damned. In Puritan preachers like Richard Baxter and John Bunyan, this feeling of despair led to the vision that business success could be interpreted as a sign of election. Asceticism, achievement and rational conduct of life became an inner motor of the individual, in contrast to the merely external device of Catholic (and Lutheran) church discipline.

Schriften und Reden 1904–1911, ed. Wolfgang Schluchter and collab. Ursula Bube (Tübingen: Mohr Siebeck, 2014; MWG I/9), which also contains the papers by Fischer and Rachfahl; Max Weber, *Die protestantische Ethik und der Geist des Kapitalismus. Die protestantischen Sekten und der Geist des Kapitalismus. Schriften 1904–1920*, ed. Wolfgang Schluchter and collab. Ursula Bube (Tübingen: Mohr Siebeck, 2016; MWG I/18); the magisterial introduction by Schluchter (ibid., 1–59) is indispensable for an appreciation of the historical context of the PE and also provides the best guide to the textual differences between its two versions (ibid., 35–43).

II. 2. Asceticism and capitalism. This forms the logical climax of the argument. Once more Puritanism, again with Baxter as the crown witness, who is now quoted extensively: his idea of a general duty to work, *against* its social refraction in the traditional exemption of clergy and nobility; his stress on effort and performance, with the explicit advocacy of enhanced efficiency through the division of labour and occupational diversification, *against* sinful avarice; his justification of wealth when used productively: capital formation through an ascetic compulsion to save, *against* luxury and meaningless wastefulness. In a brief excursion concerning Jews (Baxter refers mainly to the Old Testament), it is argued (against Sombart) that they are capitalist adventurers. The social carriers of modern capitalism are said to be the rising sections of the commercial and industrial middle classes.

At the end, a grim prognosis is given. The rational conduct of life, rooted in the Protestant notion of the calling (and this in turn in Christian asceticism) turns into the opposite: vocational commitment is bound to become the doom of modern society.

MODERN CAPITALISM (1): THE BASIC MODEL

In both methodological and substantive terms, the PE rests on Weber's ideal type of modern capitalism. The close methodological link is given through the 'objectivity' paper of 1904 in which Weber introduced the concept of the 'ideal type'. This was a programmatic manifesto, significant not only because it was Weber's first major publication (with the 'sigh paper' on Roscher and Knies as a prelude) after his long illness since 1898, but also because it went along with his new strategic role as joint editor, from 1904, with Sombart and Edgar Jaffé, of the *Archiv für Sozialwissenschaft und Sozialpolitik* (ASWSP).[8] While the 'objectivity' paper gave a general outline of the 'ideal type', the PE was the first material application of that concept, ostensibly only with respect to the 'spirit of capitalism', but the underlying substantive idea was the ideal type of modern capitalism.

---

[8] Max Weber, 'Roscher und Knies und die logischen Probleme der historischen Nationalökonomie', and 'Die "Objektivität" sozialwissenschaftlicher und sozialpolitischer Erkenntnis', both in his *Gesammelte Aufsätze zur Wissenschaftslehre*, ed. Johannes Winckelmann (Tübingen: Mohr Siebeck, 1968), 1–145, 146–214.

Weber held that greed for material wealth, striving for excessive profit and lust for conspicuous consumption were as old as history and thus did *not* help us to understand what modern capitalism was about. They belonged to what he called 'adventure capitalism', which was found even in classical antiquity. The adventurer made a fortune by mere chance, by force, or by both. He tapped whatever resources he got hold of. Hence the brutal exploitation of human resources in all pre-capitalist modes of production, where slavery and serfdom were the social norm. By contrast, *modern* capitalism, in Weber's understanding, is distinguished by four characteristic features.[9]

1. Modern capitalism transcends the mere distribution of goods and penetrates the production process itself.
2. Profit is not dumped unproductively or squandered, but recycled productively in the form of reinvestment. Weber's trenchant formula: 'accumulation of capital through ascetic compulsion to save' (*Kapitalbildung* durch *asketischen Sparzwang*).[10]
3. Economic integration is attained by means of a particular institution: the market. This is not the market place or the fair as the physical meeting point of traders, something also found in all pre-modern civilizations. The pre-modern market is a closed arena of limited exchange based on privileges and protected as well as

[9]The clearest systematic juxtaposition of pre-modern and modern capitalism is to be found in the 'Prefatory Remarks' of 1920: Weber, *PE* (Kalberg), 208–214; *PE* (Parsons), 17–24; MWG I/18, 101–121, but it also features prominently in the PE itself: Weber, *PE* (Kalberg), 74–76, 87; *PE* (Parsons), 58, 76; MWG I/18, 163–176 (with long extensions of the original 1904 text) and 206–207. See also Weber, *PE* (Kalberg), 392–393, 431–435, for the relevant passages in Weber's lecture course on General Economic History (1919–1920); Max Weber, *Abriß der universalen Sozial- und Wirtschaftsgeschichte*, ed. Wolfgang Schluchter and collab. Joachim Schröder (Tübingen: Mohr Siebeck, 2011; MWG III/6), 317–320, 380–396. On Weber's concept of modern capitalism, see also the two chapters by Johannes Berger, '"Kapitalismus" und "Abendländischer Kapitalismus"? – Zur Vergangenheit und Gegenwart eines Weberschen Grundbegriffs', in *Max Weber-Handbuch. Leben – Werk – Wirkung*, ed. Hans-Peter Müller and Steffen Sigmund (Stuttgart: Metzler, 2014), 71–74, 375–382.

[10]Weber, *PE* (Parsons), 116. At this point, I prefer Parsons' simple translation (though he dropped Weber's italics) to the rather clumsy rendering by Kalberg: '*the formation of capital* through *asceticism's compulsive saving*' (152). German text: MWG I/9, 412; MWG I/18, 466.

controlled by the authorities. By contrast, the modern market is an abstract system of unlimited exchange of all commodities on the basis of the formal equality of all market participants. The free exchange of commodities extends to human labour.

4. Labour is the crucial point. To the extent that wage labour is also found in pre-modern societies, it is a marginal feature, since agrarian production, the most important economic sector in terms of both value and employment, is typically based on the exploitation of unfree or 'bound' labour: slaves, peasants, bondmen, serfs. By contrast, modern capitalism is based on the exploitation of formally free labourers.

On these four points, Weber saw himself in full agreement with Marx. This may seem surprising, given the widespread inclination to read Weber *against* Marx, with the PE in particular often said to have shown that Marx had got it all wrong and that historical progress was a matter of ideas rather than material forces. But in their critical assessment of modern capitalism, which was not concerned with contingent individual cases of social evil, but devoted to the strict theoretical ('cold') analysis of the inner logic of the system, Marx and Weber were intellectual twins.[11] The extent to which their models of capitalism converge is difficult to assess, though, as Weber hardly ever referred to (or even quoted from) Marx's works in precise detail—it is almost as if Marx was

[11] The first scholar to see this clearly (as early as 1932) was Karl Löwith. See his 'Max Weber und Karl Marx', *Archiv für Sozialwissenschaft und Sozialpolitik* 67 (1932), 175–214; *Max Weber and Karl Marx* (London: Allen & Unwin, 1982). Later discussions of that issue include Anthony Giddens, 'Marx, Weber and the Development of Capitalism', *Sociology* 4 (1970), 289–310; Anthony Giddens, *Capitalism and Modern Social Theory: An Analysis of the Writings of Marx, Durkheim and Max Weber* (Cambridge: Cambridge University Press, 1971), 190–195, 243–247; Jürgen Kocka, 'Karl Marx und Max Weber im Vergleich. Sozialwissenschaft zwischen Dogmatismus und Dezisionismus', in *Geschichte und Ökonomie*, ed. Hans-Ulrich Wehler (Cologne: Kiepenheuer & Witsch, 1973), 54–84; Wolfgang J. Mommsen, 'Kapitalismus und Sozialismus. Die Auseinandersetzung mit Karl Marx', in his *Max Weber. Gesellschaft, Politik und Geschichte* (Frankfurt: Suhrkamp, 1974), 144–181, 265–271. See also the useful collection by Robert J. Antonio and Ronald M. Glassmann, eds., *A Weber-Marx Dialogue* (Lawrence: Kansas University Press, 1985) (with English translations of the papers by Kocka and Mommsen); Gregor Schöllgen, *Max Webers Anliegen. Rationalisierung als Forderung und Hypothek* (Darmstadt: Wissenschaftliche Buchgesellschaft, 1985), 44–79; and Gregor Schöllgen, *Max Weber* (Munich: Beck, 1998), 76–105.

simply so important to Weber that he found it unnecessary to quote him.[12] But it is clear that Weber never left any doubt about his deep respect for Marx as a theorist and, in 1920, he went so far as to praise Marx (along with Nietzsche) as the most important intellectual force of his day.[13]

THE MORAL FOUNDATION OF MODERN CAPITALISM: PROTESTANT ETHIC

The 'Protestant ethic' as the heart of the 'spirit' of capitalism marks a point where Weber claims to have seen further than Marx. Again, with Marx he insists that modern capitalist business, based on entrepreneurial rationality and the exploitation of free labour, is a historical novelty. But Weber thinks that in his analysis of the capitalist system, Marx has not gone far enough. First, Marx cannot explain how it was that labour was released from all bonds of domination and thrown upon the market as a free commodity, *against* the perennial historical experience of the ruling classes of all pre-modern civilizations that the exploitation of unfree labour provides the easiest way to increase wealth and power. Second, there is the question of the psychological drive that guides the modern capitalist. Again, Weber agrees with Marx that the mentality of the adventurer does not explain anything here. On the contrary, extraordinary courage and pleasure in playing at high risk are typical of all daring merchant capitalists like Jakob Fugger.[14] Hence the deep suspicion about trading enterprises in all traditional societies and the idea, in evidence

[12] I have borrowed this phrase from Jürgen Osterhammel who used it to suggest why Schumpeter hardly ever quoted Weber, 'Spielarten der Sozialökonomik: Joseph A. Schumpeter und Max Weber', in *Max Weber und seine Zeitgenossen*, ed. Wolfgang J. Mommsen and Wolfgang Schwentker (Göttingen: Vandenhoeck & Ruprecht, 1988), 147–195, at 159.

[13] As reported by Eduard Baumgarten, *Max Weber. Werk und Person* (Tübingen: Mohr Siebeck 1964), 554–555: 'Die Redlichkeit eines heutigen Gelehrten [...] kann man daran messen, wie er sich zu Nietzsche und Marx stellt. Wer nicht zugibt, daß er gewichtigste Teile seiner eigenen Arbeit nicht leisten könnte, ohne die Arbeit, die diese beiden getan haben, beschwindelt sich selbst und andere'.

[14] Jakob Fugger is explicitly mentioned in the PE to this effect: Weber, *PE* (Kalberg), 71; *PE* (Parsons), 51; MWG I/18, 155–157. It is significant that this reference to Fugger is preceded and followed by extensions of the original 1904 wording in the 1920 text, pointing out the difference from *modern* capitalism.

since ancient antiquity, that exchange for the sake of profit was against nature. Moreover, pre-industrial elites were not only suspicious of trading, but also detested all manufacturing business. Naturally, they did appreciate wealth, preferably when based on landed property, which was seen as the 'natural' form of wealth. It was also regarded as natural that those who owned landed estates were normally also invested with domination over the people attached to them, so that they could draw considerable resources and incomes from the soil without ever having to soil their own hands. Wealth from landed property enabled them to enjoy leisure and devote themselves to noble and honourable duties such as politics or culture. The necessity to work for a living was a social stigma. Manual labour in particular was the unmistakable sign of inferior social status. In traditional society, the ruling classes were therefore socially and culturally blocked from engaging in productive business.

According to Weber, Protestantism broke with that tradition in that it found a genuinely positive appreciation of labour and employment which led to a distinctive ethic of work. We need not discuss this at any length. But it is nevertheless worth taking a brief look at the precise point where the argument sets in within the PE. This is the consideration of 'Luther's conception of the calling' (*Beruf*), a stunning exercise in historical semantics which extends far beyond its humble title. Beginning with Luther and his translation of the Bible, moving on to the Protestant Bible translations in all major European languages, and then discussing that evidence against the background not only of the original Hebrew, Greek and Latin wording of the Scripture but also of medieval exegesis and homiletics, Weber provides nothing less than a systematic analysis of the landslide shift brought about by Protestantism in the entire semantic field of 'vocation' and 'duty', 'occupation' and 'employment', 'work' and 'labour'.[15]

Methodologically, this analysis is guided by Weber's idea of unintended consequences as a mover of historical change.[16] The shift in the meaning of work was not due to any explicit master plan or conscious decision. Rather, it occurred almost in passing, as though Luther himself did not know what he was doing. Two short passages are sufficient to illustrate the point. The first one is to be found in the book *Ecclesiasticus* or *Sirach*, one of the Old Testament apocrypha; the second passage

[15]Weber, *PE* (Kalberg), 89–97 (text), 473–485 (notes); *PE* (Parsons), 79–92 (text), 204–217 (notes); MWG I/18, 209–256.
[16]Weber, *PE* (Kalberg), 96; *PE* (Parsons), 89–90; MWG I/18, 253–255.

in St Paul's first letter to the Corinthians (both quoted from the New Jerusalem Bible, 1985; italics added):

> Stick to your *job*, work hard at it and grow old at your *work*. Do not admire the achievements of sinners, trust the Lord and mind your own *business*; since it is a trifle in the eyes of the Lord, in a moment, suddenly to make the poor rich. (Sir., 11, 20–21)

> Everyone should stay in whatever *state* he was in when he was *called*. So, if when you were called, you were a slave, do not think it matters – even if you have a chance of freedom, you should prefer to make full use of your *condition* as a slave. (1 Cor. 7, 20–21)

The first passage relates to man's earthly duties in making a living. The keywords are 'job', 'work' and 'business'. The second passage relates to the moment in which someone receives God's call to his spiritual duty as a Christian, a call to duty which is said to be irrespective of social position. The keywords here are 'state', 'condition' and 'call'. These are two completely different contexts which involve completely different concepts. Yet Luther, in his translation of 1522 and 1534, uses the same German word (*Beruf*) (calling) for both passages: 'call' and 'work' are thus lumped together under the same conceptual umbrella. The implication is obvious. Whatever your social position, whatever your occupation, whatever your employment—to the extent that you do your duty, your daily work on that spot where God has placed you, at that point to which God has appointed you, you are following his 'calling'.[17]

---

[17] Needless to say, it must appear somewhat rash to report in modern English on the linguistic intricacies of Luther's translation of the Bible from ancient Hebrew, Greek and (early medieval) Latin into Early Modern High German, quoting the biblical passages from the modern wording of the New Jerusalem Bible. But for our purposes this is sufficient, the more so as it does not alter the overall message of Weber's argument. Nor is there any reason to cast doubt on this overall message in the light of the minor philological slips in Weber's analysis detected in two papers by Tatsuro Hanyu, 'Max Webers Quellenbehandlung in der "Protestantischen Ethik". Der Begriff "Calling"', *Zeitschrift für Soziologie* 22 (1993), 65–75; 'Max Webers Quellenbehandlung in der "Protestantischen Ethik". Der Berufsbegriff', *Archives Européennes de Sociologie* 35 (1994), 72–103. Hanyu claims to have demolished Weber's argument, which is difficult to accept, as he not only got some of the philological details wrong himself but apparently is unaware of the basic relevant literature on the history of the concept of *Beruf*, such as Karl Holl, 'Die Geschichte des Worts Beruf' (1924), in his *Gesammelte Aufsätze zur Kirchengeschichte*, vol. 3, *Der Westen* (Tübingen: Mohr Siebeck, 1928), 189–219, or more recently Conze (see next note).

In order to appreciate the full meaning of this new concept of 'calling', it is important to stress again that it runs entirely counter to traditional attitudes. We may also, at this point, include some of the results of modern research into historical semantics which has basically confirmed and further accentuated Weber's findings.[18] The biblical keywords in the field of 'work' and 'employment', rooted in ancient Hebrew, Greek and Latin, are *labor* (labour) and *opus* (work). While the latter carried a neutral or even slightly positive meaning, the former had harsh negative connotations: 'labour' denoted hard work, heavy drudgery, endless toil, excessive pain (remember that, to this day, 'labour' in English, as *labor* in Latin, also means pain in childbirth). Hence the deep contempt among the ruling elite for the labouring classes which is typical of all traditional societies. Cicero regarded all crafts and trades, as they involved manual labour, as inherently 'dirty'. They were tasks for slaves (whom Aristotle had called 'animated tools') and not befitting a free man. As a broad social movement with particular appeal to the lower orders, Christianity took a more positive view. At the same time, however, it introduced the idea that the true follower of Christ was to move out of this world. Monastic asceticism was seen as the proper kind of worship, a radical departure from earthly necessity, a special choice for those God had 'called' upon. This is the original meaning of 'calling', *vocatio* in Latin, hence 'vocation' in English. It refers to a special vocation, to a divine call to a spiritual state of being as opposed to any ordinary secular position.[19]

---

[18]Werner Conze, '"Arbeit" and "Beruf"', both in *Geschichtliche Grundbegriffe*, ed. Otto Brunner, Werner Conze, and Reinhart Koselleck, 8 vols. (Stuttgart: Klett-Cotta, 1972–1997), i, 154–215, 490–507; Josef Ehmer and Edith Saurer, 'Arbeit', in *Enzyklopädie der Neuzeit*, ed. Friedrich Jaeger, 16 vols. (Stuttgart and Weimar: Metzler, 2005–2012), i, 507–533; Wilfried Nippel, 'Erwerbsarbeit in der Antike', in *Geschichte und Zukunft der Arbeit*, ed. Jürgen Kocka and Claus Offe (Frankfurt and New York: Campus, 2000), 54–66; Otto Gerhard Oexle, 'Arbeit, Armut, "Stand" im Mittelalter', ibid., 67–79; and Otto Gerhard Oexle, 'Armut im Mittelalter. Die *pauperes* in der mittelalterlichen Gesellschaft', in *Gelobte Armut. Armutskonzepte der franziskanischen Ordensfamilie vom Mittelalter bis in die Gegenwart*, ed. Hans-Dieter Heimann et al. (Paderborn: Schöningh, 2012), 3–15.

[19]For futher details, see Thomas Sokoll, 'Vom äußeren Zwang zur inneren Verpflichtung. Überlegungen zur historischen Semantik von "Arbeit" und "Beruf" in Max Webers "Protestantischer Ethik"', *Österreichische Zeitschrift für Geschichtswissenschaften* 24, no. 1 (2013), 198–220, at 203–207.

Inferiority in painful labour on the one hand, and a chosen spiritual status on the other. To the extent that work and worship were thus regarded as two strictly separated human conditions, the Christian understanding might be said to have contributed to an even sharper accentuation of the ancient contempt for labour as dirty necessity. In Protestantism, however, along with the idea of the 'priesthood of all believers', work and worship were literally thrown together in the same concept of 'calling/vocation' (*Beruf*), which led to an entirely new understanding of labour, work and employment. As a consequence, monastic asceticism could no longer claim to carry a special justification before God as even the most inferior kind of work was seen as an act of prayer. In repudiating the traditional notion of asceticism as an act of worship that required one's move *out of* this world, Luther opened the door to a new kind of asceticism by fulfilling one's duties *within* this world. This is what Weber called 'innerworldly asceticism' (*innerweltliche Askese*).[20]

EARLY RECEPTION OF THE PE (1905–1920)

Most of Weber's contemporaries were not only not interested in the theological subtleties discussed in the PE, but also missed the full thrust of his argument. In particular, they ignored his distinction between modern capitalism and pre-modern (adventurous) capitalism. This may seem surprising, since eminent economists and historians like Schmoller, Sombart, Brentano and others were equally concerned with the theory and history of modern capitalism, and all were thrilled by the idea of a particular 'spirit' of capitalism once Sombart had introduced that

---

[20] It is now clear that Weber used that term only after his return from America (late November 1904). The first reference is to be found in an entry (in Weber's own hand) in the minute book of the Eranos circle at Heidelberg summarizing his talk 'Die protestantische Askese und das moderne Erwebsleben', given there on 5 February 1905, MWG I/9, 220–221 (with facsimile). In the first version of the PE, the term features, most prominently, in the headline of part II. 1, 'The religious foundations of innerworldly asceticism', but enters the text itself only towards the end of that section: Weber, *PE* (Baehr/Wells), 82; MWG I/9, 294–295. In the second edition (1920), 'innerworldly asceticism' turns up at several points where Weber expanded the original text (and the footnotes), most notably at Weber, *PE* (Kalberg), 117–118, 137; *PE* (Parsons), 120–121, 149; MWG I/18, 329–331, 403. It is noteworthy that the English translations of this key term differ: 'innerworldly asceticism' (Baehr/Wells), 'this-worldly asceticism' (Kalberg) and 'worldly asceticism' (Parsons).

term in 1902.[21] So was Weber, who took that notion (and thus part of the title of the PE) explicitly from Sombart. But whereas Sombart used the term either in a more general sense (which included commercial daring) or with a view to specific technical achievements (double-entry bookkeeping), Weber came to a radically different understanding (psychological momentum).

Weber's ideal type of the 'capitalist spirit' was increasingly lost in the process of the reception of the PE. While this is not the place to analyze that process in detail, it is necessary for our purposes to take a brief look at some of the major points of misunderstanding. As we shall see later, it is only against that unfortunate tradition of misapprehension that the complex message of the PE may be recovered as a fruitful platform for the current debates about (the history and theory of) modern capitalism (in addition, see Table 4.2).[22]

Weber's own notion of the capitalist 'spirit' was further accentuated in his debate over the PE with Fischer and Rachfahl. Time and again he insisted that he was not arguing an 'idealist' (against a 'materialist') case to the effect that 'spiritual' forces were the 'cause' of capitalism in any simple way, but again, that the PE was about the complex problem of the 'innermost' moving force of the specific conduct of life (*Lebensführung*) among the middle-class entrepreneurs whom he regarded as the social carriers of modern capitalism. It is remarkable that he introduced the term 'habitus' in this context.[23] In fact, as Wilhelm Hennis has rightly pointed out, 'habitus' was what Weber really meant, and he could have avoided a lot of misunderstanding if he had used that term from the start and never had recourse to Sombart's 'spirit'.[24]

[21]Werner Sombart, *Der moderne Kapitalismus*, 2 vols. (Leipzig: Duncker & Humblot, 1902), i, 378–397 ('Die Genesis des kapitalistischen Geistes'). The text is readily available in the useful anthology by Bernhard vom Brocke, ed., *Sombarts, Moderner Kapitalismus'. Materialien zu Kritik und Rezeption* (Munich: Deutscher Taschenbuch Verlag, 1987), 87–106.

[22]The best account of the reception history of the PE up to 1980, with a balanced exposition of the most pervasive misunderstandings, is Gordon Marshall, *In Search of the Spirit of Capitalism: An Essay on Max Weber's Protestant Ethic Thesis* (London: Hutchinson, 1982).

[23]MWG I/9, 585, 730; PE (Baehr/Wells), 252, 312 (respectively first and second rejoinder to Rachfahl, 1909 and 1910).

[24]Wilhelm Hennis, 'Max Weber's "Central Question"', *Economy and Society* 12 (1983), 135–180.

Table 4.2   Weber's PE: Fields of discourse, reception and transmission (1850–2016)

Theory of modern capitalism
Marx/Engels *Manifesto* 1848
Marx *Capital* I-III 1867/85/94

[Nietzsche]

(Bücher, Schmoller)

Sombart *Mod. Kap.* 1902

Fischer/Rachfahl: Critiques of PE 1907-10
> Troeltsch *Soziallehren* 1912
Sombart *Juden* 1911; *Bourgeois* 1913
Brentano *Anfänge mod. Kap.* 1916
Sombart *Mod. Kap.*² I/II 1916

Sombart *Mod. Kap.*² III 1927

Weber
'Objectivity' 1904
PE¹ 1904-5
'Churches' and 'Sects' 1906
Anticritiques 1907-10

Soc. of Religion (= ES II, chap. 6) [1911-13]
Econ. Ethic of World Rel. [15]1-14] 1916-18

General Econ. Hist. (chap. IV 9) [1919/20]
PE² 1920 (= GARS I)
Prefatory remarks GARS I

Global historical comparison

Theory of modernity

Sociological orthodoxy
PE Engl. 1930 (Parsons)
Parsons *Structure of Social Action* 1937

Modernization theory
Eisenstadt *PE/Modernization* 1968
Seyfarth/Sprondel *Rel. ges. Entw.* 1973

Postmodern discourse
Schluchter *Webers Sicht okzid. Christentums* 1988
Lehmann/Roth *Weber's PE: Origins, Evidence, Contexts* 1993
Lehmann/Ouédraogo *Webers Rel. soz. interkult. Persp.* 2003
Schluchter/Graf *Asket. Prot./'Geist' d. Kap.* 2005
Swatos/Kaelber *PE Turns 100* 2005

Critical edition
PE¹ + related texts (1904-11) = MWG I/9, 2014
PE² + Prot. Sects (1920) = MWG I/18, 2016

ES *Economy and Society* ed. Roth/Wittig 1968
GARS *Gesammelte Aufsätze zur Religionssoziologie*
MWG *Max Weber Gesamtausgabe*

However, Weber missed that chance. He did not take up the notion of 'habitus' but stuck to 'spirit' in the revised text (1920) of the PE (and dropped the quotation marks from the title). But he did provide further clarification, not least by inserting 'modern' before 'capitalism' at several places in the original text.[25] He also inserted new long footnotes (as if the old ones were not cumbersome enough) in which he dealt with Sombart and Brentano—oddly enough, the discussion with these eminent and revered colleagues was buried in footnotes and never entered the plain text, which marks a striking contrast to the extensive, excited and offensive polemic Weber had earlier launched against Fischer and Rachfahl. But then, whatever there was in terms of scholarly exchange about the PE between Weber on the one hand and Sombart, Brentano and other celebrities on the other never turned into open dispute in the first place. Looking at the entire discursive field in which the PE was located, that is the project of a 'bourgeois' theory of modern capitalism and social reform as it had emerged from the Younger Historical School of German political economy (*Nationalökonomie*), the impression is that the parties involved tended to indulge in cultivated conversation in which conflicting views were played down and the decisive differences never really addressed.[26]

They would talk past each other. Sombart and Brentano came up with all sorts of explanations of the 'roots' and 'origins' of modern capitalism, ranging from the minority status of Jews in medieval society, the greed of the crusaders and the commercial enterprises in Renaissance Genoa and Florence to the early modern state and its military campaigns. But apparently it never entered their mind that all this was beside (or rather, below) the point Weber had made in the PE.[27] More specifically, when Sombart discussed the 'early-capitalist spirit' (*frühkapitalistischer Geist*)

---

[25] MWG I/18, 157, 177, 190, 195.

[26] This is all the more striking as Weber was always willing to engage in fierce personal disputes with eminent colleagues when political and social issues were at stake. See Dieter Lindenlaub, *Richtungskämpfe im Verein für Socialpolitik. Wissenschaft und Sozialpolitik im Kaiserreich vornehmlich vom Beginn des 'Neuen Kurses' bis zum Ausbruch des Ersten Weltkrieges (1890–1914)* (Wiesbaden: Steiner, 1967).

[27] Werner Sombart, *Die Juden und das Wirtschaftsleben* (Leipzig: Duncker & Humblot, 1911); Werner Sombart, *Der Bourgeois. Zur Geistesgeschichte des modernen Wirtschaftsmenschen* (Leipzig: Duncker & Humblot, 1913); and Lujo Brentano, *Die Anfänge des modernen Kapitalismus* (Munich: Akademie der Wissenschaften, 1916).

in the heavily enlarged second edition of his work on modern capitalism, he not only made no reference to the PE, but fell behind it and simply lumped together the adventurous ('romantic') and rational ('bourgeois') sources of that spirit.[28] Likewise, early examples of the 'capitalist entrepreneur' included daring conquerors and adventurers.[29] Weber for his part, though he did make his own position clear against Sombart and Brentano in the endless new footnotes to the second edition of the PE, never referred to that second edition of Sombart's big book. What is more, he never really attacked Sombart and Brentano in the way he had attacked Fischer and Rachfahl, even though he would have had every reason to do so.

As a result, Weber's analytical exposition of the 'capitalist spirit' in the PE gradually dropped out of sight. To a certain extent, it was also Weber's own fault. After the debate with Fischer and Rachfahl, he did not pursue the issue any further.[30] Instead, he expanded the question of the relationship between religious beliefs and economic development onto a larger scale. From 1911, he worked on the comparative sociology of religion (as part of *Economy and Society*, which he never published himself), and then on the 'Economic Ethics of the World Religions', a giant project which he concerned himself with (alongside numerous other interests) until his death in 1920 and which drew him into investigations of Confucianism, Hinduism, Buddhism, Judaism and Islam (papers published in ASWSP, 1916–1918). This opened the horizon of global historical comparison from which Weber embarked, in the famous 'Prefatory Remarks' (1920) to the Collected Essays on Religious Sociology (*Gesammelte Aufsätze zur Religionssoziologie*) on a bold sketch of a theory of modernity which may be regarded as his

[28] Werner Sombart, *Der moderne Kapitalismus. Historisch-systematische Darstellung des gesamteuropäischen Wirtschaftslebens von seinen Anfängen bis zur Gegenwart*, vol. 1: *Einleitung – Die vorkapitalistische Wirtschaft – Die historischen Grundlagen des modernen Kapitalismus*, vol. 2: *Das europäische Wirtschaftsleben im Zeitalter des Frühkapitalismus* (Leipzig: Duncker & Humblot, 1916), vol. 2.1, 25–35. Volume 3 was published in 1927 (the entire tome, comprising 3200 pages, was reprinted in 1969 and, as a paperback, in 1987).

[29] Sombart, *Der moderne Kapitalismus*, vols. 1, 2, 836–841.

[30] He knew, of course, that his close friend Ernst Troeltsch had taken up the theme in the most congenial manner. See Ernst Troeltsch, *Die Soziallehren der christlichen Kirchen und Gruppen* (Tübingen: Mohr Siebeck, 1912).

intellectual legacy. It is as if Weber was closing a circle here, since that short essay was also his last word on the theme of the PE. With the concept of specialized professionalism (*Fachmenschentum*) on the basis of rationalism, seen as a distinctive achievement of Western civilization,[31] he referred back to the grim account, towards the end of the PE penned early in 1905, of vocational commitment (*Berufsmenschentum*) as the doom of modern society.[32] But in 1920, he had come to a more positive understanding, in that the notorious opening question of the 'Prefatory Remarks' ('what combination of circumstances…?') as to why it was that Western civilization (and *only* Western civilization) witnessed the rationalization of *all* spheres of life—from market to law to music—allowed him to embark upon a self-confident sketch of modern capitalism as the 'most fateful power of our modern life'.[33]

RECENT HISTORICAL READINGS OF THE PE (AFTER 1980)

While the PE fell into oblivion in Germany soon after Weber's death, it survived in North America from where it started its triumphal march across the globe. Lawrence Scaff has neatly described how the PE was at first only discussed in small sociological circles at Chicago, Harvard and Wisconsin, and how it then turned into a 'holy text' of sociology after the Second World War.[34] That process went along with the formation and spread of modernization theory which in turn accelerated as other Weber texts became available in English translations (while the PE has remained *the* key modernization text ever since). Modernization, of course, was a strong narrative in the context of the Cold War, the tale of the irresistible progress of Western civilization.[35]

Although essentially a sociological idea, modernization theory had pretty firm built-in historical foundations, which facilitated its critical reception and adaptation in parts of the historical community.

---

[31] Weber, *PE* (Kalberg), 207; *PE* (Parsons), 15–16; MWG I/18, 104.

[32] Weber, *PE* (Baehr/Wells), 120–121; MWG I/9, 421–423; in 1920 edition: Weber, *PE* (Kalberg), 157–158; *PE* (Parsons), 181–182; MWG I/18, 485–488.

[33] Weber, *PE* (Kalberg), 208–216; *PE* (Parsons), 17–27; MWG I/18, 105–117.

[34] Lawrence Scaff, *Max Weber in America* (Princeton: Princeton University Press, 2011), 237–304.

[35] For exemplary statements, see the anthology by S. N. Eisenstadt, ed., *The Protestant Ethic and Modernization: A Comparative View* (New York: Basic Books, 1968).

This, along with the rise of modern social and economic history, led to the rediscovery of Weber among historians since the 1960s and 1970s, and in the process Weber made his way back to German historians. Thanks to the indefatigable efforts of Wolfgang Mommsen, Hans-Ulrich Wehler, Jürgen Kocka and others, Weber's work has since become a key reference for historians as well. Today, no historian can ignore Weber's theory of social classes, charismatic leadership and bureaucracy, or his methodological contributions to the question of how to form adequate historical concepts and to the problem of value-orientation in historical research. Surprisingly, however, this renewed interest in Weber among historians has hardly ever extended to the PE.[36]

Over the last three decades, we have seen a number of major inter-disciplinary collections that are specifically concerned with the PE.[37] But in these publications, the most searching papers have all come from sociologists, even where genuine historical questions (or even particular sources) are at stake,[38] while the historians have contented themselves with historiographical exercises. Thus, we have been told that the prehistory of the PE goes back to eighteenth-century writers who praised the diligence of Protestants and blamed the idleness of Catholics[39]; or that

[36] For an assessment of Weber as a historian, see Jürgen Kocka, ed., *Max Weber, der Historiker* (Göttingen: Vandenhoeck & Ruprecht, 1986). It is symptomatic that this fine collection, with contributions from distinguished historians, lacks a chapter on the PE. For an attempt at describing this gap, see Thomas Sokoll, 'Max Webers Protestantismusthese und die Historiker. Protokoll einer Verdrängung', in *Max Weber 1864–1920. Politik – Theorie – Weggefährten*, ed. Detlef Lehnert (Cologne: Böhlau, 2016), 195–216.

[37] Wolfgang Schluchter, ed., *Max Webers Sicht des okzidentalen Christentums. Interpretation und Kritik* (Frankfurt: Suhrkamp, 1988); Hartmut Lehman and Guenther Roth, eds., *Weber's Protestant Ethic: Origins, Evidence, Contexts* (Cambridge: Cambridge University Press, 1993); Hartmut Lehmann and Jean Martin Ouédraogo, eds., *Max Webers Religionssoziologie in interkultureller Perspektive* (Göttingen: Vandenhoeck & Ruprecht, 2003); Wolfgang Schluchter and Friedrich Wilhelm Graf, eds., *Asketischer Protestantismus und der 'Geist' des modernen Kapitalismus* (Tübingen: Mohr Siebeck, 2005); and William H. Swatos, Jr. and Lutz Kaelber, eds., *The Protestant Ethic Turns 100: Essays on the Centenary of the Weber Thesis* (Boulder, CO and London: Paradigm, 2005).

[38] Lutz Kaelber, 'Rational Capitalism, Traditionalism, and Adventure Capitalism: New Research on the Weber Thesis' and Philip S. Gorski, 'The Little Divergence: The Protestant Reformation and Economic Hegemony in Early Modern Europe', both in *Protestant Ethic Turns 100*, ed. Swatos and Kaelber, 139–163, 165–190.

[39] Paul Münch, 'The Thesis Before Weber: An Archeology', in *Weber's Protestant Ethic*, ed. Lehman and Roth, 51–71.

Weber only flogged Fischer and Rachfahl so viciously because he did not have the guts to touch Sombart and Brentano[40]—which is not wrong, but not new either (Hennis had made the same point before, in a far more profound and exciting way).[41]

Historians have also come to read the PE as a source of its own time, against the backdrop of the shift, in the 1880s and 1890s, from the optimistic self-confidence of the first industrial age to the feeling of a deep crisis of modern culture.[42] Weber himself, as a child of his time, has been the subject of outstanding biographies[43] and illuminating attempts at reconstructing the 'biography' of his work.[44] From this 'historicist' interest in the PE, which is also shared by sociologists,[45] fascinating insights have emerged into the mentality of Imperial Germany before the First World War. For instance, take Weber's praise in the PE of the middle-class entrepreneur as the epitome of the modern capitalist,

---

[40]Hartmut Lehmann, 'The Rise of Capitalism. Weber versus Sombart', in *Weber's Protestant Ethic*, ed. Lehman and Roth, 195–208; in the same vein: Hartmut Lehmann, 'Friends and Foes: The Formation and Consolidation of the "Protestant Ethic" Thesis', in *Protestant Ethic Turns 100*, ed. Swatos and Kaelber, 1–22; and Hartmut Lehmann, 'Die Weber-These im 20. Jahrhundert', in *Calvinismus. Die Reformierten in Deutschland und Europa*, ed. Ansgar Reiss and Sabine Witt (Dresden: Sandstein, 2009), 378–383.

[41]Hennis, 'Weber's "Central Question"'.

[42]Detlev Peukert, *Max Webers Diagnose der Moderne* (Göttingen: Vandenhoeck & Ruprecht, 1989); Hartmut Lehmann, *Max Webers 'Protestantische Ethik'. Beiträge aus der Sicht eines Historikers* (Göttingen: Vandenhoeck & Ruprecht, 1996).

[43]Guenther Roth, *Max Webers deutsch-englische Familiengeschichte 1800–1950 mit Briefen und Dokumenten* (Tübingen: Mohr Siebeck, 2001); Joachim Radkau, *Max Weber. Die Leidenschaft des Denkens* (Munich: Hanser, 2005; rev. ed. Munich: Deutscher Taschenbuch Verlag, 2013).

[44]Wilhelm Hennis, *Max Webers Fragestellung. Studien zur Biographie des Werks* (Tübingen: Mohr Siebeck, 1987); Wilhelm Hennis, *Max Webers Wissenschaft vom Menschen. Neue Studien zur Biographie des Werks* (Tübingen: Mohr Siebeck, 1996); Wilhelm Hennis, *Max Weber und Thukydides. Nachträge zur Biographie des Werks* (Tübingen: Mohr Siebeck, 2003); Peter Ghosh, *A Historian Reads Max Weber: Essays on the Protestant Ethic* (Wiesbaden: Harrassowitz, 2008); Peter Ghosh, *Max Weber and 'The Protestant Ethic': Twin Histories* (Oxford: Oxford University Press, 2014); and Peter Ghosh, *Max Weber in Context: Essays in the History of German Ideas c. 1870–1930* (Wiesbaden: Harrassowitz, 2016).

[45]Hartmann Tyrell, 'Worum geht es in der "Protestantischen Ethik"? Ein Versuch zum besseren Verständnis Max Webers', *Saeculum* 41 (1990), 130–177; Wolfgang Schluchter, *Unversöhnte Moderne* (Frankfurt: Suhrkamp, 1996); and Stefan Breuer, *Max Webers tragische Soziologie. Aspekte und Perspektiven* (Tübingen: Mohr Siebeck, 2006).

his obsession with the habitus of innerworldly asceticism and methodical conduct of life, with rational management, diligence, thrift and hard work. This hymn of praise must also be seen as a desperate cry, a swansong against the rise of big business and financial capitalism, with the separation of the capital ownership and management functions curtailing the sense of individual responsibility, accountability and liability against the increasing bureaucratization of economic life and the loss of individual freedom under conditions of an anonymous mass society.

However, to the extent that historians have been reading the PE in that way, they seem to have lost all interest in the 'innermost' historical substance of the PE itself. Perhaps the most advanced and convincing example of this indifference is the close reading of the PE offered by Peter Ghosh. He sees the PE as a piece of intellectual history and looks at the currents of thought that influenced Weber, at the sources he used and at all the scholarly literature he drew on. Thus, he has described in minute detail how Weber composed his picture of Puritanism,[46] or more recently argued, in a stunning textual analysis of great persuasive power, that the PE is the key to the entire intellectual biography of Weber, the critical point in which the threads of *all* his works are tied together.[47] But the deeper we delve into the PE in this fashion, the more we move away from its real historical substance. It is as if we were running straight into an intellectual impasse, or more precisely, a historical deadlock, as we evade the empirical historical questions Weber addressed in the PE. Ghosh does not care whether Weber's account of Puritanism is historically tenable or not—and I say this as someone who adores Ghosh's work. But as a social historian, I hasten to add that it is precisely that question which bothers me.

The strong trend towards an ever closer 'historicist' reading of the PE and its reception must not make us overlook the work of those historians who have taken up the genuinely historical questions Weber raised in

[46]Peter Ghosh, 'Max Weber's Idea of "Puritanism": A Case Study in the Empirical Construction of the "Protestant Ethic"', in his *Historian Reads Weber*, 5–49.

[47]Ghosh, *Weber and 'Protestant Ethic'*, 218–386. This is by far the best account of the 'subtextual' history of the PE in Weber's own work between 1905 and 1920 (for a detailed assessment, see the review by Thomas Sokoll, H-Soz-Kult-Kult, 09.09.2015). See also the two brilliant pieces by Peter Ghosh, 'Protestantismus, asketischer' and 'Die protestantische Ethik und der Geist des Kapitalismus (1904–05; 1920)', both in *Max Weber-Handbuch*, ed. Müller and Sigmund, 105–107, 245–255.

the PE. Among early modern historians, Hartmut Lehmann and Kaspar von Greyerz may be singled out here as experts on the radical Protestant groups of the seventeenth and eighteenth centuries, whose religious tracts were Weber's prime source. Both have shown that Weber was mis-guided in the heavy emphasis he put on the Calvinist doctrine of predes-tination, especially with respect to Puritanism, which he regarded as the most important movement of ascetic Protestantism. Seventeenth-century Puritans, including Weber's heroes Baxter and Bunyan, were not at all bothered about predestination, but followed a providential faith accord-ing to which man was not forever condemned to desperate uncertainty about his fate but could instead, as a good hard-working Christian, hope to receive positive signs of divine mercy and goodwill. Moreover, these Puritans were not the religious lone fighters Weber had in mind but, on the contrary, members of devoted communities of believers (as Weber acknowledged in the paper on 'Sects' written shortly after the PE).[48] On the other hand, Protestantism did foster the individualization of religious experience, as witnessed in those numerous spiritual autobiographies and diaries, mostly of Puritan and Pietistic provenance, unearthed in recent research. These are indeed testimonies of systematic self-control and methodical conduct of life, occasionally even in terms of a strict account-ancy of conscience, with daily recordings of good and evil deeds.[49] There is also the example of the eighteenth-century clothier Joseph Ryder of Leeds, whose spiritual journal of 14,000 hand-written pages, cover-ing 30 years of his life, neatly displays all key features of the Protestant ethic: self-discipline, ascetic moderation, commitment to hard work and

[48] Max Weber, '"Churches" and "Sects" in North America' (1906)', in Weber, *PE* (Baehr/Wells), 203–220; MWG I/9, 435–462. Along with the revision of the PE in 1919–1920, Weber also produced a second version of the 'sects' paper, which is essentially a new text: 'The Protestant Sects and the Spirit of Capitalism', in *PE* (Kalberg), 185–199 (footnotes abridged); MWG I/18, 493–545.

[49] Hartmut Lehmann, 'Ascetic Protestantism and Economic Rationalism: Max Weber Revisited After Two Generations', *Harvard Theological Review* 80 (1987), 307–320; Kaspar von Greyerz, *Vorsehungsglaube und Kosmologie. Studien zu englischen Selbstzeugnissen des 17. Jahrhunderts* (Göttingen: Vandenhoeck & Ruprecht 1990); Kaspar von Greyerz, 'Der alltägliche Gott im 17. Jahrhundert. Zur religiös-konfessionellen Identität der englischen Puritaner', *Pietismus und Neuzeit* 16 (1990), 9–28; Kaspar von Greyerz, 'Biographical Evidence on Predestination, Covenant, and Special Providence', in *Weber's Protestant Ethic*, ed. Lehman and Roth, 273–284; and Kaspar von Greyerz, *Religion und Kultur. Europa 1500–1800* (Göttingen: Vandenhoeck & Ruprecht, 2000), 146–154.

conscientious use of time. These examples may suffice to show how the PE may still be used imaginatively as a fruitful platform for historical research.[50]

However, I would go even further and suggest that the historical reconsideration of the PE has still missed its most important asset, that is, the chapter on Luther. This may seem pointless, not only because most historians have paid scant attention to that chapter compared to those on Calvinism and Puritanism, but also, and more importantly, because Weber himself basically did the same. He saw the Luther chapter only as a preliminary methodological consideration which enabled him to clarify the question without yet providing the answer (given in the second part of the PE). But he was wrong, and he misled himself in dismissing Luther as a backward social traditionalist. *Against* Weber, I contend that the Luther chapter is the true pearl within the PE as it provides a brilliant exercise in the historical semantics of our modern concept of 'work', rooted in the notion of vocational commitment. Hence the considerable space I have given to it above, and my point that subsequent research has, if anything, lent further support to Weber's argument that Luther's notion of the earthly duty of all Christians to work for their living not only marked a radical departure from the cynical contempt for manual labour among the ruling classes of traditional societies, but also set the foundation for the habitus of 'innerworldly asceticism' as a promoter of modern capitalism.[51]

Modern Capitalism (2): The Moral Dilemma of the Market

The particular emphasis in the PE on the sanctification of work, which includes even the most menial types of manual labour, is closely related to the idea of a decidedly new ethos of work which involved self-discipline, frugality, diligence and rational time management. Weber had no doubt that by the early twentieth century (when he penned the PE), these features had long become purely *secular(ised)* ethical habits.

[50]Margaret C. Jacob and Matthew Kadane, 'Missing, Now Found in the Eighteenth Century: Weber's Protestant Capitalist', *American Historical Review* 108 (2003), 20–49.

[51]See also Sokoll, 'Vom äußeren Zwang zur inneren Verpflichtung', 200–201. For a similar appreciation of the Luther chapter in the PE, see Lehmann, *Webers 'Protestantische Ethik'*, 46–47.

But originally, he held, they were based on *religious* norms, attitudes and beliefs. Benjamin Franklin's creed that 'time is money' was nothing but the secularized version of the idea that the faithful Christian was not allowed to spoil even a single moment of his life—the time span God had given to him. It was within Protestant discourse on the economic conduct of everyday life that that fundamental change in economic mentality occurred which provided the psychological lever for the emergence of modern capitalism.

The psychological thrust in Weber's argument is crucial. But it is also misleading. On the face of it, we are only concerned here with the inner self of the individual obediently working for his living to please God. In fact, however, it is specifically *not* the independent economic agent as an isolated individual. The institutional setting is the capitalist entrepreneur and his wage labourer. And, of course, these are both market participants. It is true that the market does not feature in the PE (other than in a metaphorical sense).[52] But this is only because the sources on which the PE draws abstract from any specific working conditions or market relationships while it is nevertheless clear that their authors have an advanced market economy in mind, most notably Baxter in his discussion of the division of labour (which Weber reads as an anticipation of Adam Smith's) and of individual 'profitability' (*Profitlichkeit*).[53] At any rate, Weber himself left no doubt whatsoever that the PE was about modern capitalism, and that this included the market system in general and the modern labour market in particular.

It is worth carrying this point a little further, placing it in a wider theoretical context. In an undated fragment on 'market association' (*Marktvergesellschaftung* or *Marktgemeinschaft*, the text bears no title), Weber made a sharp distinction between the modern market as an impersonal system of universal exchange based on the principle of rational

---

[52] The key reference, though, is significant enough. This is the last paragraph of part II.1 (see Table 4.1), with the juxtaposition of monastic and innerworldly asceticism, where the decisive turn from the former to the latter is evoked as the moment when the Church, after 'slamming the doors of the monastery behind it', entered the 'market place of life' (*Markt des Lebens*): Weber, *PE* (Baehr/Wells), 105. Unfortunately, both Kalberg (140: 'hustle and bustle of life') and Parsons (154: 'daily routine of life') have missed that point in their translations. There is no textual reason, as the German wording is identical in both versions (1905 and 1920): MWG I/9, 356–366; MWG I/18, 411.

[53] Weber, *PE* (Kalberg), 143–146 (reference to Smith, 144); MWG I/18, 426–437 (Smith, 429).

choice and the traditional market as a particular place of regulated exchange. More specifically, he stressed the artificial character of the modern market system and pointed out that it was historically exceptional for human labour to be treated as a commodity like any other commodity.[54] This idea was later developed further, from the wider cross-cultural perspective of comparative economic anthropology, by Karl Polanyi, who defined the modern market as a 'self-regulating market', which required the institutional separation of the economy from all political, social and cultural interference. This, he held, was a long and painful historical process because normally the economy in general and the market in particular were always 'embedded' in society at large, and subject to cultural norms, legal restrictions and political control. Pre-industrial societies, far from being 'primitive' economies, were typically imbued with far-reaching trading networks involving all sorts of goods, but with the exception of land, money and human labour.[55] Strictly speaking, land, money and labour could never be turned into commodities in the full sense, in that their very production (and not just their exchange) followed the law of supply and demand. But the modern market system, as a system of self-regulating exchange, depended on the universal extension of the 'commodity fiction' to *all* goods. Land, money and labour were therefore 'fictitious commodities'.[56]

While Weber himself had not yet heard of 'fictitious commodities', we may use precisely that term to highlight, once again, his concept of modern capitalism as underlying the argument of the PE. Weber insists on the artificial character of the modern market system, and when he comes to explain its world-historical novelty (again, the 'Prefatory Remarks' of 1920 provide the clearest exposition), he sees the most decisive feature

---

[54] See Max Weber, *Economy and Society*, ed. Guenther Roth and Klaus Wittich (New York: Bedminster Press, 1968), 635–640; extract in Weber, *PE* (Kalberg), 427–429. German text: Max Weber, *Wirtschaft und Gesellschaft. Grundriß der verstehenden Soziologie*, ed. Johannes Winckelmann, 5th ed. (Tübingen: Mohr Siebeck, 1972), 382–385; Max Weber, *Wirtschaft und Gesellschaft. Die Wirtschaft und die gesellschaftlichen Ordnungen und Mächte. Nachlaß*, part-vol. 1: *Gemeinschaften*, ed. Wolfgang J. Mommsen and collb. Michael Meyer (Tübingen: Mohr Siebeck, 2001; MWG/I/22-1), 193–199.

[55] Karl Polanyi, *The Great Transformation: The Political and Economic Origins of Our Time* (Boston: Beacon Press, 1953), 43–67. Alongside anthropologists like Malinowski, Thurnwald and Firth, Polanyi also refers to Weber's posthumous General Economic History.

[56] Polanyi, *The Great Transformation*, 68–76.

in the 'capitalist organisation of *work*', the 'rational organization of *free labour* in industrial *enterprises*'.[57]

The political as well as theoretical implication is that we ought to extend our understanding of the ethical discourse within the PE and read it as a powerful moral justification of modern capitalism. In discussing Weber's own political 'ethic' within the Protestant ethic, a distinction is normally drawn between the narrative of *emerging* modern capitalism as told in the PE and the fully developed capitalist system lying beyond the proper scope of the PE. For example, Wolfgang Schluchter has argued that there are two opposing theses in the PE about the relationship between ethics and capitalism. For the rise of modern capitalism, religiously founded ethical attitudes were decisive. However, once properly established, modern capitalism turned into an 'an-ethical' economic system, a system of ethical neutrality. The market is not *un*ethical, but 'an-ethical' in that it follows the formal logic of free exchange void of all ethical considerations (other than the basic procedural principle that all market participants obey the rules of good faith).[58]

Against this, I want to suggest a reading of the PE that goes beyond that distinction and extends the ethical 'potential' of the PE to capitalism in its fully developed form. After all, Weber was a passionate advocate of modern rational capitalism who was convinced that the social conflicts and economic distortions inevitably and inherently associated with modern capitalism could only be addressed from within the system itself.[59] In his later political writings, he made the distinction between acting according to an 'ethic of conviction' (*Gesinnungsethik*) and according to an 'ethic of responsibility' (*Verantwortungsethik*). My point here is that this distinction may be projected back onto the distinction made in the PE between monastic and innerworldly asceticism. The former is guided by the firm belief in moral principles which must not be violated under any circumstances—in cases of doubt, immaculate acting can only be attained by fleeing the real world. By contrast, the latter rests on the idea of reliability and proper performance *within* this world, which means that moral conduct is subjected to the rational assessment of possible

---

[57] Weber, *PE* (Kalberg), 212–213; *PE* (Parsons), 22–23; MWG I/18, 112–113.

[58] Wolfgang Schluchter, 'Ethik und Kapitalismus', in his *Unversöhnte Moderne*, 200–222.

[59] A clear indication may be found in his position on the labour movement in imperial Germany. See the brilliant discussion in Wolfgang J. Mommsen, *Max Weber und die deutsche Politik 1890–1920* (Tübingen: Mohr Siebeck, 1974), 97–132.

alternatives, a situation where the individual is answerable for the consequences of his or her behaviour.[60] To the extent, then, that innerworldly asceticism forms the moral background of modern capitalism, the concomitant option of economic acting within this world may be seen as an enduring moral commitment to perform responsibly even within the fully developed system of modern capitalism.

CODA

In retrospect, we may name several reasons why the PE has been misrepresented, at least as a historical study (as distinguished from a sociological one), for so long now that any attempt at its historical reconsideration seems almost like fighting a losing battle. For economists and historians at the time, and also later, Weber's notion of modern capitalism was apparently too complex. It was regarded as too strict with respect to the image of the rational capitalist as a heroic pioneer, and at the same too elusive with respect to the idea of spiritual forces as his inner psychological drive. Irritation may also have arisen from the fact that Weber embarked on the historical reconstruction of the moral foundations of modern capitalism, but at the same time, following Marx, insisted that modern capitalism, as an economic system, rested on the self-regulating market as an institution within which moral values were utterly irrelevant. It may also be said that Weber, as he moved from the spirit of capitalism in Europe to the process of rationalization in Western civilization and from there to the global spread of modernization, loaded onto the PE an increasing burden of proof which simply became too heavy for it to carry.

Against all this, I would argue that for us as historians it is still worth going back to the initial process, as described in the PE, where modern capitalism and rational business enterprise went together, under the specific work ethic associated with radical Protestantism. And I would hold *with* Weber that this was a cultural achievement of world-historical significance, because the drive to accumulation is also found in pre-capitalist societies, whereas only the modern capitalist entrepreneur is

---

[60] The record of the sources is somewhat complicated here, but there is a convenient guide in Martin Endreß, 'Ethik (Gesinnungs- und Verantwortungsethik)', in *Max Weber-Handbuch*, ed. Müller and Sigmund, 52–54. See also Giddens, *Capitalism and Modern Social Theory*, 136–138.

driven by the same work ethic which he inflicts upon his labourers. This ethical drive to productive work *within* the ruling class itself is historically unique. It seems to have originated in Western Europe, from the Protestant idea of work as a 'calling'—a spiritual concept turned into a purely secular economic motivation, but as such arising from (and only sustainable as) an inherently ethical imperative. Without that moral foundation of modern capitalism, which includes the close linking of enterprise with individual ownership, and of managerial expertise with individual responsibility and accountability, we might all too easily fall back into the worst forms of adventure capitalism—as the recent recurrent crises of global financial capitalism have shown only too clearly.

PART II

Capitalism and the Political

CHAPTER 5

'We Only Want to Pay What Is Fair': Capital, Morals, and Taxes in Canada 1867–1917

Elsbeth Heaman

Capitalism is always intertwined with the state because it is regulated in nation-state frameworks, even when it globalizes. Consumers and producers, buyers and sellers, inevitably bring moral choices to bear on their market-oriented behaviour, but the regulating and taxing state, as the centre of deliberative decision-making, remains the most obvious lever with which to discipline capital. No nation finds it easy to formulate consensual and effective tax policies. People don't agree as to what constitutes fair taxation, and wealth can distort the deliberations. It can mass-market propaganda, silence critics, and buy off legislators. Every nation has its own history of state, capital and taxation, each one a Tocquevillian case study in the conjunction of political will, state capacity, and notions of

Material from *Tax, Order, and Good Government: A New Political History of Canada, 1867–1917*, reprinted courtesy of McGill-Queen's University Press.

E. Heaman (✉)
Department of History and Classical Studies,
McGill University, Montreal, QC, Canada
e-mail: elsbeth.heaman@mcgill.ca

© The Author(s) 2019
S. Berger and A. Przyrembel (eds.), *Moralizing Capitalism*,
Palgrave Studies in the History of Social Movements,
https://doi.org/10.1007/978-3-030-20565-2_5

fairness. Here, I offer Canadian tax policy during the period 1867–1917 as a case study in the de- and re-moralization of capital.

I draw upon new work in 'fiscal sociology' and tax history that has been slow to come to Canada.[1] Tax revolts figure prominently in many national historiographies, and particularly so in the three nations that most shaped Canadian history: Britain, France, and the United States. Historians identify fierce fights over wealth, poverty, and taxation at the centre of those national stories. By comparison, most writing about Canadian history has focused on disputes over identity rather than over the governance of wealth and poverty. That focus on identity has had exceptionalist consequences and has tended to isolate Canadian historiography from international currents. It has also misled scholars into thinking that Canada lacked serious progressive reform movements. But Canada also had a progressive reform era and movement, one closely conversant and even integrated with American progressivism.[2] If we apply the new fiscal sociology to the study of Canada, we see a population remarkably engaged with international debates about how to discipline capital and, indeed, capturing the attention of the world in doing so. Amidst fierce debate around the core liberal perplexity—how could the state govern capital when active governance was understood to be a check upon capital?—Canadian progressives leveraged the complex meanings of 'value' to mediate between moral and economic ideas; in the process, they proclaimed public ownership over property.

---

[1] See Isaac William Martin, Ajay K. Mehrotra, and Monica Prasad, eds., *The New Fiscal Sociology: Taxation in Comparative and Historical Perspective* (Cambridge: Cambridge University Press, 2009); also works by tax historians Sven Steinmo, Margaret Levi, Avner Offer, Frank Trentmann, Robin Einhorn, Romain Huret, Robert D. Johnston, Nicolas Barreye, Michael Kwass, Nicolas Delalande, and others cited below. Full references are in E. A. Heaman, *Tax, Order, and Good Government: A New Political History of Canada, 1867–1917* (Montreal and Kingston: McGill-Queen's University Press, 2017).

[2] E.g. Bruce Smardon, *Asleep at the Switch: The Political Economy of Federal Research and Development Policy Since 1960* (Montreal and Kingston: McGill-Queen's University Press, 2014), 17. Important American studies give no more than nominal attention to Canadian participation, including Daniel T. Rodgers, *Transatlantic Crossings: Social Politics in a Progressive Age* (Cambridge, MA: Harvard University Press, 1998); Thomas C. Leonard, *Illiberal Reformers: Race, Eugenics, and American Economics in the Progressive Era* (Princeton: Princeton University Press, 2016) who describes the United States as 'uniquely … the land of antitrust' (46). Canada passed antitrust legislation in 1889, one year before the United States. On continental integration, see Damien-Claude Bélanger, *Prejudice and Pride: Canadian Intellectuals Confront the United States, 1891–1945* (Toronto: University of Toronto Press, 2011).

Canada reconstituted itself in 1867 as a federation because it needed a new tax deal; the old one fell victim to cultural and fiscal antipathies. That year was a high-water mark for liberal political economy, so Canada's constitution reflected liberal suspiciousness of the regulating and taxing powers of the state. Legislators aimed to direct capitalism and morality into distinct jurisdictions, so as to liberate national economic policy from the trammels of misguided morality. Federally, prosperity alone would be the measure of good governance, while social, cultural, and religious elements of identity would become provincial responsibilities. The next half century saw Canada evolve towards plutocratic rule, as measurable by its deeply regressive tax policies. An Ontario economist, Oscar Skelton, argued in 1912 that 'there is probably no civilized country to-day in which the rich man pays a smaller proportion of taxation than in Canada'.[3] Even Tsarist Russia looked progressive in comparison.[4] But in 1917, almost exactly half a century after Confederation, liberal economics met their match in an Income Wartime Tax Act that wrote moral and social considerations back into the national political arena. Governance would henceforth be governance of wealth *and* poverty; wealth, too must doff its cap to a moral reckoning higher than itself. I will sketch that process of de- and re-moralization of capital, from its deep constitutional causes in 1867 to its bitterly polarizing consequences in 1917.

DEMORALIZING CAPITAL

Canada needed a new constitution in the 1860s because it was paralyzed by cultural and fiscal resentments. Successively under Indigenous, French, and British control, Canada had a diverse population and pluralist institutions. After 1760, governors had to reconcile a British heritage of securing consent through elections and taxation with their deep-seated distrust of majority Catholic, French-speaking subjects.

---

[3] *Queen's Quarterly* 20 (July 1912): 112–113; Barry Ferguson, *Remaking Liberalism: The Intellectual Legacy of Adam Shortt, O.D. Skelton, W.C. Clark and W.A. Mackintosh, 1890–1925* (Montreal and Kingston: McGill-Queen's University Press, 1993), 169; J. Harvey Perry, *Taxes, Tariffs and Subsidies: A History of Canadian Fiscal Development* (Toronto: University of Toronto Press, 1955), 2 vols.

[4] Yanni Kotsonis, *States of Obligation: Taxes and Citizenship in the Russian Empire and Early Soviet Republic* (Toronto: University of Toronto Press, 2014), 208.

They established legislative assemblies in Upper and Lower Canada (contemporary Ontario and Quebec) in 1791, but relations broke down around taxation in the early nineteenth century. Local taxes to pay for prisons in Lower Canada polarized the electorate, as French-Canadian farmers, who were modest consumers, demanded consumption taxes, while English Canadians preferred land taxes. Aggravating matters, all the ports were in Lower Canada, whose legislators were in no hurry to transfer customs revenues into Upper Canada. And in the 1820s when French-Canadian politicians tried to use the power of the purse to discipline an irresponsible executive, they were denounced as backwards, superstitious, impoverished tax evaders. 'They pay no taxes for perhaps the same reason that you can't tak the breeks off a Hielandman', declared the embattled governor general, Lord Dalhousie, in the 1820s. The pre-eminent nationalist Toronto historian, Donald Creighton, wrote his earliest article on that financial conflict, seeing in it no minor dispute but a clash of civilizations: 'At the bottom of the struggle was a difference of social heritage as fundamental as the differences of race, language, or creed'. It pitted 'a governing class whose deepest instincts were towards improvement, expansion, and prosperity' against 'the sullen, inert opposition of men who accepted unquestioningly the purposes, pursuits, and habits of their forefathers'.[5]

Polarization became violent in the 1830s, leading to constitutional reform in the 1840s, as the two Canadas were given a shared legislature with shared revenues. But by the 1860s mutual antipathy was again making the fiscal constitution unworkable. Each side was convinced that it was unfairly subsidizing the other. Quebecers-to-be thought that spending was disproportionately in the direction of the western frontier, Ontarians-to-be thought that it was to eastern state services that should have been local charges. Along the western frontier, resentment reached fever pitch. There the Toronto *Globe* newspaper, published by nativist George Brown and widely read, insisted that 'Upper Canadians paid 75% of all taxes'. Because his data was weak (the government kept its bureaucracy small and partisan), his rhetoric was particularly vituperative. But French Canadians voted as a political block and, allied with a cronyist Tory minority from Upper Canada, could control the political process. But the more that Brown complained of the fiscal transfers as

[5] Donald Creighton, 'The Struggle for Financial Control in Lower Canada, 1818–1831', *Canadian Historical Review* 12, no. 2 (1931): 120–144.

reflecting 'eastern' and 'Catholic' domination, the more the governing alliance of John A. Macdonald and George-Étienne Cartier had to spend to prop itself up, and the more taxpayers they alienated. Reformers could not convincingly oust them, but could poison the atmosphere and block money votes, making Canada ungovernable. Sympathetic newspapers as far away as Halifax repeated Brown's complaint as gospel: 'The half civilized people of the sterile shores of the Saguenay – the shivering squatters away up by the Temiscouata Lake – had more political power vested in them than the wealthy, and substantial farmers and tradesmen on the shores of Lake Huron, or Lake Erie. The latter paid the taxes, the former controlled them'.[6]

'Rep by pop' or representation by population was, famously, Brown's solution, but what he really wanted was 'rep by prop' or representation by property. Britain, which must approve any constitutional reform, did not have rep by pop but did restrict power to the more highly propertied. Brown wanted a constitutional reset to give Ontario ratepayers either autonomy or superiority, not their current fiscal and political bondage. But how to get a better tax deal when French Canadians enjoyed veto power in the legislature? 'What Finance Minister', Brown asked mournfully in 1863, 'would propose direct taxation while Lower Canada maintains her present control over the affairs of the Province? He would not remain in office a week after committing such an act of folly'. The American example of separate state and federal revenues, the one taxing directly and the other indirectly, was Brown's ideal, but he knew Lower Canadians would never relinquish the power of the purse. And while Canadians paralyzed themselves with fiscal squabbles, the expanding American economy steamrollered its way across the continent.

The fiscal reform that we call Confederation resolved the problem. Confederation created two levels of government, a federal one to pursue national prosperity, and a provincial one that would pursue regional prosperity but must grapple with identity politics as it did so, through governance of schools, churches, asylums, and similar institutions. English Canadians could only poverty-proof their wealth by culture-proofing it. They had to stop clientelist religious, ethnic, or regional

[6] P. B. Waite, *The Life and Times of Confederation 1864–1867: Politics, Newspapers and the Union of British North America* (Toronto: University of Toronto Press, 1962), 41; J. M. S. Careless, *Brown of the Globe, Statesman of Confederation 1860–1880* (Toronto: Dundurn, 1996).

political bosses from translating identity claims into fiscal raids. They had to write both culture and fiscal transfers out of the constitution. The Constitutional Act of 1867 did not achieve hermetic separation but it put Canada on the road towards separation. The colonies becoming provinces would all lose their major source of revenue, their tariff, so they must receive federal subsidies. But, after some very tense constitutional negotiations in 1864, legislators from New Brunswick, Nova Scotia, and the Canadas agreed to enter into Confederation based on a funding formula of 80 cents per head. The sum would remain fixed at those levels, so that a province that doubled its population would receive only 40 cents per capita. Federal subsidies would become insignificant in expanding regions, which must either shrink their state or turn to direct taxation. The pitifulness of the subsidies instantly created an 'Anti' Confederation movement in the Maritime Provinces but, nonetheless, the deal was done with only minor concessions following in subsequent years. Brown exulted in the deal done: 'Is it not wonderful? French Canadian domination entirely extinguished'.[7]

Wealth and morality had distinct jurisdictions. Where morality divided, wealth united, so it was thought. If those shivering Quebec *habitants* insisted on throwing up cultural obstacles to the full and free play of economic liberalism, they might hold back their own province but should find few federal allies. The other British North American colonies, governed by Protestant, Anglophone majorities, were expected to prefer prosperity to culture. The western prairies were peopled by Indigenous and Métis peoples whose culture didn't look progressive or liberal, but immigration was expected to resolve that problem in the long term. Viewed nationally and over the longue durée, the government of Canada could focus on transcontinental economic development. Government had to protect property and sustain rule of law, of course, so as to lend confidence to investments and contracts, but its general mandate was not to mediate between economic and non-economic interests so much as run interference for the economic interests. (An important exception was an 1885 federal Chinese head tax of $50, later rising to $500, designed to discourage immigration from China, as a concession to public opinion in British Columbia, where economic grievances were profoundly racialized.)

---

[7] Christopher Moore, *Three Weeks in Quebec: The Meeting that Made Canada* (Toronto: Allen Lane, 2015), 221.

Macdonald made that mandate explicit in his negotiations with aggrieved Nova Scotia soon after Confederation when the first federal tariff too ostentatiously privileged central Canadian business interests. The pro-Confederation party was humiliated, the 'Anti' party vindicated, and the popular mood ugly. Politicians, merchants, even the Catholic bishop of Nova Scotia flooded the inbox of John A. Macdonald, now prime minister, with warnings that the tariff would systemically impoverish the region and stoke unrest, even violence. Macdonald's reply was cavalier. Poverty, he asserted, was not a political problem and not his problem: '[R]emission of the duty, if it were within the power of the Government, which it is not, would be of no appreciable value to those destitute people. Meanwhile, you must remember that we have got a distinct policy in view as to our dealings with the United States, and that policy must not be interfered with from any accidental poverty in one section of the Dominion. It would be the duty if private or municipal charity is insufficient of the Local Legislature to look after those poor people, and it would be much better for the Central Parliament to supplement any such relief rather than to change their policy'.[8] Here was capital demoralized indeed. Poverty had no claims upon the state or economic policy because the untrammelled pursuit of wealth was the best avenue to national well-being. The new Canadian constitution was designed to work like the English New Poor Law of 1834. Poverty, dressed up as ethnic, regional, and religious solidarity, had wielded real political heft before 1867 but, in theory, would do so no longer. In fact, as political tensions intensified, as his regional allies and even Westminster (petitioned by Nova Scotians) urged responsiveness, Macdonald did modify the tariff and did improve the subsidies. In the process, he ruptured Brown's fiscal straitjacket. Fiscal payoffs would remain the gold standard of Canadian politics. In Ontario, reformers fumed fruitlessly, while politicians from all the other regions flooded to Macdonald's big-tent liberal-conservative party.

[8]Library and Archives Canada, Macdonald fonds, letterbook, vol. 11, 333–334, Macdonald to McCully, 2 January 1868; see Phillip Buckner, 'CHR Dialogue: The Maritimes and Confederation: A Reassessment', *Canadian Historical Review* 71, no. 1 (1990): 1–45; also Andrew Smith, 'Toryism, Classical Liberalism, and Capitalism: The Politics of Taxation and the Struggle for Canadian Confederation,' *Canadian Historical Review* 89, no. 1 (March 2008): 1–25.

Protectionism enhanced the payoffs. In late Victorian Canada, pandering to business interests meant pandering to protectionism. Manufacturers insisted that foreign capital threatened Canadian prosperity, thereby giving Macdonald a mandate for protection. He personally leaned towards free trade principles, but after his party and the national economy both took a tumble in the mid-1870s, Macdonald worked himself back into public favour with a decisive turn towards economic protection. Shut out of American markets and undermined by Americans dumping their surplus in Canada, Canadian manufacturers demanded and in 1879 Macdonald gave them a new, regressive protective tariff. (It was a dirty secret in Canadian politics that the cheaper goods that could be easily produced in Canada were most heavily taxed.) The process created transnational corporations, combines, and associations that enhanced both the economic and political power of the leading businessmen, many of whom took their business interests directly into parliament. A continual flood of propaganda trumpeted the tariff's success. Posters showed farmers and workers prospering together with the 'resistless might of a great army marching to victory', or hoisting Macdonald on their shoulders, while Liberals were shown pimping out Miss Canada to a leering Uncle Sam or snatching hard-earned money from farmers' hands.[9] Canadians were proud of their loyalist heritage and tended to see Americans as always-already immoral, whether they were violently rebelling against the British, violently enslaving Black and dispossessing Indigenous peoples (Canada did both of those things but on a smaller scale), or corrupting the world by making a fast buck. In Canada, being anti-American was, like being wealthy, a practical demonstration of your judgment and virtue. But Macdonald also had a common touch and he won the loyalty of many workingmen by insisting that the tariff created jobs. There were also concessions to regional interests, including bounties and protection for iron and steel in the Maritimes, that secured growth rates comparable to those in central Canada.

Macdonald died in office in 1891, but his successors perpetuated his policies. There was too much wealth and power at stake to do otherwise. The rival Liberals complained that the national tariff didn't just impose

[9] *The Canadian Manufacturers Association* (n.p., 1890), 11; J. J. B. Forster, *A Conjunction of Interests: Business, Politics, and Tariffs, 1825–1879* (Toronto: University of Toronto Press, 1986); and R. T. Naylor, *The History of Canadian Business, 1867–1914* (Montreal and Kingston: McGill-Queen's University Press, 2006; reprint).

an import tax but a whole series of corrupt fiscal transfers as well. One Liberal opposition critic observed in 1891: '[T]here are two kinds of taxation – the kind of taxation that goes into the treasury, and the taxation which goes into the pocket of the combines, and of those in whose behalf the National Policy has largely been created'.[10] There was also a third fiscal transfer. Because the government had such powers to protect or annihilate an industry or company, it was continually subjected to lobbying and bribery that went to party rather than government coffers. Donations from the big corporations, such as the Canadian Pacific Railway, could run above a million dollars. Under such conditions, remarked business historian Michael Bliss, elections must have been close to meaningless. According to a *Globe* editorial of 1894: 'Superficially, the question before civilization to-day is a question of taxation; fundamentally, it is a question of justice between man and man. Our nineteenth-century "noblesse" do not wish to be taxed. They are succeeding splendidly in their attempt at permanent immunity from taxation'.[11]

Canada, in short, had one of the most clientelist governments in the world, openly run by and for capital. Even Liberals must fall in with the national paradigm: Sir Wilfrid Laurier led them to electoral victory in 1896 by promising reformers a measure of tariff reform and businessmen a measure of tariff stability. The latter impulse won and Canada's tariff remained more entrenched and lucrative than ever. American muckrakers marvelled at the unabashed, naked hegemony of wealth in Canada.[12] How to moralize capital under such conditions?

REMORALIZING CAPITAL: LOCAL BEGINNINGS

Like other countries, progressive-era Canada was replete with progressive reformers seeking restraints upon unbridled capitalism, but they had almost no federal political purchase. Prohibitionists, suffragists, social gospellers, socialists, Knights of Labor, Grangers, single taxers, Bellamyite nationalists, and all sorts of other cross-border North American reform movements proliferated, and they focused their efforts

---

[10] Canadian *Hansard*, 22 July 1891, p. 2294.

[11] Michael Bliss, *Right Honourable Men: The Descent of Canadian Politics from Macdonald to Mulroney* (Toronto: HarperCollins, 1994), 22–29; Toronto *Globe*, 3 February 1894.

[12] Gustavus Myers, *History of Canadian Wealth* (Chicago: Charles H. Kerr, 1914).

on provincial and local reforms. Unbridled crony capitalism was even more prevalent provincially than federally, albeit with a core focus on natural resources—the booming pulp and paper, mining, and hydroelectricity sectors. That left only municipal governments, and that's where capitalism met its match in Canada.

Reformers enjoyed their greatest political successes at the municipal level. Fiscally, the crucial variable was widespread support for a single tax on land values. The single tax was advocated in an 1879 book, *Progress and Poverty*, by American radical Henry George, who had an unusually absolute distinction between public and private. Labour was private and the government had no right to tax it. Forced labour was slavery and, therefore, so were taxes on labour. Land, on the other hand, belonged to the whole people of the earth, and the state should use confiscatory taxes to transfer its value back to public ownership. The value of land, George argued, rose as society grew up around it, but landlords were appropriating those incremental increases in value. Valuable urban property should be taxed upon that 'unearned increment' to the point of nationalization. George's theory became known as the 'single tax' because he rejected all other taxes on grounds that they unjustly taxed industry and poverty. *Progress and Poverty* sold in the millions; John Dewey estimated that it 'had a wider distribution than almost all other books on political economy put together'.[13]

Liberals and economists were horrified by both George's diagnosis and prescription, unearned wealth, and confiscatory taxation. No wealth was unearned, and no property should ever be confiscated; even land speculators helped to develop the west, they argued, pointing to unimproved, collectively held 'Indian' land.[14] But George gave lecture tours in Canada that drew turnaway crowds in 1881 and again in 1889; the turnout in Toronto included leading politicians and intellectuals, and popular enthusiasm grew. However, municipal policy frameworks were made provincially. Ontario's government vigorously rejected single tax

---

[13] Allan Mills, 'Single Tax, Socialism and the Independent Labour Party of Manitoba: The Political Ideas of F. J. Dixon and S. J. Farmer', *Labour/Le Travail* 5 (Spring 1980): 33–56; Ramsay Cook, *The Regenerators: Social Criticism in Late Victorian English Canada* (Toronto: University of Toronto Press, 1985); and Gregory J. Levine, 'The Single Tax in Montreal and Toronto, 1880–1920: Successes, Failures and the Transformation of an Idea', *American Journal of Economics and Sociology* 52, no. 4 (October 1993): 417–432.

[14] Toronto *Daily Mail*, 13 June 1887; Toronto *Globe*, 13 April 1911.

reforms as revolutionary confiscation in 1889 and continued to do so as the single tax movement gained strength and breadth throughout Ontario and western Canada. (The movement was much less successful in Quebec and more easterly provinces where land values rose more slowly.)

What became known as the 'Canadian experiment' both thrilled and appalled international audiences as municipalities across western Canada began to heap taxes on land value and reduce them on buildings. Big business in that region—mining and railway companies and the Hudson's Bay Company—generally owned large tracts of land and resisted paying municipal taxes on them. In March 1911, when Alberta's case against the Canadian Pacific Railway for millions in arrears failed in the courts, a popular farming magazine, the *Grain Growers' Guide*, explained just how badly the decision would hit small communities. They would have to tax settlers 'to the limit in order to procure a school, and then possibly they will have to arrange for the school to be open only a few months in the year'. Many could afford no schools at all.[15] You didn't have to believe the single tax was a panacea to see that it had a certain political utility in such regions, one that radicals and even liberals could rally around. This was an important battle against large landed interests, which, political theorists argue, tend to be 'authoritarian opponents of democracy'.[16] Westerners also knew that the single tax was incompatible with the detested protective tariff. Every vote for a single tax mayor reinforced anti-tariff platforms. Small wonder that provincial governments in western Canada fulsomely welcomed single tax legislation or that many municipal governments passed single tax bylaws that exempted buildings and taxed land values in the years before the First World War. Small wonder that Ontario, as a protected manufacturing heartland, obstinately resisted permissive single tax legislation, notwithstanding the Toronto referendum in 1912 that called for a single tax by 25,773 votes to 6440 and notwithstanding all the other petitions, coming from 325 municipalities and 200 labour unions, not to mention the 168 editorial endorsements by Ontario newspapers. The most that Ontario's provincial government ever conceded to single tax reformers was base tax exemptions for the poor.

---

[15] *Grain Grower's Guide*, 25 May 1910 and 11 March 1911.

[16] Francis Fukuyama, *Political Order and Political Decay: From the Industrial Revolution to the Globalization of Democracy* (New York: Farrar, Straus and Giroux, 2015), 407.

But the single tax had other uses for fiscal reformers in Ontario. There the strength of big business was less in tangible property like land and more in intangible property, above all in finance capital. Financialization of the industrial economy came wholesale to the United States and Canada. The first wave saw the development of price-setting combines in the 1880s that prompted anti-combines legislation (1889 in Canada, 1890 in the United States); the second wave took the form of corporate mergers and trusts. Trusts were large corporate holding companies that could bring entire sectors into one firm. American historian James Livingston observes that 'in 1891-92 an industrial company with a capitalization in excess of $10 million was still extremely rare. In 1902, by contrast, nearly a hundred industrial corporations had attained that size'.[17] Canadian historians see a similar 'distinct surge' in corporate consolidation in the 1890s and 1900s. Trusts were hard to tax and intangible capital was particularly hard to tax. Early provincial tax codes tended to follow early American tax codes in focusing on tangible property, like land, that was relatively easy to see, evaluate, and tax. Intangible property—complicated instruments of credit initially developed to fund state debts, extended to railway corporations around the middle of the century, and now extended to the industrial economy as a whole—was comparatively invisible. You couldn't tax finance capital without taxing stocks and bonds. But bonds were classified as debt, which was exempted from taxation, while stocks traded hands too rapidly to be tracked. Moreover, governments, especially municipal governments, had scant power to access lists of stockholders. Toronto ruefully admitted as much in 1876, after the Toronto Street Railway had managed to overturn municipal taxes on its railway easements. The Ontario Court of Appeals had concluded that such utilities companies were being doubly taxed and should only be taxed on their corporate stock. But the city assessors reported that such taxation was 'almost inoperative'.[18] Two worlds, the one material and the other a tissue of money, credit, and reputation in perpetual motion, perplexed tax assessors, not only because the relationship between the two worlds was so complex and volatile but also because they could not tax one without letting the other go free

[17]James Livingston, *Origins of the Federal Reserve System: Money, Class, and Corporate Capitalism, 1890–1913* (Ithaca: Cornell University Press, 1986), 56, 50.

[18]City of Toronto Archives, *Minutes of Proceedings of the Council of the Corporation of the City of Toronto for the Year 1876* (Toronto: City of Toronto, 1877), Report #208.

and could not tax both without imposing double taxation. Either way, they failed to tax all property 'equally' as legislation everywhere required them to do.

In short, the more that wealth financialized, the more it exempted itself from taxation. Tax assessors began to discover in the 1870s that the more a given community prospered, the less it tended to tax that prosperity. While taxes on real estate rose as the price of land increased, taxes on 'general property' plummeted, testifying to widespread evasion. New York led the way, its assessors charted that process, and other jurisdictions joined in the production of comparative tables that confirmed the trend. The financialization of the industrial economy in the 1890s and 1900s massively increased the trend towards tax exemption for all but landed property. Finance capital transformed the meaning of property and in the process it hollowed out tax codes. Fiscal reformers and municipal tax officers could not win this battle unless they developed their own mechanisms for redefining property and value. Henry George gave them the necessary tools to do so, by writing popular moral economies into the very meaning of capital.

Canadian capitalism had a Trojan horse in the local taxation of property. Trade and commerce were federal responsibilities but property fell under provincial jurisdiction. The Judicial Committee of the Privy Council, the final court of appeal, continually reaffirmed that decision, despite Macdonald's attempts to use the federal veto so as to make the 'vested rights of property' a federal concern. Property was intrinsically a moral construct because it rested on the concept of value. Value was two-edged, pulling hard in two directions. It meant the monetary worth of something—as in 'land values'—and it also meant morality, as in 'traditional values'. You couldn't have property without some conception of value hardwired into it, and that value was irreducibly social. The value of land just *was* what people wanted to pay for it, according to a whole host of eclectic considerations. Tax assessors had to turn those shifting values into statist forms of knowledge rigorous enough to withstand judicial review. That put them at the heart of political fights over value, as corporate lawyers, fiscal radicals, and liberal political economists all tried to impose their own definitions of it.

Value was already at the heart of the political and fiscal confrontations around trusts. Financialization was no good to financiers unless they could engineer and control value. Local governments in the United States, beginning in New Jersey in the early 1890s, competed to attract corporate capital by loosening regulatory regimes. Permitting one company to hold another was one such loosening; another was insider valuation of stock. Such innovations put a premium on stock watering. The waterers—corporate insiders—issued bonds and preferred shares secured by tangible material assets and actual earning power, but they also issued large quantities of common shares that represented more speculative 'intangible assets and expected income'. The preferred shares, with their regular dividends, were sold to the general public; the common shares, representing actual control and speculative profits, remained in the hands of financial insiders. The complex mix of tangible and intangible assets made value subject to reputation, predicted performance, and a thousand other complex and subtle qualities beyond the ken of uninformed investors and tax assessors.[19] Stock watering and financialization proceeded together, as insiders constructed millions of fictitious dollars so as to extract millions more from uninformed investors. The financiers insisted on their right to sell stocks at inflated prices, reflecting expert prediction of future value, while they resisted any movement towards taxation of that inflated value.

Corporations rebuffed municipal assessments with complicated arguments that made mincemeat of prosaic tax codes. If a tax assessor pursued tangible property, corporate lawyers insisted that value was intangible, and vice versa. When assessors identified wealth as local, the lawyers insisted it transcended the local, and vice versa. Above all, when assessors identified market value, the lawyers proved that markets were fictions. The two most notorious such rulings, in 1897 and 1898, both saw the calamitous defeat of assessment codes. In 1897, when Toronto tried to tax the corporate earnings of Consumers' Gas Company, the courts permitted the assessment in principle (overturning the ruling of 1876) but insisted it must be on a ward-by-ward basis. No such ward-level value could be found to exist. And when Hamilton tried to tax Bell Telephone Company on its wires, the notorious 'scrap iron decision' of 1898 established that those wires could only be assessed for their physical resale value, as scrap iron, not on the basis of any supposed value to the corporation. Whereas a homeowner could be taxed on the resale value of a house, Bell and kindred corporations wanted to be taxed on

---

[19] Lawrence E. Mitchell, *The Speculation Economy: How Finance Triumphed over Industry* (San Francisco: Berrett Koehler, 2007); Jonathan J. Baskin and Paul Miranti Jr., *A History of Corporate Finance* (Cambridge: Cambridge University Press, 1997), 150–156.

the resale value of the bricks and mortar in their buildings. Bell, as a franchised utility, had a special legal status that prevented its selling those wires in an open market. The legal power to *use* utility property was subject to political oversight that, according to Bell, negated any attempt to reason from market value. The corporate lawyers carried the argument one step further: utilities corporations (they told a commission of inquiry) must be specially protected from confiscatory taxation because, unlike manufacturers, they could not relocate and were dangerously subject to 'the caprices of local agitators and very often to the caprices of local councils themselves'.[20] The greater the public agitation, the lower the value of the property. In that sense, society controlled the value of their property, but the more that that fact was known, debated, and calculated, the more that value was impaired.

But could you really monetize public opinion without admitting that the larger public had a stake in it? Wasn't there something essentially democratic about value? That point was made by two very different schools of economic thought: marginal utility theorists and unorthodox single taxers. Columbia economist John Bates Clark built on Henry George's observation that popular demand determined value, and applied it to other kinds of artefacts that were, unlike land, potentially unlimited. Consumer demand, not labour or source inputs, determined value for Clark. He saw demand as autonomous and individualized, but for his colleague and occasional collaborator at Columbia, E. R. A. Seligman it was a social construct. 'Value in society depends upon the fact not only that each individual measures the relative urgency of his own different wants, but that he compares them consciously or unconsciously with those of his neighbors'. I might not want a locomotive but if my neighbour does then it has an indirect or social utility for me.[21] Individual choices thus reflected both individual need and a determinative public opinion. Seligman was a tax specialist and was reasoning from the ways in which real estate was valued. As a progressive economist

[20] *Report of the Ontario Assessment Commission, being the Interim or First Report and Record of Proceedings* (Toronto: L. K. Cameron, 1901), 415; see also Christopher Armstrong and H. V. Nelles, 'Private Property in Peril: Ontario Businessmen and the Federal System, 1898–1911', *Business History Review* 47, no. 2 (Summer 1973): 158–176.

[21] Rosanne Currarino, *The Labor Question in America: Economic Democracy in the Gilded Age* (Urbana: University of Illinois Press, 2011), 80.

straddling high theory and banal taxation practices, in the journals he edited, organizations he presided, and graduate students he supervised Seligman was enormously influential. He did more than anyone else to professionalize public finance in the United States, and his influence was hardly less felt in Canada. Every tax debate referenced his voluminous writings, and he was a regular correspondent of Canadian economists as well as an outspoken critic of the western Canadian single tax experiment. Seligman's ruling principle was 'ability to pay'. He devoted his life to rebuffing capital taxes and installing graduated income taxes. Seligman was the son of a wealthy banker and he considered trusts were a steadying anti-democratic influence. He was, therefore, an inveterate enemy of the single tax, a veritable Javert to George's Jean Valjean. No self-respecting and professional economist, he insisted, could subscribe to single tax precepts.[22]

For radical Georgeites, on the other hand, you could bring down the trusts and the banks if you could tax finance capital on the basis of its social inputs, its public value. Finance capital might *seem* hard to tax because of those complicated instruments of debt financing that made it so volatile and invisible. But the logic behind monetization, debt financing, was to reify value and make it interchangeable at an abstract and objective level so that it could be freely exchanged on the market. Ultimately, all debt measures social value.[23] That made it fair game for confiscatory taxes on unearned increments. In a world where all values were irreducibly social, enforcing a general property tax meant asking the public: 'How much is this transaction, this factory, this bank, worth to you?' No corporation could have welcomed that conversation; each must have valued its own services more than did the public. Property so easily reassessed by an unreliably democratic public could not play the role of political and economic ballast that Edmund Burke had assigned it a century earlier.

These were not arcane, specialized debates but were played out in heated public confrontations before packed audiences. The corporate tax revolt of the late 1890s sent Ontario municipalities into sudden fiscal crisis: Toronto's tax rate shot up from 17½ to 19½ mils on the dollar. Railways paid a tenth in Ontario what they paid to American states.

[22] A. J. Mehrotra, *Making the Modern American Fiscal State: Law, Politics, and the Rise of Progressive Taxation, 1877–1929* (Cambridge: Cambridge University Press, 2014).

[23] David Graeber, *Debt: The First Five Thousand Years* (New York: Melville House, 2011).

Outraged ratepayer associations lobbied hard for reforms and mayoral candidates explicitly referenced the tens of thousands in revenue lost to the scrap iron decision as they denounced unfair double standards: 'It is utterly wrong that private citizens should be compelled to pay for the protection, opportunities, and other advantages that the city gives to wealthy corporations enjoying extensive privileges and earning large profits'.[24] In 1900, the province responded with a comprehensive Ontario Assessment Commission that held extensive hearings that drew large audiences and newspaper coverage. Corporate lawyers defended the loopholes and insisted that their clients only wanted to pay 'what is fair'; tax assessors defended their ability to formulate both rigorous and fair criteria for taxation if the politicians and judges would only let them; and populists demanded confiscatorial taxation of social inputs. Effective nationalization would, remarked single taxer Alan C. Thompson, 'simplify the matter very materially'.[25]

In progressive-era Canada, corporate lawyers effectively dismantled municipal tax codes when they persuaded judges that tax codes imposed fictitious and dangerous encroachments upon capital. Fiscal reformers began to rebuild those codes according to the newly politicized understandings of value. They realized that democratic control of property taxes could check insider valuations and corporate tax exemptions. Progressive economists who had warned that capital taxation in any form was a serious threat to capitalism everywhere, now saw the argument begin to turn against them. They saw the public waking up to capital taxation as a viable option in progressive and thriving cities. Liberal economists like Skelton and Adam Shortt at Queen's University and James Mavor at the University of Toronto threw their energies behind the Seligmanian project of shifting the incidence of taxation to income. Relieved Ontario legislators seized upon income tax to resolve the turn-of-the-century crisis and to fend off the demands for capital taxation. But the debate was far from over.

Municipally and even provincially, progressive tax reforms were beginning to enjoy success. In some regions, income tax resulted; in others, the trend was towards capital taxation. But everywhere, grassroots social movements were reshaping fiscal policies according to popular moral

[24] Toronto *Daily Mail and Empire*, 25 December 1900.

[25] *Report of the Ontario Assessment Commission*, 150, 422, and *passim*.

economies that insisted on 'fair taxation' and rewrote the criteria of fairness. Such prominent mid-Victorian liberals as Goldwin Smith and John
Stuart Mill had considered graduated income tax the fairest in principle
but pragmatically impossible to achieve, on grounds that they required
inquisitorial state powers and provoked class warfare.[26] Fiscal reformers demanded and instituted new empirical criteria for taxation and new
state powers to measure wealth. Above all, they inscribed wealth *and*
poverty into taxation. They whittled away the mid-Victorian arguments
for formal, legal equality in taxation and exploded tendentious liberal
distinctions between private and public. They didn't just demand fiscal
redistribution between haves and have-nots but made existing definitions
of property unworkable. The fiscal reformers forced liberals to concede
that legal definitions of property, devoid of moral and social considerations, could not undergird tax regimes. There must be some sense of a
public interest, with social relationships inscribed in that public interest.

Remoralizing Capital: The Nation-State

Local government provided a good space to debate first principles of taxation. But you could only go so far towards implementing them before
you ran headfirst into what remained an extraordinarily unresponsive
and regressive federal state. While local jurisdictions were being recon-
structed by grassroots fiscal reform movements, the federal government
went about its usual business, nurturing prosperity and largely disen-
gaged from the economic struggles of ordinary people. It was locked
into a waltz with big business, its only dancing partner. If radical principles of reform found their early successes at the local level, they were
never going to be content with local action alone. Every significant local
tax reform had federal tax implications. It remains to conclude with a few
words about how the remoralization of capital percolated from the
local to the federal arena.

By 1910, Liberal Prime Minister Wilfrid Laurier, like American
President Howard Taft, was under serious pressure to reform the embar-
rassingly lucrative tariff. As prices soared upwards, so did consumption
taxes. Organized farm and labour everywhere demanded tax relief and
freer trade. When Laurier went on a western speaking tour he was

---

[26]Martin Daunton, *Trusting Leviathan: The Politics of Taxation in Britain, 1799–1914*
(Cambridge: Cambridge University Press, 2007).

mobbed by free-traders, who followed him home to stage a massive 'siege of Ottawa' that drew thousands. And early in 1911 a deal was done, as the two countries came to terms around reciprocity in natural goods. Initially dismayed by the deal, Conservatives quickly rallied against it, their nerve stiffened by Toronto businessmen. Tory leader Robert Borden, a wealthy corporate lawyer, won the 'Reciprocity election' of 1911 by arguing that it was better to be ruled by Canadian tycoons than by American ones. Bankers and manufacturers joined him at the platform to insist that they would offer apolitical expert business-like rule and they flooded the country with propaganda and bribes. One Toronto railway baron supposedly wrote a blank cheque that was eventually redeemed for $2,000,000.[27] The most devastatingly effective businessman-orator of the campaign was Thomas White, a Toronto financier who had originally put himself through law school by working in the Toronto assessment office. White had been such a devastatingly effective assessor (the attempt to tax corporate earnings at their head office had been his idea) that, soon after graduation in 1900, he was invited to become manager of the National Trust. A decade later, he so winningly championed corporate capital that, after the election, Borden pressed him into service as finance minister. White and Borden were two of what an aghast Liberal press described as 'seven reputed millionaires' in the cabinet, with others waiting in the wings. Until 1911, big business gave marching orders to politicians; in 1911 it began to rule the country directly. Rule by plutocrats: what could possibly go wrong?

Things went very wrong very quickly. Borden's government pledged to unviable transcontinental railway projects (in which ministers were directly interested), saw debt and interest payments skyrocket. Lower-level governments were in even worse straits, drowning in debt: single tax jurisdictions were particularly hard hit. The cost of living rose inexorably through the period, and the outbreak of war in August 1914 drove it still higher. It also drove ethnic tensions higher. This was a popular war, one embraced with unprecedented patriotism across Canada, but not so ardently embraced in French Canada. French Canadians enlisted at lower rates than English Canadians. They were war shirkers, the nativists insisted, just as they had always been tax shirkers. Many nationalist politicians had built their political careers on that Brownian complaint,

[27] Patrice Dutil and David MacKenzie, *Canada 1911: The Decisive Election That Shaped the Country* (Toronto: Dundurn, 2011), 120–121.

among them Clifford Sifton, the malevolent architect of a school-tax crisis in Manitoba in the 1890s, who denounced Catholic schools as enemies of a common national life. Sifton crossed the floor in 1911 to join Borden's government and mastermind his campaign, and he did some more of that malevolent masterminding in 1917.

Through 1916 into 1917 the wartime demands on Canada increased inexorably. The terrible Battle of the Somme in 1916 saw more than twenty thousand Canadian casualties. In his budget that year, White introduced a tax on 'excess' wartime profits, but because the tax rose with prices and profits, the effect was inflationary; so too was the fact that loans rather than taxes still paid for almost the entirety of the war effort. Workers were outraged as rising prices turned necessities into luxuries, and salaried white-collar workers, including university professors, were similarly hard hit. Manufacturers were no less outraged: like fiscal reformers, they couldn't understand why production was taxed but not finance capital or personal income. Where other Allied countries were now taxing wealth heavily, above 50%, Thomas White was still protecting it. Even the United States, once it entered the war in April of 1917, immediately increased its tax rates to 67% to put the burden of wartime finance onto taxation rather than loans.[28] April was also the month that saw Canadians emerge victorious in the Battle of Vimy Ridge that instantly became a powerful symbol of national pride. But when White introduced his budget a few weeks later, incredibly, income and capital remained untaxed. White uniquely feared the dangers that 'fair' taxation must pose to finance capital in a country where single tax logic was all too prevalent. Industrial capital, its value more or less 'earned' through labour, could protect itself, but finance capital, if not exempted, was too vulnerable to confiscatory taxation of its social inputs. White was sacrificing everything else to the protection of finance. Even his old employer at National Trust, Joseph Flavelle, who was now running the Imperial Munitions Board, deplored that choice as inimical to the war effort.[29] Liberals and the left went into paroxysms of outrage. Farmers and workers were already highly organized; they began to form new political parties to carry their demands more directly into parliament.

---

[28] Kenneth Scheve and David Stasavage, *Taxing the Rich: A History of Fiscal Fairness in the United States and Europe* (Princeton: Princeton University Press, 2016).

[29] Queen's University Archives, Flavelle fonds, 2237–46, Flavelle to White, 21 April and undated April 1917.

In May, Borden returned from a visit to the troops and announced that he would support conscription. Two things immediately followed. First, there must be an election: Laurier would neither permit suspension of statutory limits any longer, nor would he accept Borden's invitation to join a union government. Second, there must be graduated income tax so as to ensure that even if Laurier, with his political base in Quebec, dared not accept the invitation, progressive Liberal politicians whose base was outside Quebec dared not reject it. They must rally to conscription and political union with Borden, but they demanded progressive income tax as their price. In June, income tax became official policy; in September it was enacted by Borden's union government.[30] And when an election was called for December of 1917, income tax and conscription were the leading planks.

But if the Income Wartime Tax Act sufficed to carry progressive politicians, it did not carry the wider population. Farmers and workers, socialists and liberals, from across Canada—including Quebec where capitalism had first begun to industrialize and financialize—understood that it was designed as much to protect as to tax wealth. On the one hand, the rates were much lower than in other Allied countries; on the other hand, wealth invested in a new Victory Bonds campaign was exempt from taxation. Finance capital, especially Toronto finance capital, poured millions into Victory Bonds and would enjoy virtual tax exemption for many years to come. So while the new income taxes satisfied some progressive reformers, others demanded much more searching taxation. Where White insisted that taxes would only be on income, not on 'accumulated wealth', fiscal reformers noisily demanded both. Indeed, moderate and radical demands were so intermingled that White and Borden saw liberal agitation being put to subversive, anti-capitalist purposes. In Winnipeg, both the liberal *Free Press* and the socialist *Voice* wanted conscription of wealth but they harboured very different ideas of it, with the latter demanding confiscatory taxes on 'hoards of cash and liquid securities'.

By the late autumn of 1917, people across Canada demanded taxation of wealth, for its own sake as an act of economic justice rather than

---

[30] See Shirley Tillotson, *Give and Take: The Citizen Taxpayer and the Rise of Canadian Democracy* (Vancouver: UBC Press, 2017); David Tough, *The Terrific Engine: Income Taxation and the Modernization of the Canadian Political Imaginary* (Vancouver: UBC Press, 2018).

as a pragmatic accommodation with prosperity. They insisted that if it did not 'hurt', then it was not fair taxation. Borden and White had held out for too long and offered too little. With Laurier still leading the Liberal party, Quebec was solidly against them of course, but Laurier's focus on profiteering and regressive taxation was attracting fiscal reformers and radicals elsewhere to rally around the Liberal party. Even fortress Ontario was turning against the Tories. In late November, Sifton, White, and others persuaded Borden that he was in danger of losing the election. One consequence was an offer of exemption from conscription for farmers' sons; another was a vicious attack on French Canadians as backwards, selfish evaders of war service and war financing. The financiers understood that capital was much safer in an ethnically polarized nation. There followed the most virulently racist campaign ever seen in Canadian history. Jack Granatstein and J. M. Hitsman argue that the Khaki election was 'deliberately conducted on racist grounds' and 'heavily dependent on corporate contributions from Toronto and Montreal'.[31] The same Toronto financiers, former colleagues of White at the National Trust, who presided over the Toronto and national branches of bond-dealers associations and Victory loan committees (the national association of bond dealers was formed for Victory loan purposes), also spearheaded the 'nonpartisan' Citizens' Union Committee to propagandize for Borden's re-election. It circulated cartoons that openly declared the real stakes were not conscription but power and money. They showed a nationalist politician from Quebec installed as finance minister, his feet on the coffers, telling Old Man Ontario to speak French. A new and heavily subsidized national press association and a new federal propaganda department, run by White's half brother publisher M. E. Nichols, helped to orchestrate virtual unanimity in English-language newspapers across Canada, as editorials and cartoons denounced Quebec as a 'foul blot on Canada' and insisted that a 'united' French Canada must be squarely defeated by a 'united' English Canada. The result was crushing defeat for French Canada: a grimmer and more effectual replay of Confederation to produce real rather than nominal extinguishment of 'French Canadianism'. Borden's speechwriter, Sir John Willison, proclaimed that a union of 'Eastern Conservatives with Western Liberals'

[31] J. L. Granatstein and J. M. Hitsman, *Broken Promises: A History of Conscription in Canada* (Toronto: Oxford University Press, 1977).

would 'destroy the ascendancy of Quebec in Canadian affairs. That has been done but Quebec will be well treated'.[32]

Nonetheless, progressive income tax was on the books. Its beginning was inauspicious and, indeed, Thomas White initially harboured hopes for repeal. But the Canadian state was so deeply indebted, its interest payments so heavy into the 1920s, that there could be no repeal. Financial investors benefitted from the continuing payouts and Canadian income inequality, newly measurable, briefly soared above American rates.[33] A new prime minister, William Lyon Mackenzie King, would gradually reorient federal fiscal policy. He had a PhD, having done graduate studies under progressive American economists, and he would eventually dethrone Macdonald as the longest-serving prime minister. Capital would no longer reign unchecked in the federal parliament; it must henceforth seek accommodation with poverty and with popular moral economies. In the long run, income tax would become a practical calculus of fairness grounded in principles of social solidarity.

CONCLUSION

Early Canadian tax history conveys some terrible lessons. Liberal politics became social politics in Canada amidst fierce debate about the debt that the individuals owed to society and the dangers that organized capital posed to electoral accountability. Taxes framed that confrontation. If taxes aren't strategically designed to engineer fairness, then they will be strategically designed to engineer unfairness. The matter is too important to be left to experts. When ordinary people relax their vigilance, the consequence stretches far beyond economic inequality. Canadian tax history teaches us that, unchecked, the rich will tax the poor and stigmatize them as tax evaders, and wherever possible increase both indignation and taxation by racializing that stigma. Capital knows it is safer in an ethnically polarized world. This remains a pertinent lesson.

---

[32] Richard Clippingdale, *The Power of the Pen: The Politics, Nationalism, and Influence of Sir John Willison* (Toronto: Dundurn, 2012), 324–325; John English, *The Decline of Politics: The Conservatives and the Party System, 1901–20* (Toronto: University of Toronto Press, 1977), 113–115.

[33] Thomas Piketty, *Capital in the Twenty-First Century*, trans. Arthur Goldhammer (Cambridge, MA: Harvard University Press, 2014), 316.

CHAPTER 6

Humanizing Capitalism: The Educational Mission of the Ford Foundation in West Germany and the United States (1945–1960)

Wim de Jong

Moralizing capitalism has historically been a task taken up by social movements, political parties and intellectuals, among others. An often overlooked but obvious domain in the moralizing of capitalism has been that of philanthropies, from which much of the pressure for bettering social circumstances has originated. Of particular interest are corporate philanthropies, at the same time progenitors and forces in the moral adjustment of capitalism as well as products of such attempts. In corporate philanthropies, there is a tension between the social goals they strive for and the outlook of their founders, mostly business magnates (whether Rockefeller or Zuckerberg). Not infrequently, the people who the philanthropist charges with disbursing their money, come to the job with developed social consciences and look down on the way the organization has earned its money. They may tend to perceive capitalism, which is the root of the organization's existence, as the cause of

W. de Jong (✉)
Open Universiteit, Heerlen, The Netherlands

© The Author(s) 2019
S. Berger and A. Przyrembel (eds.), *Moralizing Capitalism*,
Palgrave Studies in the History of Social Movements,
https://doi.org/10.1007/978-3-030-20565-2_6

the social problems it tries to combat. In the words of historian of philanthropy Olivier Zunz: 'The philanthropists were the titans of industry who caused the very afflictions the reformers sought to undo'.[1]

At the same time, corporate philanthropy differs fundamentally from anti-capitalist moralizers of capitalism: the former were and are commonly led by the view that a certain version of capitalism and its cultural values is not the cause of the world's problems but their solution. This makes corporate philanthropies particularly worthwhile to explore; ideals and values of capitalism are contested, showing how capitalism can be seen as a cultural construct and a contested concept. The clash of moral values takes place within and in response to the activities of philanthropies, which are key in the diffusion of moralities of capitalism, and of cultural meanings attached to it.

Post-World War II American corporate philanthropies like the Ford Foundation aimed to shape the world through their programs.[2] They helped to create, moralize and legitimize a culture of capitalism and a liberal reformist Cold War culture. In 1948 the Ford Foundation acquired 90% of the Ford Motor Company stock, enabling it to embark on activities dwarfing other philanthropies, with an endowment amounting to some $417 million.[3] Pursuing good relations and influence around the globe, from 1949 onwards it set up domestic and foreign sections for Europe and Asia, subsidizing exchange programs and cultural institutions. It became key in globally spreading the idea of safeguarding democracy by making the world safe for capitalism. Post-war Western political and intellectual elites sensed that to fend off totalitarianism, democracy had to be instilled in their populations. To lend credence to the notion of democracy as identical with a capitalist, 'free' society, capitalism needed to be humanized.

In the psychological war with communism, the Foundation delivered cultural criticism of authoritarian and antisocial versions of capitalism at home and abroad that exalted individual instead of collective

---

[1] Olivier Zunz, *Philanthropy in America: A History* (Princeton: Princeton University Press, 2012), 20.

[2] Chay Brooks, '"The Ignorance of the Uneducated": Ford Foundation Philanthropy, the IIE, and the Geographies of Educational Exchange', *Journal of Historical Geography* 48 (2015): 36–46, 36.

[3] Sonja M. Amadae, *Rationalizing Capitalist Democracy: The Cold War Origins of Rational Choice Liberalism* (Chicago: University of Chicago Press, 2003).

responsibility. Its New-Deal-oriented anticommunism centred around progressive values. Liberalism promised to prevent more radical and disharmonious unrest. An enlightened corporatist capitalism would be the way to pacifically develop the world. Notably, its first director within this new framework (from 1950 to 1953), former chairman of the Economic Cooperation Administration (ECA), Paul G. Hoffman, claimed the Cold War necessitated a cosmopolitan worldview.[4]

In this chapter, three arenas of the Ford Foundation's attempts at spreading humanized capitalism are examined. First, during American attempts at re-education of the German public between 1945 and 1955, it took on many former Marshall Plan officials. The American strategy for democratizing Germany emphasized 'modern' industrial relations. The Foundation supported these ideas, based on a belief in economic justice in an enlightened capitalism, and supported its dispersion through magazines, the Freie Universität Berlin, and exchange programs. The Amerikahaus Berlin, developed from the American reading rooms in post-war Germany, from 1948 onwards served as one of the local hubs of these activities.

The second arena is that of domestic adult educational projects. In this domain, methods were deployed that were analogous to the effort to export democracy through peaceful industrial relations. Hoffman believed in fostering dialogue and discussion, and as Foundation director he supported its Fund for Adult Education (FAE), a massive project of liberal education that ranged from Great Books study groups to a Test Cities program to kick-start adult education in local communities. Liberal education was to morally elevate American consumers above narrow materialism. Foundation gurus Hutchins and Adler believed in free enterprise but strove for transcendence of the shortcomings of consumerist society. Capitalism should be made more equitable. The project was shot through with the discourse of commerce, staying firmly within capitalist moralization of capitalist society.

A third front of moralizing capitalism was business and management education. After the 'one-worldist' cosmopolitanism of Hoffman

---

[4]Christopher Endy, 'Power and Culture in the West', in *The Oxford Handbook of the Cold War* (Oxford University Press, 2013), 323–338, 329. The ECA was a US government agency set up in 1948 to administer the Marshall Plan. It reported to both the State Department and the Department of Commerce.

and Hutchins brought them into conflict with Henry Ford II, the Foundation took a more pragmatic course from the mid-1950s onwards, and focused on reform of the curriculum of management education in the United States. It became instrumental in the setting up of business schools all over Europe, transmitting a democratic repertoire of cooperation, harmony and humanistic managerial values.

The Ford Foundation has been criticized as an example of elites trying to stop democratization. Thus Amadae claims philanthropies coalesced with governments and 'impartial' social scientists to remove decisions from the control of democratic politics. This cultural-industrial-scientific complex created a technocratic elite, 'at odds with a model predicated on a communicative and dialogic public sphere'.[5] This interpretation reduces phenomena like the Ford Foundation to a cover for a special interest, whether the RAND Corporation, the CIA or the State Department, not taking their own liberal economic vision of democracy seriously.[6]

The Ford Foundation certainly was firmly entrenched in the corporate-governmental establishment, but was also engaged with civil rights, which brought it into Joseph McCarthy's firing line, and supported popular participation in democratic politics.[7] It exercised a liberal moral influence, embedded in a progressive capitalist vision of democracy.[8] As Hoffman put it already in 1945, 'We [the Committee for Economic Development, WdJ] did not subscribe to the idea that what helps business helps you, but rather what helps you and every other American, helps business'.[9] The Ford Foundation intended to strengthen capitalist society by humanizing it, through the promotion of industrial harmony, cultural elevation of consumers, and reform of management education.

---

[5] Amadae, *Rationalizing Capitalist Democracy*, 31, 37.

[6] Frances Stonor Saunders, *The Cultural Cold War: The CIA and the World of Arts and Letters* (New York: New Press, 1999/2013), 116.

[7] Charles R. Acland, 'Screen Technology, Mobilization and Adult Education in the 1950s', in *Patronizing the Public: American Philanthropy's Transformation of Culture, Communication, and the Humanities*, ed. William J. Buxton (Lanham, MD: Lexington Books, 2009), 261–280, 273.

[8] Robert F. Arnove, *Philanthropy and Cultural Imperialism: The Foundations at Home and Abroad* (Bloomington: Indiana University Press, 1982), 1.

[9] Paul G. Hoffman, 'Business Plans for Postwar Expansion', *The American Economic Review* 35, no. 2 (1945): 85–90, 88.

The historical perspective taken here provides a clearer view of the moral values attached to capitalism, their diffusion and development, and capitalism's links with democracy, citizenship and education in this determining phase for Western societies in the latter half of the twentieth century. Among the sources for this contribution are the Amerikahaus Berlin, the records of the FAE in the Syracuse Special Collections, and the Truman Library.

RE-EDUCATING GERMANS: HUMANIZED CAPITALISM AS A STRATEGY TO INSTIL DEMOCRACY

Already during World War II, American authorities acknowledged that to rebuild Europe, Germany had to be incorporated in the realm of democracy.[10] American authorities thought that in addition to free elections, political parties and reform of the capitalist system, 'mentally sick Germans' needed re-education.[11] Many American policymakers in Europe supported the promulgation of a 'modern' American capitalism, based on a New Deal-like corporatism, and joined the Ford Foundation after 1949. Ideological affinities and connections with other parts of the American intelligence and psychological warfare complex made it a logical continuation of their careers.

In the first phase of United States occupation, from 1945 to 1949, while direct power was exercised over the occupied zone, a mission headed by educational administrator George Zook described democracy as a 'humane spirit', treating every human being 'on the level'. Schools should instil the democratic *method* of living and secure equal liberty of thought and open opportunity of action. The fault in Germans was their disdain for politics, Zook's report declared, and their hierarchical attitude in both politics and industrial relations.[12] Zook professed that capitalists needed to admit there 'must be rules of the game governing the

---

[10] Mark Mazower, *Dark Continent: Europe's Twentieth Century* (New York: Knopf Doubleday, 2009).

[11] Walter Ruegg and Jan Sadlak, *A History of the University in Europe: Volume 4, Universities Since 1945* (Cambridge: Cambridge University Press, 2010), 76.

[12] George F. Zook, ed., *Report of the United States Education Mission to Germany* (US Government Printing Office, 1946), 12.

rights of the employer, the employee, and the consumer, and that these should be defined and modified through the democratic process'.[13]

To change the authoritarian attitude, new history textbooks, educational system reform (which failed due to German resistance), magazines, radio, books, movies, theatre, music, lectures and town meetings were employed. American reading rooms and *Amerikahäuser* were hubs of this ideological warfare. From mid-1947 onward, the Military Government relaxed unpopular denazification rules[14] and shifted from re-education to reorientation and cooperation, furthered by the Cold War, which necessitated winning over the German population.[15] The cultural-ideological influence of Allied and Soviet forces continued after the military occupation, up to the point where West Germans started copying American speech and cheeseburgers as a kind of 'self-colonization'.[16]

From the end of 1947, the Marshall Plan got underway with a huge propaganda effort to convince Germans of the merits of American-style consumer capitalism.[17] The Americans wanted to force through a break with German syndicate and trust capitalism, seen as responsible for a closed hierarchical culture which was not in the interest of consumers. Competition in business, a 'dynamic capitalism' as the Marshall Plan's ECA director Hoffman called it, was essential for an open society.[18] This policy was inextricably linked with democratic re-education. In a speech

[13] George F. Zook, 'Education and the Present World Order', *Annals of the American Academy of Political and Social Science*, vol. 265, Critical Issues and Trends in American Education (September 1949), 1–9, 3.

[14] George N. Shuster, 'German Re-education: Success or Failure', *Proceedings of the Academy of Political Science* 23, no. 3 (1949): 12–18, 13.

[15] Beate Rosenzweig, *Erziehung zur Demokratie? amerikanische Besatzungs- und Schulreform in Deutschland und Japan* (Stuttgart: Steiner, 1998), 211.

[16] Natalia Tsvetkova, *Failure of American and Soviet Cultural Imperialism in German Universities, 1945–1990* (Leiden: Brill, 2013); Mel van Elteren, *Americanism and Americanization: A Critical History of Domestic and Global Influence* (Jefferson, London: McFarland, 2006), 136.

[17] Jennifer Fay, *Theaters of Occupation: Hollywood and the Reeducation of Postwar Germany* (Minneapolis and London: University of Minnesota Press, 2008), 88.

[18] Volker Berghahn, 'Rheinischer Kapitalismus, Ludwig Erhard und der Umbau des westdeutschen Industriesystems 1947–1957', in *Deutschland als Modell? Rheinischer Kapitalismus und Globalisierung seit dem 18. Jahrhundert*, ed. David Gilgen (Bonn: Dietz Verlag, 2010), 89–116, 98.

for the Amerikahaus in 1950, Edward G. Miller, Jr., Truman's Assistant Secretary of State, said: 'Democracy depends on education, an enlightened electorate and an economy that offers equally favourable opportunities to all'.[19]

At the same time American capitalism was framed in terms of democratic participation by workers, to deflect its stigma of class struggle and individualism. One of the media channels in the psychological war was *Internationale Arbeitsmitteilungen*, the Amerikahaus publication for German trade unions.[20] It printed speeches by e.g. Truman Labor Secretary Maurice Tobin, a New Deal man, who agitated against Republican Senator R. Taft's anti-union proposals, which he saw as at odds with individual liberty in a democracy: 'This could lead to conflicts that bring an industry to a standstill. And that could shake an entire country to its foundations. But to a point this is the price we must pay for the sake of freedom – in this case, the freedom of the labour movement'.[21]

What were these 'democratic' and 'free' American industrial relations? The Special Services Branch wrote in 1952 on the 'causes of industrial peace' which allegedly made strikes in the United States the exception rather than the rule. Through planning, harmonious relations between employers and workers were achieved, if workers were 'democratic' and responsible, and employers raised wages and did not try to disrupt trust in the union. All involved should be amenable and flexible.[22] Industrial democracy and humanization of capitalism were part and parcel of the horizontal mentality the American authorities tried to get across. Creating a sense of responsibility was essential: if treated more 'on

---

[19]'Demokratie beruht auf Erziehung, auf einer aufgeklärten Wählerschaft und einer Wirtschaft, die allen gleich günstige Möglichkeiten bietet', *Internationale Arbeitsmitteilungen* 3, no. 28 (15 September 1950): 6.

[20]J. F. Tent, *Mission on the Rhine: 'Reeducation' and Denazification in American-Occupied Germany* (Chicago: University of Chicago Press, 1984), 152; Zook, *Report of the United States Education Mission*, vi.

[21]'Dies könnte zu Konflikten führen, die eine Industrie zum Stillstand bringen. Und damit könnte die Ordnung eines ganzen Landes erschüttert werden. Dies ist jedoch bis zu einer bestimmten Grenze der Preis, den wir um der Freiheit willen, d.h. der Freiheit der Gewerkschaftsbewegung, zahlen müssen', *Internationale Arbeitsmitteilungen* 3, no. 37 (17 November 1950): 14.

[22]*Internationale Arbeitsmitteilungen* 5, no. 3 (1 February 1952): 9.

the level', workers would feel responsible, and industrial harmony would result. If superseded by a humane capitalist work-community, capitalism would cease to be merely an antonym of socialism. Irving Brown, chairman of the AFL-CIO and the World Federation of Trade Unions, in 1950 insisted that social justice could be secured only in a political democracy, and also called on German workers to fight for industrial democracy.[23]

Exchange programs for journalists, women's groups, youth leaders, teachers, labour officials and students offered 'participation in the cultural life of the country'.[24] In one such exchange, organized by the Manpower Division of the Military Government in 1949 in cooperation with AFL-CIO, 50 German unionists visited Washington and cities where the unions had a leading role, staying at the homes of American unionists. They could show them the 'Principles of the corporate leadership in the work places and factories […] How they conclude contracts and compromises, how they are themselves led democratically, and how they are part of the construction of democratic government'.[25] It is ironic that American trade unions were lecturing on industrial democracy when German trade unions already had a tradition of cooperative thinking and were even more radical in their demands for co-determination than their American counterparts.[26]

In this second phase of US activity in post-war Germany, many former government workers poured into the Ford Foundation. Corporate philanthropy was increasingly involved, for example in financing exchange programs by the Institute of International Education.[27] This Institute,

---

[23] *Internationale Arbeitsmitteilungen* 3, no. 10 (12 May 1950): 2. A year before, Brown's colleague George Meany had made similar statements on his visit to Berlin. *Internationale Arbeitsmitteilungen* 2, no. 26 (12 August 1949): 7.

[24] Shuster, 'German Re-education', 14.

[25] 'Maximen der Betriebsleitungen in den Gewerkstätten und Fabriken' (…) 'wie sie Verträge und Abkommen abschliessen, wie sie selbst demokratisch geleitet werden und wie sie am gewarnten Aufbau der demokratischen Regierung beteiligt sind', *Internationale Arbeitsmitteilungen* 2, no. 16 (April 1949): 3.

[26] Marie-Laure Djelic, *Exporting the American model: The Postwar Transformation of European Business* (Oxford University Press, 1998), 259–260.

[27] Brooks, 'The Ignorance of the Uneducated', 37. Hoffman was joined by Milton Katz, who worked for the ECA Special Representative in Paris, and Shepard Stone, the former Public Relations official of John McCloy in Berlin, who also after his job in Germany in 1953 came to the Foundation to expand its international program.

founded in 1919, pioneered international student exchange with the United States, which greatly expanded in the 1950s.[28]

Henry Ford II used the huge endowment of the Foundation for a plethora of national and international projects in education, social science research, and community building. H. Rowan Gaither, attorney and chairman of the RAND Corporation, was asked to compile a programmatic report in 1949. It identified five key areas where the Foundation would promote human welfare: the economy, democracy, peace, education, and individual behaviour and human relations. The emphasis was on research, but also on social action.

The report matched the ideas about economy and democracy in the Amerikahaus Berlin. The broad international political responsibilities of the United States made a stable free enterprise system with full employment and industrial peace essential, as 'depressions cause human misery and […] create social and political tensions'.[29] A more complete knowledge of 'effective organization and administration in business firms and unions, a more complete understanding of human behavior', and democratic internal government of trade unions were needed: not only should they represent workers, but they should also have a 'responsible government within [their] own organization, while observing the rules of justice for the public and members alike'.

A democracy should have 'a relatively more stable and more healthy economic system with greater opportunity for personal initiative, advancement and individual satisfactions'. Instead of cowboy capitalism, Gaither spoke of a mixed economy with some government intervention in which economic activities worked to the benefit of the whole of society. Economic concentration in the hands of a few trusts was vulnerable to abuse; a free enterprise system knew real competition. On the other hand, the Study Committee thought big firms were not inherently a bad thing. Here the report showed its corporate inclinations in criticizing anti-business tendencies in Truman's administration.[30]

---

[28] Seth Spaulding, James Mauch, and Lin Lin, 'The Internationalization of Higher Education: Policy and Program Issues', in *Changing Perspectives on International Education*, ed. Patrick O'Meara, Howard D. Mehlinger, and Roxana Ma Newman (Bloomington: Indiana University Press, 2001), 194.

[29] H. Rowan Gaither, *Report of the Study for the Ford Foundation on Policy and Program* (Detroit: Ford Foundation, 1949), 34.

[30] Ibid., 48, 36.

The warm connections with the ECA were underlined when Ford asked Hoffman to head the Ford Foundation in 1951. Like many of his ECA colleagues, Hoffman was a former captain of industry. At Studebaker he promoted peaceful labour relations.[31] Hoffman saw making the world safe for democracy as synonymous with making sure Europe would become a prosperous consumer society. He epitomized the post-war interweaving of business, government and 'philanthropoids' (managers of big philanthropic organizations). On his departure from the ECA, acclaimed journalist Eric Sevareid said Hoffman 'demonstrated how an able businessman can make government work', a good example of those who did not see the New Deal as a 'plot to destroy private business'.[32] Already during the war, Hoffman was convinced that the interests of business were best served by not losing sight of the general welfare.[33]

From 1949 onwards, Hoffman was already supporting the Foundation's activities, especially those intended to strengthen third world economies like India; this effectively made some Ford activities into subcontracted Marshall Plan work.[34] Hoffman coordinated a major propaganda drive in the United States to garner public and congressional support for foreign aid. He tried to convince conservatives of the utility of foreign aid in winning the ideological war against the Soviets; the United States needed a strong Europe in order not to become a garrison state itself. His foreign aid agenda carved out a third way between laissez-faire capitalism and communism. Developing countries benefited most from 'responsible, progressive capitalism', Hoffman maintained, even though he grumbled privately about how multinational corporations abused poor countries.[35] He legitimized foreign aid as enlightened self-interest. In 1960 he wrote that the third world was experiencing

[31] Alan Raucher, *Paul G. Hoffman, Architect of Foreign Aid* (University Press of Kentucky, 1985), 25.

[32] Eric Sevareid, Broadcast CBS, 25 September 1950, http://www.trumanlibrary.org/whistlestop/study_collections/marshall/large/documents/pdfs/7-9.pdf.

[33] Raucher, *Hoffman*, 50.

[34] Memorandum of Conversation with Paul Hoffman and Other Representatives of the Ford Foundation, 3 April 1951; Anthony Carew, *Labor Under the Marshall Plan: The Politics of Productivity and the Marketing of Management Science* (Detroit: Wayne State University Press, 1987), 194.

[35] Raucher, *Hoffman*, 68, 153.

a great awakening, a 'renaissance of aspiration and determination', which profoundly altered the world situation. 'Out of the yearnings of these millions of people can come a better world, or, if the yearnings are ignored, a very dangerous world for the people of the richer nations'.[36]

The danger of course was communism, as illustrated by Cuba in 1957. But the larger context of the belief in the necessity of a humanized capitalism was the mitigation of world tensions. According to the Gaither study, these were 'intensified by the atomic arms race' and 'of the first urgency'. The United States should pursue this mitigation through diplomatic pressure on foreign countries, domestic public opinion and the United Nations.[37] Hoffman and his aides were strongly committed to one-sided nuclear disarmament, and a world police force to ensure peaceful co-existence among capitalist, socialist and communist nations.[38] Secretary of State Dean Acheson in 1952 responded rather sceptically to these idealistic pleas.[39] This 'one-worldism' also aroused the suspicions of the House Un-American Activities Committee, where Hoffman had to defend the Foundation's adherence to the American way of life and free enterprise.

Part of selling American-style humanized capitalism in Europe was showing that American culture was about more than mass oriented materialism, in order to counter the anti-Americanism of Europe's economic and intellectual elite.[40] In Europe, the Ford Foundation supported the intellectual magazine *Der Monat*, which promoted liberal anticommunism and was sponsored by the US High Commissioner

[36] Paul G. Hoffman, 'Foreword', in *How United Nations Decisions Are Made*, ed. John G. Hadwen and Johann Kaufmann (Leiden: Sijthoff, 1960).

[37] Gaither, *Report of the Study for the Ford Foundation*, 52–53.

[38] Memorandum of Conversation with Paul Hoffman of the Ford Foundation, Mr. Milton Katz, and W. Park Armstrong, 17 January 1952. Secretary of State File. Acheson Papers (Harry S. Truman Library); Grenville Clark and Louis B. Sohn, *Peace Through Disarmament and Charter Revision: Detailed Proposals for Revision of the United Nations Charter* (1953).

[39] Memorandum of Conversation with Paul Hoffman and Other Representatives of the Ford Foundation, Assistant Secretary of State Willard Thorp, and Mr. Armstrong, 3 April 1951, Acheson Papers.

[40] Volker R. Berghahn, *America and the Intellectual Cold Wars in Europe: Shepard Stone Between Philanthropy, Academy, and Diplomacy* (Princeton: Princeton University Press, 2002), 211; Saunders, *The Cultural Cold War*, 117.

McCloy[41] as well as James Laughlin, publisher of *Perspectives USA*.[42] Most notably, during the 1950s there was a growing commitment to the Free University Berlin, which taught American-style social sciences and fostered a fruitful intermigration of scholars.[43] The continuity with re-education was clear: in 1956 the Foundation had former deputy of the High Commissioner in Bavaria George Shuster write a report on the FU which led to further financial support.[44] The Foundation's trustees, however, prioritized domestic programs. Some thought it should avoid setting itself up like a state-within-a-state in Europe and Asia.[45] Due to these internal disagreements, until 1956 the public involvement of the Ford Foundation in Europe stayed largely limited to the FU Berlin, and subsequently also the Congress for Cultural Freedom.[46]

So a first arena of the Ford Foundation's moralization of capitalism was its investment in American cultural colonization. Foundation officials believed in progressive capitalism which mitigated authoritarian corporate hierarchies, promoted worker responsibility and decartelization, would let capitalism work more in the interest of consumers and pave the road to economic stability. The belief that an enlightened capitalism was in the best American interest, and the claim that American culture was about more than materialism, were however not only directed overseas but at least as much at American society itself, as its domestic mission of liberal education makes clear.

[41] Francis X. Sutton, 'The Ford Foundation in Europe: Ambitions and Ambivalences', in *The Ford Foundation and Europe, 1950's–1970's: Cross-Fertilization of Learning in Social Science and Management*, ed. Giuliana Gemelli (Brussels: Interuniversity Press, 1998), 30, 171.

[42] Berghahn, *America and the Intellectual Cold Wars in Europe*, 174; Kathleen D. McCarthy, 'From Cold War to Cultural Development: The International Cultural Activities of the Ford Foundation, 1950–1980', *Philanthropy, Patronage, Politics* 116, no. 1 (1987): 93–117, 96.

[43] Detlef Junker, ed., *The United States and Germany in the Era of the Cold War, 1945–1990: A Handbook*, vol. 1 (Washington: Cambridge University Press, 2004), 166.

[44] Stefan Paulus, *Vorbild USA? Amerikanisierung von Universität und Wissenschaft in Westdeutschland 1945–1976* (Munich: Oldenbourg Verlag, 2010), 193.

[45] H. Welch, 'Philanthropy Uninhibited: The Ford Foundation', *The Reporter*, 17 March 1953, 22–25, 25; Sutton, 'The Ford Foundation in Europe', 28–29.

[46] P. Gremion, 'The Partnership Between the Ford Foundation and the Congress for Cultural Freedom in Europe', in *The Ford Foundation and Europe*, ed. G. Gemelli, 137–164, 146.

Humanizing Capitalism Through Great Books: The Fund for Adult Education

Just as the Ford Foundation perceived the American capitalist system at home as in need of moral elevation, it also felt the consumers within it had the same need. The Foundation advocated the nurturing of 'mature and responsible' citizenship in a free enterprise system. The Gaither report stressed consumer education, raising the level of 'economic understanding' among citizens, because 'those with little or no economic understanding cannot judge intelligently the alternatives presented to them and may easily be swayed by propaganda and emotion'.[47] This was to be achieved through a broad program of liberal cultural elevation to foster critical citizenship within a capitalist framework; citizens should become loyal but critical members of the 'free' world. The Foundation's domestic program wedded progressive social reform with the maintenance of social order and cultural edification. The Foundation wanted to safeguard critical democratic liberties, leading it to support, inter alia, desegregation during the McCarthyist period. Its FAE wanted to raise capitalist consumers above a materialist mentality.

The FAE was the brainchild of the dean of the University of Chicago, Robert Hutchins, who was close with Hoffman. Community education had been around since the Depression, consisting of a range of informal activities aimed at the leisured, such as dramatic performances, forums, lectures, arts and crafts.[48] At the end of the 1940s, Hutchins and philosopher Mortimer Adler sought to revitalize this tradition, as they hoped to save American citizens from becoming anomic mass men, as well as from the communist temptation. They brought together refugee intellectuals at a festival in Colorado to celebrate the bicentennial of Goethe's birth, with lectures by Albert Schweitzer, José Ortega y Gasset and Thomas Mann.[49]

Hutchins' civilization-saving mission was about opening up American education to cosmopolitan values, which made him in the eyes of

---

[47] Gaither, *Report of the Study for the Ford Foundation*, 37.

[48] Joseph F. Kett, *The Pursuit of Knowledge Under Difficulties: From Self-Improvement to Adult Education in America, 1750–1990* (Stanford: Stanford University Press, 1994), 423.

[49] Mary Ann Dzuback, *Robert M. Hutchins: Portrait of an Educator* (Chicago: University of Chicago Press, 1991), 155.

conservatives a 'one-worldist'.[50] Hutchins was critical of capitalism, which needed to be made 'just', but did not think socialism as a system was inherently better. He told his friend, the progressive journalist Milton Sanford Mayer, that 'as long as we have tremendous concentrations of private power, we are not going to have the kind of country we ought to have'. Mayer noted critically that Hutchins did not follow this up, but rather saw the fault in the mentality of men, whatever the system they lived in, while at the same time 'he said nothing to scandalize the rich beyond their bearing… he was an eccentric one of them, but still one of them, the establishment's anti-establishmentarian'.[51]

Adler, the high-minded originator of the Great Books program, even co-wrote Louis Kelso's *Capitalist Manifesto* in 1958, and *The New Capitalists* in 1961. Adler thought 'Democracy requires an economic system which supports the political ideals of liberty and equality for all. Men cannot exercise freedom in the political sphere when they are deprived of it in the economic sphere'.[52] Political freedom demanded economic emancipation; rather than seeing the New Deal as 'creeping socialism', Adler followed Kelso in promoting a third way between free market and socialization. Kelso was the inventor of the controversial 'binary economics', which combines private property and free markets with interest-free loans and employee-owned joint stockholding companies. Part of this theory is the creation of 'new capitalists' through asset building: through broad capital distribution across the population a more equitable capitalist system is achieved. Kelso and Adler went beyond mainstream asset building theories, proposing to liberate citizens from the 'tyranny of savings' if the central bank could give them interest-free credit, which would lead to real economic freedom and from there to human fulfilment.[53]

Even though Hutchins' alternative order stayed more abstract, he and Adler both had the same goal in mind: a just society in which modern man could find his highest destiny in high culture. Their Great

[50]John U. Nef, 'The Chicago Experiment', *The Forum* 111, no. 1 (January, 1949): 1–6, 3.

[51]Milton Sanford Mayer, *Robert Maynard Hutchins: A Memoir*, ed. John Hicks (Berkeley: University of California Press, 1993), 335–336.

[52]Mortimer Adler and Louis Kelso, *The Capitalist Manifesto* (New York: Random House, 1958/2000), 4.

[53]Adler and Kelso, *The New Capitalists*.

Books study groups were initially confined to the leisured class of businessmen.[54] With the FAE they wanted to develop every citizen's mature, critical and creative potential. In its ten-year report the FAE stated that 'as a citizen of a free society the individual is the means for the preservation and continual improvement of the kind of society which makes possible the fullest development of his own capacities and those of his fellow citizens'.[55] This emphasis on the individual in a free society rested on the assumption of free enterprise—the word capitalism was preferably not used.

'New York intellectual' Dwight MacDonald thought the Foundation's adult education activities amounted to a chaotic splurging of millions of dollars, famously calling it 'a large body of money completely surrounded by people who want some'. He described Hoffman and Hutchins, the instigators of the Fund, as amateurish men with 'extremely large ideas' of world peace.[56] In this vein, the Test Cities project is often derided as a failed attempt at spreading humanistic education through discussion groups, a focus which gave way to emphasis on civil liberties after the mid-1950s.[57] The FAE however was remarkably well organized, given its hasty setup in the beginning of the 1950s. There is more to say for the view that it helped create a liberal, commodified middle-class culture with its commercially successful Great Books program, which was linked to the Encyclopaedia Britannica venture, both the brainchild of Mortimer Adler.[58]

The FAE worked with study-discussion groups such as the Great Books program. Like Hoffman, it believed that 'discussion' would lead participants to world understanding through face-to-face confrontation of problems and 'objective analysis of world affairs, politics, economics,

[54] Kett, *The Pursuit of Knowledge*, 424.

[55] *A Ten Year Report of the Fund for Adult Education 1951–1961* (White Plains, NY: Fund for Adult Education, 1962).

[56] Dwight MacDonald, *The Ford Foundation: The Men and the Millions* (New York: Transaction, 1989/1956) 3, 143.

[57] Kett, *The Pursuit of Knowledge*, 424: 'when it ceased operations in 1961, the FAE had relatively little to show for its decade of experiment with popular adult education'.

[58] Timothy Lacy, *The Dream of a Democratic Culture: Mortimer J. Adler and the Great Books Idea* (New York: Palgrave, 2013), 63–81; P. Edelson, 'Socrates on the Assembly Line', paper presented at the Annual Conference of the Midwest History of Education Society (Chicago, IL, 18–19 October 1991), 25.

and the humanities'.[59] The FAE's Experimental Discussion Project combined film with essays and small group discussions. Session leaders schooled in group dynamics should be smooth process coordinators, not authorities on topics.[60] The first two programs in 1951 involved 20,000 participants in some 1000 groups.[61] The FAE boasted that in 1960 the program had over 42,000 participants, in more than 1100 communities, discussing issues of public policy.[62] Foundation-subsidized organizations developed programs on such subjects as 'World Affairs are Your Affairs' and 'Great Men, Great Issues', centring around great American historical figures such as Hamilton and Jefferson.

The FAE devised a plan to systematically popularize liberal education, using 'opportunities for self-education by adults in American urban communities'.[63] The 'test cities' project from 1952 to 1955 was envisioned as a 'cooperative enterprise' with 12 carefully selected medium-sized communities in 12 states representing a variety of geographic, vocational and economic situations, such as Little Rock (Arkansas), Akron (Ohio) and San Bernardino (California). Project coordinators Robert Blakely and John Osman described the project as a community laboratory, where 'the exercise of mature and responsible citizenship must begin and be firmly rooted if our free society is to survive and flourish'.[64] A local coordinator would be the 'program engineer' and the link between local and national adult education programs. Ultimately the community would take over, and grow in self-awareness and reflexivity.[65]

The corporate background of the FAE staff was visible in the economic discourse. The Foundation 'invested' in liberal education, and

---

[59] Archives Fund for Adult Education, Syracuse Special Collections, Test City evaluation suggestions and proposed check sheet, by R. B. Pettengill, Box 2.

[60] *Ten Year Report*, 28.

[61] Charles R. Acland, 'Screen technology, Mobilization and Adult Education in the 1950s', in *Patronizing the Public: American Philanthropy's Transformation of Culture, Communication, and the Humanities*, ed. William J. Buxton (Lanham: Lexington Books, 2009), 261–80, 270.

[62] *Ten Year Report*, 30.

[63] *Ten Year Report*, 43.

[64] Report to the Board of Directors of the FAE on the test cities project, by Blakely and John Osman, 12 September 1952, box 2 FAE.

[65] Letter Osman to coordinators, 6 August 1952, box 2 FAE.

wanted a 'maximum dividend', by creating a permanent infrastructure.[66] Osman emphasized local leadership, a person who could bring together program 'products' and program 'consumers'. The coordinator would be a 'wholesaler' of ideas and programs, including those projects supported by the FAE. But such an organizer-manager should be an educator, more than just a 'salesman' or a 'middle man'.[67] Here there was a characteristic tension between a corporate managerial point of view and the wish to transcend it, aptly summarized by the historian Edelson as 'Socrates on the assembly line'.[68]

There was some criticism of these consumerist tendencies. Anna Lord Strauss of the League of Women Voters wrote to FAE Director C. Scott Fletcher in 1952: 'I wondered whether on occasion a preconceived idea of course was sold to the council or leaders in the community, instead of getting them to think through their own needs and come up with their own suggestions'.[69] In a follow-up, Blakely claimed liberal adult education was not 'sold' in an advertising sense, 'though I hope that the fervent belief of the staff of the FAE in what they were suggesting made the project appear important and desirable'.[70]

The Experimental Discussion Project then, was a scientific experiment, characterized by a corporate tendency to expect defined yields, which clashed with the insistence on spontaneity. The program proved a limited success; coordinators did not create enough local leaders, and Osman felt the participants were not a good cross-section of the community—not enough men, not enough from business and industry.[71] In fact, the largest portion of them consisted of middle-class consumers in search of cultural enrichment. Ultimately they accepted that this was their main clientele. Osman noted in 1953, 'it is evident that a vertical

[66] 25 April 1953, Osman to Blakely, box 2 FAE.

[67] Statement Osman to Board of Directors on TC-project, 1954; FAE box 2.

[68] Edelson, 'Socrates on the Assembly Line'.

[69] FAE box 2, Anna Lord Strauss to Scott Fletcher, 27 August 1952; Scott Fletcher to A. Lord Strauss, 9 September 1952.

[70] FAE box 2, C. Scott Fletcher/Blakely to Lord Strauss, 18 September 1952.

[71] History of the Project, FAE box 13, 11. In his study of FAE discussion groups in 1960, Kaplan found that in general they were dominated by women, although there were not as many female leaders as men. Abbott Kaplan, Study-Discussion in the Liberal Arts (1960), 10.

distribution among all levels of the community is difficult to achieve'.[72] Despite this, Osman believed the American people were ready for liberal education.[73] The FAE at the end of the 1950s dropped into the background.[74]

The links between liberal education, the liberal political position of the Ford Foundation and its business attitude were well described by FAE chairman Frank Abrams, who in 1952 spoke of a 'crisis in education'. The Cold War in his opinion generated hysteria and confusion over what education was for. It was not about teaching people what to think, but how to think; 'the American Tradition' had to be carried on, epitomized in the 'belief in the individual, in the capacity of the free man to shape his destiny by his own efforts'. Suspicions against the education system originated in a fear that technology and specialization had diluted the self-reliance of people, who then started leaning on government; people grew too conformist when what they should do was experiment and progress.[75]

Abrams simultaneously showed how this attitude connected with a managerial discourse. He argued in a magazine article that the spirit of private enterprise perfectly suited liberal education. The modern corporation was no longer an inhuman, Fordist undertaking: 'Business organizations now are frequently found among those in the forefront of social pioneering and progress. [...] Our teachers must be strengthened in their belief in the American system of democratic capitalism by a more equitable participation in the rewards of that system'.[76] Education and business should cooperate more closely—business humanized and education more open to commerce—a development that Abrams did not think would endanger the independence of educational institutions.

Liberal education as a second way to moralize capitalism was an attempt to create open-minded, responsible citizen consumers who would raise capitalist society to a higher standard. Directed as it was against mass man and materialism, it would seem to be anti-capitalist;

[72] Report Osman to Blakely 1st year project, 13 June 1953.

[73] Report Osman to Blakely, 28 December 1952, on Test City Project June–December.

[74] *Ten Year Report*, 42; Scott Fletcher to Allen B. Kline, President American Farm Bureau Federation, 30 November 1954.

[75] F. Abrams, 'A Businessman Looks at Education', *The Saturday Review*, 19 April 1952, 13.

[76] Ibid., 71.

but Adler and Hutchins saw it as a moral strengthening of free societies within a capitalist framework, and other Ford executives thought it was perfectly suited to the spirit of free enterprise. In fact, the gains of the FAE projects were used in the reform proposals to put business education on a more liberal footing by the end of the decade.

MANAGEMENT EDUCATION AS A MORAL GOSPEL OF CAPITALISM

Hoffman's tenure at the Ford Foundation ended badly when the trustees fired him in 1953 over irritations about his loose management style, intensive involvement in Eisenhower's campaign in 1952 as well as with UNESCO and civil rights in the McCarthy period, which unnerved Henry Ford II[77] as the House Committee on Un-American Activities started probing into philanthropies, suspecting them of being 'soft on communism'.[78]

H. Rowan Gaither took over its leadership until 1956. In his 1949 report he had underlined peace and strengthening democracy, but his tone in international matters was more Cold-Warrior-like, stressing 'leadership', and the need of a disciplined democracy to survive the nuclear threat. In 1957 his Gaither report went down in classic Cold War history, advising an intensification of the arms race after the 'Sputnik crisis' caused by the Soviets putting the first artificial satellite into space.[79] Nonetheless, Gaither tacitly supported the civil rights activism of the Fund for the Republic, a sub-Fund of the Ford Foundation whose board Hoffman chaired from 1953 onwards, with Hutchins as president. The Fund for the Republic became enmeshed in civil rights strife, leading to tensions with Henry Ford II; but with Hoffman and Hutchins safely sidelined to the Fund, Gaither steered the Foundation away from the idealistic discussion-oriented approach of liberal education. Hoffman's and Hutchins' version of moralizing capitalism was aimed at the faculties of lay people of reasonable deliberation, which would

[77]Paul G. Hoffman, *Peace Can Be Won* (New York: Doubleday, 1951), 67.

[78]Raucher, *Hoffman*, 99.

[79]*Deterrence and Survival in the Nuclear Age* (Security Resources Panel of the Science Advisory Committee 1957); H. Rowan Gaither, Jr., 'We Must Have Courage: Law, National Security and Survival', *American Bar Association Journal* 44, no. 5 (1958): 425–430.

mitigate world tensions by humanist elevation, and saw the achievement of world peace as lying in the promotion of discussion and foreign aid to help countries like India build up a free enterprise system. Gaither took a more pragmatic approach, focusing on the kind of people naturally akin to the Ford Foundation and the natural allies of American capitalism—managers.

Gradually, Foundation-sponsored organizations such as the American Foundation for Political Education turned towards a business clientele, creating 'executive seminars' and focusing on leadership training. In Europe as well as the United States, the Foundation increasingly concentrated on management education, and the FAE, with its liberal arts emphasis, gradually came to a close. This was a much more technocratic, and less controversial, way of spreading the values of humanized capitalism. The Ford Foundation became a standard-bearer of post-Fordism, evangelizing and exporting the managerial revolution both in the United States and Europe. Where the Foundation in the cultural Cold War avoided overt ideological imperialism, its export of 'management' was avowedly imperial in nature: in 1966 the Foundation even published a report with the triumphant title *Management Education: A New Imperialism*.[80] Since 1954, it had a program to reform business education curricula, introducing more social science, and tailoring it to the needs of professional management. Ford's generous support of the Harvard Business School fostered the spread of its model through the United States.[81]

The business education agenda of the Ford Foundation centred on leadership and ethics, as the seminal study *Higher Education for Business* (1959), commissioned by it, epitomized.[82] It had a dramatic impact on the United States and the global development of business education. Its authors emphasized the professionalization of business education, while underlining the need for a good liberal arts component in management

[80] Giuliana Gemelli, 'From Imitation to Competitive Cooperation: The Ford Foundation and Management Education in Western and Eastern Europe (1950s–1970s)', in *The Ford Foundation and Europe, 1950's–1970's*, ed. Gemelli, 167–306, 168.

[81] Scott Kohler, 'Program to Strengthen Business Education: Ford Foundation, 1954', in *Casebook for the Foundation: A Great American Secret, How Private Wealth Is Changing the World*, ed. Joel Fleishman, Scott Kohler, and Steven Schindler (New York: Public Affairs, 2007), 76–78.

[82] Robert A. Gordon and James E. Howell, *Higher Education for Business* (New York: Columbia University Press, 1959).

education as well as the social responsibility of the manager. Gordon and Howell wrote: 'The need for competent, imaginative, and responsible leadership is greater than ever before; the need becomes more urgent as business grows ever more complex and as the environment with which it has to cope continues to change at an accelerating tempo.'[83]

On closer examination, there are striking similarities between management education and liberal education, especially regarding education for democracy. The FAE was cosmopolitan, going beyond pre-war Americanism, as was business education; it too aimed for the creation of responsible, internationally minded managers with some liberal arts training. Thomas H. Carroll was a director at the Ford Foundation from 1953 to 1961, himself a product of the Harvard Business School, and author of *Business Education for Competence and Responsibility*.[84] He explained that the focus should be on leadership, not solely on economic techniques. A broad imaginative grasp of social problems and public affairs was needed, a 'framework or a scheme of values'. Crucial was the *way* it was taught: 'a course in business law can become a means for transmitting a set of legal rules or it can be used as a truly liberating vehicle in education with emphases on moral and ethical values as they are applied by individuals in the business setting'. If the antithesis between specialization and liberal education could perhaps not be eliminated, at least business education should be made the vehicle for liberal as well as specialized or professional education.[85]

In its European activities, the Foundation focused on transplanting knowledge, sponsoring social science research at European universities. Richard Bissell Jr., who came from the ECA to the Foundation to set up its European activities, said the Marshall Plan had lacked a thought-through plan to change the mentality of the 'relatively decadent managerial class', particularly in France and Italy. The Ford Foundation took up this task with exchange programs for managers, exporting American know-how and business administration practices.[86] The Ford Foundation

---

[83] Ibid.

[84] Thomas H. Carroll, *Business Education for Competence and Responsibility* (Chapel Hill: American Association of Collegiate Schools of Business, 1954).

[85] Thomas H. Carroll, 'Towards a Liberal Education for Business', *California Management Review* 1, no. 3 (1959): 73–78.

[86] Interview with Richard Bissell Jr. by Harvey Mansfield, Sam van Hyning, Guy Horsley, and 'HBP', 19 September 1952, Truman Library: http://www.trumanlibrary.org/whistle-stop/study_collections/marshall/large/documents/pdfs/7-3.pdf.

also subsidized business schools, e.g. in Italy,[87] and the training of future European professors of business administration in American universities through the European Productivity Agency (EPA).[88]

The Foundation educated trade unionists about the struggle against communism.[89] The EPA organized numerous adult education courses and exchanges for union and university personnel, financed partly by the FAE. By 1958 it had trained 15,000 people.[90] The Foundation helped set up European management schools, arranged visits and consultancies by American experts, and funded summer courses on American campuses.[91] Gaither's successor Henry Heald (1956–1965) wrote in 1959 that the exchange programs could 'act without the restrictions or suspicions sometimes attached to government-sponsored programs. Their flexibility, objectivity, and precision make them particularly suited for the task of helping others get access to the knowledge that is the basis for human advancement'. Foreigners could learn business and government administration practices; it could conversely be a 'bridge of knowledge' to help American citizens understand international problems and the need for peaceful cooperation.[92]

The Ford Foundation's colonization of European management schools exemplified the turn from 1949 onwards from re-education, understood as imitation, to cooperation. Business education fitted with this seemingly more neutral type of social engineering. The Ford Foundation really entered its European colonization phase after 1955, when its export of management techniques was expanded. Ford's emphasis on exchange was aimed at elevating the American businessman as well as the European one to adopt a broadly socially responsible, horizontal and humanistic outlook. A properly morally educated manager

---

[87] Giuliana Gemelli, 'The "Enclosure" Effect: Innovation Without Standardization in Italian Post-war Management Education', in *Management Education in Historical Perspective*, ed. Lars Engwall and Vera Zamagni (Manchester: Manchester University Press, 1998), 127–144, 139.

[88] Djelic, *Exporting the American Model*, 212, 214.

[89] Carew, *Labor Under the Marshall Plan*, 195.

[90] Robert R. Locke, *The Collapse of the American Management Mystique* (New York: Oxford University Press, 1996), 45.

[91] Gemelli, 'From Imitation to Competitive Cooperation', 194.

[92] Henry T. Heald, 'Foundations for the Bridge of Knowledge', *The Rotarian*, October 1959, 18–20.

would be able to respond to different and complex circumstances, and would also treat his personnel in a 'modern way'—the American way.

CONCLUSION

Corporate philanthropies like the Ford Foundation offer excellent examples in the transnational history of moralizing capitalism. Their cultural imperialism was key in the diffusion of the ideology of a humanized capitalism, which helps explain the widespread acceptance in the West of capitalism in the second half of the twentieth century. Philanthropies like the Ford Foundation are a promising field for efforts to identify the tendencies involved with moralization of capitalism from within. Between the idealist progressivism of Hoffman, whose frame of reference was at the same time that of a captain of industry, the otherworldly idealism of Hutchins, Adler's vision of property-owning citizens, and the pragmatic stance of Gaither, a range of different paths towards moralizing capitalism were charted.

Three domains of moralization of capitalism have been explored here. The first was post-war American propaganda overseas for a democratic mentality that broke with closed hierarchies and cartels, one of harmonious industrial relations in which workers could participate, a mentality of close personal links between states and corporate philanthropy.

A second arena back home in the United States was liberal education for responsible citizenship in a capitalist society. Hoffman and the FAE were very idealistic, indeed sometimes naïve in their faith in the potential of liberal adult education to breed critical democratic citizens. The Experimental Discussion project aimed to create responsible and mature citizens who could deliberate on democracy and engage critically with their surroundings. Nonetheless, a constructive attitude was expected of them, one not put at risk due to social conflict. While the Experimental Discussion Project had no apparent economic goal, aimed as it was at cultural edification, an economic discourse was nevertheless discernible in the semantics of 'wholesaling' and the 'product' of liberal education to the population.

The dominant paradigms within the Ford Foundation shifted during the 1950s under the pragmatist H. Rowan Gaither. Under his leadership a turn towards a third domain, the moralization of business education through the breeding of socially responsible and open-minded managers set in, aimed at both Europe and the United States. This business education had striking similarities with liberal education: the model of the responsible citizen taking care of his community was transplanted to become the responsible manager with some liberal arts training who takes the human element into account. In its initial stage, the study-discussion groups had consisted of businessmen, and from 1955 onwards the Ford Foundation increasingly focused on management education, suffusing it with the same values it had tried to put across in liberal education, such as leadership and humanism.

This managerial repertoire of democracy emanated from the Foundation as corporate philanthropy. The training of European union personnel was clearly designed to make the world safe for capitalism by humanizing and democratizing it, and they made no secret of that. Ironically, the Ford Foundation became a main proponent of post-Fordism.

CHAPTER 7

'Corporate Citizens' at the United Nations: The 1973 GEP Hearings and the New Spirit of Multinational Business

Christian Olaf Christiansen

INTRODUCTION

In the beginning of the 1970s, multinational corporations and their evolving role in world political and economic affairs became a source of high tension in international politics. A range of concerns regarding multinational corporations prompted a series of new investigations, research and high-flown political debates at the United Nations. More specifically, the United Nations Economic and Social Council (ECOSOC) resolution 1721 LIII of 1972 mandated the establishment of a so-called 'Group of Eminent Persons' (GEP), who were to study the role of multinational corporations in development and international relations. In 1973, as part of their work, the GEP held high-profile hearings in New York and Geneva, thereby facilitating a new global exchange of ideas on the subject of multinational corporations and their impact upon international relations and developing countries.

C. O. Christiansen (✉)
Aarhus University, Aarhus, Denmark
e-mail: idecoc@cas.au.dk

© The Author(s) 2019
S. Berger and A. Przyrembel (eds.), *Moralizing Capitalism*,
Palgrave Studies in the History of Social Movements,
https://doi.org/10.1007/978-3-030-20565-2_7

This chapter is about these GEP hearings. It is about how the political and legitimacy crisis of multinational corporations gave birth to a new spirit of multinational business as 'corporate citizenship'. It is a case study on how the world political economy of an increasingly globalized capitalism was moralized in an international and a global context. The hearings bear witness to how representatives of multinational corporations—in the face of much critical scrutiny and public attention—needed to defend, justify and legitimize their activities in developing countries. In the early 1970s, the political and legitimacy crisis of these corporations prompted business representatives to craft a more positive imaginary of multinational corporations. More specifically, representatives of businesses often invoked the rhetorical trope of transnational corporations being *corporate citizens* in host countries. As Val Duncan of the Rio Tinto Zinc Corporation said, 'We should be good corporate citizens'.[1] Or in the words of Jacques Marchandise (Pechiney-Ugine-Kuhlmann), 'Subsidiaries have always made it a rule to act as good citizens'.[2] Or to quote the renowned front figure of the FIAT car company, Giovanni Agnelli, 'In our overseas operations, we seek to relate our activities to the development needs, priorities, and programme of the host country, where our basic policy has always aimed at being good and loyal citizens'.[3] Revisiting the hearings conducted by the GEP reveals how this new image of multinational corporations as both beneficial to developing countries and capable of moral self-regulation emerged. At the time, ideas of corporate social responsibility (CSR) were already a familiar trope in the American national context.[4] But what was new was that this idea of corporate citizenship was being articulated in a unique new *global* exchange of ideas on multinational corporations, facilitated by the UN.

[1] United Nations Department of Economic and Social Affairs (UNDESA), *Summary of the Hearings Before the Group of Eminent Persons to Study the Impact of Multinational Corporations on Development and on International Relations* (New York: United Nations, 1974), 174.

[2] Ibid., 304.

[3] Ibid., 148.

[4] See, e.g., Committee for Economic Development, *Social Responsibilities of Business Corporations: A Statement on National Policy by the Research and Policy Committee* (New York: CED, 1971).

Whereas other scholars have studied the history of the United Nations and its relationship with multinational corporations, relatively little attention has been given to the GEP hearings and their background.[5] The literature that does exist has tended to focus upon the history of the development of a 'code of conduct' for multinational corporations (a set of international rules for foreign direct investment).[6] Such a code was definitely one of the issues addressed at the time, and it was presented in the 1973 UN report *Multinational Corporations in World Development* which served as a pre-circulated point of reference for discussions in the hearings. But as I will demonstrate here, code of conduct was only one of many issues addressed. At its root, the debate over multinational corporations was about nothing less than economic and political *sovereignty* in a post-colonial, Cold War era.

Secondly, while the subject of CSR has received an enormous amount of scholarly attention, much less attention has been given to historicizing it. The historical scholarship that does exist has tended to investigate it within a national context, most often the American one.[7] Other works often state that ideas about the social responsibilities of business have existed for centuries, but then typically go on to note their emergence as an academic field of study in early 1950s America and thereafter focus on the trajectory of the concept in the American context of management theory and business ethics.[8] This literature says little about when these

---

[5] Tagi Sagafi-Nejad, *The UN and Transnational Corporations: From Code of Conduct to Global Compact* (Bloomington and Indianapolis: Indiana University Press, 2008).

[6] For key work on the history of the United Nations code of conduct, see Jennifer Bair, 'Corporations at the United Nations: Echoes of the New International Economic Order?' *Humanity* 6, no. 1 (2015): 159–171; Jennifer Bair, 'Taking Aim at the New International Order', in *The Road from Mont Pèlerin: The Making of the Neoliberal Thought Collective*, ed. Philip Mirowski and Dieter Plehwe (Cambridge, MA: Harvard University Press, 2009), 347–385, 350; Sagafi-Nejad, *The UN and Transnational Corporations*, and Karl P. Sauvant, 'The Negotiations of the United Nations Code of Conduct on Transnational Corporations: Experience and Lessons Learned', *The Journal of World Investment & Trade* 16 (2015): 11–87.

[7] Christian Olaf Christiansen, *Progressive Business: An Intellectual History of the Role of Business in American Society* (Oxford: Oxford University Press, 2015); Gabriel Abend, *The Moral Background: An Inquiry into the History of Business Ethics* (Princeton: Princeton University Press, 2014).

[8] Archie B. Carroll, 'Corporate Social Responsibility: Evolution of a Definitional Construct', *Business & Society* 38, no. 3 (1999): 268–295; David Birch, 'Corporate

ideas entered into a global context and the larger social field in which they took place. Furthermore, while there is today highly elaborate and sophisticated sociological and political science literature on the responsibilities of business, the dominant tendency in this literature is to place the main emphasis on the 1990s, to speak of the 'latest decades', of an 'emerging discourse' or of a new, 'emerging field' around CSR.[9]

Finally, scholarship in the tradition of the sociology of the spirit of capitalism has convincingly suggested that there is a link between critiques of capitalism and the development of a 'new spirit': criticism and contestation trigger new justification and legitimization.[10] This scholarship, however, has also tended either to focus upon national contexts or to concentrate on the period from the 1990s to the present day. In this chapter, I seek to reposition the attention in an earlier decade, arguing that the early 1970s GEP hearings bear witness to how a global discourse on the responsibilities of business was being articulated then. The idea of CSR as a new 'spirit of capitalism' emerging in the globalization decades of the 1990s and onwards thus needs to be seen against this historical backdrop of globalization in the early 1970s.[11]

Social Responsibility: Some Key Theoretical Issues and Concepts for New Ways of Doing Business', *Journal of New Business Ideas and Trends* 1, no. 1 (2003): 1–19; William C. Frederick, 'From CSR_1 to CSR_2: The Maturing of Business-and-Society Thought', *Business & Society* 33, no. 2 (1994): 150–164; and N. Craig Smith, 'Corporate Social Responsibility: Whether or How?' *California Management Review* 45, no. 4 (2003): 52–76.

[9] Andreas Georg and Guido Palazzo, 'The New Political Role of Business in a Globalized World—A Review of a New Perspective on CSR and Its Implications for the Firm, Governance, and Democracy', *Journal of Management Studies* 48, no. 4 (2011): 899–931; Ronen Shamir, 'Socially Responsible Private Regulation: World-Culture or World-Capitalism?' *Law & Society Review* 45, no. 2 (2011): 313–336; and Leslie Sklair and David Miller, 'Capitalist Globalization, Corporate Social Responsibility and Social Policy', *Critical Social Policy* 30, no. 4 (2010): 472–495.

[10] The key work in this genre focused upon French history. See Luc Boltanski and Eve Chiapello, *The New Spirit of Capitalism* (London: Verso, 2006).

[11] Authors who have argued that CSR is the new spirit of capitalism have focused mainly upon the latest decades of globalization (Bahar A. Kazmi, Bernard Leca, and Philippe Naccache, 'Corporate Social Responsibility: The Brand New Spirit of Capitalism', paper presented at the Critical Management Studies Research Workshop, Los Angeles, 2008).

Four Reasons Why Multinational Corporations Became a Key Issue in International Politics

Before turning to the GEP hearings and the emergence of corporate citizenship, however, we need to look into the historical context of multinational corporations and why they became such a pressing issue in international politics and diplomacy. Overall, the late 1960s to early 1970s was a period of profound transition and crises. Indeed, the future of multinational corporations in particular—and the economic and political world order in general—looked very uncertain. The renowned management theorist Peter F. Drucker even warned that 'it is [...] entirely possible that the multinationals will be severely damaged and perhaps even destroyed within the next decade'.[12] In terms of economic and political events, it was a remarkable period: from 1971 the US dollar could no longer be converted into gold; 'stagflation' prevailed and discredited Keynesianism; the oil crisis caused by OPEC in 1973 indicated potential shifts in the power balance between non-Western and Western countries. The period also marked the end of unprecedented economic growth and initiated a new crisis of the welfare states. Famously, the German philosopher Jürgen Habermas would later write about the 'legitimacy crisis' of capitalism in an age of late-modernity.[13] It was in this context that multinational corporations became the centre of attention in the political and public sphere.

The debate over the role of multinational corporations in the international political economy was very polarized; as Tagi Sagafi-Nejad notes, 'multinational corporations were viewed as either saints or demons in an increasingly polarized and fractured global economic policy environment'.[14] One crucial issue was how multinational corporations affected the hosting 'underdeveloped' or 'third world' countries in which they operated: Was foreign direct investment to the benefit only of the corporations themselves, or was it also of benefit to the host countries? The rising issue concerning the role of multinational corporations in relation to development and international relations had several contexts and players. Multinationals were critiqued by the Soviet Union for

---

[12] Peter F. Drucker, 'Multinationals and Developing Countries: Myths and Realities', *Foreign Affairs* 53, no. 1 (1974): 121–134.

[13] Jürgen Habermas, *Legitimation Crisis* (London: Heinemann, 1976).

[14] Sagafi-Nejad, *The UN and Transnational Corporations*, 48.

being the extended arm of Western imperialism.[15] Latin American and African intellectuals voiced many critiques as well. In the US and in other Western countries, there was much criticism of businesses and multinational corporations.[16] Additionally, reflecting the emergence of the New Left and its critiques of capitalism as well as the Vietnam War, multinational corporations were heavily critiqued by American Marxist economists.[17] More generally, anti-corporate ideas became mainstream in the US public in this period.[18]

More specifically, four factors can explain why multinational corporations become a new centre of attention for international politics and the United Nations at the beginning of the 1970s, and why ECOSOC decided in 1972 to establish a 'GEP' who were given the task to 'study the role of multinational corporations and their impact on the process of development, especially that of developing countries, and also their implications for international relations'.[19]

Post-war globalization. There was rapid growth in multinational corporations in the post-war era. While this economic factor is by no means

---

[15] Sagafi-Nejad, *The UN and Transnational Corporations*, 53.

[16] See Sagafi-Nejad, *The UN and Transnational Corporations*, 230 (notes 3–8) for a useful overview of critical work on multinational corporations. Notable among those are: Charles Kindleberger, ed., *The International Corporation: A Symposium* (Cambridge, MA: MIT Press, 1970); Raymond Vernon, *Sovereignty at Bay: The Multinational Spread of U.S. Enterprises* (New York: Basic Books, 1971); Jean-Jacques Servan-Schreiber, *Le Défi Américain* (Paris: Éditions Denoël, 1967; Eng. trans. *The American Challenge*, New York: Atheneum, 1968); Richard J. Barnet and Ronald E. Müller, *Global Reach: The Power of Multinational Corporations* (New York: Simon & Schuster, 1974); Kari Levitt, *Silent Surrender: The Multinational Corporation in Canada* (New York: St. Martin's Press, 1970); Stephen H. Hymer, 'The Multinational Corporation and the Law of Uneven Development', in *Economics and the World Order: From the 1970s to the 1990s*, ed. Jagdish Bhagwati (New York: Macmillan, 1972); Stephen Hymer, 'The Efficiency (Contradictions) of Multinational Corporations', *American Economic Review* 60, no. 2 (1970): 441–448; and Osvaldo Sunkel, 'Big Business and "Dependencia": A Latin American View', *Foreign Affairs* 50, no. 3 (1972): 517–531.

[17] See, for example, Paul Baran and Paul Sweezy, *Monopoly Capital: An Essay on the American Economic and Social World Order* (New York: Monthly Review Press, 1966). See also Charles Perrow, ed., *The Radical Attack on Business* (New York: Harcourt Brace Jovanovich, 1972).

[18] David Vogel, *Lobbying the Corporation: Citizen Challenges to Business Authority* (New York: Basic Books, 1979).

[19] United Nations ECOSOC Resolution 1721 LIII.

a sufficient explanation of why multinational corporations became a key theme in international politics in the early 1970s, it provides important background. To be sure, multi- or transnational corporations had existed for a long time, as is clear when one looks into the history of trading companies, or at other phases of globalization.[20] But the post-war era was characterized by an increasing internationalization of the economy, especially in the West (even if it was the 1980s that marked the real turning point towards 'reglobalization').[21] This growth was facilitated by the new international trade regime of the Bretton Woods institutions and the fixed exchange rate system, which were created against the backdrop of pre-war economic protectionism and nationalism. The growth also reflected the American Marshall Plan in post-war Europe.[22] And even though the greater part of foreign direct investment flowed from developed countries to other developed countries (and not to developing countries), the issue became especially urgent for developing countries. During the 1970s, a lot more manufacturing and consumer goods corporations began investing in the Global South. As the GEP hearings demonstrate, many contemporary experts struggled to understand and conceptualize the rising importance of multinational corporations and of renewed economic integration across borders—or what was later to be referred to as 'globalization'.

The Global South and the New International Economic Order. Decolonization and the withdrawing of visible *political* dominance made the *economic* relations between former colonizers and former colonized nations more visible. Indeed, economic relations were also political relations, as many critics of the existing world economic and political order would point out. New political alliances formed in the Global South, most notably the 'Non-Aligned Movement' in Bandung in 1955 and later the Group of 77 (G77). Indeed, some of the voices at the very first

---

[20] Jürgen Osterhammel and Niels P. Petersson, *Globalization: A Short History* (Princeton: Princeton University Press, 2005).

[21] Ronald Findlay and Kevin H. O'Rourke, *Power and Plenty: Trade, War, and the World Economy in the Second Millennium* (Princeton: Princeton University Press, 2007).

[22] This growth in economic integration was also reflected linguistically: a Google N-gram search on the terms 'transnational corporation' and 'multinational corporation' shows that the usage of these terms was nonexistent or miniscule in the 1950s, it then proliferated in the late 1960s, exploded through the 1970s, ending with a peak in the usage of the terms around 1980.

meeting of The United Nations Conference on Trade and Development (UNCTAD) in 1964 wanted to bring more attention to the issue of multinational corporations. In this context, the Latin American concept of *dependencia* became a key intellectual term for grasping the unequal economic relationships in the world economy. It articulated the concern that while developed countries would tend to industrialize and develop further, developing countries would continue to be providers of primary (low-tech) commodities—a concern that was also raised in the GEP hearings. In step with decolonization and the admission of new nation states to the General Assembly, the Global South became more vocal in the United Nations. Among the issues they would bring to the international agenda were questions about development, international distributive justice, national sovereignty, and the economic and political world order in the post-colonial, Cold War era.

Indeed, the United Nations work on multinational corporations in the early 1970s should be seen in conjunction with the rise of the Global South and their demand for a 'New International Economic Order' (NIEO). The peak of this development was the passing of the 1974 United Nations resolution on the NIEO, which was marked by ambitious and radical ideas about more global distributive justice and the right of the newly freed sovereign nation states to their own territory and natural resources. In the words of Nils Gilman, the 'fundamental objective of the NIEO was to *transform the governance of the global economy to redirect more of the benefits of transnational integration toward "the developing nations"* – thus completing the geopolitical process of decolonization and creating a democratic global order of truly sovereign states'.[23] Among the key aims of the NIEO was a restructuring of the global political economy that would include, for example, the right of developing countries to re-appropriate their natural resources and to regulate multinational corporations.[24] For developing countries 'foreign' multinational companies owned (and run) primarily by foreigners were often seen as signifying the continued dominance of developed countries. In brief, developing countries were the key drivers in putting the issue of multinational corporations on the international political agenda in the early 1970s.

---

[23] Nils Gilman, 'The New International Economic Order: A Reintroduction', *Humanity* 6, no. 1 (2015): 1–16 (quote from p. 1).

[24] Ibid., 3.

The Chile Affair. The 1972 political events in Chile were a prox-
imate cause of ECOSOC's decision to look further into the issue of
multinational corporations.[25] That year it was revealed publicly that the
American communications company ITT had, allegedly with the help
of the CIA, tried to prevent the election of socialist Salvador Allende as
President of Chile in 1970.[26] ITT was concerned about nationalization
and expropriation of their assets in Chile (the Allende government did
usher in a wave of nationalization and expropriation). These revelations
had an impact on the national American political scene where congressional hearings were initiated in the aftermath of the Chile revelations,
bringing further attention to issues concerning corporate bribery and
corporate scandals at the time.[27] They also directly affected international
politics: it was the Chilean delegation who in the summer of 1972 at
the ECOSOC meeting brought this issue to the forefront of the United
Nations.[28]

The Cold War. The events in Chile directly prompted the closer scrutiny at the United Nations of the issue of multinational corporations.
The Chile case was also closely tied to the broader context of the Cold
War with its economic, ideological and geopolitical factors. At stake
were the economic interests of American companies, of Chile, and of the
United States; but there were also the ideological clashes between capitalism and socialism. Geopolitically, US involvement in Latin America
was part of the Cold War context of big-power interference in nation
states. External interference in other countries' domestic political and
economic affairs, either by governments and intelligence agencies or by
multinational corporations, was part of the impetus for the new critical attention towards multinational corporations. In several countries,

[25] Sagafi-Nejad, *The UN and Transnational Corporations*; Bair, 'Taking Aim', 367.

[26] The name of the American journalist who revealed this backstory was Jack Anderson.
The allegations were about the actions of the ITT and its links to the CIA during the presidential elections of 1970. The revelations in 1972 and 1973, however, are almost infini-
tesimal compared to later revelations after 1999–2000 when CIA documents were released
as part of the Chile Declassification Project authorized by Bill Clinton. These showed that
American businesses and the CIA had been involved in Chilean political affairs from the
early 1960s and onwards, in order to hinder 'another Cuba', i.e. another socialist takeover,
and that they were successful in ensuring that Allende did not get elected in 1964.

[27] From 1973 to 1974, the Securities and Exchange Commission investigated corporate
bribery scandals.

[28] Bair, 'Corporations at the United Nations', 161.

such as Cuba after the Cuban Revolution (1953–1959), or Iran under Prime Minister Mohammad Mossadegh (1951–1953), governments had turned towards nationalization and expropriation of foreign company assets, and were in turn met with various political, economic and military counter-measures imposed by the West (as the Soviet Union was all the while clamping down on opposition in the Eastern bloc). First and foremost, this long list of interferences raised the indivisible issues of *political and economic sovereignty*, crucial in the renewed international political attention towards multinational corporations in the early 1970s.

The 'Group of Eminent Persons' Hearings on Multinational Corporations

It was in this historical context that the United Nations was to facilitate a new 'global dialogue' on multinational corporations, especially through the GEP and their hearings.[29] Prior to the hearings, the Secretariat for the UN Department of Economic and Social Affairs prepared the 1973 report *Multinational Corporations in World Development*, which was circulated to the witnesses who were to give testimony there and which served as the specific 'discussion paper' for the hearings.[30] The report dealt with the major issues concerning the effect of multinational corporations on developing countries and the political and economic sovereignty of (developing) countries vis-à-vis multinational corporations, including sub-themes ranging from technology and capital transfer to taxation, post-colonial global justice and ownership of natural resources. Given the context of a high degree of polarization, it is no surprise that the report sought a balanced view that would acknowledge both key negative as well as key positive aspects of multinational corporations.

---

[29] The issue of transnational corporations and rules for foreign direct investment was also taken up in other international organizations in the 1970s. From 1973 the ILO would look into the relations between transnational corporations and social policy, and in 1976 the OECD adopted their guidelines on transnational corporations, as these had earlier been advocated by the International Chamber of Commerce. During the GEP hearings business representatives would often refer favourably to these ICC guidelines, which were based upon voluntary adherence.

[30] United Nations Department of Economic and Social Affairs, *Multinational Corporations in World Development* (New York: United Nations, 1973).

It tried to steer clear of the two extremes of liberalist-capitalist (pro-corporate) and Marxist-socialist (anti-corporate) political economy, in the spirit of a knowledge-based and pragmatic approach to the issues: 'Multinational corporations, which are depicted in some quarters as key instruments for maximizing world welfare, are seen in others as dangerous agents of imperialism. The basic facts and issues still need to be disentangled from the mass of opinion and ideology and a practical programme of action still awaits formulation'.[31]

The GEP was not a decision-making body. But the result of their work—a report written on the basis of the GEP hearings—was intended to inform individual governments as well as the subsequent international negotiations on multinational corporations.[32] The GEP consisted of high-ranking members from business, government, labour and academia who were chosen to achieve broad geographical coverage (although the members were not there in the capacity of representing their countries). The very selection of the people to form the GEP was a delicate and important affair for the UN staff, as the issue of multinational corporations had surged to new heights in the field of international politics, fuelled by the events in Chile. Philippe de Seynes, Under-Secretary-General for ECOSOC and a very important figure in driving the process forward, informed all senior officials at the UN that he would take personal responsibility for the process of appointing the members, given the 'nature of this subject'.[33] He also stressed that establishing the GEP was 'one of the most difficult such tasks that I have had to undertake'.[34] Invitations from then Secretary-General Kurt Waldheim to potential members of the GEP (sent out between late 1972 and spring 1973) also bear witness to the delicacy of the multinational issue. In them Waldheim

[31] Ibid., 1.

[32] According to the UN resolution, they were to 'formulate conclusions which may possibly be used by Governments in making their sovereign decisions regarding national policy in this respect, and to submit recommendations for appropriate international action'.

[33] Inter-office memorandum, 25 January 1973. UN folder: S-0897-007-06. The following quotes stem from the United Nations archival folders (retrieved at the United Nations Archives and Record Management in New York): S-0897-0007-05, S-0897-007-06.

[34] Inter-office memorandum from Philippe de Seynes to the Secretary-General, 29 March 1973. UN folder: S-0897-007-06.

stressed that 'It is quite clear to me, given the emotions which surround the multinational corporations, that the group will gain credibility only if it is established at the highest level of political wisdom, backed of course by expert and professional advice'.[35] Waldheim also underlined that 'a phenomenon of this importance and complexity, with so many political implications, could not remain away from the forum of the United Nations'.[36] Even though such invitations usually stress the import of a potential member's involvement, Waldheim and de Seynes were clearly not exaggerating when they highlighted the political tensions concerning the issue of multinational corporations.

In June 1973 the GEP was announced, consisting of 20 members. During the GEP hearings, the group called in 47 people to give testimony. Additionally, they made use of consultants such as the famous Argentinian UN economist Raúl Prebisch. The witnesses were intended to represent all relevant major perspectives and viewpoints regarding the question of multinational corporations and their impact upon development and international relations. Among them were high-standing business representatives, academics, government officials, labour representatives and representatives from various international organizations such as the Commission of European Communities and the Food and Agriculture Organization. The first round of hearings took place in New York in September 1973. During these hearings, Salvador Allende died during the military coup in Chile (on 11 September 1973)—an event which had a 'sobering effect on the Group and its staff'.[37] The second (and larger) session took place in Geneva in November 1973.[38]

The Stakes of the Game for Multinational Corporations

In the hearings, a spectacular new 'game' around multinational corporations and their role in the world economy unfolded before the very eyes of these early 1970s observers: developing countries trying to attract

[35] Letter from Waldheim to Sicco L. Mansholt (president for the Commission of the European Economic Community), 27 December 1972. UN folder: S-0897-007-06.

[36] Letter from Waldheim to Roy Jenkins (MP, UK House of Commons), 27 December 1972. UN folder: S-0897-007-06.

[37] Bair, 'Taking Aim at the New International Economic Order', 380.

[38] These written testimonies were published along with questions raised by members of the GEP and the answers given by those testifying before the committee (see *Summary*).

foreign capital and technology, but in a way that would support their own development goals; rich countries' populations and labour unions fearing capital flight, outsourcing and corporate tax evasion; multinational corporations using their threats of exit to 'shop' for the most lax regulatory regime. These today well-recognized dynamics of globalization were crystallizing in front of the experts involved in the GEP hearings, at a historical moment of great uncertainty regarding the emerging economic and political world order.

The stakes were high on all sides.[39] Generally, the home countries would have an interest in protecting their overseas corporations and their investments, and retaining access to foreign goods and resources, while preserving their tax base. However, there were also conflicts of interests within home countries, particularly around questions concerning deindustrialization.[40] Critics argued that multinational corporations were highly evolved institutions with their own logic of profit maximization, which was aligned with neither host nor home countries. One typical viewpoint was that they needed to be politically directed and channelled. As José Campillo Sainz, Mexico's Under-Secretary for Industry and Commerce, put it: 'Organizations seeking only financial gain [...] become pressure groups in international political life and create problems for the co-existence of nations. [...] their power must be channeled towards solidarity and justice'.[41] The host countries (often developing countries) were concerned that they benefited too little from the operation of multinationals: that the latter would exploit their natural resources and interfere with or support local government elites against the will and interests of populations, possibly in alliance with foreign political and economic powers (with Chile and the Republic of South Africa as main examples).[42]

---

[39] Given such high stakes, it is not surprising that definitional matters were taken up by several of those who gave testimony, bringing into question the very definitions of 'multinational', 'transnational', and the terminology of 'home' versus 'host' countries.

[40] See, for example, the statement by the research representative of the American Federation of Labor and Congress of Industrial Organizations Nathaniel Goldfinger: *Summary*, 44.

[41] *Summary*, 22.

[42] Host countries in the hearings were mostly developing countries, as the GEP was tasked with studying the impact of transnational corporations on development. However, the economic integration was much stronger between developed countries themselves (in terms of developed countries being the most typical home and host countries of foreign direct investment) than between developed and developing countries.

At the same time, the developing countries also expressed their worries about being deeply dependent upon rich countries and the inflow of foreign capital and technology. A main concern was thus to find a balance between bringing the goals of multinational corporations into closer alignment with those of developing countries and taking care to avoid making demands which would provoke multinational corporations to exit to other countries (for example, those concerning regulation, ownership, management participation, or different forms of 'FDI regulations'). As Jamaica's permanent representative to the United Nations said, 'the participation of multinational corporations as an important source of private capital is welcomed. However, such participation must result in meaningful benefits and not compromise the legitimate aspirations of the Jamaican people and their right to regulate their affairs within a sovereign state'.[43] Representatives of developing countries were thus very well aware of the dilemmas that they faced in the game around foreign capital. As one adviser to the Australian government explained, Australia had been successful in establishing a favourable milieu for multinational corporations, but the flipside was increased foreign ownership.[44] Other dilemmas concerned how to build alliances to increase bargaining power vis-à-vis multinational corporations, and whether the imported production technologies would be too capital-intensive (rather than labour-intensive), thereby leading to higher unemployment (which was already exacerbated by steady population growth in developing countries).

The trans- or multinational corporations had an interest in continuing their business and making a profit, using a variety of tactics to do so; their interests were in avoiding external interference, regulation and control, and decreasing their expenditures, including paying taxes. Above all, they had an interest in not being nationalized or expropriated by their host developing countries. Often the concern was raised that they desired a 'secure' and durable investment climate, in which their property would be fairly protected, where they would not be treated worse than local and national businesses, and where they, in general, would be

---

[43] *Summary*, 426. Written statement by H. S. Walker, Permanent Representative of Jamaica to the United Nations in Geneva.

[44] *Summary*, 431. Written statement by Sir Ronald Walker, Special Adviser to the Government of Australia on Multinational Corporations.

able to make long-term plans. National and international labour organizations opted to enforce or secure labour standards.[45]

Finally, the task of United Nations civil servants was to shape a diplomatic world-organization vehicle that could propose compromises for a new 'global investment regime' more balanced than the current situation in which the West was highly favoured, while avoiding escalation of the very manifest conflicts between North and South, and West and East.[46]

If these were the major interests involved in the high-stakes game of foreign capital, the GEP hearings also bear witness to what were the most important points of discussion and of major disagreement. In brief, four main issues can be teased out.

1. *Development.* In the main, representatives of multinational business claimed that developing countries were benefiting from multinational corporations; socialists claimed that there were other and better alternatives; and representatives of developing countries most often claimed that they did benefit from multinational corporations, but that much more could be done to increase those benefits and to align the activities of multinational corporations with their development goals.

2. *Power.* In general, representatives of multinational companies argued that they operated on the principle that they were satisfying human needs (operating on market terms), and that they did not have any economic or political power, leading to asymmetries in their dealings with developing countries (such as asymmetrical bargaining power, influencing domestic politics, gaining monopoly power). They also tried to draw attention to the actions of even so-called weak nation states in nationalizing or expropriating property of multinational corporations or passing legislation that was unfavourable to companies, as proof that nation states had much more power than corporations. Another controversial issue concerning power (which again had to do with sovereignty) was the question concerning the interference by multinational corporations

---

[45] Several business representatives were thus asked during the hearings about whether they would be willing to accept international labour standards. See, for example, the interview with Giovanni Agnelli, President of FIAT. *Summary*, 152–155.

[46] See Sauvant, 'The Negotiations', for a detailed account.

in internal political relationships, again with the Chile case as the most obvious ongoing example.[47]

3. *Ownership and property rights.* With the NIEO project, the question was why the former colonies, which had now gained their political independence and national sovereignty, should not also gain greater economic independence and sovereignty. It was discussed whether it was fair (and wise) for the new nation states to nationalize or appropriate foreign-owned industries, and whether and to what extent they were then obliged to compensate foreign companies and 'home states' (again with the events in Chile as a main point of reference). They also dealt with different models for how ownership could be transferred from or shared with multinational corporations, most notably through joint ventures with national or local groups in developing countries, through divestment, and through opening up trade in stocks on local stock exchanges. One idea was that of a transition phase in which 'foreign' ownership would gradually be succeeded by full 'home' ownership. They also dealt with questions about which industries should be transferred to national and public ownership.

4. *Control.* Questions concerning control had political as well as legal dimensions. Several representatives of businesses testified that local participation in management was high. Other crucial elements were transparency and taxation of corporate profits: through so-called 'transfer-pricing', multinational corporations were trading with themselves in order to move their profits to countries with the lowest tax rate (or to tax havens). Taxation was related to the questions of ownership, power and sovereignty. It involved international legal and political questions about creating worldwide taxation on corporate profits.

The most controversial and 'hardest' issues concerned development, power, control, property rights, the impact of multinational corporations and questions of post-colonial justice. At their base, they were all related

---

[47] For example, György Adam, head of the Economic Research Section at the Computer and Automation Institute, Hungarian Academy of Sciences, referred to the events in Chile, but also mentioned other such cases of violation of national sovereignty (Ecuador, Guatemala, Iran, Jamaica and Peru). *Summary*, 139–145.

to the big questions of national political and economic *sovereignty*. The stakes in this game were thus very high on all sides. It was in this hostile environment that the idea of multinational corporations as 'corporate citizens' was articulated.

Imagining Multinational Corporations in the World Economy: Four Visions

The spectacular political and legitimacy crisis concerning multinational corporations prompted a new battle of ideas about how to understand and interpret their role in a world of growing international economic integration. To simplify matters, at least four basic ways of thinking about multinational corporations and their relationship to developing countries were articulated during the hearings. As Weberian ideal types, they can be summarized as four different perspectives on corporations.

1. *The 'invisible hand'* perspective: leave multinational corporations be, as they are already benefiting developing countries, already satisfying specific needs, etc.;
2. *The radical alternative:* dissolve multinational corporations and look for alternative, socialist forms of economic organization;
3. *The internationalist and developmentalist perspective*: find new ways to regulate multinational corporations through new international agreements, law, machinery, and 'channel' or 'direct' the multinational corporations in directions more favourable to developing countries;
4. *The corporate citizenship perspective*: multinational business corporations can self-regulate and continue to be of net positive benefit to developing countries through voluntary measures such as a non-binding code of conduct.

The critical test which framed the discursive context in which business representatives had to navigate was whether the multinational corporations were to the benefit of developing countries or not. Business representatives opted for a 'soft law' regime of self-regulating, socially responsible business enterprises. They defended multinational corporations on the grounds that they were beneficial to developing countries (in relation to matters such as economic development, technology transfer, influx of foreign capital, and in respect of local participation in ownership and control); that they ultimately served consumers and satisfied a variety of different demands; and that they did not exercise or possess any power which threatened the sovereignty of nation states. A couple of quotes will demonstrate their rhetoric. As Pierre Liotard-Vogt from Nestlé said, 'the larger the company, the more it should be fully conscious of the part it plays in the economy of the country where it is situated, and of its social and human responsibilities both to its staff and to its Government'.[48] Or as Marcus Wallenberg (Skandinaviska Enskilda Banken) said, 'Nobody needs the MNC [Multinational Corporation] more than the developing countries'.[49] The fact that advocates of multinational business were under pressure to demonstrate how multinational corporations were benefiting developing countries explains why they would often invoke the vocabulary of 'corporate citizenship' rather than the imaginary of 'the invisible hand'. They were critically aware of the need for some form of international rules which could also be of benefit to international business. However, their stance was that such a 'code' for foreign direct investment would not only apply to companies but should also apply to host governments (thereby restricting the power of governments to nationalize and appropriate at will—a position that was advocated by American Secretary of State Henry Kissinger in later negotiations about a 'global investment regime'). Notably, many business representatives were in favour of a 'soft' regime of international rules. More specifically, many referred to the 1970 'Guidelines for International Investment' drafted by the International Chamber of Commerce (the world's leading representative of international business, founded in 1919).[50] The chairman of FIAT, Giovanni Agnelli, referred to them directly when he stated:

> we clearly need better rules governing the relations between multinationals and Governments. But a binding multilateral agreement between developed and developing countries in the form of a 'GATT for Investment' does not seem practical at the moment. Instead, the idea of developing a

[48] *Summary*, 282.

[49] *Summary*, 443.

[50] These 1970 guidelines by the ICC were also mentioned in United Nations, *Multinational Corporations in World Development*.

voluntary code on the rights and responsibilities of the multinational corporations seems to be an attractive one.[51]

Indeed, the most common imaginary among business representatives of multinational corporations in the world economy was not that of simple laissez-faire, but rather this new vision of a 'code' ('soft law') which emphasized 'corporate citizenship' of multinationals. Emphasizing responsibilities towards developing countries and a 'moral' view of the corporation, this represented an alternative, 'fourth way' between the laissez-faire model and a juridical (hard law) approach to regulation— and of course to the more radical project of the NIEO. Out of the critique and the crisis concerning the role of multinational corporations in relation to developing countries a new idea was born: the morally and socially responsible multinational business corporation that had a net positive impact upon developing countries. This new imaginary of the 'benevolent' multinational corporation had something to offer business representatives: a new source of business legitimacy at a time in which the normative sources of laissez-faire and free trade were drying up. Here, it seems that the trope 'corporate citizen' was the one favoured by several business representatives.

At the other end of the spectrum, socialists and radicals were also represented at the hearings.[52] Hungary's representative referred directly to the involvement of the American company ITT in the internal political affairs of Chile. He then moved on to make a more general point about alternatives to private capital for development: 'The myth that foreign Western private capital is indispensable for the development of the developing countries is waning', he stated, and then mentioned various forms of alternative, such as state-owned enterprises, and wrote about the willingness of the USSR to assist developing countries, invoking solidarity with the Third World: 'As a citizen of a socialist country, may I claim

---

[51] *Summary*, 149–150. 'Summary of Written and Oral Statement' in reference to the General Agreement on Tariffs and Trade (GATT) by Giovanni Agnelli, Chairman, FIAT, S.P.A.

[52] There were two from the Soviet bloc who testified before the committee: György Adam, Head of the Economic Research Section, Computer and Automation Institute, Hungarian Academy of Sciences, and Romuald Kudlinski, Director, Institute for Economic Science, Warsaw University, Representative of the Government of Poland.

a part for the community of socialist nations in offsetting the asymmetry in economic capabilities between multinational corporations and the Third World?'[53] Similar critical concerns about multinational corporations were voiced by other socialists and radicals from developing countries as well as the US. For example, Osvaldo Sunkel (Latin-American Faculty of Social Sciences, Santiago, Chile), was 'generally skeptical' about the programme for action outlined in the report, as he believed that 'there are basic contradictions between the development strategy needed for developing countries and the kind of developing strategy induced through the multinational corporate system'.[54] Stephen Hymer, an economist from the New School for Social Research, also gave a very critical appraisal of the secretariat and its report, as it had 'accepted the current structure of the world economy as given and concentrated on how life could be made easier within it', thereby failing to address 'the problem of dependency', and avoiding 'two questions of crucial importance'. These were, firstly, whether 'a world system based on private multinational capitalism ever achieves the development goals we all desire', and secondly, whether there are 'alternative systems of organizing the world economy which rely much less on private multinational capital and are more promising for reaching these goals'.[55] Hymer pointed towards a solution: 'a system of independent socialist countries is needed in which information and technology flow freely between countries, but capital, i.e. power, does not'.[56]

Where business representatives had spoken of multinational corporations being beneficial to developing countries, the radical and socialist critics rejected capitalist principles altogether. Interestingly, representatives of developing countries did not often invoke such extreme perspectives as those, for example, of the American Marxist Hymer. Several among the former spoke about the benefits brought to them by

[53] *Summary*, 142–143. 'Summary of Written and Oral Statement' by György Adam.

[54] *Summary*, 133. 'Summary of Written and Oral Statement' by Osvaldo Sunkel. Sunkel (an economist) penned several articles in these years about the Latin American concern for 'dependencia'. See Sunkel, 'Big Business and "Dependencia"'.

[55] *Summary*, 215–216. 'Written Statement' by Stephen Hymer. Due to his untimely death, the testimony of Hymer was printed in full in the Summary publication. Hymer's key intellectual contribution to the debates about the economic and political world order in these years was the concept of the 'law of uneven development'.

[56] Ibid., 217.

multinational corporations, but insisted upon their own sovereignty in political and economic affairs, including securing better means for steering their development process, and in particular deciding when, for example, nationalization would be legitimate. It would thus be inaccurate simply to generalize representatives from developing countries as airing only radical or socialist (anti-capitalist, anti-market, or anti-world economic integration) views. In reality, several of them were not critiquing private property rights or international trade as such, but were rather concerned with the foreign ownership of corporations located in their countries. They also tended to favour fairer rules for international trade and investment.

It is worth noting that although many positions in the battle of ideas for representing the 'true' image of the multinational corporation were of course wholly irreconcilable (as they ranged from pro-capitalist to full-blown socialist), there were still signs of a common denominator. There was thus a sense in many of the participants' testimonies that theirs was a new era of world economic entanglements. For example, Osvaldo Sunkel, representing a socialist and radical view, wrote that 'The emergence of the Multinational Corporations cannot be understood in its full socio-economic and cultural dimension without reference to the transformations which this process is bringing about in the global capitalist system', also referring to this as 'contemporary transnational capitalism'.[57] And similar attention to the novelty of the world economy—but more positively evaluated—was expressed by the chairman of FIAT, Giovanni Agnelli: 'We have almost become one world economically, but we are still far from being one world politically. […] In a sense, the network of multinational companies represents in embryonic form the central nervous system of an emerging global economic order'.[58] Or as was stated in a similar spirit by another business representative, Irving S. Shapiro, Vice Chairman of E. I. Du Pont de Nemours: 'I am a devoted and optimistic advocate of what I call one-world economics'.[59] (He and others also pointed towards new communication and information technologies as being central to the new economy of the post-World War II era.) Of course, participants would

---

[57] Ibid., 128, 130.

[58] Ibid., 147.

[59] Ibid., 123.

disagree strongly about the nature of this 'emerging global economic order' of globalization and which interests it would serve. But there was a shared understanding that a new economy was emerging in the post-war, post-colonial era. This shared experience of the emergence of more world economic integration, however, should not make us forget that the positions were irreconcilable.

The United Nations officials did their best to persuade the business community that the imaginary of the invisible hand was no longer tenable: the powers and activities of multinational corporations would have to be channelled in a direction more beneficial to developing countries—setting multinational corporations loose would not in itself create more global justice and equality. Western businesses would need to understand that a more balanced world economic order would not come about simply through the long-cherished ideas about the benefits of free trade, now in an age of multinationals. As Under-Secretary-General de Seynes stated in an address at an Academy of International Business Annual Dinner Meeting:

> [S]ome of the more extravagant claims, at times bordering on utopia, seem to have been considerably toned down. The picture of an internationalization of production whereby the most productive use of world resources is arrived at through the instrument of multinational enterprises with their mastery of modern technology, their innovative spirit, their managerial skills, their marketing arrangements, and also their ability to mobilize capital is somewhat receding. To be sure, it is recognized that multinational corporations, like classical trade, may be a powerful engine of growth providing a means for allocating world resources to their best use, judged by market considerations. But hardly anyone today would contend that this is the same thing as a model of world equity in which for instance the less developed countries were able to integrate harmoniously.[60]

While de Seynes was addressing business people, in forums elsewhere business representatives were making arguments about multinational

---

[60]Address by Philippe de Seynes, Under-Secretary-General for Economic and Social Affairs, at the Academy of International Business Annual Dinner Meeting, New York Sheraton Hotel, 27 December 1973 (UN folder: S-0897-0007-05). According to de Seynes, the last six or seven years of 'extensive research' had given new insights into the real workings of the multinationals, and he was referring to that new empirical research as a means of contesting the free-trade ideology.

business in developing countries acting as 'good corporate citizens'. As we have seen from the GEP hearings, a new 'moral economy' of multinational capitalism was in the making: a new spirit of self-regulating, morally responsible, 'progressive' multinational business corporations that would exhibit 'corporate citizenship' and be beneficial to developing countries in a broad range of ways.

CONCLUSIONS

This chapter can be read as a case study of how the world political economy of an increasingly globalized capitalism was 'moralized' in an international context of high contestation of multinational corporate capitalism. The early 1970s controversy about multinational corporations was a political crisis because the question of multinational corporations was a central part of North–South as well as East–West tensions at the time. But it was also a *legitimacy crisis* of multinational corporations which involved an intellectual and ideological struggle—a 'battle of ideas'—about how to interpret the increasingly integrated world economy and the role of multinational corporations. The crisis was a product of several factors colliding: the Cold War, growth in multinational corporations, decolonization and the rise of the Global South, and the more immediate events in Chile. The idea that 'free trade' and complete freedom of manoeuvre for multinational corporations would be beneficial to developing countries (and eventually put them on an equal footing with the developed world) was challenged by the various Marxist, socialist, developmentalist and internationalist perspectives represented at the GEP hearings. A somewhat paradoxical effect of these hearings was that the critique of multinational corporations prompted new defences and justifications, ultimately leading towards a new 'moral economy' of multinational capitalism: the spirit of self-regulating, morally responsible multinational business corporations that would act as 'good corporate citizens' in developing countries.

The debates about multinational corporations in the early 1970s took place in a context of high contestation of both capitalist globalization and of the North–South balance of power. Where the UN declaration on the NIEO in 1974 can be seen as a peak moment in that history, the North–South debates came to a dead end around 1980, giving way to a new era of neoliberal reform, third world debt accumulation, structural adjustment programmes, and what was later to be known as the

'Washington Consensus'.[61] Those trends involved an increased openness of the developing world to foreign capital. At the same time, attempts to bring corporations under an international regulatory regime went to a large degree without any significant results until well into the post-1989 era. The UN Global Compact (2000) and the UN Guiding Principles on Human Rights and Business (2011) are the most recent UN initiatives for ushering corporations into a soft law regime of human rights and labour and environmental standards. These initiatives are clearly examples of contemporary attempts to put pressure on multinationals to become 'corporate citizens', a term that is still widely used today.[62] However, it is clear that they have played out against the historical backdrop of more radical visions for political and economic sovereignty of developing countries (e.g. national ownership of natural resources such as oil).

This chapter certainly does not argue that foreign direct investment has ultimately been bad (or good) for developing countries, a question that falls outside the scope of the study. What I have claimed, however, is that contemporary ideas of 'corporate citizenship', CSR and the like must be seen against the historical backdrop of early 1970s globalization, and not confined to the 1990s. Secondly, when viewed in that expanded context, present-day attempts to 'embed global corporations into global values' should also be placed against the more radical alternatives of political and economic sovereignty of developing countries which came to a halt in the 1980s. For better or worse, the international debate about multinationals was de-radicalized. Global capitalism may certainly have become more thoroughly 'moralized' since the 1970s, meaning that pressure on multinationals to act in a socially conducive way and to be 'corporate citizens' is stronger now than then. But it has remained exactly that: a global—and not a national—way of life, ultimately more committed to shareholders, wherever they may be, than to local and national stakeholders.

---

[61] John Williamson, 'What Washington Means by Policy Reform', in *Latin American Adjustment: How much Has Happened?* ed. John Williamson, https://piie.com/commentary/speeches-papers/what-washington-means-policy-reform.

[62] Klaus Schwab, 'Global Corporate Citizenship', *Foreign Affairs* 87, no. 1 (January/February 2008): 107–118.

Acknowledgements Thanks to Paul S. Adler (Harvard University), Steven L. B. Jensen (Danish Institute for Human Rights), Jacob Jensen (Aarhus University), the participants of the conference 'Moralizing Capitalism: Agents, Discourses and Practices of Capitalism and its Opponents in the Modern Age' in Berlin in March 2016, and to the participants at the workshop on the history of international organizations in Aarhus in December 2016 for comments on earlier versions of this chapter. This research was supported financially by the Danish Council for Independent Research and its research career programme Sapere Aude.

PART III

Ethics and Merchants

Dr Jekyll and Mr Hyde: Commercial Honour at the New York Stock Exchange During the Progressive Era

Boris Gehlen

In 1896, the future president (1898–1903) of the New York Stock Exchange (NYSE), Rudolph Keppler, articulated on behalf of a minority of Stock Exchange members a serious discomfort about the Unlisted Department. It had been established in 1885 in order to attract transactions (and capital) in riskier securities than regularly dealt with at the NYSE. The NYSE was known for—and proud of—only putting high-standard, low-risk securities with a sound performance history on its stock list. To be listed at the NYSE, securities had to be approved by the Committee on Stock List and meet comprehensive disclosure standards. But as markets had shifted towards shares in newly founded industrial corporations—both promising and risky—the NYSE did not want

B. Gehlen (✉)
Economic and Social History,
Bonn University, Bonn, Germany
e-mail: b.gehlen@uni-bonn.de

S. Berger and A. Przyrembel (eds.), *Moralizing Capitalism*,
Palgrave Studies in the History of Social Movements,
https://doi.org/10.1007/978-3-030-20565-2_8

to yield the floor to rival exchanges inside and outside New York, and so established said Unlisted Department.[1]

The Unlisted Department's ambiguous position always aroused opposition within the exchange, finally leading to a review in 1896. While a majority still concluded that its advantages outweighed the disadvantages, Keppler and his allies stressed the double standard which they regarded as capable of causing lasting damage to the Exchange:

> As that committee is at present constituted, the Chairman of the Committee on Stock List is unfortunately placed in the position not unlike that of the famous Dr. Jekyll and Mr. Hyde; laboring to elevate the standard of financial and corporate morality through the medium of his Committee on Stock List, and compelled to work evil by lowering that standard through the Unlisted Department.[2]

By referring to Robert Louis Stephenson's contemporary novel *Strange Case of Dr Jekyll and Mr Hyde* (1886), this voice from inside the NYSE sheds a particular light on the basic problem of morality at stock exchanges. In Stephenson's novel, Dr Jekyll was a renowned member of society, fully abiding by its formal and informal rules while using his alter ego, Mr Hyde, to circumvent accepted norms and act out even his lowest urges—ending up as a criminal. At that point, Jekyll acknowledges his self-deception but still denies being responsible for Hyde's transgressions.[3] The novel addresses the inner disunity of a human being between conformity and individual freedom and, in particular, between a rational acceptance of taming moral standards and non-rational, untamed 'animal spirits'—a term not by chance used by the economists and Nobel laureates George A. Akerlof and Robert J. Shiller to explain inter alia

---

[1] Ranald C. Michie, *The London and New York Stock Exchanges 1850–1914* (London: Allen & Unwin, 1987), 198; Mary O'Sullivan, 'The Expansion of the U.S. Stock Market, 1885–1930: Historical Facts and Theoretical Fashions', *Enterprise and Society* 8 (2007): 489–542.

[2] Special Committee on Unlisted Department. Minority Report (Rudolph Keppler), 22 January 1896, 2–3, NYSE Archives, RG 1-2.—The author gratefully acknowledges the assistance of Janet Lynde and Steven Wheeler from the Archives of the New York Stock Exchange.

[3] Robert Louis Stephenson, *Strange Case of Dr Jekyll and Mr Hyde* (London: Longmans, Green, 1886).

irrational and non-rational behaviour in financial markets.[4] The conclusion of both Stephenson's novel and the book by Akerlof and Shiller is, in short, that mankind clearly is not able to entirely separate the 'good' from the 'bad'.

This inner disunity can be found in stock exchanges and their history as well. While there are 'good' exchanges that set high (moral) standards in and for the economy, there are also 'bad' exchanges offering incentives to indulge in unwanted market behaviour. Consequently, stock exchanges were—and are—frequently subject to discourses about ethics, morality and virtuous behaviour in the economy in general and in stock markets in particular, ever since 'modern' exchanges were established during the nineteenth century.[5]

To break sophisticated discourses down into a simple contraposition, two main narratives circulate about what happens at stock exchanges.[6] The more popular (and populist) narrative is iconically represented by Gordon Gekko's infamous speech in the movie *Wall Street* (1987) arguing that 'greed is good'. Gekko moreover represents a negative example par excellence of a stock broker: greedy, ruthless, free from any ethical scruple, and only interested in pursuit of profits. In the language of the early twentieth century, some would conceive of him as 'a low wretch', a 'parasite', or 'a social excrescence'.[7] The other narrative, widely embraced within stock exchanges and by a majority of financial economists, describes stock exchanges as the most efficient type of market with the most sophisticated rules in the economy—or as the secretary of the NYSE, William C. van Antwerp, stated in 1914, 'Commercial honour is what counts, and within these four walls it is raised to a high plane and maintained with reverence'.[8]

---

[4] George A. Akerlof and Robert J. Shiller, *Animal Spirits: How Human Psychology Drives the Economy, and Why It Matters for Global Capitalism* (Princeton: Princeton University Press, 2009).

[5] For a comprehensive overview of the development of securities markets see Ranald C. Michie, *The Global Securities Market: A History* (Oxford and New York: Oxford University Press, 2006).

[6] Cf. Sven Grzebeta, *Ethik und Ästhetik der Börse* (München: Wilhelm Fink, 2014), 15–19.

[7] William C. van Antwerp, *The Stock Exchange from Within* (Garden City and New York: Doubleday, 1931), 261.

[8] Ibid., 264.

Obviously, dealing on stock exchanges is a moral issue, or at least has a moral impact, especially as the exchanges are fairly said to be the epitome of capitalism. Outsiders frequently stress the exchanges' morally negative impact on the whole of society; insiders highlight their outstanding virtue. While historians (and contemporary economists) have examined the 'morality of stock exchanges' quite extensively in the German case,[9] stock exchanges in the US, and especially the New York Stock Exchange, have been analyzed either with a 'pure' economic history perspective focusing primarily on market developments[10] (including financial crises)[11] or—with a more cultural approach—as one aspect of morality and capitalism during the Gilded Age and especially during the Progressive Era with its demand for more comprehensive governmental regulation of (big) business.[12]

[9] Richard Ehrenberg, 'Börsenwesen', in *Handwörterbuch der Staatswissenschaften: Volume 2*, ed. J. Conrad et al., 2nd ed. (Jena: Gustav Fischer, 1899), 1024–1052; Oswald von Nell-Breuning, *Grundzüge der Börsenmoral* (Freiburg: Herder, 1928); Christof Biggeleben, *Das 'Bollwerk des Bürgertums'. Die Berliner Kaufmannschaft 1870–1920* (München: C.H. Beck, 2006); Knut Borchardt, 'Einleitung', in *Max Weber. Börsenwesen. Schriften und Reden 1893–1898*, ed. Knut Borchardt (Tübingen: Mohr Siebeck, 1999), 1–111; Rainer Gömmel, 'Entstehung und Entwicklung der Effektenbörse im 19. Jahrhundert bis 1914', in *Deutsche Börsengeschichte*, ed. Hans Pohl (Frankfurt a. M.: Fritz Knapp, 1992), 135–290; and Boris Gehlen, '"Manipulierende Händler" vs. "dumme Agrarier": Reale und symbolische Konflikte um das Börsengesetz von 1896', *Bankhistorisches Archiv* 39 (2013): 74–90; see also Andreas Fahrmeir, *Ehrbare Spekulanten: Stadtverfassung, Wirtschaft und Politik in der City of London, 1688–1900* (München: Beck, 2003).

[10] E.g. Richard Vernon, *The Regulation of Stock Exchange Members* (New York: Columbia University Press, 1941); Robert Sobel, *The Big Board: A History of the New York Stock Market* (New York: Free Press, 1965); Alexander Engel and Boris Gehlen, '"The Stockbroker's Praises Are Never Sung": Social Practices in Stock and Commodity Exchanges—Lessons from the USA and Germany, 1870s to 1930s', *Archiv für Sozialgeschichte* 56 (2016): 109–137.

[11] Robert Sobel, *Panic on Wall Street: A History of America's Financial Disasters* (New York: Macmillan, 1968); Robert F. Bruner and Sean D. Carr, *The Panic of 1907: Lessons Learned from the Market's Perfect Storm* (Hoboken: Wiley, 2007).

[12] Rowena Olegario, *A Culture of Credit: Embedding Trust and Transparency in American Business* (Cambridge, MA: Harvard University Press, 2006); Jackson Lears, *Something for Nothing: Luck in America* (New York: Penguin Books, 2004); Ann Fabian, *Card Sharps, Dream Books, and Bucket Shops: Gambling in Nineteenth-Century America* (Ithaca: Cornell University Press, 1990); Jane Kamensky, *The Exchange Artist: A Tale of High-Flying Speculation and America's First Banking Collapse* (New York: Viking, 2008); Stephen Mihm, *A Nation of Counterfeiters: Capitalists, Con Men, and the Making of the United States* (Cambridge, MA: Harvard University Press, 2007); Susie Pak, *Gentlemen*

The main findings of these contributions are accordingly contra-dictory to some extent. On the one hand, Richard Vernon, Ranald C. Michie and others stressed the achievements of self-regulation at the NYSE, especially the implementation of a sophisticated system of market rules which gradually evolved by closing loopholes and improving defi-cient regulations. Moreover, the recent law and finance literature con-firms these findings and argues that the most efficient way to organize exchanges is self-regulation and competition between exchanges.[13] On the other hand, publications that focus on the discourses and social effects of speculation—with exchanges as crucial actors—do not fully endorse the narrative of regulatory success, highlighting the numerous transgressions at exchanges and their severe consequences for society, especially for people not involved in speculative frenzy. This discrepancy can be explained, of course, in terms of their divergent perspectives. The latter view is more comprehensive and looks at the exchanges as symbols and symptoms of usually multi-factorial crises within capitalism.[14]

Arguably, the two perspectives—exchanges as organized markets and exchanges as capitalist symbols—are complementary. They agree at least on the ultimate goal: to promote a good and virtuous exchange and to tame the bad one. Therefore, this chapter analyzes how a morally charged concept of 'commercial honour' influenced the organization and self-perception of the NYSE. It looks more closely at internal processes than the public debates that always framed and influenced internal dis-cussions. The chapter argues that the NYSE indeed pursued a virtuous Jekyllian vision but was not entirely able to tame Mr Hyde.

Bankers: The World of J.P. Morgan (Cambridge, MA: Harvard University Press, 2013); Sven Beckert, *The Monied Metropolis: New York City and the Consolidation of the American Bourgeoisie, 1850–1896* (Cambridge: Cambridge University Press, 2001); Julia C. Ott, *When Wall Street Met Main Street: The Quest for an Investors' Democracy* (Cambridge, MA: Harvard University Press, 2011); Stuart Banner, *Speculation: A History of the Fine Line Between Gambling and Investing* (New York: Oxford University Press, 2017).

[13] Rafael La Porta et al., 'What Works in Securities Laws?', *The Journal of Finance* 61 (2006): 1–32.

[14] Charles P. Kindleberger et al., *Manias, Panics, and Crashes: A History of Financial Crises*, 7th ed. (Basingstoke, UK: Palgrave Macmillan, 2015); for some recent re-eval-uations of capitalism as an analytical concept see Jürgen Kocka and Marcel van der Linden, eds., *Capitalism: The Reemergence of a Historical Concept* (London and New York: Bloomsbury Academic, 2016). See in particular the essays of Youssef Cassis about Economic and Financial Crises' and of Harold James about 'Finance Capitalism'.

Virtuous Insiders, Vicious Outsiders? Self-Regulation and the Vision of Commercial Morality

From a formal point of view stock exchanges are not very exciting. They are organized—in many cases self-regulated—markets to buy and sell securities at a certain price. Even in countries with public exchange regulation, self-regulation has remained more important than the incidence of state intervention suggests.[15] The historical relevance of self-regulation—and the critique thereof—can be largely summarized in five points:

- The rules of stock exchanges have been to a large extent implemented by stock brokers themselves;
- Many professional stock brokers or affiliated bankers have been wealthy and some politically influential;
- Banks and stock exchanges have not been that affected by economic and financial crises than other parts of the economy;
- In normal times transactions on stock exchanges have seemed to be relatively transparent;
- Deviant, fraudulent and illegal transactions have occurred more often during strong bull markets.

Arguably, the first point is the crucial one. Self-regulation cuts both ways. On the one hand it enables stock exchanges to react quickly and appropriately to market challenges, while on the other hand the lack of (democratic) legitimation has meant that good arguments have had to be put forward to preserve stock exchanges' freedom. From time to time the self-regulation of particular stock exchanges has come under scrutiny. In the case of the New York Stock Exchange, the reaction has been a twofold strategy: underlining its sophisticated commercial morality in public discourses, and reassessing and readjusting the rules laid down in its constitution and various by-laws.[16]

This twofold strategy has not been merely an opportunistic approach to get off cheaply. External criticism often drew attention to regulatory

---

[15] Boris Gehlen, 'Zielkonflikte bei Aktienerstemissionen? Regulierung und Zulassungspraxis am Beispiel der Berliner Börse (1870 bis 1932)', *Jahrbuch für Wirtschaftsgeschichte* 2018/1: 39–76.

[16] For some evidence see Engel and Gehlen, 'Stockbroker's praises'.

deficiencies which came to light when something had gone wrong. Already in 1873, Thomas Denny, Jr., a NYSE member, referred to public discomfort and argued that 'the present method of speculating [...] has been found defective at periods of unusual excitement, and the sad results of the last few weeks make it manifest that the Stock Exchange must adopt some new plan for speculative dealing'. He then made some suggestions to improve the relevant by-laws.[17] This was a somewhat pioneering remark as in the following decades it became the tacit strategy of the NYSE to react to market deficiencies.

In the view of stock brokers such deficiencies were acceptable side-effects of a dynamic market but should perhaps be remedied to avoid problems in the future; meanwhile, public opinion often assumed a general badness of financial markets. This discrepancy of interpretation resulted from different concepts of morality. Commercial morality, as the value system of stock brokers, means essentially to fulfil contracts always, at any time and completely, or otherwise to personally accept responsibility for failures. It therefore followed that when internal charges of dubious transacting arose, members of the NYSE had to defend themselves and were not allowed to be represented by counsel.[18]

As the ultimate purpose of commercial honour could be said to be to make markets work and thus was open to opportunistic reinterpretation when markets changed, it was never meant to be a general moral model. Arguably, the model has been amoral. Commercial morality focuses on the market process and implicitly considers market results as always 'good' in the long run, while 'public morality' mainly focuses on results (especially of speculation) seen as negative. In this latter view, if stock exchanges contributed to bad market outcomes they themselves must be bad institutions.[19]

However, both 'moralities' agreed in their ultimate moral goals: in economic terms, they both aimed to prevent market failures in the form of negative externalities. But to a greater or lesser extent they both also

---

[17] Thomas Denny, Jr. to the members of the Stock Exchange (ca. 1873), Governing Committee, Minutes, Correspondence, Report F 1, NYSE-Archives RG 1-2.

[18] Art. XVII, sec. 12, Art. XVII, *Constitution of the New York Stock Exchange with Some Resolutions Adopted by the Governing Committee. Amended to March 1902* (New York: Charles A. Searing, Stationer and Printer, 1902), 32.

[19] For a nuanced overview of 'good' and 'bad' speculation see Nell-Breuning, *Grundzüge*, pp. 162–163.

regarded greed and vicious behaviour as unavoidable. This meant it simply had to be tamed: 'The temper to speculate will always exist. It is well that it should. But being so it should be governed by rule which will protect the speculator against every other misfortune than the error of his own judgment; [...] methods which adapted themselves to yesterday have outgrown their usefulness to-day, and tomorrow are behind the age'.[20]

The NYSE and the market it covered had highly developed mechanisms available which, moreover, were continuously refined. It was thus beneficial to be an insider, i.e. a member of the NYSE. However, membership was restricted to 1100 persons. Being so desirable, membership was costly and it became an instrument of social exclusion. Although van Antwerp might claim that social background was immaterial—'It has nothing to do with the size of one's purse, nor the blue in one's veins; it takes no account of what a man has been nor of what his ancestors were'[21]—the NYSE increasingly became an elitist circle, hardly surprising when membership cost 160 times the annual wage of a blue-collar worker.[22]

The NYSE wanted to enlist only the financial elite and did so mostly by self-recruitment. Insiders were virtuous and honourable *businessmen* merely by virtue of their group affiliation, while outsiders—and especially non-specialized 'retail' *speculators*—had to be protected or excluded: 'Our duty is to protect these victims against the consequences of their own folly by closing down the doors now open to them'.[23] This distinction between valued insiders esteemed as (honourable) businessmen or brokers and hazardous amateurs termed speculators was not confined to the United States; elsewhere too, vicious 'speculators' always were the other players.[24]

---

[20] G. H. J. Collins to the members of the Stock Exchange, 18 July 1887, Governing Committee Minutes, Correspondence, Report F 2, NYSE-Archives RG 1-2.

[21] Van Antwerp, *Stock Exchange*, 264.

[22] Engel and Gehlen, 'Stockbroker's Praises', 160.

[23] Digest of the preliminary work of the Special Committee, 25 June 1913, Special Committee on Bucket Shops, NYSE-Archives RG 1-2, 42.

[24] Kim Christian Priemel, 'Spekulation als Gegenstand historischer Forschung', in *Jahrbuch für Wirtschaftsgeschichte* 2013: 18–19.

MORAL AMBIVALENCES: FIGHTING BUCKET-SHOPS, PROMOTING UNREGULATED MARKETS

This kind of repression is reminiscent of one motif in Stephenson's novel: Dr Jekyll repeatedly persuaded himself that Mr Hyde was no part of his personality. Jekyll tried to compensate for Hyde's failures. Likewise, the NYSE engaged in a fight against bucket shops. The 'business model' of the bucket shop was quite simple: Customers could put money on the rise or decline of securities' quotations. These quotations, however, were collected from exchanges—quite often via dubious means. In consequence, customers bet on 'real' quotations without influencing them. In contrast, purchasing or selling securities at regular exchanges affected quotations, as these transactions altered demand and supply and thus influenced price formation. Of course, it was common at stock exchanges to speculate on securities' price differences, but whether this was profitable depended on brokers' information, assessment, and experience; and it constituted a real transaction. In bucket shops the only material variable was luck. Since the late nineteenth century, the NYSE, other established stock and commodity exchanges and public authorities joined forces to stamp out bucket shops. Although they all wanted to abolish these institutions because '[…] the speculator of limited means and experience—the typical bucket shop patron—became a moral and economic problem', their motivations differed. Public authorities, indeed the public in general, put the argument in moral terms and severely criticized bucket shops' promotion and encouragement of gambling, with all its morally detrimental effects.[25]

Economically, bucket shops became an issue for two reasons. For one, they withdrew money from the financial system and competed with the exchanges for customers. They also gave their customers to believe that they conducted real transactions in the stock market, which they obviously did not. In consequence, the betting on price differences on the basis of quotations of the NYSE damaged the latter's reputation by implicating it in shady transactions. Moreover, the NYSE and

[25] David Hochfelder, '"Where the Common People Could Speculate": The Ticker, Bucket Shops, and the Origins of Popular Participation in Financial Markets, 1880–1920', *The Journal of American History* 93 (2006): 337.

the Chicago Board of Trade, the largest commodity exchange in the US, feared a general detrimental effect on business conduct: 'Gambling business methods are […] of so insidious and undermining a character and so widespread, as to demand the concerted and vigorous action of the principal commercial bodies […] for their utter suppression'.[26] Finally, they benefitted from the rising public discomfort about gambling and public authorities finally abolished bucket shops. However, the NYSE in particular had for a long time hesitated to demand federal public regulation, preferring instead action at the local level.[27] Coping with gambling had not been a moral issue per se for the NYSE; rather, it was mainly motivated to stop the abuse of its quotations and the consequent reputational damage.

Arguably, the struggle against bucket shops, which was successful, had been the NYSE's Dr Jekyll face; its Mr Hyde face showed up (again) in its inconsistent stance on speculative markets outside its walls. Already the existence of the Unlisted Department as a regular component of the Stock Exchange pointed to the fact that Wall Street had a less honourable story, that of less-regulated or even unregulated speculation. The most striking example was the curb stone brokers who placed their bids and offers directly in front of the NYSE building, using the information and money of members of the exchange while dealing not in sound and safe securities but in highly speculative, risky stock. The Curb—as well as the Unlisted Department—was virtually a trial market for the honourable NYSE without its honourable regulations. Unlike, e.g., the Consolidated Stock Exchange—which in the 1880s had been the major and heavily opposed rival of the NYSE[28]—the Curb was able by the Exchange's grace to develop into a regular market. The Curb was more of a complementary market than a replacing one and thus no competitor for the NYSE. However, for a long time the NYSE could claim no formal relationship existed between it and the curb stone brokers.

---

[26] Jackson to the board of directors of the Chicago Board of Trade, 2 February 1904, Law Committee, Reports and Resolutions F 2, NYSE-Archives RG 1-2.

[27] Meeting of the Law Committee, 1 February 1900, Law Committee Minutes vol. 1:166-168, NYSE-Archives RG 1-2.

[28] For the competition in the New York Stock markets see beside Michie, *London and New York*, and O'Sullivan, 'Expansion', e.g. Eugene N. White, 'Competition among the exchanges before the SEC: Was the NYSE a natural hegemon?', *Financial History Review* 20 (2013): 29–48.

Whenever speculative excesses worried Wall Street, the NYSE argued that it had nothing to do with these machinations and that its regulations, moreover, prevented its members from engaging in such speculative folly. This, however, was only true in a formal sense. The NYSE implemented a rule that its members only could deal with curb stone brokers if the latter remained on the street outside its building. If the Curb had moved indoors, any dealings between NYSE and Curb would have been prohibited: 'Hence, the Curb Association, a body with its own regulations […] is forced to remain in the street and to surrender to the big Exchange whatever business in securities the latter may from time to time elect to take from the Curb an unto itself. It is hard to believe that such things are possible'.[29]

REGULATING BUSINESS CONDUCT: GROUP CONFORMITY INSTEAD OF NORM CONFORMITY

For the NYSE's functionality as well as for its credibility it was vital not only to point out morally questionable developments outside its organization but also to do everything possible to hamper detrimental business conduct by its members or at least to convey the impression that it did so. Accordingly, the NYSE implemented a comprehensive code of conduct for its members and, finally, a standing Committee on Business Conduct in 1913.[30] It was a duty of the governing committee to monitor norm conformity and in case of doubt to charge a member and to probably suspend or expel them. The governing committee had far-reaching powers and, moreover, its decisions were irreversible; the committee was the only body to judge members' misconduct and there

---

[29] Samuel Untermyer, *Speculation on the Stock Exchange and Public Regulation of the Exchanges. An Address delivered before the American Economic Association at Princeton, N.J.*, 29 December 1914: 11; George Garvy, 'Rivals and Interlopers in the History of the New York Security Market', *Journal of Political Economy* 52 (1944): 139; Jones/Baker, *The History of the New York Curb* (New York, 1916); and New York Curb Exchange, *New York Curb Exchange: Summary of Report of Committee on Stock Exchange Investigation of the National Association of Securities Commissioners on the New York Curb Exchange* (New York: 1929).

[30] Meeting of the Governing Committee, 25 February 1913, Governing Committee Minutes, vol. 7: 1; Report of the Special Committee in regard to transactions by members outside of the Exchange in securities listed on the Exchange, 20 February 1914, Governing Committee Minutes, vol. 7: 66–67, NYSE Archives RG 1-2.

was no avenue of appeal.[31] This internal rule had nothing to do with fair trials in a juridical sense, but it was repeatedly confirmed by regular courts that the members had to submit to the governing committee's jurisdiction because they had voluntarily accepted the terms of the Exchange's constitution.[32]

The governing committee thus enjoyed enormous latitude when enforcing the rules at the NYSE. Peer judgment ensured not only norm conformity but also—and in particular—group conformity. This was crucial for shaping commercial honour. That which determined what was right or wrong at the NYSE was not superior standards like law or morality in a broad sense but the judgement of commercial specialists. The exchange's watchword was functionality of the market; business conduct was regarded as appropriate so long as it did not disturb dealings at the NYSE. Starting in the 1880s the NYSE implemented several rules which could be regarded as morally founded: stock brokers were not allowed, for example, to use indecorous language, to circulate (false) rumours, or to run on the floor.[33] These regulations arguably had a double rationale, on one hand simply distilling the behaviour expected of gentlemen, but at the same time enshrining fair business conduct. Inappropriate language and movements could disrupt regular business transactions, especially as stock brokers had to decide quickly about transactions and unequivocally communicate their bids and offers; any disturbance therefore had to be prevented. Circulating rumours, moreover, could influence investors' decisions and thereby distort market outcomes.

However, until the 1890s the NYSE rarely impeached members for contravening the rules. When such transgressions came to light

[31] *Constitution of the New York Stock Exchange 1885*: 26, NYSE-Archives Publications 1-C-2.

[32] E.g. 'Not Given a Fair Hearing', *New York Times*, 16 March 1884; Neukirch v. Keppler, Appellate Division of the Supreme Court of New York, First Department; 56 App. Div. 225 (N.Y. App. Div. 1900); Neukirch v. Keppler, Court of Appeals of the State of New York; 174 N.Y. 509 (N.Y. 1903).

[33] E.g. Meetings of the Governing Committee, 8 July 1891, Governing Committee Minutes vol. 4: 376, NYSE-Archives RG 1-2; summarized: Art. XVII, *Constitution of the New York Stock Exchange with some Resolutions adopted by the Governing Committee. Amended to March 1902* (New York: Charles A. Searing, Stationer and Printer, 1902), 27–29.

the governing committee were more inclined to rebuke brokers than sentence them—especially if the charges related only to 'individual' harm.[34] Usually the NYSE confined itself to tightening the rules and regulations in order to prevent similar incidents in future—or explicitly restated existing ones. While running on the floor had been forbidden since 1883, the governing committee had to remind its members from time to time of this rule.[35]

But times were changing in the 1890s and especially after the panic of 1893. During the Progressive Era the effects of the structural transformation of the US economy became an issue and public demands for economic state intervention rose in volume. The stock exchanges were well aware that they could not avoid being caught up in these public discourses. The NYSE therefore had to underline that commercial honour was not just an empty phrase but was actually built into the way the exchange operated. Accordingly, it revised its constitution, detailed offences against commercial honour and raised the severity of penalties (see Table 8.1).

The last point in particular deserves closer attention. Since the 1902 constitution, the governing committee could intervene in nearly every transaction if it detected an act detrimental to the exchange's welfare. This 'misconduct rule' was an effective tool in disciplining members. They were threatened with suspension or even expulsion if they did not play by the rules. As only members could directly access the market provided by the NYSE, suspension immediately meant a loss of earnings. Moreover, the decision of the NYSE was published inside and outside the Exchange and stigmatized every infringer as a (for the moment) dishonourable businessman—with significant effects. One expelled member, Charles Neukirch, put it this way: 'I have suffered the severest penalty in the power of the Exchange to inflict, with all the disgrace and dishonour attaching to it in social, business and financial relations'.[36]

---

[34] Meetings of the Governing Committee, 28 March 1888, Governing Committee Minutes vol. 4: 94–95 and 107–108, NYSE-Archives RG 1-2.

[35] Meetings of the Governing Committee, 8 July 1891, Governing Committee Minutes vol. 4: 376, NYSE-Archives RG 1-2.

[36] Governing Committee: Minutes, Correspondence, Reports F 3 (Charles Neukirch): 1. NYSE, RG 1-2.

Table 8.1 Offences and maximum penalties as listed in the Constitution of 1902

Offence	Penalty (maximum)
Fraud or fraudulent acts	Expulsion
Misstatements to Committee on Admission	Expulsion
Direct communication connections to other Exchanges in New York City	Suspension up to one year or expulsion
Transactions with non-members in rooms of the Exchange	Suspension up to one year
Wilful violation of Constitution, by-laws, and regulations (including conduct inconsistent with just and equitable principles of trade)	Suspension or expulsion
Not granting access to business documents; destroying evidence; not appearing as a witness, refusing to testify	Not specified [cross-referred to 'Acts detrimental…']
Acts detrimental to Welfare of the Exchange	Suspension up to one year

Source Art. XVII, Constitution of the New York Stock Exchange with some Resolutions adopted by the Governing Committee. Amended to March 1902 (New York: Charles A. Searing, Stationer and Printer, 1902), 27–29

The Neukirch case was a tricky one, because the Exchange maintained its verdict even after he presented mitigating evidence. For the governing committee there was no alternative, as otherwise any of its decisions could potentially be reversed. Moreover, it could not allow room for doubts to be cast on its assessment of deviant behaviour. The governing body was essentially infallible—and it had to be relentless if markets were to be kept workable. Thus, Neukirch became a scapegoat. He admitted that he had manipulated prices, but stressed that for one thing the constitutional penalty for his offence would only have been suspension but not expulsion, and for another thing that his manipulations had been quite common at the NYSE for a long time.[37] Arguably, Neukirch was unlucky. He was one of four members to be expelled in the period 1895-1898—in the aftermath of the panic of 1893. In the 40 years prior only one member had been expelled. Moreover, no new by-laws had been brought in, and so Neukirch and the others seemed to be victims

---

[37] Governing Committee: Minutes, Correspondence, Reports F 3 (Charles Neukirch): 5. NYSE, RG 1-2.

of the stricter construction of its existing rules by which the governing committee had reacted to the rising public demand for stock exchange regulation.[38]

Again, this is an obvious case of double standards. As long as stock exchange practices were of no public interest, even doubtful transactions were accepted among brokers. In this way, dishonest or manipulative dealings became a habit. Immoral transactions arguably undermined the NYSE's vaunted commercial honour. A prominent critic of self-regulated exchanges in the US, Samuel Untermyer, went to the heart of the matter when he observed 'that the most reckless and unconscionable forms of gambling, dishonesty, misrepresentation and manipulation [...] have been so long tolerated that the members are obsessed on the subject of their right to continue these illicit transactions'.[39] Phases of detrimental speculative excitement were actually facilitated by the governing committee's omnipotence, in Untermyer's often expressed view. It was on those occasions when it suddenly enforced its rules, like in the case of Neukirch and others, that it could be seen to be acting opportunistically.

The strategy to put commercial honour at the heart of its public relations had a quite ironical effect: It implied to be more lenient towards the most honourable men on the higher levels in the Exchange's hierarchy than to inferior brokers at the bottom of this hierarchy. If an eminently respectable member were to be expelled by an exchange that claimed to host the most honourable businessmen, this could only do damage to the exchange's reputation as well. Put another way, these 'most honourable businessmen' got off lightly more often than inferior members. Hierarchy and (financial) power obviously mattered.[40] A financial tycoon like John Pierpont Morgan even could use his influence over rulings in order to get of rid of bothersome rivals, it was claimed.[41] Very occasionally, downright horse trades could be observed, as well: In 1893 one member withdraw from the NYSE in order to save a very prominent

---

[38] 'C. Neukirch expelled', *New York Tribune*, 29 April 1897.

[39] Untermyer, *Speculation*, 3; for empirical evidence see Timothy A. Kruse and Steven K. Todd, 'Price manipulation at the NYSE and the 1899 battle for Brooklyn Rapid Transit shares', *Financial History Review* 20 (2013): 279–303.

[40] E.g. Meetings of the Governing Committee, 12 December 1896, Governing Committee, Minutes, Vol. 5: 72–75.

[41] 'Exchange Governors suspend Weidenfeld', *New York Times*, 25 February 1903.

peer from being expelled. The withdrawal was part of a deal which, however, was very controversial among the NYSE's members.[42]

It must be admitted that such highly doubtful arrangements were rare exceptions and even critics like Untermyer certified that the NYSE indeed was the hub of commercial honour: 'In some respects the code of ethics is above that encountered in any other calling', he asserted.[43] Such accolades were without doubt a victory for the exchange's public relations. It was widely believed that the NYSE left no stone unturned in the cause of improving commercial honour. In 1902, Camille Weidenfeld, a member of the NYSE, was tried for fraud and blackmail in a regular court. His offences had nothing to do with his membership of or transactions at the NYSE, but the judge Charles F. Adimon called on the NYSE to also discipline Weidenfeld. He explicitly mentioned the high standards of commercial honour at the exchange as indicative that Weidenfeld's conduct could not be left unsanctioned by them. In consequence, the governing committee suspended him for one year for criminal transactions that had occurred well beyond the NYSE's authority.[44]

The NYSE drew on this self-initiated perception of its association with commercial honour when arguing for maintenance of the existing mode of self-regulation. The argument was in any event not without merit. There is plenty of evidence that self-regulation did indeed root out unwanted behaviour. There had been several charges brought in response to rumours and misconduct, for example, at the NYSE during the 1890s, but after that time nearly none. Either the offence was henceforth regarded to be irrelevant and therefore was not prosecuted anymore or—more likely—bad conduct had disappeared. Admittedly, some members now occasionally fell foul of new provisions on misstatements to the committee on admission and the like.[45] But the problem of insolvencies at the NYSE acknowledges the general impression that the NYSE was able to improve business conduct. However, insolvencies are a characteristic risk of any business and hardly to prevent. But according to

---

[42]'Interest in the Bache case', *New York Times*, 12 March 1893.

[43]Untermyer, *Speculation*, p. 3.

[44]Meetings of the Governing Committee, 14 January 1903, Governing Committee Minutes vol. 5: 646–662, 668–669, NYSE-Archives RG 1-2.

[45]These are some preliminary results of a larger examination of charges at the NYSE. An article by the author about 'Stock brokers in Court' is still work in progress.

a contemporary study, insolvency ratios at the NYSE were by comparison always among the lowest.[46]

In general, it always was up to the exchange and its governing committee to decide what was (morally) 'good' or 'bad', virtuous or vicious. As it mainly focused on the functionality of the market and not on superior ethical standards, it never could be a moral authority in a strict sense; the NYSE was an authority of 'commercial honour', no more, no less. Yet, despite several moves to impose public regulation on exchanges, it was able to continue all the way to the Great Depression before a governmental agency—the Securities and Exchange Commission—was put in charge to regulate stock markets and exchanges in 1934.

CONCLUSION: TAMING MR HYDE—TO SOME EXTENT

How to moralize an association that probably is—like Dr Jekyll and Mr Hyde—at the same time good and evil? Stock exchanges in general, and the NYSE in particular, were and are essential institutions within capitalism. As such, they are subject to the same analytical problems as capitalism itself. Stock exchanges are controversial because they, like capitalism, have generally positive economic effects but also certain detrimental ones. Within a capitalistic framework there remains room for manoeuvre to tame speculation and to tame stock exchanges so that negative effects are reduced to a minimum. There have been financial crises in the past that were triggered by stock exchanges, but never have they solely caused one. Assuming this to be the case, it should follow that stock exchanges do not pose a general moral problem, if one is prepared to accept capitalism itself—with all its inherent moral problems.

Nevertheless, from time to time criticisms have been raised and challenged the exchanges as institutions. The NYSE responded to these challenges in the Progressive Era with a twofold strategy: communicating commercial honour and integrity as essential principles of the exchange, and adjusting its rules and organization. With regard to moral issues, however, the NYSE never was a strictly ethical institution; its focus was not on rigidly governing members and transactions as a moral end in itself, but on the market's functionality. It did whatever was needed

---

[46] J. E. Meeker, *Insolvencies on the Stock Exchange* (New York: New York Stock Exchange, The Committee on Library, 1925), 2.

to keep the market workable—including some morally questionable approaches. It was not right in a moral sense to punish high-ranked members more leniently than inferior ones; nor was it right to randomly scapegoat members when it seemed opportune. It was not right to claim the highest business standards for its own organization while turning a blind eye to the curb business; and it was surely not morally right to implicitly condone doubtful business conduct while society's attention was elsewhere but to severely punish it when exchanges came under the spotlight. But all this was necessary to maintain a workable market—and, moreover, it worked very well, as the NYSE went on to develop the most sophisticated rules in American business. To a large extent, though, this was a result of the fact that stock exchanges always have been carefully scrutinized by the general public. What happened at stock exchanges obviously was relevant for the economy and for society in general. Thus, the pressure from public monitoring and from public opinion more generally about stock exchanges encouraged the NYSE to intensify its regulatory efforts, thus in the end improving commercial morality. Hence, the general public helped Dr Jekyll to tame Mr Hyde—but not to overcome him.

CHAPTER 9

Bankruptcy and Morality in a Capitalist Market Economy: The Case of Mid-Nineteenth-Century France

Jürgen Finger

In a draft for his *Théorie de l'unité universelle* (1822/1823), Charles Fourier (1772–1837) gave a colourful account of the reckless practices of commerce. He presented bankruptcy as the vice of merchants in what he called the 'civilized' era of human development: a free market economy. And insolvency was no more than a socially accepted façade for (fraudulent) bankruptcy.[1] The 1789 Revolution and its unsteady aftermath had

[1] Charles Fourier, 'Section ébauchée des trois unités externes (19e section du plan général)', *La Phalange. Revue de la Science sociale*, 1ère série in-8 14, no. 1 (1845): 3–42, esp. 23–42. A slightly truncated German translation of the draft was published by Friedrich Engels: Friedrich Engels and Charles Fourier, 'Ein Fragment Fouriers über den Handel', in *Die Lage der arbeitenden Klasse in England und andere Schriften von August 1844 bis Juni 1846*, ed. V. Adoratskij, vol. I/4 of Marx/Engels Gesamtausgabe (Glashütten Ts.: Auvermann, 1970), 409–453. Fourier inserted an excerpt of the section in: Fourier,

J. Finger (✉)
Department of Contemporary History,
German Historical Institute Paris, Paris, France
e-mail: JFinger@dhi-paris.fr

© The Author(s) 2019
S. Berger and A. Przyrembel (eds.), *Moralizing Capitalism*,
Palgrave Studies in the History of Social Movements,
https://doi.org/10.1007/978-3-030-20565-2_9

shaped Fourier's writings. Backed by suggestive anecdotes resonating with both economic naivety and anti-Semitic slurs, he proposed an elaborate hierarchy of bankrupts. This 'utopian' socialist (the epithet later used to belittle him) postulated the perversity and insubstantiality of a modern market economy, which lacked the social embeddedness of old-style retail and was precariously based on promissory notes and cheque book money.

Fourier was aware of the various reasons and motivations for, and mechanisms of, bankruptcy, lying along the spectra of incapacity vs. cool calculation, premeditated deception vs. precipitate withdrawal of funds, and singular event vs. chain insolvency. Nevertheless, he identified bankruptcy as a social crime and as theft.[2] He even disparaged those insolvents with honourable intentions, eager to satisfy the claims of their creditors: They simply had not yet figured out that bankruptcy would be an accepted path to enrichment in a market economy. Fourier's stance certainly was inconsistent. He blamed both the personal character of the merchant and the economic system: 'I have observed that bankruptcy is the only social crime that is epidemic, and that necessarily makes the reliable man [*l'homme probre*, in the sense of the Latin *vir probatus*] imitate the rogue'.[3] Despite his cutting critique of the merchant class, he did not see much point in moralizing against the individual merchant, as civilization itself had forced him into such behaviour.[4] He reads like a dispirited moralist, who bemoans the moral defects of the market economy and is torn over whether to blame the actors for it.

Théorie de l'unité universelle, Section 4 of *Œuvres complètes*, 2nd ed. (Paris: Société pour la propagation et la réalisation de la théorie de Fourier, 1841), vol. 3/4, 121–129.

The project leading to this publication was supported by the P.R.I.M.E. program of the German Academic Exchange Service (DAAD), co-funded by the European Union's Marie Skłodowska-Curie Actions (grant number 605728 under FP7-PEOPLE-2013-COFUND) and the Federal Ministry of Education and Research.

[2] See also Charles Fourier, *Théorie des quatre mouvements et des destinées générales*, Section 1 of *Œuvres complètes* (Paris: Société pour la propagation et la réalisation de la théorie de Fourier, 1841), 341–354.

[3] Fourier, 'Section ébauchée', 42. All translations into English by the author.

[4] Fourier, *Théorie des quatre mouvements*, 333–334. This corresponds to Fourier's drive theory, which saw wealth as the first source and precondition of human happiness and, thus, as a legitimate goal of human existence. Cf. Lorenz von Stein, *Die industrielle Gesellschaft. Der Sozialismus und Kommunismus in Frankreich von 1830 bis 1848*, vol. 2 of: *Geschichte der sozialen Bewegungen in Frankreich von 1789 bis auf unsere Tage* (München: Drei-Masken-Vlg., 1921), 281–291.

Morality as a regulative idea guiding the actions of economic stakeholders would only be reinstated in a future state of civilization, the awaited age of 'societary' competition, characterized by the renewed social embeddedness of a morally bounded economy. This clearly referred to small-scale communities like his *Phalanstères*, an early-socialist and experimental heterotopia.[5] Only then would the merchant class submit to the interests of industrialists, farmers and landowners—as a writer of the 1820s he still omitted the working class—and cease to be a 'class of parasitic and unproductive agents'.[6]

Fourier provides us with central arguments of the nineteenth-century debate on bankruptcy. Firstly, debt represents a social relation between debtor and creditor. Secondly, Fourier's rejection of the modern market economy and his desire for small-scale alternatives imply a critique of impersonal, abstract or dematerialized economic activity and its supposed lack of individual responsibility. Supra-regional and international supply chains seemed to loosen creditor–debtor relations, as they made trade less a matter of peer-to-peer commerce. Finally, debt and bankruptcy were always a question of morality. Not only were the relations between individual stakeholders moralized, this was also the case for relations with society and with an idealized merchant community. 'Moralizing' was meant to discourage all stakeholders, debtors as well as creditors, from opportunistic behaviour. The increasingly abstract, de-individualized credit nexus, the challenges to its moralization, and the consequences of

---

[5] Anne Kwaschik, 'Gesellschaftswissen als Zukunftshandeln. Soziale Epistemologie, genossenschaftliche Lebensformen und kommunale Praxis im frühen 19. Jahrhundert', *Francia* 44 (2017): 189–211, esp. 209–211. For the concept of heterotopias see: Michel Foucault, 'Des espaces autres', in *Dits et écrits 1954–1988*, ed. Daniel Defert and François Ewald (Gallimard–Nouvelle revue française, 1994), vol. 4, no. 360, 752–762, esp. 755–756. Fourier's idea of social and moral bounds, proper to both old-style retail and future 'societary' commerce, apparently is too narrow. He arbitrarily negates the possibility of moral and social relations in a market economy, as it has been analysed in recent research by means of the term *embeddedness*. Mark Granovetter, 'Economic Action and Social Structure: The Problem of Embeddedness', *American Journal of Sociology* 91 (1985): 487–504; Chrostof Dejung, 'Einbettung', in *Auf der Suche nach der Ökonomie: Historische Annäherungen*, ed. Dejung, Monika Dommann and Daniel Speich Chassé (Tübingen: Mohr Siebeck, 2014), 47–71; and Jens Beckert, 'The Great Transformation of Embeddedness: Karl Polanyi and the New Economic Sociology', in *Market and Society: The Great Transformation Today*, ed. C. M. Hann and Keith Hart (Cambridge: Cambridge University Press, 2009), 38–55.

[6] Fourier, *Théorie*, 331–334.

industrialization (which Fourier could not have foreseen): these were the conflict zones in which the nineteenth-century debate about bankruptcy evolved.

This chapter will use the example of bankruptcy (in the broad sense of the term, as used in American English) as indicative of these structural and discursive challenges to traditional ways of moralizing the economy of debt in the age of capital.[7] Although bankruptcy was a rare and extreme situation in the life of an individual merchant, legislators and civil society of the nineteenth century always approached it as a question of principle, presuming it to affect the functionality of trade and the national economy in general. How did moralizing discourses about bankruptcy evolve, and how did they translate into the text and practice of commercial law? How did the discursive link between individual misconduct and common interest evolve, oscillating between public and private realm? What ensured the persuasiveness of moral arguments in public discourse, and why were the instruments of moralization questioned?

This analysis of the ways of 'moralizing' is not undertaken to search for evidence for an alleged dismal moral condition of economic life. Instead, morality and moralizing are understood as analytical tools to better understand the transition from the French merchant economy to an industrialized and capital-intensive economy. Morals and morality, the act of moralizing the behaviour and character of others, are based on customs and accepted standards of behaviour (in the literal sense of the Latin *mos/mores*). These are moral by convention and common practice, not by ethical deliberation and universal validity.[8]

The French Revolution of 1848 serves as a case study for this analysis. After a short contextualization of the economic problems in revolutionary and republican France, I introduce the juridical basics of French bankruptcy law. The chapter then investigates debates on bankruptcy from 1848 to 1850/1851, which reflected the changing moral evaluation

---

[7] Eric J. Hobsbawm, *The Age of Capital 1848–1875* (New York: Vintage Books, 1996).

[8] 'Lemma "Moral, moralisch, Moralphilosophie"', in *Historisches Wörterbuch der Philosophie*, vol. 6, eds. Joachim Ritter and Karlfried Gründer (Basel: Schwabe, 1984), col. 149–168, esp. col. 149; Karl-Heinz Ilting, 'Sitte, Sittlichkeit, Moral,' in *Geschichtliche Grundbegriffe: Historisches Lexikon zur politisch-sozialen Sprache in Deutschland*, vol. 5, eds. Otto Brunner, Werner Conze and Reinhart Koselleck (Stuttgart: E. Klett; G. Cotta, 1984), 863–921, esp. 863–864; and Marion Fourcade and Kieran Healy, 'Moral Views of Market Society' *Annual Review of Sociology* 33, no. 1 (2007): 14.1–14.27, https://doi.org/10.1146/annurev.soc.33.040406.131642.

of creditor–debtor relations. I show that inability to settle a debt, once a question of common interest, became a predominantly private problem. This changed the need for moralization, the instruments of moralization and the legitimacy of these instruments. Bills, parliamentary discussions and official documents, as well as petitions to the legislators and to the Prince-Président Louis Napoleon Bonaparte, later Napoleon III, elucidate the political, juridical and economic assessment of bankruptcy. Beyond that, these sources are also indicative of the moral evaluations common among stakeholders in mid-nineteenth-century French commerce.[9]

Belated Debates, Belated Reactions

The 1840s saw a world 'out of balance', where huge economic, technical and social change proceeded in the absence of political and institutional reform.[10] A European economic crisis fed the already endemic political discontent, and rising prices for grain and potatoes since 1846/1847 finally triggered the February Revolution in France. The subsistence crisis necessitated food imports, thus draining capital out of the country. The capital market, already burdened by the unprecedented capital demands of railway corporations, was hit by a severe credit crisis. From 1848 the pendulum swung in the opposite direction. Subsequent good harvests and the general depression caused corn prices to collapse even below the pre-crisis level, now generating major discontent in rural areas even while the Revolution was in its heydays.[11] The economic shock of 1846–1851 had launched the Revolution and before long also contributed to the failure of the Second Republic. This ushered in the productivism of the Second Empire and its promise of a new economic boom, partially inspired by Saint-Simonianism.[12]

---

[9] Lex H. van Voss, 'Introduction: Petitions in Social History', *International Review of Social History* 46, no. 9 (2001): 1–10, https://doi.org/10.1017/s002085900100030x.

[10] Eric J. Hobsbawm, *The Age of Revolution 1789–1848* (New York: Vintage Books, 1996), 303–308.

[11] Maurice Agulhon, *The Republican Experiment 1848–1852* (Cambridge: Cambridge Univ. Press, 1993), 7–8, 35–36, 82–85; William Fortescue, *France and 1848: The End of Monarchy* (London and New York: Routledge, 2005), 43–45; and Jonathan Sperber, *The European Revolutions 1848–1851* (Cambridge: Cambridge University Press, 1994), 24–26, 105–107.

[12] Agulhon, *Republican Experiment*, 35–45, 82–85, 178–183.

The number of insolvencies (*faillites*) generally grew throughout the nineteenth century and stabilized only during the post-1890 Belle Époque, when France experienced a boom for almost two decades. This increase correlated with the general proliferation of businesses during the century. Political and economic development did correlate, but in a roundabout way.[13] Spikes in bankruptcy statistics accompanied the revolutionary moments of 1830 and 1848 as well as the Franco-German war and the *Commune* uprising in 1870/1871. In a context of growing supranational trade and investment, the London 1847 panic, the 1869 Black Friday and finally the Paris stock market crash in 1882 all had considerable influence. The news reporting of the time reflected the awareness of such interdependency; the *Moniteur universel*, for example, noted a growing number of bankruptcies of British industrial companies and merchant banks engaged in overseas trade in 1847.[14] In an atmosphere of general crisis, the *Times* found it worthy of note that on one day there had been no new bankruptcies.[15]

The number of bankruptcies typically dropped, and to a significant extent, after such moments of political and economic turbulence. The previous wave of bankruptcies had amounted to a market adjustment, so that the remaining businesses were deemed more stable. French governments also cushioned the viability of these surviving businesses by extending the terms of payment and by decreeing temporary rules for bankruptcy procedures during the violent transition phases of 1848 and 1870, and again in 1919–1922.[16] This trend can also be discerned at the time of the 1848 revolution: after having reached an all-time high in 1847, the number of bankruptcies significantly

---

[13] For the following, see: Luc Marco, *La montée des faillites en France, XIXe–XXe siècles* (Paris: l'Harmattan, 1998), 5–8, partially own calculations based on data 165, 173.

[14] *Le Moniteur universel* 1847, 670, 2111, 2648, 2651, 2672, 2700, 2704, 2708, 2714, 2724, 2738, 2798, 2802.

[15] *Le Moniteur universel* 1847, 2724 (21 October 1847).

[16] Jean-Marie Thiveaud, 'L'ordre primordial de la dette: Petite histoire panoramique de la faillite, des origines à nos jours', *Revue d'économie financière* 25, no. 2 (1993): 67–106, https://doi.org/10.3406/ecofi.1993.1989, esp. 89, 95; Léonce Thomas, *Études sur la faillite: De la faillite dans le droit français et dans le droit étranger. Observations sur quelques points spéciaux de la législation française en matière de faillite* (Paris: Larose, 1880), 16–17.

decreased during the Republican years. Surprisingly, the monetary volume of the 1848/1849 settlements was unusually high. The ratio of assets to liabilities was about 6:4 in 1848 and 1:1 in 1849, which was much higher than during regular years when the assets were out-numbered by the liabilities with a ratio between 1:2 and 1:3. This means, that insolvency procedures had struck merchants who still had important assets and under normal circumstances would not have been considered overindebted.[17] The controversy about bankruptcy in the aftermath of the 1848 revolution came too late for most of the affected businesses. Yet, the discussion about inefficient procedures, deserving and undeserving bankrupts clearly addressed a relevant problem of the time.

FLAWS OF THE 1807 NAPOLEONIC BANKRUPTCY LAW

Already during the first French Revolution, economic troubles, scandals, and the collapse of merchant houses revealed an economy and society in a state of severe disorder. Napoleon started a vast legislation pro-gram to harmonize and modernize French law. Public order was to be re-established, and morality reintroduced into the economy. The *Code de commerce* of 1807 offered a comprehensive regulation of commercial activity by replacing the 1673 *Ordonnance sur le commerce*. Frequent cases of bankruptcy incited Napoleon to tighten the measures against bankrupts.[18]

French bankruptcy law sought to balance protections for private inter-ests (primarily the claims of the creditor against his debtor) with protec-tion of the public good. A government circular letter issued during the elaboration of the *Code de commerce* proves how individualizing morali-zation and reference to the common good went hand in hand, and how this union was usually emphasized with strong rhetoric:

[17] Marco, *Montée*, 165.

[18] Thiveaud, 'Ordre', 84–87. This is not the place to retrace the revisions of the *Code de commerce*, or to describe the institutional development of commercial courts: Corinne Saint-Alary-Houin, ed., *Qu'en est-il du Code de commerce 200 ans après: État des lieux et projections* (Toulouse: Presses de l'Univ. des sciences sociales de Toulouse, 2009); Catherine Delplanque, ed., *Bicentenaire du Code de commerce, 1807–2007* (Paris: Dalloz, 2008).

> In general, it is impossible to end the *malpractices* to which insolvencies give an opportunity without strict laws: but, as you know, there is *no trade without credit, no credit without guarantees*. Strict laws against *bad faith* are protecting *probity* and, by purging the theatre of business of the *adventurers* who had *usurped* it, they shall tend to bring back the *morality* that *honours* trade, *consolidates* it and assures *public trust* in it.[19]

This reasoning would stand for decades to come. It integrated the (personal) creditworthiness of the merchant, trust in an abstract *commerce* (thus favouring public credit and state financing) and, finally, public order and morality. As I will show, the specific mixture of the individual and collective level became problematic during the nineteenth century, in an era of growing individualism. Curiously, the moral rigour of the distinctly modern Napoleonic codifications was in stark contrast to the relative laxity of early modern merchant practices. The latter often were embedded in kin and peer networks allowing for amicable arrangements in case of over-indebtedness. As Natacha Coquery maintains, the early modern 'commercialist' concept of bankruptcy was less rigorist and more pragmatic, more about stabilizing the relation instead of ending it and squeezing out what was owed by means of the law.[20]

French nineteenth-century legislation distinguished between an imbalance of assets and liabilities in a balance sheet, which led to a cessation of payments and insolvency (*faillite*), and cases of bankruptcy, which were liable to criminal prosecution (*banqueroute*). The first had to be declared at the Tribunal de Commerce, the commercial court, by submitting a balance of accounts (*dépôt de bilan*). The latter was punishable and covered acts of deceiving the creditors, whether by negligence, gambling or excessive borrowing (*banqueroute simple*) or by fraud and

---

[19] Italics added by the author. Circular letter of the Minister of the Interior to the Chambers of Commerce, survey on the project of a Code de Commerce, 18 June 1806, Archives Nationales (AN), AN/F/12/866.

[20] Laurence Fontaine, *L'Économie morale. Pauvreté, crédit et confiance dans l'Europe préindustrielle* (Paris: Gallimard, 2008), 281–296, esp. 288–898, 302–303; Natasha Coquery, 'Credit, Trust and Risk. Shopkeepers' Bankruptcies in 18th-Century Paris', in *The History of Bankruptcy. Economic, Social and Cultural Implications in Early Modern Europe*, ed. Thomas M. Safley (London: Routledge, 2013), 52–71, esp. 51–54, 61–66.

in bad faith (*banqueroute frauduleuse*).[21] These provisions, as well as the *Code de commerce* in general, only applied to merchants (*commerçants*), whereas the *Code civil* defined a specific form of private bankruptcy for all other citizens (*déconfiture*).[22] Both forms of bankruptcy (in the narrow sense) regularly included criminal charges as the debtor generally was suspected to harm the interests of some or all of the creditors by removing or hiding assets or by conspiring with selected creditors. 'Simple' bankrupts faced imprisonment for up to two years. Fraudulent bankrupts and their accomplices were to be punished with heavy labour in a *bagne*, a jail in seaports reminiscent of the former punishment on prison hulks (*galères*). Napoleon III replaced these by penitentiary camps in the colonies but the name *bagne* was kept.

As a preventive against fraudsters, the commercial court, after verification of the balance sheets, established the date of imbalance—referring to the hypothetical fact that after a certain point there were more *passifs* than *actifs* in the accountancy books. This point in time did not necessarily correspond with the date of *dépôt de bilan*. Meanwhile, potentially malicious transactions had to be reversed. Merchants who tried to save their company by avoiding a cessation of payments, bargaining, pleading for delay and restructuring debt, ran the danger of filing for insolvency too late. The merchant then could be accused of having disguised the imbalance and deceived new business partners.[23]

---

[21] For the following: *Code de commerce* ([Paris: 1807]), 3rd book, titles 1 (especially 1st chapter) and 4, art. 437–448, 586–603. The general elements did not change much in the first half of the century, as a concise overview of the procedure in a report to the National Assembly shows: *Le Moniteur universel* 1850, 2244–2245 (Report by Bravard-Veyrières). Victor Dalloz, *Jurisprudence des faillites, de la banqueroute, de la déconfiture, ou collection complète des arrêts rendus par les Cours de France et des Pays-Bas sur cette matière: Précédée de l'exposé des principes de la législation et de la doctrine des auteurs sur ces diverses matières* (Brussels: H. Tarlier, 1830).

[22] The definition of a 'merchant' was tautological, as in most commercial legislation: 'Sont commerçants ceux qui exercent des actes de commerce [sic!], et en font leur profession habituelle' (C. com., 1st book, art. 1). The state of *déconfiture* was not treated by civil law as systematically as *faillite* and *banqueroute* were in commercial law. Neither the *Code Civil* nor the *Code de procédure civile* had a special section. Its effects were mentioned inter alia in: (An XII = 1804) *Code civile des Français [...] suivi des lois transitoires sur l'adoption, le divorce et les enfants naturels*, 2 vols (Paris: Journal du Palais), art. 1267, 1613, 1913, 2003, 2032.

[23] Thomas, *Études*, 23–24.

Each insolvent was threatened with immediate imprisonment in a *maison d'arrêt pour dettes*, a debtors' prison, irrespective of the nature of the insolvency. Under the regulations of the commercial code, the court arrested the debtor, seized his possessions by affixing seals (*scellés*), and nominated a trustee (*syndic*) for the administration of the property as well as a bankruptcy judge (*juge commissaire*) for overseeing the syndic.[24] In the meantime, the debtor's property rights were substantially curtailed; his rights of disposal were transferred to the *syndic* and the *juge commissaire*. A complete cessation of the business usually was the result. If the imbalance had not been a major one at the outset, it would become so now.

However, the declaration of insolvency also protected the merchant, as an individual request for *contrainte par corps* (coercive arrest) could not be filed against a declared insolvent. The common interest of the creditors as a collectivity had priority. Curiously, demanding a *contrainte par corps* against a merchant could trigger an insolvency, which then helped the debtor to avoid coercive arrest. This, however, was only a Pyrrhic victory, as imprisonment by order of the bankruptcy judge was then imminent.[25]

The *contrainte par corps*, not to be confused with the automatic arrest of the insolvent, literally meant to get hold of the debtor's body in order to force him to pay. It was the thematic anchor par excellence for a moral and functional evaluation of bankruptcy law, even though the *contrainte* seemed to have been enforced on merchants rarely. It seems to have provided a false focal point for the discussion, as the idea that trade and *crédit public* could be promoted by arresting defaulting merchants was at odds with the reality of business life.[26] For many creditors, automatic arrest and *contrainte* represented the ultimate guarantee of outstanding debts, a last resort. The debtor, in contrast, faced debtors' prison as a temporary and limited, form of civil death.

---

[24] Dalloz, *Jurisprudence*, 86–99; Thiveaud, 'Ordre', 86–7; C. com., art. 455, 568.

[25] Raymond T. Troplong, *De la contrainte par corps en matière civile et de commerce: Commentaire du titre XVI, livre III, du Code civil* (Paris: C. Hingray, 1847), 275–284, 297–300.

[26] Pierre-Cyrille Hautcœur, 'La statistique et la lutte contre la contrainte par corps: L'apport de Jean-Baptiste Bayle-Mouillard', *Histoire et mesure* 23, no. 1 (2008): 167–189, http://journals.openedition.org/histoiremesure/3093 (accessed 1 February 2018), esp. par. 28–30.

An 1838 revision of the so-called *Code des faillites*, the third book of the commercial code, addressed the practical inadequacies of the highly moralistic and complex 1807 provisions. It sought to accelerate and simplify procedures, to facilitate settlements and to clarify the rehabilitation procedure for those debtors who were cleared of suspicion of fraudulent misconduct and had fulfilled all claims, even those claims waived by the creditors in an earlier settlement.[27] Successful settlement did not of itself lift the status of *failli*. Only formal rehabilitation allowed a debtor to make a fresh start; his full political rights were restored, such as to serve on juries or as an officer in the National Guard, membership in the chamber of commerce, and, not least, access to the stock exchange. Only the rehabilitation procedure ended the symbolic and social exclusion of the defaulting debtor.[28] From the moralizing perspective, formal rehabilitation was ambiguous. For a start, moralization was bound to an act of misconduct, but aimed at the debtor's character. When all liabilities were fulfilled and the restoration of order was acknowledged, moralization was suspended. Morality, finally, seemed less to be a question of character than one of the ability to meet the expectations of the peers.

Both institutions, *contrainte par corps* and formal rehabilitation, represented asynchronies in nineteenth-century law. These relics of the early modern regime of commercial morality, paradoxically reinforced by the Napoleonic modernization of the commercial code, equated each cessation of payments to a crime against society and public weal. The *contrainte* violated the personal freedom of the debtor for the sake of enforcing private claims. A creditor could detain his debtor in a public prison, without any criminal charge, without the approval of a criminal judge, for a relatively long period, and at the debtor's own expense. In the new age of codifications and of normative individualism, the *contrainte par corps* represented an inappropriate mixing of private law, public law and the penal system. The *contrainte* became a systemic problem.[29]

---

[27] Thiveaud, 'Ordre', 87–89.

[28] C. com., art. 604–614.

[29] Horace Émile Say, *Avant-propos à la discussion d'une nouvelle loi sur les faillites* (Paris: Guillaumin et Cie., 1837), 1–7, 52–57; Jérôme Sgard, 'Bankruptcy, Fresh Start and Debt Renegotiation in England and France (17th to 18th century)', in *The History of Bankruptcy*, ed. Safley, 223–235, esp. 223–224.

The traditional approach of moralizing the debtor by seizing and punishing him faced a substantial backlash from the ethical reasoning of modern individualism and liberal ideas of the rule of law.

French legislators were aware of this confusion of realms. The *contrainte* was subject to the back and forth of French political history. Abolished for the first time by the Convention on 9 March 1793, it was reintroduced by the same Convention on 14 March 1795 (*loi du 24 ventôse, an V*). The Directory regime proceeded to refine the rules for its application (*loi du 15 germinal, an VI* = 4 April 1798). Napoleon integrated the *contrainte* into his codifications of civil law, civil procedure, and commercial law without discarding the prior laws. Reformed and modernized in 1832 during the July Monarchy, the *contrainte* was abolished by the provisional government of 1848. The Assemblée reintroduced it again on 1 September of the same year. Only in 1867 was the *contrainte* finally abolished in matters of private and commercial law. From then, coercive arrest could only be applied in matters of public interest (penal law, enforcement of fees and taxes, etc.).[30]

Legal Technicality Instead of High Expectations

The February Revolution provided an occasion to reflect on the nature both of bankruptcy and of the bankrupt person. Although a general reform was never on the agenda, the *journées révolutionaires* and the following two years seemed propitious for reforming the so-called *Code des faillites*. The success of these attempts at reform was limited: brought forward at the zenith of the Second Republic, and discussed at length, the window of opportunity for a reform quickly closed.

Four contentious issues can be identified. The first three were the ranking of workers' wages in claims on the insolvent; short-term relief for merchants whose businesses were affected by revolutionary turmoil; and the reform of settlement procedures. Finally, one bill addressed misconduct in insolvency procedures.

---

[30] Hautcœur, 'Statistique', par. 28–30; Troplong, *Contrainte*, 508.

Challenges of Industrialization

During the initial phase of the Republic, working-class representatives introduced a bill to rank workers' wages (to a maximum of three months) among the privileged liabilities. Louis Marius Astouin (1822–1855), a representative in the Constituent Assembly for the Bouches-du-Rhône, was a leader of the influential porters' corporation of Marseille Harbour. In June 1848, the moderate democrat, who regularly sat in the Assembly in workers' clothes, introduced the bill 'in the name of my brothers, the workers'. Astouin invoked the traditional differentiation of incomes from productive ('real') work and from capitalist speculation—a distinction as popular in Christian theology as in early socialism. If workers did not participate in the employer's profits, why should they participate in a loss in the case of insolvency? Astouin also suspected that insolvency had become a business model for merchants providing a smokescreen for failed speculation at the expense of the workers.[31]

Astouin's bill met considerable opposition. Doubts were raised as to whether the proposition really would strengthen the position of workers, as employers might exercise 'moral' pressure on them to forgo wage payment during an economic downturn. Workers would have to rely on the legally protected but uncertain claim to a future insolvency estate. Moreover, such a privilege would produce high uncertainty for investors. Arrears of wages over as much as three months would constitute a considerable liability. The liberal position was clear: In the ongoing crisis, workers needed work; there was no work without liquidity; and the Astouin bill would restrict liquidity and credit, and hinder capital circulation.[32] To the liberals, then as now, being social (and moral) meant creating jobs.

[31] *Le Moniteur universel* 1848, 1307 (8 June 1848, Astouin), 1722–1723 (21 July 1848, Astouin); Adolphe Robert and Gaston Cougny, *Dictionnaire des parlementaires français: comprenant tous les membres des Assemblées françaises et tous les Ministres français depuis le 1er Mai 1789 jusqu'au 1er Mai 1889* (Paris: Bourloton, 1889), vol. 1, 103.

[32] *Le Moniteur universel* 1848, 1675 (report by Rouher, 15 July 1848), 1722–1724 (21 July 1848, Levavasseur, Dabeaux, Bravard-Veyrières).

Liberals also pointed out that workers (usually paid on a daily or weekly basis) who did not insist on the payment of their wages simply became creditors of their employer. Advocates of the bill acknowledged this, but they put it into perspective and interpreted debt as a social relation. During an economic crisis—a kind of sellers' market amidst an abundant human workforce—the self-interest of workers would lead them to continue working without collecting their wages, as they would not want to lose either their workplace or the money already owed by the employer. The conservative representative Joseph de Laboulie maintained: 'he [the worker] is chained to his master precisely because of the debt constituted by his salary, which has not been paid to him'.[33]

After the violent *Journées de Juin* (22–26 June 1848) and the anti-socialist backlash of the bourgeois Republic, the window of opportunity for such legislation closed. The bill simply disappeared from the agenda. Nonetheless, the threat of insolvencies by large (industrial) companies added new, large-scale problems to the question of financially and morally bankrupt merchants. In 1848, the scope of these problems of future industrial capitalism was only starting to be understood. Wages would be added to the list of privileged claims only in 1889.[34]

A Law of Exceptions for an Exceptional Event

The second political intervention had a limited objective and better suited the taste of the Constituent Assembly's majority: protecting businesses on the verge of bankruptcy.[35] The provisional government had already issued a decree on 20 March 1848 allowing the commercial courts to grant a general extension of the terms of credit to up to three months.[36] After the *Journées de Juin*, a debate about further emergency measures began. The original idea to reform the procedures for 'amicable settlements' (*concordats amiables*) encountered strong resistance.

[33] *Le Moniteur universel* 1848, 1722–1723 (Laboulie, Rouher).

[34] Thiveaud, 'Ordre', 93.

[35] *Le Moniteur universel* 1848, 1307 (8 June 1848), 1440 (20 June 1848), 1987 (report by Bravard-Veyrières).

[36] 'Projet de moratoire des effets de commerce. Sursis aux déclarations de faillite', AN/F/12/6835/B, Dossier 1848.

In the end, no fewer than seven different propositions, together with a substantial number of amendments, were debated. Many pointed to unconfirmed numbers of about 6500–7000 cessations of payment registered in Paris since 20 February 1848. Others queried how many of these went back to the prerevolutionary crisis. The data given above suggests that more insolvencies arose from a structural crisis in 1846/1847 than from the political events of 1848. Nonetheless, in the words of one representative, 'Capital was frightened, it hid'. All his colleagues shared this analysis, though they were unable to agree on the means by which credit and stability could be restored: whether this should be attempted using all available emergency measures, or by relying on the existing system of guarantees in the commercial code.[37]

Even socialists like Victor Considérant (1808–1893) adhered to the idea of promoting commerce by allowing debtors more room to manoeuvre. The social philosopher and promoter of Fourier's Phalanstère movement pleaded for debtors to be empowered against their creditors to ensure tranquillity and equity in French commerce.[38] In contrast, the conservative Pierre de Sainte-Beuve (1819–1855), who already had supported the reintroduction of the *contrainte*, mocked his colleagues and suggested insertion of a clause into the original bill stipulating that all 'debtors are exempted from the duty to repay their debt'.[39] This sarcastic remark was typical of the general mood of the liberal and conservative majority and aligned with the position of the Cavaignac government. During the third reading, Finance Minister Michel Goudchaux (1797–1862) finally rejected moves to facilitate *concordats amiables*, observing that the Republic should not be built on a law of exceptions.[40]

After extensive debate, what was adopted on 22 August 1848 was a decree with limited scope. As a purely transitional measure, all cessations of payment since the end of the July Monarchy on 24 February 1848 until the date of publication of the decree were to be presumed

---

[37] *Le Moniteur universel* 1848, 1985–1989, 2046–2052, 2061–2065, 2077–2082, 2105–2111, the citation 1986.

[38] *Le Moniteur universel* 1848, 2062–2063.

[39] *Le Moniteur universel* 1848, 2080; Robert and Cougny, *Dictionnaire*, vol. 5, 249.

[40] *Le Moniteur universel* 1848, 2106.

not to be *faillite*. The decree temporarily reversed the norm (that every cessation is *faillite*). The commercial courts were authorized to forego the arrest of the debtor, the concomitant suspension of business, and the affixing of the seals; debtors were to be enabled to liquidate businesses themselves.[41]

French merchants were divided. One group pleaded for a utilitarian approach and were in favour of government intervention to avoid the risk to stability and public order that the collapse of businesses and subsequent unemployment would pose. For them, the primary objective of the law should not be to prevent the rare cases of fraudulent behaviour and inability to manage a business but rather to protect all merchants. They saw the revolution as an unforeseeable case of force majeure.[42] This utilitarian view was able to invoke modernizing arguments advanced by liberal economists and statisticians like Jean-Baptiste Bayle-Mouillard and Horace E. Say, a liberal economist in the tradition of his father, Jean-Baptiste Say.[43]

The second group of merchants feared losing the guarantees for their outstanding accounts. Instead of helping an allegedly small minority of *commerçants malheureux*, they were concerned that the decree would clear the way for unsound and fraudulent racketeers. This group was aware that the utilitarian and the moral approaches were partially incompatible: If the decision on the cessation of payment and the exact time of its declaration ceased to be a moral question, reinforced by the 'salutary fear' of incarceration, insolvency would become an acceptable risk. In other words, it would become a business option for debtors.[44]

[41] *Le Moniteur universel* 1848, 2155 (Décret relatif aux concordats amiables du 22 août 1848).

[42] 'Notes of the *Délégués du Commerce de Paris* "Des vraies raisons de décider dans la question dite des Concordats Amiables"', AN/F/12/6835/A; 'Merchants of the City of Blanc (Indre) to the *Citoyens membres du Gouvernement Provisoire*' (30 March 1848), AN/F/12/6835/B.

[43] Hautcœur, 'Statistique,' par. 15–17; Say, *Avant-propos.*

[44] 'Observations présentées à l'Assemblée Nationale par le Comptoir National d'Escompte de Paris sur les projets de Décrets relatifs aux concordats amiables'; 'Avis de M. Gautier, sous-gouverneur de la Banque [de France]' (2 July 1848); 'Lyon Chamber of Commerce to the Minister for Agriculture and Commerce' (10 June 1848); 'Reims Chamber of Commerce to the Minister for Agriculture and Commerce' (16 June 1848); for the citation 'crainte salutaire': 'Paris Chamber of Commerce to the Minister for Agriculture and Commerce' (16 June 1848), AN/F/12/6835/A.

But both groups shared common reference points. They desired to re-establish trust within French commerce and to further the *crédit public*—a multifaceted concept popular since the end of the eighteenth century, including the creditworthiness of the state, trust in the performance of an imagined national economy and, thus, the readiness of the citizens to grant credit to each other. And although they drew different conclusions, both based their moral argument on the idea of commercial utility. The liberals, who had approved the emergency measures in part, later were reticent. The effects of the decree seemed to confirm the doubts of the conservatives. In hindsight, Pierre Bravard-Veyrières (1804–1861), representative for the Puy-de-Dôme, professor at the Sorbonne law faculty and author of a manual on commercial law, gave a disillusioned report on the abuses of the law. It was not a question of force majeure, he felt, if most merchants passed through the crisis 'without bowing'. The legislation committee had been 'touched by the misfortune of a certain number of notable merchants and moved by a sentiment of merciful equity'. Bravard-Veyrières sarcastically emotionalized the motives of his colleagues and countered them with sober economic arguments. The law professor believed that the decree, finalized in a rush, was internally inconsistent and an example of poor legislation. Yet he was confident that the courts were able to distinguish deserving and undeserving insolvents.[45] Even a utilitarian liberal like Bravard-Veyrières thus had a specific idea of worthiness that a defaulting debtor had to prove.

Cases of allegedly ruthless merchants who invoked the decree even after it had expired motivated Bravard-Veyrières to request a clarifying resolution. The decree seemed to have offered the possibility of judicial liquidation to those who allegedly had not merited it. The relevant committee of the Assembly, too, questioned the benefit of a measure 'made for an exceptional and temporary situation'. It may have been 'profitable' for individual *commerçants*, but not necessarily for French commerce as a whole. Without further discussion, the Assembly approved the resolution in autumn 1849 and stopped the application of the exemption clauses.[46]

[45] *Le Moniteur universel* 1848, 2583–2584 ('Observations sur l'application du décret du 22 août 1848, relatif aux concordats amiables, par M. Bravard-Veyrières'); Robert and Cougny, *Dictionnaire*, vol. 1, 473–474.

[46] *Le Moniteur universel* 1849, 3424 (committee report on the bill of Bravard-Veyrières), 3463–3464, 3521, 3606 (second committee report), 3643 (adoption without discussion); *Le Moniteur universel* 1850, 438 (excerpts from a booklet by Bravard-Veyrières).

Deficiencies of Legal Practice

The third topic concerned the simplification of the *concordats par aban-don*, a special form of settlement where the debtor assigned all or part of his property to the creditors, who then were responsible for selling it on their own—and at their own risk. This practice existed in a legal vacuum, but an increasing number of assignments were accepted by commercial courts, which in the process set aside the risks to creditors and accepted overt procedural deficits. Bravard-Veyrières brought forward a bill to ensure all creditors received timely information about the settlements' details. The court's approval of such *concordats* was to be published for the attention of creditors who had not participated in or accepted the settlement.[47] The bill generally was welcomed, but during the third reading, the topic was first delayed and then taken off the agenda. Eugène-Émile Loyer (1807–1880), an entrepreneur from Rouen, did not see any need for reform at all, and seems to have blocked the bill using procedural tactics.[48]

The last bill by representatives Pierre Henri Sevaistre (1801–1851) and Joseph de Laboulie (1800–1867), did not address a systemic problem, but focused on specific forms of misconduct in bankruptcy procedures. The representatives pointed out institutional deficits at the commercial courts and unlawful acts by the syndics. This bill ran aground already during the preliminary discussion in the assembly.[49] Laboulie's charges were serious: 'You have created a new class, a new industry at the commercial courts, called the bankruptcy syndicate'. The only interest of this *syndicat des faillites* would be to never bring any proceeding to an end.[50] Sevaistre's and de Laboulie's overt attack on commercial courts and syndics may have been a reason why this bill failed.

---

[47] *Le Moniteur universel* 1850, 894–895 (committee report by Laboulie on the Bravard-Veyrières bill), 2244–2245 (committee report by Bravard-Veyrières on his own bill).

[48] *Le Moniteur universel* 1850, 1200–1201 (discussion), 3325 (second reading), 2244–2245, 2259–2260 (committee report by Bravard-Veyrières on his own bill); *Le Moniteur universel* 1851, 1397, and supplement III–IV (additional committee report by Bravard-Veyrières), 2167 (third reading).

[49] *Le Moniteur universel* 1850, 3688 (committee report); *Le Moniteur universel*, 1851, 145–147 (discussion).

[50] *Le Moniteur universel* 1851, 145–147 (discussion: Laboulie).

Rhetorics and Arguments

Numerous representatives participated in these debates, but some among them stood out. In many cases, their opinion on bankruptcy did not follow in a straightforward way from their general political leaning. Astouin and his friends spoke solely for the interests of the workers and were barely interested in technical questions of commercial law. Bravard-Veyrières was described as politically conservative, sitting on the right side of the house, but liberal in legal matters. His moderately modernizing reports and bills indicate his distinctly modern grasp of the problem. In contrast, the conservative Laboulie and the small-town entrepreneur Sevaistre focused on institutionalized misconduct and displayed a moralizing and individualizing stance. Their bill against the syndics was the fruit of a non-partisan alliance. Sevaistre was the owner of a small spinning factory in Elbeuf (Seine-Inférieure). Former president of the local commercial court there, he was thought to be an independent seated on the left in the assembly. The former Bourbonic legitimist Laboulie was an independent right-wing representative for the Bouches-du-Rhône. All withdrew from politics after Napoleon's coup, unlike Eugène-Émile Loyer who had fervently opposed the last two bills. Loyer, a former lawyer, represented the Seine-Inférieure and was director of a spinning factory, active in the same industry as Sevaistre. But unlike Sevaistre, Loyer was to become a Bonapartist magnate in the important port city of Rouen.[51]

The debates were characterized mostly by legal observations, but always underpinned with anecdotal evidence and hypothetical cases. Particularly scandalous examples and allegedly all-too-common behaviour were brought up to illustrate grievances and abuse of the law. It was the same anecdotal approach that promoted the moralization of bankruptcy and the individualization of its causes in works of fiction by realist and naturalist authors like Honoré de Balzac and Emile Zola. They used the calamity of bankruptcy as a springboard to explore the decadence of the French bourgeoisie, their decay as a class, and the general shallowness of their time.[52]

---

[51] Cf. footnotes 31, 39, 45; Robert and Cougny, *Dictionnaire*, vol. 3, 484–485; vol. 4, 193; vol. 5, 311.

[52] The original title of Balzac's most pertinent novel on the subject is 'Histoire de la grandeur et de la décadence de César Birotteau, parfumeur, chevalier de la Légion d'honneur, adjoint au maire du deuxième arrondissement de Paris' (1837–1839). With Zola, the topic is omnipresent in his Rougon-Macquart series, e.g. in 'La Curée' (1871), 'L'Argent' (1891) and 'Le débâcle' (1892).

Empirical knowledge in the form of statistical information was introduced only on rare occasions. Sevaistre communicated statistical information from his own observation about the outcome of procedures at an unnamed commercial court—most probably in Elbeuf, where he had been president. Bravard-Veyrières evaluated the effects of the 1848 decree within the circuit of the Tribunal de Commerce of the Seine Department.[53] Statistical data on the *contrainte par corps* and its effects appear not to have been brought to bear on the political and juridical discussion. Jean-Baptiste Bayle-Mouillard's study *De l'emprisonnement pour dettes*, awarded a prize by the Academy of Moral and Political Sciences in 1835, had only limited effect.[54]

Openly moralizing, sometimes emotional rhetoric contrasted sharply with a measured and primarily technical style of argumentation. Sevaistre explicitly evoked the need for 'moralization of commerce' and the 'just and moralizing mindset' of Napoleonic bankruptcy law. His rhetoric was full of judgmental expressions: abuse, equity, extreme, fraud, good/bad faith, grave, honourable, illegitimate, incapable, justice, *malheur*, merit, scandalous. Quite to the contrary, the liberal jurist Bravard-Veyrières hardly ever evoked the 'malheur' of an otherwise honest merchant.[55] This oft-cited 'misfortune' was a deeply moralistic term, in a certain sense even a romantic notion, which can best be illustrated with reference to the ship owner Pierre Morrell in Alexandre Dumas' 'Comte de Monte-Christo' (1844–1846). The idea of *malheur* had also influenced French jurisprudence; sentences acknowledged the existence of bankrupts who were 'unfortunate but with good faith', victims of the 'too-hazardous chances of commerce', struck by 'inevitable misfortune'.[56] Even creditors could be moralized, when a settlement was not approved and when opaque tactics by some of them aimed at the arrest of the debtor—risking the dividends of the other creditors.

---

[53] *Le Moniteur universel* 1850, 438; *Le Moniteur universel* 1851, 145.

[54] Hautcœur, 'Statistique,' par. 19–34.

[55] *Le Moniteur universel* 1851, 145 (Sevaistre); *Le Moniteur universel* 1850, 894 (committee report by Laboulie on the Bravard-Veyrières bill); versus 2244–2245, 2259–2260 (committee report by Bravard-Veyrières).

[56] Dalloz, *Jurisprudence*, 1, 99.

The personal enemy, who tried to press home an advantage, and the malicious asset stripper, who extorted a preferential treatment, were frequent topoi of the debate.[57]

To a certain extent, all discussants still clung to the 'fantasy, if not always the reality, of personal, individual responsibility', as Rebecca Spang put it when discussing eighteenth-century affairs.[58] This individualizing tone was compatible with the views of classic economists (J.-B. Say, A. Smith). Apart from an early contribution by Jean de Sismondi, a new economic contextualization of bankruptcy emerged only in the second half of the nineteenth century. Economists like Karl Marx, Rudolf Hilferding, Werner Sombart and Joseph Schumpeter began to understand bankruptcy as an adaptation crisis at the individual level, a purgatory in which small, undercapitalized and dispensable market actors were liquidated.[59]

Industrial growth irrevocably changed the game. Kinship networks of mutual assistance once had provided credit and were the last resort for merchants in trouble; additionally, they were effective barriers against opportunistic behaviour by debtors and creditors alike. Such networks began to lose their relevance, as was already attested by the 1848 debates. During the following decades it became evident: industrialization and external financing for companies had a disruptive effect—especially after the liberalization of the Sociétés Anonymes in 1863 and 1867. The organizational structure of companies changed, the sole proprietorship went into decline and—in the medium term—the entrepreneurial role was separated from ownership during the

---

[57]'Minister of Justice to the Minister of Agriculture and Commerce' (12 April 1848), AN/F/12/6835/A. The minister was also evoking the idea of a 'reliable but unfortunate merchant'.

[58]Rebecca L. Spang, *Stuff and Money in the Time of the French Revolution* (Cambridge, MA and London: Harvard University Press, 2015), 19–56.

[59]Marco, *Montée*, 23–30; Jean-Clément Martin, 'Le commerçant, la faillite et l'historien' *Annales HSS* 35, no. 6 (1980): 1254–1266, https://doi.org/10.3406/ahess.1980.282700, esp. 1265–1266; Luc Marco, 'Faillites et crises économiques en France au XIXe siècle' *Annales HSS* 44, no. 2 (1989): 355–378, https://doi.org/10.3406/ahess.1989.283597, esp. 355–360. For the continuity since the eighteenth century see: Jean-Pierre Hirsch, 'Honneur et liberté du commerce: Sur le libéralisme des milieux du commerce de Lille et de Dunkerque à la veille des Etats Généraux de 1789', *Revue du Nord* 55 (1973): 333–346, https://doi.org/10.3406/rnord.1973.3200, esp. 340–344.

so-called managerial revolution. Organizing (joint) responsibility—including shared control, knowledge and motivation—became a problem, discussed up to the present day under the keywords principal-agent problem and compliance. Finally, the integration of companies into the capital market increased the vulnerability of firms during the new types of economic crisis of the second half of the nineteenth century.[60]

In 1848, the understanding of these impending changes obviously was limited. Even for liberal modernizers, insolvency still was understood as a problem between businessmen; the merchant with unlimited liability continued to be the recipient of the commercial law's moralizing message. The points of reference (economy, society, *crédit public*) remained abstract. Only seldom, as with the Astouin bill on workers' wages, was the focus shifted to the growing relevance of industrial labour.

Traditionally, the *failli* was legally (e.g. by syndics), symbolically (by the *scellés*), rhetorically (via the loss of reputation), and physically (by coercive arrest, expulsion from the stock exchange) excluded from the merchant community. From the middle of the nineteenth century, this conception of moralization by exclusion was questioned. Not by a purely utilitarian argument: all discussants more or less shared a utilitarian perspective, they simply drew different conclusions from the situation. The true novelty was that the legitimacy of the moralizing instruments was at stake. The same Napoleonic commercial code, which had reinforced the moralizing features of bankruptcy law, also provided, together with other codifications of the time, the modernizing judicial and ethical framework that would bring the individual, his rights and freedoms, to the fore. The evolution of bankruptcy law and of the moralizing discourse can be understood as a double transition: from the close ties of early modern trade to a new moralism in the late eighteenth and early nineteenth centuries and, again, from the Napoleonic era to industrial capitalism. The reinforced moralization of bankrupts in the first half of the nineteenth century was a paradoxical feature of modernization.

---

[60] Thomas, *Études*, 27; Martin, 'Commerçant'; Werner Plumpe, *Wirtschaftskrisen: Geschichte und Gegenwart* (München: C. H. Beck, 2013), 26–54; Marco, 'Faillites', 363–376; and Sgard, 'Bankruptcy, fresh start and debt renegotiation', 229–230.

During the Second Empire and the Third Republic, the debate about the 1807 commercial code, often disparaged as the 'shopkeepers' act' (*code des boutiquiers*), continued. Repeated petitions requested the reform of bankruptcy law and the abolition of the *contrainte par corps*. Only the style of petitions occasionally changed. Whereas the tone of the 1848 *citoyens représentants du peuple* was insistent, some years later, when merchants from 50 French cities pleaded for a reform, the style was deferential again. The petitioners simply threw an imperial cloak over the Republican style of their original address: The previously collected signature lists were bound in green leather embossed with Napoleon III's gilded imperial monogram and with bees, a heraldic symbol of both Napoleonic Empires.[61]

HEDGING THE UBIQUITY OF DEBT

The German economist Lorenz von Stein (1815–1890) was a fine connoisseur of French political ideologies of the nineteenth century in general and of French socialist thinkers like the above-cited Charles Fourier. He believed that *die Fallissemente* (a German loan word from *faillite*) were a symptom of the social and economic development of a society. Speculation, the degree of entanglement in credit–debt relations and the capitalist orientation towards future profits would provoke more cases of bankruptcy. The growing demand for capital would make companies take considerable risks in order to be competitive. Von Stein deplored the deficiency of moral and legal institutions needed to set bounds on the growing dependency on capital.[62]

In fact, these social institutions were highly controversial in nineteenth-century France, especially the pre-modern features of the Code de Commerce, and they provoked highly moralized questions: Were you a *failli* or a *banqueroutier*? Did you act negligently or in bad faith? Were your transactions risky but above board? Was it a matter of bad luck or an unexpected economic downturn? Would you go to debtor's prison, or did you qualify for rehabilitation? Was it your fault—or was it fate?

---

[61]'Le Commerce à Napoléon III. Projet de Réforme du Code des faillites' [1853], AN/F/12/9419. Cf. for further petitions: 'Inmates of the Clichy debtors' prison to Napoléon III' (18 July 1859), AN/F/70/60; 'Droguerie Épicerie [...] Thiers-Chave, Marseille, to the Minister of Finance, Achille Fould' (14 January 1855), AN/F/70/68.

[62]Von Stein, *Industrielle Gesellschaft*, 29–30.

The asynchrony of the traditional features of bankruptcy law in an epoch of liberal and individualist legislation was created by the tension between the individual and social dimensions of bankruptcy, between individual and public realm. Even today, the basic lines of this conflict are still to be found in public debate. Some European commentators, for instance, responded with amazement when Donald Trump in a Republican candidates' debate congratulated himself for never having gone 'bank bankrupt'. He had successfully used the provisions of American bankruptcy law, namely the chapter 11 procedures (US Code, Title 11, chapter 11), reorganized his companies and liquidated loss-making activities—or, as he put it: 'I used the law four times and made a tremendous thing. I'm in business. I did a very good job'.[63] This apparent embrace of insolvency as a business option—a proposition that continues to unsettle public opinion in Europe today—represents the worst fears of some of the protagonists of 1848 come true.

The example of bankruptcy helps in analysing the construction of economic morality at a crucial point in the life of a merchant. Unpaid debt refers to the relational character of both debt and morality, as all stakeholders were mutually bound by means of the money owed—both before and after filing for bankruptcy. Debt, mostly in the form of trade credits, was and is omnipresent and essential for capitalism. Trade credits ensure liquidity and constitute the major part of the floating capital; they dematerialize transactions; their reproducibility and reciprocity stabilize the system of debt and contribute to its expansion.

Written-off claims, the debts of a bankrupt were a moral problem precisely because debt in general was an integral part of the economic system. This became evident in a time of economic and political crisis like the 1848 Revolution, when all creditors ran the risk of becoming defaulting debtors themselves.[64] This ambiguity may explain the

---

[63] CNN, Transcript of the GOP Presidential Debate. Aired 16 September 2015, 8:10–11:15p ET., http://transcripts.cnn.com/TRANSCRIPTS/1509/16/se.02.html (accessed 1 February 2018).

[64] *Le Moniteur universel* 1848, 1987; for the omnipresence of the credit nexus cf. Margrit Schulte Beerbühl, 'Zwischen Selbstmord und Neuanfang. Das Schicksal von Bankrotteuren im London des 18. Jahrhundert', in *Pleitiers und Bankrotteure. Geschichte des ökonomischen Scheiterns vom 18. bis 20. Jahrhundert*, eds. Ingo Köhler and Roman Rossfeld (Frankfurt am Main and New York: Campus, 2012), 107–128, esp. 108–110.

eagerness to punish those who 'failed', in the moral as well as in the business sense.[65] If this was true, even when debating about particular cases the system itself was always at issue. Although, during the nineteenth century, the traditional instruments of commercial moralization—discursive, symbolic and physical exclusion—lost their force, moralizing bankruptcy still was about building a firewall between the collapsed *faillis* and a legitimate culture of debt.

[65] Coquery, 'Credit, trust and risk', 65.

PART IV

Social Movements and Moral Concerns

CHAPTER 10

US Catholicism and Economic Justice: 1919–1929

Giulia D'Alessio

INTRODUCTION

During the years of Benedict XV's and Pius XI's pontificates Catholics still represented one of the poorest minorities in the US society—among there were the Italian, the Irish and the Polish communities. A focus on social action thus marked American Catholicism, particularly during the early decades of the twentieth century and Franklin Delano Roosevelt's first term. Accordingly, in our analysis of the organization of the Catholic presence in the United States and of the role it played in the American social-political context, we will lay particular emphasis on the pursuit of two main goals: on the one hand the achievement of social integration for the catholic minorities, and on the other hand their legitimation by the US political institutions.

The Catholic Church's marginalization on the political level went on for a long time in the United States but it never meant a lack of presence in the US social context. Since the nineteenth century the majority of the immigrants to the United States was Catholic: through its relationship

G. D'Alessio (✉)
Dipartimento di Storia Antropologia Religioni Arte Spettacolo, Sapienza
Università di Roma, Rome, Italy

© The Author(s) 2019   233
S. Berger and A. Przyrembel (eds.), *Moralizing Capitalism*,
Palgrave Studies in the History of Social Movements,
https://doi.org/10.1007/978-3-030-20565-2_10

with 'New Americans' the US Church managed—firstly on the local and then on the national level—to reinforce its role and its contribution to the country's cultural and political debate.[1]

The US Catholic Church has been traditionally perceived, before and after the period analysed within our research, as a 'conservative institution', especially on the basis of its firm opposition to all form of radicalism. In the context of the early Cold War, for example, important Catholic figures like New York Archbishop Francis Spellman were strongly committed to anti-Communism, even in its more virulent and persecutory facets.[2]

This interpretation, however, fails to take into account other important aspects. Emblematic of a greater richness and variety of approaches adopted by the Catholic Church in the United States is, in fact, its stake in the Social question. This was particularly evident during the Interwar period. By focusing on what the Catholic Social teaching has meant

[1] For a detailed account of the history of Catholic immigration in the United States and, more generally, of the events related to Catholicism in USA see: John T. Ellis, *American Catholicism* (Chicago: University of Chicago Press, 1956); Jaroslav Pelikan, *The Riddle of Roman Catholicism* (New York and Nashville: The Abingdon Press, 1959); Theodore Maynard, *The Story of American Catholicism* (New York, NY: Macmillan, 1960); Thomas T. McAvoy, ed., *Roman Catholicism and the American Way of life* (Notre Dame, IN: University of Notre Dame Press, 1960); Harold J. Abramson, *Ethnic Diversity in Catholic America* (New York, NY: Wiley, 1973); Andrew M. Greeley, *The American Catholic. A Social Portrait* (New York, NY: Basic Book, 1977); James J. Hennesey, *American Catholics: A History of the Roman Catholic Community in the United States* (New York: Oxford University Press, 1981); Gerald P. Fogarty, *The Vatican and the American Hierarchy from 1870 to 1965* (Stuttgart: Hiersemann, 1982), George Gallup, Jr. and Jim Castelli, *The American Catholic People* (New York: Doubleday, 1987); Stephen M. De Giovanni, *Archbishop Corrigan and the Italian Immigrants* (Huntington, IN: Our Sunday Visitory Publication, 1994); Charles R. Morris, *American Catholic* (New York: Random House, 1997); Daniela Saresella, *Cattolicesimo italiano e sfida americana* (Brescia: Morcelliana, 2001); Matteo Sanfilippo, *L'affermazione del cattolicesimo nel Nord America: élite, emigranti e Chiesa cattolica negli Stati Uniti e nel Canada, 1750–1920* (Viterbo: Sette Città, 2003); Peter R. D'Agostino, *Rome in America: Transnational Catholic Ideology from the Risorgimento to Fascism* (Chapel Hill and London: The University of North Carolina Press, 2004); Patrick W. Carey, *Catholics in America: A History* (Westport, CT and London: Praeger, 2004); Matteo Sanfilippo, 'Parrocchie ed emigrazione negli Stati Uniti', *Studi Emigrazione* 168 (2007): 993–1005; Matteo Sanfilippo, 'L'emigrazione italiana verso gli Stati Uniti negli anni 1889–1900: una prospettiva vaticana', *Giornale di storia contemporanea* 1 (2008): 54–78; and Massimo Di Gioacchino, 'Religione e società nelle Little Italies statunitensi (1876–1915)', *Una rassegna tra studi e fonti* 11 (2015): 95–108.

[2] See, among others, John Cooney, *The American Pope: The Life and Times of Francis Cardinal Spellman* (New York: Times Books, 1984).

in the United States, it is possible to highlight the original contribution that some of the main protagonists of the American Catholicism, and especially the American Catholic Bishops, gave to the political-intellectual debate and the concrete US institutional choices and policies.

In the context of the pursuit of both a legitimation by the institutions and integration in the US society, the American Catholic Church increased its intellectual and organizational efforts in order to consolidate its action in the socio-economic field. The legitimation, on the political and the institutional level, was possible thanks to the definition of a social thought and a political action both based on a reinterpretation of the Catholic Social doctrine that could correspond and adapt to the cultural, economic and social context of the United States. Between the end of the nineteenth century and the first three decades of the twentieth century, the US Catholic church produced—on the pattern laid down by Leo XXIII's *Rerum Novarum*—theories and proposals in the socio-economic field, a significant number of which would later be put into effect, on the legislative level, during the Thirties. The latter represented indeed a pivotal decade for American Catholicism, also because of the increased institutional understanding between the US government and the Holy See: several documents kept at Vatican Secret Archives, F. D. Roosevelt Presidential Library, the Archives of Catholic University of America, show that the process of rapprochement between Washington and St. Peter had begun to significantly develop during the initial phase of the first Roosevelt Presidency.[3]

We will not analyse all the complicated events that, at the end of nineteenth century, led to the breaking of official relations between the White House and the Holy See. It is well known that it was the result of misunderstandings and problems of both ideological and political order:

---

[3] For a detailed account of American Catholicism during the FDR Administrations and the New Deal years see, among others: Francis L. Broderick, *Right Reverend New Dealer: John A. Ryan* (New York: Macmillan, 1963); David J. O'Brien, *American Catholics and Social Reform: The New Deal Years* (New York: Oxford University Press, 1968); George Q. Flynn, *American Catholics & the Roosevelt Presidency, 1932–1936* (Lexington: University of Kentucky Press, 1968); Stefano Luconi, *Little Italies e New Deal. La coalizione rooseveltiana e il voto italo-americano a Filadelfia e Pittsburgh* (Milano: Franco Angeli, 2002); Kevin E. Schmiesing, 'Catholics Critics of the New Deal: 'Alternative" Traditions in Catholic Social Thought', *Catholic Social Science Review* 7 (2002): 145–159; and David B. Woolner and Richard G. Kurial, *FDR, The Vatican, and the Roman Catholic Church in America, 1933–1945* (New York: Palgrave Macmillan, 2003).

the legal principles that provided a clear separation between Church and State in the United States, contrasted with the possibility of maintaining official contacts with an institution that had at his top a religious leader.

What we wish to stress, instead, is that the arrival of F. D. Roosevelt at the White House marked a decisive change of perspective, and that the significant convergence of views between the New President and the Vatican on issues relating to economic and social policy played a major role in this development. Roosevelt famously expressed his high consideration of the 1931 encyclical letter *Quadragesimo Anno* ('*Quadragesimo Anno* is as radical as I am, is one of the greatest documents of modern times' the President said during a 1932 speech in Detroit[4]), and his positive view of Pius XI's social doctrine represented an important step in the direction of a deeper social and political integration of the American Catholics.

In order to understand the origins of this process, it is important to underline that the US Bishops—especially through the official statements of the NCWC, the National Catholic Welfare Council (later the National Catholic Welfare Conference')—had been expressing their position on social-economic issues since the end of World War I, when they published the 1919 statement entitled *Program for Social reconstruction*.[5] The 1920s, on the contrary, were a phase of relative silence of the US clergy: the official statements of the US bishops on the Social question represented a thing of the past.

In the United States as well as in the other belligerent countries, the First World War and the post-war period witnessed a redefinition of the concept of citizenship and of the patterns of inclusion in—and exclusion from—the national community of wide sections of the population. The experience of the United States was however peculiar as compared to those of developed European countries or colonial territories. The First World War represented, in fact, a watershed in the history of immigrant communities in the United States and in the gradual acquisition of a more than simply formal citizenship by individuals hitherto on the margins of the social, economic and political-institutional system of their

[4] Franklin D. Roosevelt, Detroit Speech, October 2, 1932, in George Q. Flynn, *American Catholics and the Roosevelt Presidency, 1932–1936* (Lexington: University of Kentucky Press, 1968), 17.

[5] Bishop's Program of Social Reconstruction, National Catholic Welfare Conference, Washington, 1919.

'new homeland'. The conflict, moreover, was a harbinger not only of thrusts towards the integration of the minorities that were present on US soil, since the exceptional context of the war led to the spreading of a climate of suspicion towards those 'Hyphenated-Americans' who were perceived and singled out as internal enemies. As a result, several provisions were adopted that restricted civil liberties. These specular inclusive/exclusive thrusts were not limited to the chronological boundaries of the Great War: they were picked up, in different forms and with different protagonists, in the post-war period and re-emerged again later. The forms assumed by the American Melting Pot, in continuous mutation both in terms of numbers and geographical origin, were the subject of a famous speech given by Theodore Roosevelt in 1915. Roosevelt highlighted the need for the multiplicity cultures and origins to find its synthesis in the common American identity: 'There is no room in this country for hyphenated Americanism. When I refer to naturalized Americans. When I refer to hyphenated Americans, I do not refer to naturalized Americans. Some of the very best Americans I have ever known were naturalized Americans, Americans born abroad. But a hyphenated American is not an American at all'. These words were pronounced in front of the Knights of Columbus, protagonists of the secular Catholicism in the United States, who paired the daily declaration of allegiance to the constitutive values of the United States with the affirmation of Catholicism as an integral part of the society and culture of the country. Catholicity had traditionally constituted a motive of prejudice against those who, even once naturalized Americans, were suspected of double fidelity: to the Pontiff, as well as to the American state institutions.

Starting from 1917, the modalities of the integration of the immigrant Catholic communities in the United States, started with the 'Soldier's Naturalizations', were strongly connected to the efforts made by both the laity and the ecclesiastical hierarchies to favour the full inclusion of Catholics in the social and economic fabric of the country, in the context of ever increasing phenomena of exclusion, demonization and marginalization of specific Catholic communities in the United States.[6]

---

[6]One can just think of the events that invested the Irish, and, even more, the German community. Prejudice against the Irish-Americans had quickly spread based on the hypothesis of their lack of involvement alongside the British ally, due to the strong bond with the land of origin in which the independence thrusts were ever stronger. Woodrow Wilson,

In this social and political framework, pivotal is the role played, with a view to the acquisition of a not only formal citizenship by immigrants of the Catholic faith, by the National Catholic War Council, founded in 1917 immediately after the entry into war of the United States. The leaders of the American Catholic hierarchy met for the first time since 1884, especially for the purpose of coordinating the activities of the Catholic world in the context of the war engagement. In peacetime, the body changed its name to the National Catholic Welfare Council (and then Conference), and (as early as 1919) it identified the triumph of Social Justice as the only 'possible pacification' in a Country torn by great contradictions and characterized by the absence of legislation to protect the weakest subjects. The First World War represented the starting point for a series of changes in the society and in the political-institutional choices whose impact would be felt also in the following decades. The logic of the identification and repression of the 'internal enemy' would give rise to the Red Scare of the Twenties, during which the Catholic Social thought became marginal on the public level and the Bishops seldom expressed their views on the problem of the economic justice.

This attitude changed dramatically after the 1929 Wall Street Crash and during the Great Depression, when the NCWC published three fundamental documents: the *Statement on unemployment* (1930), the *Statement on the Economic Crisis* (1931) and the *Statement on the Present Crisis* (1933). They were inspired by the Catholic Social teaching but also by the ideas of Mgr. John A. Ryan, one of the main figures of the American Catholicism, among the most influential US Catholic social reformer and a great supporter of FDR'S New Deal.[7]

---

during the Paris Peace Conference, said he was annoyed by the attitude of Irish Catholics during the war, saying: 'My first impulse was to tell the Irish to go to hell but, feeling inside me that this way of saying would not have been a gesture worthy of a statesman, I denied myself this personal satisfaction'. The attitude of mistrust and hostility towards immigrants from the territories of the central empires was also very harsh. Before the US entry into the war, many had enrolled in the German and Austrian armies and this was the basis of a feeling of mistrust and intolerance also towards those who, though coming from these countries, had remained in their new homeland, and in 1917 would participate in the war in the armed forces with stars and stripes.

[7]Cfr. Francis L. Broderick, *Right Reverend New Dealer: John A. Ryan* (New York: Macmillan, 1963); Patrick W. Gearty, *The Economic Thought of Monsignor John A. Ryan* (Washington, DC: Catholic University of America Press, 1952); and Aaron I. Abell,

As we shall see in a moment, the analysis of the US Bishops' pastoral letters on economic justice, as well as the political trajectories of some of the most influential figures of American Catholicism, shows that during the Great Depression the US Catholic Church often displayed an interventionist and critical attitude towards the 'errors and distortions' of American 'economic system', promoting their distinctive version of 'moralization of Capitalism'.

John A. Ryan and the 1919 'Bishops' Program for Social Reconstruction'

The analysis of the US Bishops reaction to the First World War, should be based on the study of the thought and action of John Augustin Ryan—the Director of the Social Action Department of the National Catholic Welfare Conference and one the most important exponent of the Catholic social thought in the United States, who was later to become a great supporter of FDR and to play a fundamental role in the New Deal. Both his publications and concrete action in defending the American workers must be connected to the official pronouncements of the US Bishops (which constantly produced documents and pastoral letters concerning the socio-economic field), and were deeply based on the points made by Ryan.

The *Bishops' Program for Social Reconstruction* (February 1919) is one of the first official documents by the US Bishops focused on the social question and contains the position of the American hierarchy on the issues connected to the reorganization of the Country after one year from the end of First World War: Social justice is identified as the main concept on which the possible and desirable pacification among the different parts of the society could be based. Ryan's thought and action was mostly focused—in the context of a more general discourse that aimed at analysing the whole set of problems linked to the employment—on the struggle for minimum wage[8] and for child labour

---

'Monsignor John A. Ryan: An Historical Appreciation', *The Review of Politics* 8, no. 1 (1946): 128–134.

[8] On this specific issue is clear the influence of the thought of Liberatore on Ryan's ideas. In his 'Principi di economia politica' (1889) Liberatore wrote about minimum wage as commitment of primary importance for governments.

regulation[9]: Ryan's involvement in the battle for the minimum wage goes back to its strong support for the proposals and concrete action of the National Consumers' League, in 1910, which first emphasized the need to work towards the enactment of the Law on Minimum Wage. Ryan was one of the members of the committee formed for the purpose of drawing up the bill: its active engagement in favour of the minimum wage was of such extent that the request of a law on minimum wage was often dubbed as the battle for the Living Wage (referring to the book by Ryan, who was identified as the real creator of the bill). The first State to adopt the minimum wage law was Massachusetts, in 1912. In 1913 it was the turn of another eight countries: Utah. Oregon, Washington, Minnesota, Nebraska; Wisconsin, California and Colorado. Two years later, Arkansas and Kansas adopted the law on the minimum wage, and in 1917 the example was followed by Arizona. In 1918, the legislation on the minimum wage was adopted in Texas and North Dakota. The law concerned only female and child labour, did not apply to the adult male employees, but at least protected the rights of those (women and children) who represented the weakest component of the workers and was traditionally unassisted. Ryan had managed to approve, in Minnesota (his homeland) the guarantee of a much higher salary than that which was usually perceived by women and minors. In 1923 the minimum wage laws were, however, declared unconstitutional by the Supreme Court (following the 'Atkins Decision' of the same year). The reason behind such a decision related to an interpretation of the Constitution, and in particular of the 5th amendment, which defined the 'freedom of contract' as a fundamental freedom. The imposition by law of a minimum wage was judged as a violation of the 'freedom of contract' and this argument, in its final outcome, would have led to the unconstitutionality of the minimum wage. Ryan had been one of the main protagonists of a battle of a very important symbolic significance for those who were committed to the improvement of living conditions of US workers: for he had fought against attempts to declare the law unconstitutional as early as 1913, the year in which began the long series of interventions by the Supreme Court Against the Minimum Wage. Following the judgement of 1923 Ryan was very critical of the Supreme Court.

[9] On the US Catholic Church and Child Labor see Vincent A. McQuade, *The American Catholic Attitude on Child Labor Since 1891* (Washington, DC: The Catholic University of America, 1938).

The judgement in fact seemed to arbitrarily interpret the constitutional text, which is nowhere explicitly in contrast with the idea of the establishment of a minimum wage by law.

Ryan's ideas influenced the large part of the US Catholic Hierarchy, which promoted a self organization through the foundation (at the end of WWI) of the National Catholic Welfare Council, the predecessor of the United States Conference of Catholic Bishops: the organization updated and expanded the competences of the National Catholic War Council, created previously during the war period. One of the most direct influences on the work of John Ryan was the thought of Matteo Liberatore, one of the authors of the *Rerum Novarum*: He belongs, next to Giuseppe Toniolo and Sturzo, to those Catholic scholars who, at the turn of the nineteenth and twentieth century, 'supported the State presence in economic activities as an active role in reducing the class conflict, the sufferings of the workers, the arrogance of the landowners, and so on'.[10] Ryan's approach to the study of the socio-economic issues aimed at combining ethical and religious assumptions of Catholic social doctrine and Pontifical documents with economics knowledge. Ryan was particularly inspired by these Sects. (44–45) of the RN:

> To labor is to exert oneself for the sake of procuring what is necessary for the various purposes of life, and chief of all for self preservation. "In the sweat of thy face thou shalt eat bread" (33). Hence, a man's labor necessarily bears two notes or characters. First of all, it is personal, inasmuch as the force which acts is bound up with the personality and is the exclusive property of him who acts, and, further, was given to him for his advantage. Secondly, man's labor is *necessary;* for without the result of labor a man cannot live, and self-preservation is a law of nature, which it is wrong

---

[10] See Piero Barucci, 'I cattolici e il mercato', *Studi e note di economia* 3 (1998): 18. In particular, as noted by Barucci (p. 20) in the works of Liberatore (*Principii di economia politica*, Trattato, Roma, 1889) and Luigi Sturzo (Note e Appunti di Economia sociale del Sac. Dott. Luigi Sturzo, prof. nel Seminario Vescovile di Caltagirone, 1900, in L. Sturzo, La battaglia meridonalista, a cura di G. De Rosa, Laterza, Bari (1979): 195–242) is not fully deployed the organicistic conception of society and voluntarist conception of the economy of Toniolo. Liberatore with a fierce criticism of the influence exerted on the economic science by modern liberalism reiterates the necessary subordination of the economy to politics and morals, and affirm the need for the public power action to defend the weak and manage the strong; however, if some state intervention in economic facts is needed, one can find also severe criticism of Socialism by the Jesuit, as well as a clear defence of private property.

to disobey. Now, were we to consider labor merely in so far as it is personal, doubtless it would be within the workman's right to accept any rate of wages whatsoever; for in the same way as he is free to work or not, so is he free to accept a small wage or even none at all. But our conclusion must be very different if, together with the personal element in a man's work, we consider the fact that work is also necessary for him to live: these two aspects of his work are separable in thought, but not in reality. The preservation of life is the bounden duty of one and all, and to be wanting therein is a crime. It necessarily follows that each one has a natural right to procure what is required in order to live, and the poor can procure that in no other way than by what they can earn through their work. Let the working man and the employer make free agreements, and in particular let them agree freely as to the wages; nevertheless, there underlies a dictate of natural justice more imperious and ancient than any bargain between man and man, namely, that wages ought not to be insufficient to support a frugal and well-behaved wage-earner. If through necessity or fear of a worse evil the workman accept harder conditions because an employer or contractor will afford him no better, he is made the victim of force and injustice. In these and similar questions, however - such as, for example, the hours of labor in different trades, the sanitary precautions to be observed in factories and workshops, etc. - in order to supersede undue interference on the part of the State, especially as circumstances, times, and localities differ so widely, it is advisable that recourse be had to societies or boards such as We shall mention presently, or to some other mode of safeguarding the interests of the wage-earners; the State being appealed to, should circumstances require, for its sanction and protection.[11]

In two of his most relevant works—*A living Wage* (1906) and *Distributive Justice* (1916)[12]—Ryan expressed his opinion on the minimum wage and on the proposal for a family living wage, writing that the minimum wage had to become a law. Behind all his work on the social question there was the idea that the State had to play a main role in the

---

[11] For a detailed account of the impact of the Rerum Novarum in the United States see Aaron I. Abell, 'The Reception of Leo XIII's Labor Enclyclica in America, 1891–1919', *The Review of Politics* 7, no. 4 (1945): 464–495; On the Rerum Novarum see, among others Giovanni Antonazzi and Gabriele De Rosa, ed., *L'Enciclica Rerum Novarum e il suo tempo* (Rome: Ediz. di Storia e Letteratura, 1991).

[12] John A. Ryan, *A Living Wage: Its Ethical and Economic Aspects* (New York: Macmillan, 1906); John A. Ryan, *Distributive Justice: The Right and Wrong of Our Present Distribution of Wealth* (New York: Macmillan, 1916).

regulation of the socio-economic issues: the latter assumption was high-lighted in the *Bishops' Program for Social reconstruction.*

US Church thus proposed its own model for the reconstruction of the post-war societies in the same years of the delivering of President Woodrow Wilson's 'Fourteen Points'. The Bishops stressed the importance of social justice as a primary condition for a peaceful future also underlying that no one should be excluded from the right for dignified living condition. The *Bishops' Program* caused negative reactions among the entrepreneurs: the Bishops were accused of being misled by the socialist thought so that they wrote a document full of destabilizing contents that, once applied, could have undermined the US institutions.[13] The *Program* clearly shows Ryan's attempt at giving to the political-economic autonomy from analysis than the religious issue. The most programmatic contents of the document could be easily ascribed to a lay organization. The references to the Catholic doctrine are rare and can be found only in the introduction and in the final section of the text. A few months after the first edition of the document, American Bishops expressed with a Pastoral Letter (September 1919) a much more moderate line if compared with some of the statements contained in the previous version of the document. While inside the *Bishops' Program* published in February 1919 one could read that 'the majority of workers must not remain mere wage earners but somehow become owners, or at least in part, of the instruments of production',[14] the September version lacked any reference to the opportunity for the workers to have granted, beside the minimum wage, the notion of taking part in owning those same instruments of production. The February *Program* strongly supported the idea of starting social security policies and presented a list of issues where action was needed, such as social insurances for illness, injury, old age, unemployment; a public housing project; the creation of a National Agency for employment; price control measures; equal pay for

[13] Particularly relevant in this respect was the position expressed by the president of the National Association of Manufactures which wrote that the Program of the bishops could be said to be a 'Socialist propaganda document'.

[14] Pastoral Letter of the Archbishops and Bishops of the United States, September 26, 1919. SRSS AAEESS = Segreteria di Stato, Sezione per i Rapporti con gli Stati, Archivio Storico, Archivio della Sacra Congregazione per gli Affari Ecclesiastici Straordinari, Affari Ecclesiastici Straordinari (AAEESS), America, IV, P.O. 172, fasc.14–18, fasc.17.

women; banning child labour. Those proposals and issues seemed much less forthright and had no such emphasis.

This partial shift towards much moderate behaviour would have been constitutive of the future 'Red scare', in a clime of general fear for a diffusion of socialism in the United States. The real Red hunt that lasted during all the Twenties had an impact on the Catholic Church and on Ryan: just as the majority of the US Catholic hierarchy, he thus became more and more moderate on a political level. This is especially evident if compared with some publications such as *Bolshevism in Russia and America*[15] by Reverend Raymond A. McGowan, written for the Social Action Department of the National Catholic Welfare Council at the beginning of the Twenties. In the pamphlet one could read, in 1920, that:

> Capitalism is a newcomer on the stage of the world and late indeed in the United States. Capitalism is a kind of society in which the predominant means of production and distribution are owned and controlled by a comparatively small part of the people, while the propertyless section, which is very large, is forced by the hard facts of life to work for a livelihood on other people's property for other people's primary advantage and profit. So long as capitalism last we are not safe from Revolution.

AFTER THE WALL STREET CRASH

Unemployment was the most negative consequence of the Wall Street Crash: it would soar between 1929 and 1933 until it impacted on one-third of the American population.[16]

The political debacle of Al Smith (the first Catholic candidate running for US Presidency in 1928) caused great frustration among the Catholics: but, at the dawn of the Thirties they were able to go over that political failure and disillusion restarting from what represented, during the previous two decades, the strongest expression of the Catholic experience in the United States. An evaluation of the mid-late 1910s and of the early 1920s highlights the developing of the Catholic thought on

---

[15] Raymond A. McGowan, *Bolshevism in Russia and America* (New York: Paulist Press, 1920).

[16] See Richard Lowitt and Maurine Beasley, *One Third of a Nation* (Urbana: University of Illinois, 1981).

the socio-economic issues as the real positive achievement from which was worth trying to start again taking a new political inspiration, new ideas and new energy. US Catholics could 'speak' again through public statements on the possible resolution of the Crisis. The Catholics were then ready to become protagonist, and not only passive observers, of the political and social changes that were taking place in the United States, especially during the first F. D. Roosevelt Administration.[17]

The growth of unemployment was one of the most tragic results of the Crisis and the US Bishops decided to devote to that issue their first public statement on social question after the *Program* and the Pastoral letter on 1919. On November 12, 1930, through the *Statement by the bishops of the the Administrative Committee of the NCWC on Unemployment*[18] (written by the Archbishop of San Francisco Edward J. Hanna), the US Bishops expressed themselves on the dramatic situation of the unemployed and underlined the need for a strongest State involvement in the economy as a possible solution for the most catastrophic consequence of the Crisis. The main references of the 1930 *Statement on unemployment* references were the *Rerum Novarum* and the 1919 *Bishops' Program* and Pastoral Letter. The *fil rouge* which tied the *Statement* of 1930 and the *Program* of 1919 was evident and the restoration of that original document (almost shelved and forgotten during the Twenties) coincided with the re-evaluation of thought and action of John A. Ryan, the 'real author' of the 1919 *Program*. In 1930 the Bishops made clear that it would have been better if the politicians, the US society and Catholic world had paid attention to the passage which in 1919 stated that no peace would have been achieved without social justice.

In the *Statement* of 1930, the Bishops underlined that unemployment was nothing new to the United States, because it represented a problematic issue that cyclically came back in its economic history, thus

---

[17] See Francis J. Lally, *The Catholic Church in a Changing America* (Boston: Brown and Company, 1962).

[18] Statement by the bishops of the Administrative Committees of the NCWC on Unemployment, November 12, 1930, in Raphael Huber, *Our Bishops Speak: National Pastorals and Annual Statements of the Hierarchy of the United States* (Resolutions of Episcopal Committees and Communications of the Administrative Board of the National Catholic Welfare Conference, Milwaukee, Wisconsin, 1919–1951: The Bruce Publishing Company, 1952).

representing a constant menace for the socio-economic equilibrium of the Country. It was the 'American system' what the US Bishops were criticizing and an attack particularly towards the economic section of the system indicated such a Crisis and failure was caused by the abandoning of the Christian principles. Other connections to the 1919 *Program* can be read in the references to Ryan's quotes on the urgency for a humanistic and Christian work ethic against a purely pagan and commercial one. And a long-lasting Social justice depended on passing the sole charitable behaviour in favour of a concrete policy of support and aims for the unemployed:

> Unemployment is not due to a lack on intelligence nor any more to ignorance. It is due to a lack of good will. It is due to a neglect of Christ [...] Our Country needs, now and permanently, such a change of heart or will, intelligently and with determination, to organize and distribute our work and wealth that no one need lack for any long time the security of being able to earn an adequate living for himself and for those dependent upon him [...] More than temporary alms is necessary. Justice should be done. This unemployment returning again to plague us after so many repetitions during the century past is a sign of deep failure in our country [...] Both in its cause and in the inprint it leaves upon those who inflict it, those who permit it, and those who are its victims, it is one of the great moral tragedies of our time.

One year after the *Statement on Unemployment* the US Bishops published the *Statement on the Economic Crisis*[19] (November 12, 1931) which stressed some of the contents of the previous document, such as the need for a minimum wage and a material support for all: "Provide not only spiritual sustenance but 'the material food' essential to life and well-being of the individual, of the family, of all society". The document contained a proposal for State assistance in favour of those who lost their job. The *Statement on the Economic Crisis* was published a few month after the promulgation of the first Pius XI Social Encyclical *Quadragesimo Anno* (May 15, 1931): the references to the contents of the papal document are evident, especially the passages on the need for more State involvement in the Economy and the importance of

---

[19] Statement of the Hierarchy of the United States on the Economic Crisis, November 12, 1931, in R. Huber, *Our Bishops Speak.*

a minimum wage for workers.[20] The impact of the *Quadragesimo Anno* in the United States was even stronger than the one had by the *Rerum Novarum*. Bishop Thomas J. Shahan, the former rector of the Catholic University of America said that the encyclical represented a 'real appreciation' for John Ryan ideas and work. We think that it can be interesting reporting what he wrote about the *Quadragesimo Anno*:

> The Encyclical on Reconstructing the Social Order is not vague, remote, or academic. It realistically portrays both the evils of capitalism and the evils lurking in extreme proposals of reform. It combines a clear statement of principles with a detailed presentation of practical proposals. It faces all the facts and deals with the world of today in language which the world understands. It uses economic terminology when the subject under discussion is economic and it uses the language of ethics when moral questions are under consideration. No one can say that Pope Pius does not understand existing social and economic conditions or shrinks from proposing adequate remedies. "The Holy Father has given the world the most comprehensive, specific and adequate program of social reconstruction that we possess. Other programs may have been more detailed concerning one or other part of the problem, but none of them has been at once so fundamental, so well balanced, and so comprehensive.[21]

THE 'STATEMENT ON THE PRESENT CRISIS'

On June 1, 1933, the US Bishops published their first official document regarding the socio-economic situation in America after the promulgation of the *Quadragesimo Anno* and after the election of the new President Franklin Delano Roosevelt. The *Statement on the Present Crisis*[22] was strictly connected to the pronouncements of 1930 and 1931. Inside the document once again is stressed the tragedy of the post-war years and the Crisis is interpreted in the context of 'abandoning Jesus' and the subsequent ethical decline of the society. The core of

---

[20] See Francis L. Broderick, 'The Encyclicals and Social Action: Is John A. Ryan Typical?', *The Catholic Historical Review* 55, no. 1 (1963): 1–6.

[21] John A. Ryan, 'The New Things in the New Encyclical', *Ecclesiastical Review* 85 (1931): 13–14.

[22] A Statement on the Present Crisis, Administrative Committee of the NCWC, June 1, 1933, SVA, AAEESS, America, IV, P.O. 230, Fasc.54.

the human life is represented by Social justice and human dignity and the bishops underlined that there was a need to do something important about filling the socio-economic gap between employers and employees:

> Social justice, working in behalf of the common good, requires that the masses not possessing property rise to a degree of ownership. The chasm between owners- the relatively few -and non owners - the vast majority, must be bridged by a distribution of ownership through thrift and a real sharing of profits, not merely a profit sharing in the name.

The document wishes for harmony between capital and labour and promotes the strengthening of the trade unions. It pays attention to both the skilled and unskilled workers (the latters still represented the majority of US Catholic employees) and suggests to vote for those who are promoting great reforms in the socio-economic field: F.D.R. is never mentioned but the reference to the President and his policies is evident:

> In our form of government the obligation of bringing about a reform of the social order rests upon citizens, who by their votes give a mandate to legislators and executives. This makes evident a civic duty, and for us Catholics is also religious one governed by the virtue of piety, that is, a certain filial piety toward our country, which impels us to promote the reform of the social order by voting the competent and conscientious men of high moral principles.

On June 14, 1933, the Apostolic Delegate Amleto Giovanni Cicognani wrote a letter to the Archbishop of San Francisco (also the President of the Administrative Committee of the NCWC) and praised the *Statement on the Present Crisis* and the work of the US Catholic Bishops.[23] Two days later, on June 16, Cicognani wrote to the Secretary of State

---

[23] SRSS AAEES, America, IV, P.O. 230, Fasc.54 The letter states: 'May the statement find its way into every home and be the subject of discussion in every family'. Through sermons, conferences, instructions and lectures especially can the teaching of the Church on the Social Question be brought to the attention of our Catholic people so that they may be thoroughly acquainted with it and thus be able to explain the position of the Church to those not of our faith [...] This is but complying with the wish of the Holy Father. It will make practical His Holiness 'plan of Catholic Action. I shall be pleased to send a copy of the bishop's statement to our Holy Father'.

Eugenio Pacelli and underlined the influence of the *Quadragesimo Anno* on the document.[24]

Domenico Tardini, the Undersecretary in the Congregation for Extraordinary Affairs, on July 12 sent a letter to Cicognani in order to write him that Pius XI, once informed about the *Statement*, lauded the NCWC and the attempt of US Bishops at spreading the Catholic social doctrine and its teachings among the People of the United States.[25]

CONCLUSION

In the framework of Pius XI's pontificate arose the dialogue that was then developed between the Holy See and the United States. A fundamental role in this dialogue was played by Achille Ratti's Catholic Social Doctrine, which, also via the mediation of the American Catholic Social Thought (and especially of Mgr. John A. Ryan's thought and NCWC activities), came to confront with New Deal politics. The study of the economic debate that, both in United States and the Vatican, followed the Great Depression permits to understand one of the reasons of the rapprochement between Washington and St. Peter that took place during Franklin Delano Roosevelt's Administrations in the Thirties.

The analysis of the developments of the American Catholic Social thought and action during the first thirty years of the twentieth century is of pivotal importance in order to understand the attitude and facets of the American Catholicism before the great transformations—starting from shifting the focus of its efforts to the anticommunist action—which would affect the US Catholic Church after the breakout of the Spanish Civil War and the evolution of the Mexican political and social situation, and which shaped the role played by both the American Catholic Hierarchy and Laity during the Truman Years and the early Cold War period.

---

[24] SRSS AAEESS, America, IV, P.O. 230, Fasc.54 The letter states: 'Ho letto con attenzione lo "Statement" e l'ho trovato sostanzialmente modellato sulle recenti Encicliche del Santo Padre. Anche qui in America fortunatamente si va abbastanza consolidando tra gli acattolici, specie intellettuali, l'idea che la Chiesa Cattolica è la sola istituzione, la quale possiede in sé i principi per la soluzione della crisi sociale. Questo si legge spesso, si sente proclamato in pubblici discorsi ed in private conversazioni: e non è che il risultato delle Encicliche, particolarmente della "Quadragesimo Anno"'.

[25] SRSS AAEESS, America, IV, P.O. 230, Fasc.54.

By focusing on what the Catholic Social teaching has meant in the United States, it is possible to highlight the original contributions to the theoretical propositions and the concrete US institutional choices and politics elaborated by some of the main protagonists of the American Catholicism. 1917, the year of the entry into the WWI of the United States brought with itself, among other things, the birth of the National Catholic War Council which would become the National Catholic Welfare Council in 1919. 1929 represents a momentous turning point in the long post-war period: the explosion of the Great Crisis coincided with the end of the Red Scare of the 1920s, which had also affected some of the protagonists of Social Catholicism. The latter would initiate a dialogue with the institutions only beginning with the FDR years, when the nature of the citizenship of the Catholics started to assume a consistency that was not just formal. It was during the Great War, and then mostly during the Rooseveltian Administration throughout the Thirties, that the Americanization of immigrants underwent a strong acceleration producing a tendency to inclusion that from the formal dimension would have evolved until arriving, starting from the Kennedy age, to the recognition of civil rights for all the components of American society, even if this was not accompanied by a real overcoming of economic and social inequalities.

CHAPTER 11

The Discourse Against 'Shameful Profiteering' in Greece 1914–1925: Notions of Exploitation, Anticapitalist Morality and the Concept of Moral Economy

Nikos Potamianos

In this paper I'll attempt to elaborate on the concept of moral economy and test its relevance to a discourse with strong elements of anticapitalist morality. E. P. Thompson spoke of the moral economy of the English crowd in the eighteenth century as a set of precapitalist views about what constituted a 'fair price' and fair operation of the market that informed the food riots in this transitional period.[1] Since its first appearance in 1971, the concept has been much used in relation to a great variety of situations, views and practices. In line with Thompson's

---

[1] E. P. Thompson, 'The Moral Economy of the English Crowd in the Eighteenth Century', *Past & Present* 50 (1971): 76–136.

N. Potamianos (✉)
Institute for Mediterranean Studies—Foundation
for Research and Technology-Hellas, Rethymno, Greece

© The Author(s) 2019
S. Berger and A. Przyrembel (eds.), *Moralizing Capitalism*,
Palgrave Studies in the History of Social Movements,
https://doi.org/10.1007/978-3-030-20565-2_11

later intervention,[2] I'll argue that we should keep the concept of moral economy bounded within a specific phase of capitalist development, when the legacy of older regulations of the market still persisted and provided a kind of alternative economics to liberalism and the free market. Accordingly, I offer a different interpretation of the discourse against 'shameful profiteering' in early twentieth-century Greece, associating it not so much with defending a specific moral regime as with the diffusion of socialist ideas and the concept of exploitation in the age of rising statism. I finally propose, instead of adopting a loose usage of the concept of moral economy that limits its analytical power, to study more thoroughly the moral dimension of the anticapitalist discourse of popular movements, to reconceptualize that dimension and to place it within the framework of the struggle for hegemony.

PROFITEERING AND ITS PERSECUTION IN GREECE IN THE 1910S

The 1910s and early 1920s in Greece were years of war, intense political and class conflict, accelerated social and political transformation—including the concentration of capital and the growth of state intervention in various areas of the economy and society—unprecedented inflation and the rise of the labour movement. During this eventful period a public discourse against 'shameful profiteering' (*aischrokerdeia*) emerged and soon became the dominant explanation for the hardship experienced by Greek people.

The extremely high inflation (caused by both the printing of money and the shortage of goods) led to significant reductions in real wages. At the same time, the disruption of international commerce during the First World War particularly affected countries such as Greece, which had abandoned self-sufficiency and specialized in commercialized agricultural products instead of producing cereals. Shortages of essential goods and high prices were broadly attributed to the profiteering practices of the shopkeepers (as well as of the larger merchants), who were accused of selling expensively what they had bought cheap, and of hiding food in order to sell it at a higher price in the future. Protests and popular mobilization against profiteering and high prices remained very common in Greece until at least 1925.

---

[2] E. P. Thompson, 'The Moral Economy Reviewed', in his *Customs in Common* (London: Merlin, 1991), 259–351.

Public policy was partly based on (or responded to) perceptions of this kind. State intervention in food provisioning, besides importation of cereals and requisition of crops, included price controls, rent controls and special legislation against 'shameful profit'. Harsh penalties were imposed on merchants who were selling essential goods at prices that 'led to too much profit'. Withholding food (in order to sell it at a higher price in the future) and its adulteration were also criminalized as shameful profiteering. This legislation developed gradually, under the pressure of circumstances and popular protests against rising prices; both political blocs that governed the country in these years introduced measures of this kind.[3]

Profiteers were also strongly condemned in most countries involved in the Great War, and various measures against profiteering were adopted (alongside price controls) in the countries of Western and Central Europe—which had always been the model for Greece.[4] What might be peculiar in the Greek case was the longevity of the anti-profiteering discourse and its centrality to the critique of capitalism and its values.

The main organized social force that mobilized against high prices was the labour movement. The Labour Centre of Athens had already begun protests in 1913, and in 1916 together with the Labour Centre of Piraeus attacked profiteering merchants and demanded 'extremely harsh measures' by the state against price rises and the withholding of essential goods, the fair distribution of such goods to consumers through state shops, and the creation of local Committees of Social Defence which would ensure 'just' setting of prices.[5] In the wave of workers'

---

[3] For all the above, see Nikos Potamianos, *Oi Noikokyraioi. Magazatores kai viotechnes stin Athina 1880–1925* [Shopkeepers and Master Artisans in Athens 1880–1925] (Heraklion: Crete University Press, 2015), 464–493.

[4] Richard Wall and Jay Winter, eds., *The Upheaval of War: Family, Work and Welfare in Europe 1914–1918* (Cambridge: Cambridge University Press, 1988), 197–220; Jay Winter and Jean-Louis Robert, eds., *Capital Cities at War: Paris, London, Berlin 1914–1919* (Cambridge: Cambridge University Press, 1997); and Stephen Broadberry and Mark Harrison, eds., *The Economics of World War I* (Cambridge: Cambridge University Press, 2005).

[5] *Idrytiki praxi systasis EKA. Praktika synedriaseon 1910–1914* [Founding Act of the Labour Centre of Athens. Proceedings of the Meetings 1910–1914] (Athens, 2004), 484, 490, 506, 517, 540, 548, 554–559, 571; *Patris* 5 January 1916; *Astir* 9 February 1916; and Dimitris Livieratos, *Megales ores tis ergatikis taxis* [Significant Moments of the Working-Class Movement] (Athens: Proskinio, 2006), 98, 101–102.

mobilizations from 1918 to 1923, strikes with wage demands were combined with resolutions and protests (or even riots, as in Volos in 1921) against 'shameful profits'. The measures proposed against high prices were reinforced with demands for confiscation of the goods that were in the merchants' warehouses and their sale at a fair price, seizure of the properties that were amassed during the war, or even capital punishment for the profiteers.[6] A recurrent theme in unions' resolutions was that 'the various groups of profiteers, large capitalists, ship-owners, large businessmen and merchants became rich by the blood and sweat of the working people' and that 'the shameful profit of the merchants' was responsible for the steep decline in workers' standard of living.[7]

These protests form an essential part of what has been interpreted as 'moral economy' informing the collective action of the Greek workers in the first decades of the twentieth century. It has been argued that the early labour movement in Greece developed its demands less with a focus on wages and working hours than with a concern for issues such as food prices and control of the labour process, criticizing the free market economy from the point of view of the customary regulations of markets and production.[8]

I've tried to show elsewhere why this framework is inappropriate for the interpretation of the anti-profiteering discourse.[9] I argued that we should follow E. P. Thompson and insist on using a narrow definition of the concept of moral economy; that is, to define it not only as a set of views behind the popular mobilization against the amoral operation of an economy that has been disembedded from society, but also as popular 'alternative economics' based specifically on the paternalist preindustrial

[6] Various resolutions can be found in the General Archives of the State, archive of the Prime Minister's political office 1917–1928, file 354; Greek Literature and History Archive (ELIA), archive of Dimitrios Gounaris, file 1; ELIA, archive of Panergatiko Kentro Athinas [Labour Centre of all the Workers of Athens]; and Dimitris Livieratos, *Koinonikoi Agones stin Ellada 1923–1927* [Social Struggles in Greece 1923–1927] (Athens: Enallaktikes Ekdoseis, 1985).

[7] *Patris* 11 July 1922; *Amyna* 9 June 1920.

[8] Kostas Fountanopoulos, *Ergasia kai ergatiko kinima sth Thessaloniki (1908–1936)* [Labour and the Labour Movement in Salonica (1908–1936)] (Athens: Nefeli, 2005); Antonis Liakos, 'Peri laikismou' [On Populism], *Ta Istorika* 10 (1989): 13–28.

[9] Nikos Potamianos, 'Moral Economy? Popular Demands and State Intervention in the Struggle over Anti-profiteering Laws in Greece 1914–1925', *Journal of social history* 48, no. 4 (2015): 803–815.

customary regulation of the market.[10] The Greek workers' mobilizations against high prices in the 1910s were not the product of a traditional culture, nor did they refer to Ancien Regime regulations. I argued that actually, instead of being backward-looking, the political idiom of shameful profit was very much attuned to its era, as its emergence was related to the rise of state intervention in the economy and the modern ideological trends that legitimized it, while the idiom was extensively used by social groups with indisputably modern values such as white-collar workers.

In this paper I will examine another aspect of the issue, adding into my analysis the correlation of the discourse against shameful profiteering with the introduction of new notions of exploitation, in the context of both the rise of the socialist movement and the decline of the popular standard of living in 1910s Greece. I will also address the issue of the food riots erupting all over Europe during and after the Great War: did moral economy make a comeback under the difficult circumstances of war and food shortage?

SHAMEFUL PROFITEERING AND THE NOTION OF EXPLOITATION: AN ALTERNATIVE INTERPRETATION

An important dimension of the anti-profiteering discourse was that it translated within a widespread idiom, understood by everybody, the concept of exploitation which the rising socialist ideas brought into the public sphere of the working class as well as into broader public discussion. The mechanism of its reception existed already: some earlier denunciations of the profiteering of the merchants that found their way to the surface of the public discourse indicate the existence of a 'hidden transcript' among workers and peasants as well as among members of the educated lower-middle class.[11]

---

[10] Thompson, 'The Moral Economy Reviewed'.

[11] *Espera* 24 January and 2 March 1859; *Kairoi* 24 February 1873; *Alitheia* 26 and 31 January 1874; *Efimeris ton syntechnion* 26 February and 10 March 1891; *Acropolis* 2 September 1905; *Esperini* 16 July 1907; *Salpinx* 1 February 1909; *Efimeris ton ergaton* 17 January and 17 December 1910. Of course distrust of shopkeepers wasn't peculiar to the Greeks: Alain Faure, 'The Grocery Trade in Nineteenth-Century Paris: A Fragmented Corporation', in *Shopkeepers and Master Artisans in Nineteenth-Century Europe*, ed. Geoffrey Crossick and Heinz-Gerhard Haupt (London and New York: Methuen, 1984), 155–174; Tom Ericsson, 'Cults, Myths and the Swedish Petite Bourgeoisie

Previously, the dominant metaphor in the discourse of the labour unions and their supporters was enslavement.[12] 'We are treated like slaves' by our employers, protested the shoemakers in 1882, while in 1908 it was common to refer to workers in sweated trades as 'white slaves'.[13] In a masquerade performed in the Athens carnival parade in 1909, the 'workers in quest of bread' were not only dirty and hungry but also bound so that they couldn't escape.[14] The opposite of slavery was freedom: in 1910 the appeal of cigarette-makers for solidarity with their strike was addressed to 'liberal and free citizens', and the *Journal of the Workers* that was published by some printers often mentioned the 'liberal principles' of individuals, organizations and politicians who supported workers' demands or the establishment of labour legislation.[15]

The description of the workers' situation as slavery and the clamour for freedom formed part of an ideological complex that was by and large liberal; however, this was not the whole story. Particularly in 1908–1910 the idiom of slavery was articulated with a 'jacobin' discourse: we adopt here the term introduced by Ernesto Laclau for a specific version of populism in which the populist discourse focuses almost exclusively on the state and political relations, and identifies as the main opponent a political oligarchy that was created and reproduced around the state.[16] Liberal or 'jacobin', the discourse of workers' protest was structured to a great

1870–1914', *European History Quarterly* 23, no. 2 (1993): 237–239. For the notion of the 'hidden transcript', see James C. Scott, *Domination and the Arts of Resistance: Hidden Transcripts* (New Haven, CT: Yale University Press, 1990).

[12] For the use of the language of 'slavery' and 'tyranny' in nineteenth-century England see the comments of Robert Gray, 'The Deconstruction of the English Working Class', *Social History* 11, no. 3 (1986): 363–373, 371–373; and idem, *The Factory Question and Industrial England 1830–1860* (Cambridge: Cambridge University Press, 1996), 37–47.

[13] *Neai Ideai* 22 November 1882; *Acropolis* 28 September–22 December 1908; see also *Acropolis* 28 December 1907 and 31 January 1909, *Pyrros* 25 February 1909.

[14] *Acropolis* 10 February 1909.

[15] *Efimeris ton ergaton* 27 May 1910 (cigarette makers); 17 January, 14 and 16 May 1910; see also 21 July 1910 (resolution of Athens Labour Centre).

[16] Nikos Potamianos, 'Ti einai o laikismos? Aristeroi kai dexioi rizospastes sta chronia tou kinimatos sto Goudi' [What Is Populism? Left-Wing and Right-Wing Radicals in the Years of the Goudi Coup], in idem, *Evgeni pachiderma kai paschontes ergates. Epikaires istories apo tis arhes tou eikostou aiona* [Noble Pachyderms and Suffering Workers. Topical Histories from the Beginnings of the Twentieth Century] (Athens: Asini, 2016), 37–58.

extent by political metaphors that emphasized the oppression experienced by workers, even when their demands focused on wages.[17]

Thus, the prevalence of the discourse against shameful profiteering after 1914 can also be described as the eventual ascendancy of representations of social hierarchy that referred to the economic sphere to a larger extent than before. In this sense it constituted a significant part of the transition of popular radicalism from the liberal democratic to the socialist paradigm. This process of transition can be detected in the ever more frequent experiments in combining political and economic language, such as when the Labour Centre of Athens, in the resolution passed at its demonstration against the rent rises in 1914, asked government to 'protect the labouring people from further economic slavery and exploitation'.[18] Political and economic domination were also connected in 1910 in unions' resolutions and in the articles published in *Efimeris ton Ergaton*,[19] but eventually the newspaper put the emphasis on economic exploitation.

The references to enslavement didn't disappear in the following years; after all, the denunciation of 'wage slavery' also belonged within the rhetorical repertoire of the socialist discourse. However, it seems that they became less frequent—while the references to profiteering boomed.

Certainly, the references to the exploitation of the workers by their employers, that is to the 'unfair enrichment' of employers from 'the sweat of other people', were not entirely absent from the period before

---

[17] Perhaps this was a common characteristic in democratic pre-socialist popular radicalism; for a classical analysis of Chartism that stresses these aspects of its discourse see Gareth Stedman Jones, *Languages of Class: Studies in English Working Class History 1832–1982* (Cambridge: Cambridge University Press, 1983).

[18] Kostas Baroutas, *H kravgi ton Ellinon, 1821–1989* [The Shouting of the Greeks, 1821–1989] (Athens: Savvalas, 1992), 160. 'Economic enslavement' was an expression used as well by Minister for National Economy Andreas Mihalakopoulos in the most leftist speech he made in his political career, when discussing in parliament the law about the working hours of shop assistants: *Efimeris ton syzitiseon tis voulis* [Government Gazette] period 19΄, session B΄, meeting 68, 7 May 1914, 1518.

[19] Resolution of the presidents of labour unions of Athens in 18 June 1910 and announcement of the striking engineers of mercantile marine in April 1910: Stefanos Dragoumis archive (in Gennadeion), files 71.2 and 71.1; *Efimeris ton ergaton* 3 and 17 January, 16 March, 2 May and 25 August 1910. See also *Astrapi* 31 July and 11 August 1910 for a similar combination of economy and politics under the label of slavery in the discourse of a conservative revolutionary (A. Doufas).

the 1910s.[20] They coexisted with notions of exploitation conceived as taking profit from various opportunities and deceiving people.[21] Moreover, and not unexpectedly for a society of small proprietors, even in orthodox socialist environments there was a strong notion of exploitation according to which surplus was appropriated, not only during the production process but also in the market, by a merchant who could buy and sell at the price he wished, at the expense of both consumer and small producer.[22] This kind of conceptualization of exploitation obviously boomed in the 1910s, when attacks abounded on 'the powerful classes who exploit people in the most dreadful way'[23] as well as on the more humble 'small neighbourhood grocers who drink the blood of the poor'.[24]

The references to exploitation that were close to the notion of the appropriation of surplus value also increased rapidly in the 1910s together with the proliferation of the labour unions and mobilization,[25]

[20] *Akropolis* 28 October 1904 (on the strike of the shoemakers of Athens) and *Neon Asty* 28 October 1904 (president of their union). See also the letter of the shoemakers' union to the employers in *Neon Asty* 10 January 1905, and the letter of a printer in the radical *Neai Ideai* 29 September 1882.

[21] According to *Laos* 17 November 1908, the newspaper published by Spyros Theodoropoulos, the lawyer who founded Athens Labour Centre in 1910, 'people lack protection' and 'are exploited by cunning persons' such as selfish politicians. See also the article of the spokesman of the Military League in January 1910 about the exploitation of the people by public servants and officials: Aristeidis Kyriakos, *I Nea Ellas* [The New Greece] (Athens, 1910), 424–428. A version that combines both conceptions of exploitation was offered by the union of army boot makers when they attacked the middlemen who exploited their labour as well as the state: *Nea Ellas* 23 November 1913.

[22] A labour newspaper under the influence of a socialist group, *Efimeris ton Syntechnion* 3 February 1891, assumed that printers' and journalists' labour was exploited by the capitalist distributors of the newspapers. In 1892, when the first socialist group of Athens discussed who would have the right to become a member, objections had been expressed to the proposal to exclude only the big landowners, the managers and those who exploited the labour of workers: 'but the small merchant is an exploiter too'. Finally they decided that shopkeepers would be allowed to become members: Kostis Karpozilos, 'Stavros Kallergis: "vios eleftheros viotikon frontidon"', in *Arheio Stavrou Kallergi* [Archive of Stavros Kallergis], ed. idem (Athens: Library of Benaki Museum, 2013), 19–20.

[23] *Foni ton Syntechnion* 7 and 28 April 1916.

[24] Adamantiou Kazakopoulou, *Skepseis 1913–1948* [Insights] (Athens: Mnemon, 1998), 62–63 (diary of a judge, 1914).

[25] For instance, see *Efimeris ton ergaton* 16 May 1910 (Union of the cigarette makers); *Patris* 28 March 1919 (Union of barbers).

and with the maturation of the socialist movement that led to the foundation of the Socialist Workers Party of Greece in 1918; in the same year the first national confederation of labour unions was founded.[26] The timing of these developments contributed both to the diffusion of the concept of exploitation and to its association with 'shameful profiteering'. In Greece the emergence of the labour movement and socialist groups coincided with the First World War, during which the social discontent on the European home fronts was expressed in ways that included attacks on profiteers who sought to increase their profits instead of participating in the national effort.[27] The sudden political legitimization, in the name of the nation and the interests of the people, of the attack on the greed of businessmen created favourable conditions for the 'idiom of shameful profiteering' to become the hegemonic interpretation of skyrocketing prices and growing poverty.

Such an interpretation was urgently needed, since the 'decade of wars' from 1912 to 1922 was a watershed as regards, among other things, the decline in the standard of living. This deterioration was not expressed only in terms of averages, as a result of the integration into the Greek state after 1912 of areas which were poorer than 'Old Greece' and whose poor would become the new Greece's poorest. There were also the hardships experienced by working and agricultural households due to the continuous wars and army mobilizations until 1923; the abrupt increase of the migration of peasants to the big cities led to the growth both of proletariat and 'underclass'.[28] Last but not least, the decline in the standard of living of the working class began in the 1910s, as the huge

---

[26] For the socialist/communist party, see Alexandros Dagas, 'Kommounistiko Komma Ellados, Elliniko tmima tis kommounistikis diethnous' [Communist Party of Greece, Greek Section of the Communist International], in *Istoria tis Elladas tou 20ou aiona* [History of Greece in the Twentieth Century], ed. Christos Hadjiiossif (Athens: Vivliorama, 2002), v.B2, 155–201.

[27] Jean-Louis Robert, 'The Image of the Profiteer', in *Capital Cities at War: Paris, London, Berlin 1914–1919*, ed. Jay Winter and Jean-Louis Robert (Cambridge: Cambridge University Press, 1997), 104–132; Belinda Davis, *Home Fires Burning: Goods, Politics and Everyday Life in World War I Berlin* (Chapel Hill and London: University of North Carolina Press, 2000), 71–75, 80–81, etc.

[28] This growth is usually attributed exclusively to the arrival of the refugees from Asia Minor after the defeat by the Turks in 1922, but Aleka Karadimou-Gerolympou, 'Poleis kai ypaithros' [Cities and Countryside], in *Istoria tis Elladas*, ed. Hadjiiossif, v.B1, 64–65, has shown that this is not correct.

inflation of the 1910s and 1920s reduced real wages dramatically.[29] This was in sharp contrast to the relative prosperity experienced by the peasants, workers and petty bourgeois of the old Greece during the nineteenth century, when their living conditions had improved slowly but steadily.

The idiom of shameful profiteering was not the only available interpretation of high prices. Actually, it replaced an earlier interpretation that since the 1870s had stressed the role of political decisions: the 'idiom of taxes' attributed the limited buying power of the popular classes to the high indirect taxes and duties that burdened the price of goods. However, this liberal–radical complex of interpretation and political objectives could not work any more: it could not explain the huge inflation in the 1910s, particularly since indirect taxes had not increased. Moreover, the idiom of shameful profiteering prevailed because it was attuned to international political and intellectual trends (attacks against profiteering during the Great War, the rise of statism). Finally, the rise of the discourse against profiteering reinforced the emerging socialist politics, and vice versa.

It was, thus, under these circumstances that the tendency of merchants (and generally of businessmen) towards profiteering whenever they had the opportunity became accepted as common sense. The discourse against shameful profiteering was integrated into the stock of commonsensical beliefs of Greek society, and it articulated popular demands in ways that legitimized them as self-evident. For instance, during strikes the unions would use the discourse of profiteering against the employers, accusing them of paying low wages because they sought too much profit from workers' labour.[30] The power of the idiom derived partly from the fact that it was not one-dimensional, and it could be used for a great range of objectives. It could also be applied to quite different political projects, provided they involved the intervention of the state. The discourse against shameful profiteering could be articulated

---

[29] G. B. Dertilis, *Istoria tou ellinikou kratous 1830–1920* [History of the Greek State, 1830–1920] (Athens: Estia, 2005), v.2, 1048.

[30] 'Shamefully profiteering employers' appear, for example, in the memorandum of GSEE (General Confederation of the Workers of Greece) 26 November 1919: Archive of the political bureau of the prime minister, file 354, in GAK (General Archives of the State, Athens).

with paternalist perceptions regarding the reciprocities that should characterize the relations between the lower and the upper classes: loyalty and deference exchanged by the poor for 'protection' by the rich (a relationship that would lead to uprisings when the rich neglected their obligations).[31] At the same time, the idiom could constitute an organic part of revolutionary projects that threatened to subvert prevailing social regimes, or of more modest social-democratic projects that aimed at restricting the influence of the market in different sectors of the economy.

To conclude, the development of the discourse against shameful profiteering was placed in the midst of the transition from politics to economy as the dominant intellectual paradigm of conceptualizing social hierarchies. Of course, the popular classes did not suddenly discover economic inequalities and their importance in their lives. The difference lies rather in the politicization of the identities of the worker, the peasant, the poor etc., and in their placement next to the identity of 'people' as the dominant forms through which the popular classes conceived their selves and developed their collective action. This transition can up to a point be described as a transition from people to class: this is why I do not agree with analyzes that assume that the discourse against profiteering created political identities based on consumption instead of class.[32] In 1910s and 1920s Greece the development of the idiom of profiteering was closely related to the process of formation of the working as well as the educated lower-middle class, that is to the making of identities associated predominantly with the relations of production.

[31] It is on this exchange between elite and people that Johanna Siméant, 'Three Bodies of Moral Economy: The Diffusion of a Concept', *Journal of Global Ethics* 11, no. 2 (2015): 163–175, puts the emphasis on the concept of moral economy. She is correct in doing so, but I think we should insist on relating moral economy with the local interpersonal relations of deference between rulers and ruled, in contrast to more impersonal patterns mediated by the twentieth-century state.

[32] Paris Papamichos Chronakis, *Ellines, Evraioi, Mousoulmanoi kai Donme emporoi tis Thessalonikis 1882–1919: taxikoi kai ethnotikoi metaschimatismoi se trochia exellinismou* [The Greek, Jewish, Muslim and Dönme Merchants of Salonica, 1882–1919. Ethnic and Class Transformations in the Course of Hellenization] (PhD diss., University of Crete, 2011), 326, 332. See also the early attempt at a similar conceptualization by Dimitrios Kallitsounakis, 'I aftovoitheia ton katanaloton' [About the Self-Help of Consumers], in his *Politiki Epistimi* [Political Science] (Athens, 1925), 235–240.

What to Do with the Concept of Moral Economy: Morality and Hegemony

The notion of moral economy was originally linked by Thompson with the views and beliefs that informed the food riots in the eighteenth century. Famine constitutes a period of intense social crisis in which balances of all kinds are overturned[33]; existing loyalties and social bonds provide the basis of collective action, but they are also renegotiated or challenged; preexisting social tensions come to a head, and the power bloc and its values may be challenged. In any case, serious moral issues are raised in the context of a crisis of subsistence when the very survival of the people is at stake, and an intensification of the invocation of moral values is usually detected in the discourse of social actors. This moral rhetoric might provide the main or the only way to legitimize demands that exceed the status quo, when keystones of the social regime such as property or freedom of trade appear as obstacles to the survival of the community. My argument, however, is that we should not speak of 'moral economy' in every case of popular discourse and action which invokes intensely moral values in periods of famine, but only when this action and discourse refers to traditional regulation of the market imposed in the context of a not-so-remote Ancien Regime.

It has been pointed out that during and after the First World War a kind of revival took place of older forms of popular movements.[34] While, according to Tilly, food riots were one of the most common forms of contentious collective action in the seventeenth and eighteenth centuries, in the nineteenth century they lost their importance and actually began to be replaced by demonstrations; in 1911 nobody in France seemed to remember 'the old-fashioned blockage, seizure and forced sale' of goods.[35] Yet, in the context of food shortage and severe problems in provisioning due to the disturbance of production and commerce caused by the Great War, food riots erupted in most belligerent countries.

[33]Cormac Ó Gráda, *Famine: A Short History* (Princeton: Princeton University Press, 2009).

[34]Antoon Vrints, 'Beyond Victimization: Contentious Food Politics in Belgium During World War I', *European History Quarterly* 49, no. 1 (2015): 83–107.

[35]Charles Tilly, *The Contentious French* (Cambridge, MA and London: Harvard University Press, 1986), 270. Cf. Charles Tilly, *Popular Contention in Great Britain 1758–1834* (Cambridge, MA: Harvard University Press, 1995).

In Russia food riots triggered the revolution of February of 1917, while in Italy the *moti per il caroviveri* formed an essential part of the repertoire of popular movements of the 'red biennium' in the aftermath of war.[36] However, it was food riots that reappeared, not a moral economy as we defined it. If the form of mobilization belonged to an older repertoire of collective action, the ideas and the 'popular economics' behind it were not archaic: there was no reference to traditional regulation of the market or to the reciprocities between rich and poor. The demand for state intervention and regulation was absolutely linked to the new directive role assumed by the state in the economy during the 'total war' of 1914–1918, and, on a more general level, to the rising statism and the changing doctrines of 'political economy' (which Thompson juxtaposed to the moral economy of the crowd).[37] In the same vein, the (sometimes leading) role of women in the food riots of 1917–1919 should not be associated only with the familiar picture of their mobilization in early modern food riots and their responsibilities regarding consumption in the gender division of work in the household. The meaning of women's action in the food riots of 1917–1919 was also determined by the contemporary expansion of women's rights, the demands of the feminist and socialist movements and the (abrupt, wartime) expansion of the field of female economic activities. In short, I argue that our interpretation should insist on the historicity of the studied phenomenon, that is, on placing it in context; and the context in our case includes various

[36] Vrints, 'Beyond Victimization'; Roberto Bianchi, 'Les mouvements contre la vie chère en Europe au lendemain de la Grande Guerre', in *Le XXe siècle des guerres*, ed. Pietro Causarano (Paris: Les Éditions de l'Atelier, 2004), 237–245; Roberto Bianchi, *Bocci Bocci. I tumulti annonari nella Toscana del 1919* (Florence: Olschki, 2001); Barbara Alpen Engel, 'Not by Bread Alone: Subsistence Riots in Russia During World War I', *The Journal of Modern History* 69 (1997): 696–721; Lynne Taylor, 'Food Riots Revisited', *Journal of Social History* 30, no. 2 (1996): 483–496; Nicola Tranfaglia, *La prima guerra mondiale e il fascismo* (Milan: Utet, 1996), 90–95, 180–183; John Barzman, 'Entre l'émeute, la manifestation et la concertation: la crise de la vie chère de l'été 1919 au Havre', *Le Mouvement Social* 170 (1995): 61–84; Tyler Stovall, 'Du vieux et du neuf: économie morale et militantisme ouvrier dans les luttes contre la vie chère à Paris en 1919', *Le Mouvement Social* 170 (1995): 85–113; and Temma Kaplan, *Red City, Blue Period: Social Movements in Picasso's Barcelona* (Berkeley: University of California Press, 1992), 118–123.

[37] Roberto Bianchi, 'Voies de la protestation en Italie: les transformations de la révolte entre XIXe et XXe siècle', *European Review of History—Revue européenne d'histoire* 20, no. 6 (2013): 1047–1071, has argued that all these mark the emergence of a 'new moral economy' during the First World War. However, I opt for a stricter definition of the concept.

modern developments, among them the regulatory role assumed by the state in the twentieth century.[38]

Coming to the issue of morality, it is clear that there was an intense moral dimension in the denunciation of enslavement, exploitation and profiteering in 1910s Greece. Our case was not peculiar at all: moral values are inevitably involved in the critique of any social regime. As well as leftist movements, moral critiques of capitalist markets also include a critique in the name of Christian values, which could lead to radical Christian-socialist movements with a particular appeal to peasants.[39] Moral values were also invoked by conservative shopkeepers and master artisans in order to criticize the middle class—and not only the 'immoral' social and sexual behaviour of members of the bourgeoisie.[40] As in nineteenth-century Germany,[41] notions of justice and 'unfair competition' by bigger capitalists appear often in the discourse of the Greek petty-bourgeois militants.[42] At the same time, moral and political arguments in favour of the 'economy of the free market' abound in the discourse of its supporters, next to technocracy, science and efficiency as sources of legitimacy.[43] But let's stay in the field of anticapitalist discourse.

[38] Cf. Papamichos Chronakis, *Ellines, Evraioi*, 323.

[39] Thanassis Kalafatis, 'Thriskeftikotita kai koinoniki diamartyria. Oi opoadoi tou Ap. Makraki sti BD Peloponniso 1890–1900' [Religiosity and Social Protest. The Followers of Ap. Makrakis in the NW Peloponnesus, 1890–1900], *Ta Istorika* 18–19 (1993): 113–142. Also telling are the ideas of the pious Orthodox novelist Alexandros Papadiamantis, exposed by his persona in his 1892 novel 'Oi Chalasohorides', in *Apanta* (Athens: Domos, 1982), 401–462: 453, about 'plutocracy' as 'the persistent Antichrist of the world' that creates injustice.

[40] *Efimeris tou Chrimatistiriou* 2 June 1922 (Katsoulis); *Neai Archai* 7 July 1922 (Vrettos).

[41] David Blackbourn, 'Between Resignation and Volatility: The German Petty Bourgeoisie in the Nineteenth Century', in his *Populists and Patricians: Essays in Modern German History* (London: Allen & Unwin, 1987), 84–113.

[42] *Efimeris ton Ypodimatopoion* 24 February 1908; *Efimeris ton epaggelmation* 1 December 1927 (K. Igglesis in the first national meeting of barbers). In 1933 the foundation of a carriage factory by a big merchant was denounced as 'unfair competition' by the artisans who manufactured carriages: *Viotechnikon Vima* 15 January 1933.

[43] Paul Turpin, *The Moral Rhetoric of Political Economy* (Abingdon and New York: Routledge, 2011), provides an interesting argument about the different conceptions of morality and justice involved in the theories of liberal economists.

What do the above tell us about the concept of moral economy? I have already argued for a narrow definition of the concept of moral economy, an indispensable part of which is the reference to a legacy of pre-capitalist regulation. A looser definition might be proposed, based on the strong presence of moral values in critiques of capitalism and in proposals about the proper and fair function of the economy. In my opinion, such a conceptualization is too broad and descriptive to have any analytical power: moral values are invoked virtually in every anti-capitalist discourse in order to legitimize the critique and its objectives. Nevertheless, notions of moral economy understood more or less in this way keep recurring in the literature about social movements whenever referring to a 'soft', not socialist, anticapitalism. The reason, I believe, is that the moral dimension of the anticapitalist discourse of popular movements remains to a large extent unexplored. It is exactly because historians and political scientists have not paid enough attention to the moral aspects of politics (and specifically of the popular movements) that we are still not capable of conceptualizing these aspects without utilizing the concept of moral economy. But this has rendered the concept equal to any invocation of moral values regarding the operation of the capitalist economy, and, consequently, almost useless. Thus, it is imperative that we undertake a project of study and reconceptualization of the role of moral values in the popular discourse about capitalism and the market.

Of course there can be more operational versions of the broad definition of moral economy. For instance, the emphasis can be put on the extent to which the critique of the capitalist free market is based more on moral values, stressing the immorality of the market, and less on invoking an opposite, methodically articulated, model of economy and utopian projects of social transformation. Or, perhaps, another criterion may be whether more attention is paid to justice than to economic development—or, to put it another way, whether the working of the economy is depicted as a mainly moral issue and its technocratic aspects are minimized. However, I have the feeling that these hold true in virtually all the social movements we are going to study, and consequently they are of little interpretative value.

Another choice seems to us more productive: to study arguments about morality and immorality not only as spontaneous responses of social actors to economic change, but also as an important part of the struggle for hegemony. To use the terms and the elaborations of the early works of Ernesto Laclau,[44] morality (as a set of principles about proper social behaviour) can be seen as constituting a particular field at the broader political-ideological level where the struggle for hegemony takes place. Moral values are articulated with ideologies and 'class articulating principles'; and it is their articulation with the 'class principles' of the popular classes that produces different versions of what is usually called 'moral economy'. But this is the topic for another paper.

---

[44] Ernesto Laclau, 'Towards a Theory of Populism', in his *Politics and Ideology in Marxist Theory* (London: New Left Books, 1977), 143–199.

CHAPTER 12

Dilemmas of Moral Markets: Conflicting Narratives in the West German Fair Trade Movement

Benjamin Möckel

INTRODUCTION

The relationship between morals and markets is a recurring topic in intellectual debates about modern capitalism.[1] Its significance is obvious for the critics of capitalist societies, who regularly refer to the corrosive effects of capitalism, liberal globalization and consumerism on social inequality, culture, and the individual subjectivities shaped through market societies.[2] Other authors like Michael Sandel and Debra Satz have used the dichotomy of morals and markets in order to delineate the 'moral

---

[1] Paul J. Zak, ed., *Moral Markets: The Critical Role of Values in the Economy* (Princeton: Princeton University Press, 2008).

[2] Branko Milanović, *Global Inequality: A New Approach for the Age of Globalization* (Cambridge, MA: Harvard University Press, 2016); Luc Boltanski and Ève Chiapello, *The New Spirit of Capitalism* (London: Verso, 2007); and Rahel Jaeggi, *Entfremdung: Zur Aktualität eines sozialphilosophischen Problems* (Frankfurt am Main: Campus, 2005).

B. Möckel (✉)
University of Cologne, Cologne, Germany
e-mail: bmoeckel@uni-koeln.de

© The Author(s) 2019
S. Berger and A. Przyrembel (eds.), *Moralizing Capitalism*,
Palgrave Studies in the History of Social Movements,
https://doi.org/10.1007/978-3-030-20565-2_12

limits of markets', which they fear have become increasingly blurred in recent decades.[3] At the same time, economists, too, have begun to reflect on the question of how moral values, motives and sentiments shape the way people behave in economic transactions.[4] While this academic interest in the relationship between capitalism and moral values is not new,[5] moral sentiments themselves have now started to form part of capitalist consumer segments, constituting a consumer niche regularly referred to as 'ethical consumerism'. In the context of this development since the late 1960s, this chapter will look at a case study in which activists made use of the dichotomy of morals and markets in order to establish an 'alternative' consumer segment that challenged traditional concepts of capitalist markets and global terms of trade.

Beginning in the late 1960s, various NGOs, social movements and (alternative) corporations developed strategies to link their political campaigns with consumer products and practices. Consumer boycotts became an important protest strategy for environmental organizations and civil rights and anti-apartheid movements, NGOs like Amnesty International and OXFAM began to sell commodities and everyday items in order to raise funds and at the same time create awareness for their political campaigns, and the ecological movements of the 1970s forged new ideas of 'green consumerism' with a wide range of ecologically friendly products.[6] One of the most successful attempts to bring

---

[3] Debra Satz, *Why Some Things Should Not Be for Sale: The Moral Limits of Markets* (New York: Oxford University Press, 2010); Michael J. Sandel, *What Money Can't Buy: The Moral Limits of Markets* (New York: Farrar, Straus and Giroux, 2012).

[4] The most important contributions to this field have come from new approaches in game theory and new institutional economics. One key debate has circled around a critique of the model of the 'homo economicus' and a new emphasis on the concept of 'reciprocity' and the term 'homo reciprocans' as a new theoretical model. Cf. Irene C. L. Ng and Lu-Ming Tseng, 'Learning to Be Sociable: The Evolution of Homo Economicus', *American Journal of Economics & Sociology* 67, no. 2 (2008): 265–286; Ernst Fehr and Simon Gächter, 'Fairness and Retaliation: The Economics of Reciprocity', *Journal of Economic Perspectives* 14, no. 3 (2000): 159–181.

[5] Suffice to mention Max Weber, Werner Sombart, and Georg Simmel, who were all captivated by the social and moral mentalities which they interpreted as a necessary condition for the genesis of modern capitalism, as well as how these mentalities themselves changed through the social structures that capitalism produced.

[6] Hartmut Berghoff and Adam Rome, *Green Capitalism? Business and the Environment in the Twentieth Century* (Philadelphia: University of Pennsylvania Press, 2017); John Elkington, Tom Burke, and Julia Hailes, *Green Pages: The Business of Saving the World* (London: Routledge, 1988); and John Elkington and Julia Hailes, *The Green Consumer*

about a convergence of morals and markets was the Fair Trade movement that evolved in Western Europe and the United States in the late
1960s and early 1970s in order to create alternative modes of trade with
the 'Global South'.[7]

Today, Fair Trade products can be found in almost every supermarket,
and all major companies apply their own approaches to corporate social
responsibility, charity and philanthropy in order to claim ethical values.
'Morals', it seems, have become an integral part of how corporations
style themselves in the market place and the public sphere. One might
wonder whether this necessarily signifies a substantial turn towards moral
values or is rather a form of moral marketization. Yet in the context of
capitalist transactions, Kantian questions of deontology seem rather out
of place. To the contrary, one might even argue that when corporations
begin to take ethical considerations into account because of economic
rationales, this is the most significant sign that ethics has found its way
into the heart of modern consumer markets.

In this chapter, I will use the case study of the German Fair Trade
movement in order to discuss how the relationship between markets and
morals can be interpreted within an analytical framework. In particular,
I will refer to 'moralizing capitalism', the key concept of this volume,
and show how one can make use of the term for a historical analysis
of the Fair Trade movement. In the first part, I will discuss three concepts that have been used to analyze the relationship between Fair Trade
and modern consumer markets. In the second part, I will give a short
introduction to the history of the German Fair Trade movement, before
delineating two conceptual strands of the movement that differed significantly in their interpretation of its political and economic targets. First,
I will concentrate on the early developments of the 1970s in which the

---

Guide: From Shampoo to Champagne: High-Street Shopping for a Better Environment
(London: Gollancz, 1989).

[7] Some scholars have argued for a longer history of Fair Trade, pointing to the sale
of handicrafts from Puerto Rico or Hong Kong organized by OXFAM (UK) or 'Ten
Thousand Villages' (US) in the immediate post-war years. Even though both institutions
were (and still are) important for the development of Fair Trade, their campaigns from the
1940s and 1950s must primarily be seen as an integral part of their existing charity campaigns. It was only in the 1960s and 1970s that Fair Trade evolved as an alternative trade
model.

idea of market-driven social change appeared particularly attractive for many activists. In the last section I will focus on the developments of the 1980s when a more critical account of the relationship between Fair Trade and conventional consumer markets began to dominate the discourse and activists became sceptical about the prospects of changing capitalist societies from within. In the conclusion I will argue that it might be more productive to think of Fair Trade as an attempt to 'moralize consumers' than an attempt to 'moralize capitalism'.

MORALS AND MARKETS: COMPETING THEORETICAL APPROACHES

Scholars working on the relationship between morals and markets have regularly referred to E. P. Thompson and his concept of a 'moral economy'.[8] While Thompson used the term to analyze the moral frameworks and social dynamics of eighteenth-century food riots, subsequent scholars have tried to apply it to a diverse range of other phenomena of social unrest and economic controversy, in particular trying to prove the applicability of the concept to modern capitalist societies.[9] Thompson's concept was clearly indebted to Karl Polanyi's theory of '(dis)embeddedness', in which he argued that markets had until the mid-nineteenth century been closely embedded into social contexts and collective ideas and expectations of reciprocity.[10] Partly because of this intellectual tradition, Thompson was sceptical about applying the concept to modern market societies.[11] At the same time, it was exactly this idea of a social 'embeddedness' of markets that made the concept so attractive for many Fair Trade activists. Even though they rarely refer explicitly to either

[8] E. P. Thompson, 'The Moral Economy of the English Crowd in the Eighteenth Century', *Past and Present* 50 (1971): 76–136; E. P. Thompson, 'The Moral Economy Reviewed', in *Customs in Common* (London: Merlin Press, 1991), 259–351.

[9] Cf. for example, James C. Scott, *The Moral Economy of the Peasant: Rebellion and Subsistence in Southeast Asia* (New Haven, CT: Yale University Press, 1976); William M. Reddy, *The Rise of Market Culture: The Textile Trade and French Society, 1750–1900* (Cambridge: Cambridge University Press, 1984). For an overview of the conceptual history of the term and an analytical concept for applying the term to twentieth-century welfare democracies, cf. Norbert Götz, '"Moral Economy": Its Conceptual History and Analytical Prospects', *Journal of Global Ethics* 11, no. 2 (2015): 147–162.

[10] Karl Polanyi, *The Great Transformation* (New York: Farrar & Rinehart, 1944).

[11] Thompson, 'The Moral Economy Reviewed', 336–351.

Thompson or Polanyi, they use the concept to point out that Fair Trade sets out to create markets that are not solely concerned with the cheapest price and the largest profit, but also with ideas of long-term development and equal partnership with producers in the Global South. The term 'moral economy' has thus proven highly influential in the sphere of Fair Trade,[12] in particular in the attempt to frame Fair Trade as an effort to re-embed modern consumer markets.[13]

Thompson's concept therefore comes closest to the self-perception of many Fair Trade activists. Analytically, however, it is applied to the Fair Trade movement only with some difficulty, especially if one goes back to its original use. As Thompson conceived it, 'moral economy' was an antonym to market economy and thereby formed part of a modernization narrative in which 'moral economies' belonged to a premodern era that preceded the universal formation of markets in the context of modern capitalist societies. While this might be convincing for the case studies Thompson is dealing with, such a dichotomy of 'moral economy' and 'market economy' runs the risk of missing the most significant aspect of the Fair Trade movement, namely that it did not emerge as an ethical alternative to an existing 'market economy', but as a concept that operated—in the words of Michael Barratt Brown 'in and against the market'.[14] Fair Trade activists criticized capitalist markets, global terms of trade and Western consumer patterns, but they unavoidably operated within the framework of capitalist markets and had to constantly navigate between political and economic criticism on the one hand and some

---

[12] To cite only three examples: Bradley R. Wilson, 'Delivering the Goods: Fair Trade, Solidarity, and the Moral Economy of the Coffee Contract in Nicaragua', *Human Organization—Journal of the Society for Applied Anthropology* 72, no. 3 (2013): 177–187; Michael K. Goodman, 'Reading Fair Trade: Political Ecological Imaginary and the Moral Economy of Fair Trade Foods', *Political Geography* 23, no. 7 (2004): 891–915; and Marisa Wilson and Peter Jackson, 'Fairtrade Bananas in the Caribbean: Towards a Moral Economy of Recognition', *Geoforum* 70 (2016): 11–21.

[13] Laura T. Raynolds, 'Re-embedding Global Agriculture: The International Organic and Fair Trade Movements', *Agriculture and Human Values* 17, no. 3 (2000): 297–309.

[14] Cf. Michael Barratt Brown, *Fair Trade: Reform and Realities in the International Trading System* (London: Zed Books, 1993). Similar arguments can be found in: Eric Fichtl, 'The Fair Trade Movement in Historical Perspective: Explaining the "in and Against the Market" Predicament' (Master's Thesis, New School, New York City, 2007); Gavin Fridell, 'Fair Trade and the International Moral Economy: Within and Against the Market', Centre for Research on Latin America and the Caribbean, Working Paper, 2003.

measure of integration into consumer society on the other. It was therefore not in clear opposition to modern consumer society that activists
initiated 'fair' consumer practices but in an ambivalent relationship to
it—and it is exactly this tension that makes Fair Trade such an interesting
object for studying the competing interpretations of modern capitalist
and consumer societies.

From this perspective, the volume's 'moralizing capitalism' is a stimulating concept for analyzing the European Fair Trade movement and
other forms of 'ethical consumerism' that have emerged since the early
1970s. In contrast to 'moral economy', it is a term that describes a social
dynamic rather than a specific segment of the economy. In particular, it
avoids the dichotomy of 'moral economy' and 'market economy' and
instead points to specific movements and campaigns that aimed at changing social structures of work, trade and consumption *within* the framework of a capitalist society.

Fair Trade was only one example of a wide variety of consumer practices that emerged as means of achieving a moralization of capitalism.
From consumer boycotts to ecologically friendly products, from the professionalization of charity organizations to ethical investments, pro bono
activities and Corporate Social Responsibility, all these concepts regularly
referred to the idea of a possible convergence of morals and markets.[15]
Just as with 'moral economy', the concept of 'moralizing capitalism'
thus points to the self-perception of many activists in the realm of 'ethical consumption' who saw their campaigns as small steps towards a more
just way of organizing global trade without necessarily aiming at structural changes of the economic, social or political system. In this moral
minimalism[16] that explicitly set itself apart both from the modernization
utopias of liberal development theories of the 1960s and the left-wing
radicalism of the 1960s protest movements, ethical consumer campaigns
shared some characteristics with the way Samuel Moyn has interpreted

[15] In the case of the environmental movement this idea of a convergence of economy and
ecology was particularly popular. The most prominent example is John Elkington and Tom
Burke, *The Green Capitalists: Industry's Search for Environmental Excellence* (London: V.
Gollancz, 1987).

[16] The term 'moral minimalism' was first used by Mary Baumgartner to describe the loosening of moral bonds in 1980s New York City suburbia; M. P. Baumgartner, *The Moral
Order of a Suburb* (New York: Oxford University Press, 1988). I use the term here with a
slightly different meaning, referring to an ethics that concentrates on immediate and practical actions aiming at concrete results instead of large-scale plans and utopias.

the human rights movement of the 1970s as a 'last utopia' that came to prominence because all other political utopias had lost their mobilizing credibility.[17]

At first sight, Fair Trade appears to be a perfect example of this mode of thinking. Its campaign model is explicitly framed as a politics of small steps towards more equal global terms of trade without putting the whole economic system into question. Fair Trade thus operates within a capitalist market society, but gives consumers the chance to articulate moral concerns through their everyday consumer practices. While this describes quite adequately today's interpretation of Fair Trade, things look more complicated from a historical perspective. As I will show in the following sections, this pragmatic and hands-on approach was fiercely disputed within the movement, as was the idea of an integration of Fair Trade into modern consumer markets. While some activists saw Fair Trade as a way of reforming capitalist society and establishing more just terms of trade with producers in the Global South, a large group within the movement argued that capitalism could not be transformed and Fair Trade could therefore only be valuable as a symbolic activity of political education.

It is for this reason that other concepts based on far reaching hypotheses about the economic impact of Fair Trade are often not sophisticated enough to grasp the Fair Trade movement in its historical dimension. This is for example true of Nico Stehr's concept of a 'moralization of markets' that he outlined in 2003.[18] For him, consumer segments like Fair Trade or organic food are part of a broader transformation of modern consumer societies that began in the 1960s. From this time onwards, Stehr argues, Western consumers enjoyed greater purchasing power while becoming better informed about the global and ecological consequences of their consumer decisions. As a result, he claims, consumers attained a much more powerful position in contemporary consumer societies, not least because marketing and consumer research became more conscious about taking up new consumer demands. For Stehr, these phenomena add up to a consumer-driven 'moralization of markets', in which

---

[17] Samuel Moyn, *The Last Utopia: Human Rights in History* (Cambridge, MA: Harvard University Press, 2010); Jan Eckel and Samuel Moyn, eds., *The Breakthrough: Human Rights in the 1970s* (Philadelphia: University of Pennsylvania Press, 2014).

[18] Nico Stehr, *Die Moralisierung der Märkte. Eine Gesellschaftstheorie* (Frankfurt am Main: Suhrkamp, 2007).

'ethics' became a consumer demand that was met by a diverse range of new products, corporations and alternative trade organizations. In a broader historiographical context, this argument is part of an ongoing debate about the emergence of the 'consumer-citizen' as a new form of political citizenship in the twentieth century.[19]

Other scholars have also pointed to the surprising market success of Fair Trade, but have interpreted it within a more melancholic narrative. In this view, the success of Fair Trade in recent years should be lamented as a sell-out in which it gave up its critical and political agenda and instead focused solely on market integration, sales increases and collaboration with multinational corporations like Starbucks or Nestlé. Gavin Fridell has described this development by distinguishing between an 'embedded liberalism' model that dominated in the 1970s and early 1980s and a 'neoliberal' model of fair trade that began to emerge in the late 1980s.[20] For him, Fair Trade did not succeed in 'moralizing capitalism' but was itself absorbed by capitalist consumer society and was thereby transformed into a bourgeois lifestyle choice of 'conspicuous consumption'.[21] While Stehr points to a moralization of markets, Fridell's interpretation highlights the marketization of morals in the process of integrating Fair Trade into conventional consumer markets.

One feature both narratives share is the assumption that Fair Trade is primarily defined by its economic impact. In this way, I argue, each largely overestimates the economic influence of Fair Trade—especially for the time period from the 1970s until the mid-2000s. Even today, Fair Trade constitutes only a marginal segment of the German consumer market, claiming even for coffee—by far its most important

[19] Lizabeth Cohen, *A Consumers' Republic: The Politics of Mass Consumption in Postwar America* (New York: Knopf, 2003); Martin Daunton and Matthew Hilton, eds., *The Politics of Consumption: Material Culture and Citizenship in Europe and America* (Oxford: Berg, 2001), esp. Frank Trentmann, 'Bread, Milk and Democracy: Consumption and Citizenship in Twentieth-Century Britain', 129–163; Sheryl Kroen, 'A Political History of the Consumer', *The Historical Journal* 47, no. 3 (2004): 709–736.

[20] Gavin Fridell, *Fair Trade Coffee: The Prospects and Pitfalls of Market-Driven Social Justice* (Toronto: University of Toronto Press, 2007); Gavin Fridell, 'Fair-Trade Coffee and Commodity Fetishism: The Limits of Market-Driven Social Justice', *Historical Materialism* 15, no. 4 (2007): 79–104.

[21] Thorstein Veblen, *Theory of the Leisure Class*, Reissue (Oxford: Oxford World's Classics, 2009). On Fair Trade as a practice of 'conspicuous consumption', cf. Matthias Zick Varul, 'Ethical Consumption: The Case of Fair Trade', *Kölner Zeitschrift für Soziologie und Sozialpsychologie* [Special Issue] 49 (2009): 366–385.

product—a market share of just 2.3%.[22] Taking into account the immense attention Fair Trade attracts in public discourse, the discrepancy between its economic influence and its ability to generate public attention might indeed be one of the most significant characteristics of this movement; but historical analyzes should be careful not to confuse the two.

I therefore propose to use the idea of a 'moralization of markets' differently to the way that Nico Stehr and other scholars have done. Instead of asking whether Fair Trade was able to change the structure of global trade in a quantifiable manner by claiming considerable market shares for products like coffee, cocoa, cotton or flowers, it seems more interesting to use the concept of a 'moralization of markets' in order to assess the strategies with which the Fair Trade movement tried to attach moral meaning to economic transactions like trade and consumption. In this interpretation, 'moralizing capitalism' does not necessarily mean to create a more just economic system. Instead it refers to the more basic attempt to claim an ethical significance for the sphere of consumption. The merits of a historical perspective on the Fair Trade movement will thus not lie in quantifying its economic impact over the course of the past five decades. Instead, I will apply the term 'moralizing capitalism' to interrogate the concepts and motives of contemporary Fair Trade activists and the strategies they applied to communicate to Fair Trade buyers that their everyday consumer decisions had ethical significance. I will concentrate on the conceptual debates within the Fair Trade movement and look for the tensions and controversies that arose when these activists tried to establish an 'alternative' trade model that was meant to act as a means to 'moralize capitalism'.

The Formation of the West German Fair Trade Movement

Ideas for an 'alternative third world trade' evolved in the late 1960s and early 1970s in the context of heterogeneous but intersecting intellectual developments. The most important factor was a growing awareness among individuals, NGOs, the churches and the state of global poverty and economic inequalities. This new awareness coincided with a more

---

[22] I use the data on the market for Fair Trade products in Germany provided by *Statista*: https://de.statista.com/statistik/daten/studie/226517/umfrage/fairtrade-umsatz-in-deutschland/. Cf. also: 'Fair Trade in Deutschland—Statista-Dossier' (2015).

sceptical view on the effectiveness of third world charity projects and private and state-led development aid.[23] While the 1960s had been declared the 'decade of development' by the United Nations, large-scale projects of development and modernization were seen in a more critical light by the end of the decade. Picking up a slogan coined at the UNCTAD conferences in Geneva (1964) and New Delhi (1968), 'Trade not Aid' became the new buzz word for a more effective way of assisting 'third world' countries to develop economically.[24]

It was within this political and intellectual framework that products from the 'third world' were first used to raise awareness of global economic inequalities. In West Germany, a third factor was also important: During the 1960s, the Catholic and Protestant churches went through a process of modernization and reorientation that generated new attention to development politics and third world poverty, particularly in an attempt to mobilize their young members to participate in church activities.[25] These Protestant and Catholic youth groups organized a so-called 'peace march' in 1970 that explicitly raised the problem of third world poverty.[26] While the campaign model of a charity run stood in a tradition of third world philanthropy that the churches had established in the late 1950s,[27] the organizers also tried to use the event for articulating political protest and raising public awareness for development politics.

---

[23] A key document for this critical evaluation is the 'Pearson Report': Lester B. Pearson, *Partners in Development: Report of the Commission on International Development* (London: Pall Mall, 1969).

[24] Alfons Lemper, *UNCTAD 1968: Probleme und Perspektiven* (Hamburg: Hoffmann und Campe, 1968); UNCTAD Secretariat, ed. 'UNCTAD: A Brief Historical Overview', n.d.; Sönke Kunkel, 'Zwischen Globalisierung, internationalen Organisationen und "global Governance": Eine kurze Geschichte des Nord-Süd-Konflikts in den 1960er und 1970er Jahren', *Vierteljahrshefte für Zeitgeschichte* 60, no. 4 (2012): 555–578; and Peter van Dam, 'Moralizing Postcolonial Consumer Society: Fair Trade in the Netherlands, 1964–1997', *International Review of Social History* 61, no. 2 (2016): 226–227.

[25] Sebastian Tripp, *Fromm und politisch: Christliche Anti-Apartheid-Gruppen und die Transformation des westdeutschen Protestantismus 1970–1990* (Göttingen: Wallstein, 2015).

[26] Ruben Quaas, *Fair Trade: Eine global-lokale Geschichte am Beispiel des Kaffees* (Köln: Böhlau Köln, 2015), 82ff.; Bundesarchiv (Federal Archive of Germany): B/122/11484: 'Friedensmarsch 1970'.

[27] By the late 1950s, both the Protestant and the Catholic churches had established charity organizations that explicitly dealt with the 'third world'. The Catholic 'Misereor' was founded in 1958, the Protestant 'Brot für die Welt' in 1959. Both organizations became important institutions for the development of the Fair Trade movement in Germany.

The first concepts for an alternative trade with the third world evolved in West Germany from these initiatives. The idea had already been recently established in the Netherlands, and both the theoretical concepts and the products themselves were in the beginning imported from there—proving that Fair Trade was from the outset a transnational movement.[28] The year 1970 saw the founding of 'Aktion Dritte Welt Handel (A3WH)' ('Third World Trade Campaign'), which imported its products from S.O.S. (Stichting Ontwikkelings-Samenwerking), its Dutch counterpart. The first sales mainly took place through open-air bazaars or one-day campaigns by local church groups, but 'Third World Shops' would soon be established in most major German cities, again replicating a model that was initially established in the Netherlands, where the first 'Wereldwinkel' had opened in Breukelen in 1969.[29]

In 1975, GEPA ('Gesellschaft zur Förderung der Partnerschaft mit der Dritten Welt mbh') was founded, soon to become the leading import organization for Fair Trade products in Germany. In the same year, activists from a group of seven world shops set up the 'Arbeitsgemeinschaft Dritte Welt Läden' (AG3WL), which became the most important umbrella organization for world shops in Germany. AG3WL was crucial to the development of the German Fair Trade movement because it became a shareholder in GEPA and represented the interests of the world shops in this institution. In this capacity, it regularly came into conflict with the German church organizations as the other important (and indeed dominant) shareholders in GEPA. Thus, in the mid-1970s, the Fair Trade movement had established an institutional framework in which local shops, church-based organizations and a small number of import organizations cooperated but nevertheless continued to act comparatively independently.

In the same time period, sales began to rise. In 1975, GEPA started with a sales volume of 2 million DM, which rose to more than 5 million DM by the end of the decade. The number of world shops also increased during this period. From 1975 to 1981, membership in AG3WL rose from 7 to 43 members. The figure did not represent the total number of world shops, though, because only a minority of shops decided to join

[28] Peter van Dam, 'The Limits of a Success Story: Fair Trade and the History of Postcolonial Globalization', *Comparativ: Zeitschrift für Globalgeschichte und Vergleichende Gesellschaftsforschung* 25, no. 1 (2015): 62–77.

[29] van Dam, 'Moralizing Postcolonial Consumer Society', 234–237; Quaas, *Fair Trade*, 84.

AG3WL. Altogether, approximately one hundred shops were trading in Germany in 1977/1978 and more than 200 in 1983/1984. With this increase in numbers, the importance of world shops as points-of-sale for Fair Trade products rose. In 1983/1984, GEPA for the first time sold more products through world shops than through bazaars or other occasional sales outlets (9 million DM in total). GEPA reached its highest level of sales in 1986/1987 (18.5 million DM) before experiencing a temporary decline until Fair Trade certificates opened new sales opportunities in supermarkets and other 'conventional' shops in the early 1990s. But this new certification process did not immediately result in a major breakthrough in Fair Trade sales. For several years, world shops remained the most important space for GEPA sales; it was only in the mid-2000s that Fair Trade experienced astonishing sales increases with figures reaching 100 million euros (in total sales, not only GEPA sales) in 2006 and 500 million euros in 2012. In 2015, sales reached almost 1 billion euros.[30]

This broad outline of the economic impact of Fair Trade helps to put current research on the development of the Fair Trade market into historical context. As I have shown, Fair Trade has only attained a significant increase in sales volumes in the last 10–15 years. It is only in this time period that it has gained the attention of academic research in the fields of economics, sociology and anthropology.[31] Implicitly, this research has often been coloured by these recent developments. So even though the market share of Fair Trade products was for many decades almost insignificant and the effects both on the living conditions of workers in the Global South and on the political awareness of consumers in the Global North are very difficult to assess,[32] Fair Trade has often

---

[30] See for most of these figures the excellent coverage in: Quaas, *Fair Trade*. See also the data provided by Statista (cf. n. 21).

[31] Cf. for example, Brigitte Granville and Janet Dine, eds., *The Processes and Practices of Fair Trade: Trust, Ethics and Governance* (New York: Routledge, 2013); Keith R. Brown, *Buying into Fair Trade: Culture, Morality, and Consumption* (New York: New York University Press, 2013); and Alex Nicholls and Charlotte Opal, *Fair Trade: Market-Driven Ethical Consumption* (London: Sage, 2005).

[32] See the ambiguous findings of recent Fair Trade impact research. For an overview cf. Leonardo Becchetti, Stefano Castriota, and Pierluigi Conzo, 'Quantitative Analysis of the Impacts of Fair Trade', in *Handbook of Research on Fair Trade*, ed. Laura Raynolds and Elizabeth Bennett (Cheltenham: Elgar, 2015), 532–548. The anthropologist Sarah Besky has pointed to possible negative effects on local communities and labour rights in the case

triggered far-reaching interpretations about a presumed 'moralization of markets', the advent of an 'ethical capitalism' or the economic power of a new movement of 'conscious consumers'.[33]

As I have argued, such interpretations are most likely too far-reaching. From a historical perspective, it is not the economic success of the Fair Trade movement that is the most striking, but its ability to garner public attention for its cause over such a long time. One of the most significant aspects of the movement seems to be this discrepancy between its direct economic impact and the media and public attention it has been able to generate. A historical analysis must therefore be careful not to mistake the one for the other, but to take the discrepancy as the starting point for a history of the Fair Trade movement that would mainly focus on the conceptual debates of Fair Trade activists, the media strategies the movement implemented and the political campaigns it initiated. It is to such a conceptual history of the German Fair Trade movement that I will now turn.

Establishing Fair Trade: Early Concepts for an 'Alternative Third World Trade'

The West German A3WH 'Third World Trade Campaign' was from its outset defined by conflicting ideas and conceptualizations. Three controversies were particularly important: *First*, the Fair Trade movement defined itself as a critique of modern capitalist and consumer society. At the same time, however, it was based upon a surprisingly optimistic view on the social and political influence of individual market decisions, claiming that private consumer patterns were able to change social and economic structures. *Second*, Fair Trade was created as a twofold alternative. On the one hand, it criticized capitalist trade for increasing global economic inequalities. At the same time, however, it distanced itself from contemporary schemes of charity, philanthropy and development aid, claiming that these practices had established new forms of inequality and social and economic dependency. In contrast, Fair Trade was interpreted

---

of Darjeeling tea production: Sarah Besky, *The Darjeeling Distinction: Labor and Justice on Fair-Trade Tea Plantations in India* (Berkeley: University of California Press, 2014).

[33] See, for example, Noreena Hertz, 'Better to Shop Than to Vote?', *New Statesman*, 21 June 1999 (also *Business Ethics: A European Review* 10, no. 3 [2001]: 190–193).

as a social interaction between equal partners that did not result in the kind of social asymmetries that development aid and philanthropy regularly produced. *Finally*, Fair Trade activists referred to different goals for their initiatives. While one group saw Fair Trade primarily as an alternative trade model that should try to acquire a small but growing niche of the 'regular' economy, other activists insisted that the main purpose of the campaign was its political and educational impact. For them, Fair Trade mainly constituted a symbolic practice that was meant to trigger public interest in the inequalities of global trade. 'Raising money' and 'raising awareness' thus became buzz words for different approaches, even though both aspects were closely intertwined in the practical work of world shops and Fair Trade activists.[34]

The early draft papers of the movement reflected these conflicting interpretations.[35] After a period of improvisation in which activists had tried out different techniques of campaigning, they soon started to debate the right methods and objectives for an 'alternative trade model'. One of the key questions was the relationship of an 'alternative' trade to the capitalist consumer society it was operating in. The first theoretical paper, written by Ernst-Erwin Pioch, is a good example of the ambivalences of this relationship. Written in 1970, Pioch's text was the first attempt to theoretically reflect upon the possibilities and limitations of an 'alternative' trade with the 'third world' as a campaign model for development politics. On the one hand, Pioch argued that it was of predominant importance to distance Fair Trade from the 'regular' economy and to use the campaign to explicitly criticize 'unjust global terms of trade'. In his view, this also meant to criticize Western consumer patterns and to educate people in Germany and other industrialized countries about the destructive consequences of their consumer practices.

---

[34] Ruben Quaas, 'Selling Coffee to Raise Awareness for Development Policy: The Emerging Fair Trade Market in Western Germany in the 1970s', *Historical Social Research/ Historische Sozialforschung* 36, no. 3 (2011): 164–181.

[35] For a more detailed analysis of the conceptual debates of the West German Fair Trade movement, see Benjamin Möckel, 'Gegen die "Plastikwelt der Supermärkte". Konsum- und Kapitalismuskritik in der Entstehungsgeschichte des "fairen Handels"', *Archiv Für Sozialgeschichte* 56 (2016): 335–352. My article in the AfS focuses on the critique of capitalism formulated by Fair Trade activists in the 1970s and 1980s. By picking up the concept of a 'moralization' of capitalism, this chapter focuses more directly on the concepts for a transformation of capitalist markets that were formulated by the Fair Trade movement during this time.

At the same time, however, Pioch referred to the same consumer society in order to argue for the practicability of the Fair Trade approach. 'Department stores and mail-order', Pioch argued, 'have shown that there is a genuine interest for handicrafts from the third world in our markets'. It was therefore a worthwhile target to help cooperatives from the 'third world' to 'produce in line with [the demands of] the European market'. The task of Fair Trade co-ops was to 'sell these products in line with the market'.[36]

A similar line of thought can be found in another key document of the early Fair Trade movement. In the first years of its existence, the A3WH commissioned Gerd Nickoleit to write a report on the theoretical background and the practical implications of the 'third world trade campaign'. He called his paper 'Development of Underdevelopment',[37] a title that explicitly referred to one of the key texts of contemporary dependency theory.[38] Similar to Pioch, Nickoleit also referred to the dual character of the 'third world trade campaign' which on the one hand constituted a symbolic critique of capitalism, and on the other hand was an attempt to create an alternative and more just trade system. As Nickoleit argued, 'the third world trade campaign does not claim to be able to replace the capitalist trading system by a more just one', but as a business model that does not strive for financial profit it would 'necessarily call capitalism into question'.[39] For Nickoleit, the objective of the campaign was therefore primarily a motivational one. In the paper he argued that most people already knew a lot about the living conditions and the poverty of third world countries. The main problem, he argued, was that people would not see the connection between this knowledge and their own way of life. With this distinction between an abstract knowledge about global poverty on the one hand and a process of self-reflection on the other, Nickoleit picked up a central idea from the research on 'consciousness raising' (*conscientização*) formulated by

---

[36] Ernst-Erwin Pioch, 'Problemskizze zur Gründung einer "Aktionsgemeinschaft Dritte Welt-Handel"' (8 June 1970), in Misereor Archive Aachen, "Fairer Handel", inventory 6 (in the following citations: MAA, FH 6).

[37] 'Entwicklung der Unterentwicklung. Eine Analyse im Auftrag der Aktion Dritte Welt Handel von Gerd Nickoleit', in MAA, FH 2.

[38] André Gunder Frank, 'The Development of Underdevelopment', *Monthly Review* 18, no. 4 (1966): 17–31.

[39] 'Entwicklung der Unterentwicklung', 16.

scholars and activists like Paulo Freire, which was extremely influential within the Fair Trade movement.[40]

Even though this interpretation of Fair Trade as a model for political education and consciousness raising was not new, Nickoleit found an interesting way of linking the idea with modern consumer society. Consciousness about the economic situation of the 'third world', he argued, must begin 'exactly where our consumer patterns, our economic interests, our political affiliations are called into question, because they hinder the development of the third world'. Such information would necessarily raise resistance, and for Nickoleit it was precisely in this context that consumption became an important means of communication: 'In order to bring the European consumer-citizen (*Konsumbürger*) closer to this unpleasant truth, we need a catalyst (*Abholeffekt*, 'initiating device'). We use the drive to consume for this purpose'. Exotic handicrafts and other products would trigger interest and the consumers themselves would begin to ask questions about the products and the people that had made them. For Nickoleit, the consumer society thus had a dual dimension. On the one hand, it was a key aspect of the economic injustices that the Fair Trade movement set out to criticize; on the other hand, a presumed 'natural' inclination to consume became a means to communicate this criticism and to start an individual process of reflection about global trade inequalities.[41]

Other papers and internal debates pointed in a similar direction.[42] Most activists argued that the main objective of the campaign was to raise awareness of global economic inequalities and to criticize the 'development of underdevelopment' inscribed into the structures of global trade. Meanwhile, authors like Nickoleit, Pioch or Harry Neyer regularly referred to a rather optimistic view of the transforming potential of free markets, which accorded to individual consumers the ability to change social and economic structures through their purchasing

---

[40] Paulo Freire, *Pedagogy of the Oppressed* (New York: Herder and Herder, 1970); Paulo Freire, *Education for Critical Consciousness* (London: Continuum, 1974); and Paulo Freire, *Conscientization* (Geneva: World Council of Churches, 1975).

[41] A similar argument can be found in: Ernst Schmied, *Die 'Aktion Dritte Welt Handel' als Versuch der Bewusstseinsbildung: Ein Beitrag zur Diskussion über Handlungsmodelle für das politische Lernen* (Aachen: Aktuell-Verlagsgesellschaft, 1977), 31.

[42] Cf. for example, Schmied, *Die 'Aktion Dritte Welt Handel'*; Harry Neyer, 'Vom Bastkorb zum Guatemala-Kaffee. Trends, Tendenzen und offene Fragen bei der Aktion Dritte Welt Handel', *E + Z Entwicklung und Zusammenarbeit* 4 (1973): 19–21.

power.[43] Nevertheless they also highlighted the restrictions of this approach. To focus on individual consumers was seen as a way to communicate development politics to a segment of the population that was not intrinsically interested in such topics; but as a campaign model it would not by itself transform global terms of trade. Because of this, most activists would not have argued that the 'third world trade campaign' aimed at 'moralizing capitalism' in the sense that it would directly transform capitalist markets. Instead, they argued for a symbolic 'moralization' that aimed at criticizing market structures and consumer patterns and tried to raise awareness for alternative ways of organizing global terms of trade.[44]

This interpretation of Fair Trade as a tool of public protest was particularly important in the early political campaigns of the (European) Fair Trade movement. This is already evident in the so-called 'cane sugar campaign' that was initiated in the Netherlands shortly before the establishment of the first world shops. From 1970 onwards the campaign was also introduced in several Western European states, including West Germany. Particularly in the Netherlands it became one of the first and most important attempts to use individual consumer patterns in order to protest against tariffs, EEC subsidies and global terms of trade.[45] Shortly afterwards, similar campaigns were initiated in several European countries. In West Germany, the so-called 'Aluschok'-campaign was the most successful.[46] The name referred to aluminium and chocolate, or rather

---

[43]Pioch, 'Problemskizze', 2f.;'Entwicklung der Unterentwicklung', 17f.; and Neyer, 'Bastkorb', 20f.

[44]The importance of this distinction was made clear as early as 1972 when an activist from a small town in Lower Saxony argued for a professionalization of the 'alternative third world trade' as the only way to establish a 'true alternative' to the conventional trade with the third world. Rejecting this notion, Wolfram Walbach wrote an open letter in the name of the A3WH reminding all activists that their campaigns should not strive for a strictly economic concept of social change, but rather for raising awareness through the symbolic sale of 'third world' products. For this debate, see: Eduard Walterscheid, 'Die Entwicklung der Entwicklungshilfe', in MAA, FH 3; Wolfram Walbach, 'Dritte Welt Handel-GmbH und "Hilfe durch Handel"', in MAA, FH 3.

[45]van Dam, 'Moralizing Postcolonial Consumer Society', 232–234.

[46]On the campaign, cf. Schmied, Die 'Aktion Dritte Welt Handel', 231–246; Markus Raschke, Fairer Handel. Engagement für eine gerechte Weltwirtschaft (Ostfildern: Matthias-Grünewald-Verlag, 2009), 64–66. For a contemporary report on the campaign in the United Kingdom that shows its transnational interconnectedness, see 'Chocolate with a Bite', New Internationalist [Special Issue] 33 (1976): 16.

to the cocoa and the bauxite that were necessary to produce them. The campaign manufactured a chocolate bar (wrapped in aluminium foil) to call attention to the global trade agreements that were connected to those two commodities. An everyday item was thereby turned into a means of political protest, replacing the leaflet as the traditional protest medium. Similar to the cane sugar campaign, it was centred around the issue of global tariffs. By reading the text on the chocolate bar wrapper, the consumer learnt that the European tariff for raw cocoa was only 4% while the tariff increased to as much as 27% once the raw product was processed into cocoa butter or other products.[47] A similar argument was made in the case of bauxite. In the final paragraph the wrapper text's authors concluded, 'Our tariff policy robs the developing countries of the chance to process their raw products for themselves and thereby contain the threat of unemployment'. As a consequence, they argued, 'We must reduce our tariffs in order to grant developing countries new and fair terms of trade'.[48]

The cane sugar campaign and the Aluschok campaign relied on similar protest techniques. They used the act of consumption to transform the topic of global trade into something connected to a clearly recognizable individual decision. At the same time, both campaigns tried to prompt consumers to take initiatives that went beyond the mere act of consumption, like talking to shop keepers or sending a postcard to the federal government. The two campaigns ran similar arguments, criticizing high tariffs and EEC subsidies and calling for better market access for developing countries.

Both the theoretical concepts and the political campaigns around Fair Trade in the early 1970s thus highlighted a concept of 'moralization' that relied on a strategy of symbolic protest articulated through individual acts of consumption. On a general level these campaigns were part of a critical view of capitalism, global trade and Western consumerism. But this criticism was not a clear-cut rejection of the market society or of consumption as such, rather an attempt to point to alternatives *within* the framework of capitalist societies. In some aspects it even shared key arguments with a classical liberal view on global economic development—for example, when it referred to the political influence of

[47] MAA, FH 12.
[48] Ibid.

individual consumers or the positive effects of market access for developing countries. This interpretation of Fair Trade as a consumer model within a capitalist society was of course not without controversy. In West Germany these concepts became much more controversial particularly in the 1980s and were radically criticized by some factions of the Fair Trade movement.

ALTERNATIVE? WHAT ALTERNATIVE? CONFLICTING CONCEPTS IN THE WEST GERMAN FAIR TRADE MOVEMENT IN THE 1980S

From the statements of Fair Trade activists and the internal debates of Fair Trade groups and institutions, one gets the impression of a change in mood from the 1970s to the 1980s. The interpretation of Fair Trade as a moral transformation of capitalism partly lost ground against a more pessimistic analysis that capitalism was transforming Fair Trade itself. While in the first decade of the 'third world trade campaign' most activists had placed considerable hope in the idea of a politics of small steps toward changing contemporary consumer markets, many in the 1980s instead began to suspect a process of small steps of commodification of the trade model through a focus on balance sheets and capitalist consumer markets. Activists began to debate whether Fair Trade still constituted a real 'alternative' to the established models of trade and consumption. A key term expressing this sceptical view was the 'economy's intrinsic logic' (*ökonomische Eigenlogik*), which activists feared would in the long run trump all the political aspirations of the Fair Trade model.

It would be too simplistic, though, to put these opposite interpretations into a clear chronological sequence. Just as the market optimism of the 1970s was not shared by all activists, it was also only one faction of the German Fair Trade movement that began to articulate a more self-critical view during the 1980s. Nevertheless, some scepticism about the trade model they had established was shared by almost all activists to some degree: Did Fair Trade contribute to the establishment of new forms of economic dependency if cooperatives from the global south were integrated into European consumer markets? Did Fair Trade contribute to the expansion of monocultures by importing coffee from Tanzania or Latin America? And how should one deal with the problem that Fair Trade relied almost exclusively on exotic handicrafts and former colonial primary products like coffee, cocoa, tea or sugar?

These questions were not new, but they were posed with new urgency during the 1980s. It is therefore interesting to ask why activists began to reflect so self-critically on the campaign they were participating in. In the German case, one explanation lies with changes in the social structure of the Fair Trade movement. During the late 1970s and 1980s, a lot of activists from the West German countercultural networks (*alternative Milieu*) joined the movement,[49] founded new world shops and began to participate actively in the movement's debates. Many of these new activists favoured a decidedly political approach towards Fair Trade that differed from the more charity-based approach of some of the traditional, church-based groups. Secondly, it was primarily the activists from the world shops that articulated this new criticism of emphasis on boosting sales and integrating Fair Trade products into the market. In contrast, GEPA and the other import organizations that were often in more direct contact with the local producers generally highlighted the positive effects of increasing sales and revenues that would enable the movement to help more producers and cooperatives in the Global South. The debates outlined below thus do not represent a new self-critical consensus within *the* Fair Trade movement as such. My discussion rather highlights one significant aspect of the debate, one that was propelled by a group of activists who feared that an approach aiming for a 'moralization of capitalism' would lead to a de-politicization of the Fair Trade movement.

The debate over the political dimension of Fair Trade was mainly aired through the newsletter of the Arbeitsgemeinschaft Dritte Welt Läden (AG3WL), the umbrella organization of the world shops.[50] As outlined above, the AG3WL had originally been founded in 1975 in order to give the world shops a say in the decisions of the newly founded GEPA. In the following years it evolved into an institution through which the

---

[49] On the social structure and habitus of the West German *alternative Milieu*, cf. Sven Reichardt, *Authentizität und Gemeinschaft: Linksalternatives Leben in den siebziger und frühen achtziger Jahren* (Berlin: Suhrkamp, 2014); Sven Reichardt and Detlef Siegfried, *Das alternative Milieu. antibürgerlicher Lebensstil und linke Politik in der Bundesrepublik Deutschland und Europa 1968–1983* (Göttingen: Wallstein Verlag, 2010), 9–24.

[50] The AG3WL is today located in Mainz under the name 'Weltladen-Dachverband e.V.' The AG3WL Newsletter was first published in October 1981 and can be consulted at the office in Mainz.

world shops (that were organized in a very independent and decentralized manner) were able to discuss different theoretical and practical approaches and to establish closer links between individual groups and activists. These debates circled around one central question: how to characterize the relationship between Fair Trade as an 'alternative' trade model and the society of the 'regular market' in which it necessarily had to operate. Within the AG3WL, a majority of activists shared a rather critical view of what they perceived as an incorporation of capitalist market logic into the Fair Trade campaign model. For example, they criticized most attempts to cooperate with commercial businesses, the sale of Fair Trade products through conventional retail outlets, and efforts to 'professionalize' the operations of the world shops and the import organizations. Such criticism put AG3WL regularly into conflict with GEPA and its most important shareholders, the Catholic and Protestant churches. While many world shops continued to emphasize the priority of the symbolic and educational dimension of Fair Trade, GEPA and its church-based shareholders increasingly argued for a much stronger emphasis on the task of directly helping those partners in the Global South that were depending on expanding sales of their products.

This move towards a more profound integration of Fair Trade products into conventional consumer markets led many activists in AG3WL to ask whether Fair Trade still represented an 'alternative' model of trade and consumption. At its general meeting in 1982, a special working group called 'The Alternative Movement and Third World Shops' was constituted to discuss this question in more detail. The group arrived at a very disillusioned conclusion. They repeatedly referred to the dominance of economic rationales that hindered any substantial political campaigns. Concerning the objective of increasing sales of fair trade products, they argued: 'Rising sales create dependencies and inherent necessities (*Sachzwänge*) [...] and handicap the educative project to a large extent'.[51] As they saw it, the 'third world trade campaign' in its current approach did not constitute an alternative to conventional consumer practices. Instead, they explicitly highlighted the structural analogies to capitalist economics: 'In light of today's practice in third world

---

[51]'Thesen der Arbeitsgruppe "Alternativbewegung und Dritte-Welt-Läden"' (Archive of the AG3WL, AG3WL Newsletter no. 6, 12–14).

shops (sale, range of goods, pursuit of turnover) the term "alternative trade" seems questionable'.[52]

Again, this criticism was not completely new. What was new was the fact that the authors did not stop there. Not only did they disapprove of specific methods of the Fair Trade model, they called into question whether it was possible to establish an 'alternative' model of trade with the Global South at all. As they argued, 'trade with the third world is always based on exploitation: without it, the products could not be sold—they would just be too expensive'.[53] In an equally apodictic manner they also criticized the idea of raising awareness for global development politics through the sale of Fair Trade products. The Fair Trade movement had largely failed to achieve this goal, they claimed. In some cases it had even produced contradictory effects: 'Bulk sales [of third world products] give the impression that "a lot" is being done for the third world, thereby creating a false consciousness' about the true state of global politics.[54] In their conclusion, the authors conceded that the 'alternative third world trade' might at least provide a 'symbolic model for a less unjust global trade'. Nevertheless, they argued that it was a fatal shortcoming of the movement that both the import organizations and the world shops would continue to depend financially on the revenues generated from the trade with their partners in the Global South, and would thus remain reliant on the very thing that they had set out to put an end to.[55]

In the following years, other draft papers supplemented this critical discourse. In 1984, a group of activists from the world shop in Tübingen published an article titled 'Alternative Trade?' in the AG3WL Newsletter.[56] As these authors argued, the concept of 'aid through trade' had reached its limit; it had become increasingly evident 'that in our trade practices we remain bound to a system that lives on competition here [in the West] and exploitation there [in the Global South]'.[57] In this economic context, political objectives would regularly be marginalized by economic and commercial considerations. Even though the

[52] Ibid., 12.

[53] Ibid.

[54] Ibid.

[55] Ibid., 13.

[56] 'Alternativer Handel?' (Archive of the AG3WL, AG3WL-Newsletter no. 12, 12–14).

[57] Ibid.

authors argued in favour of a continuation of the Fair Trade model, they joined the authors of the 1982 paper in the view that world shops had to avoid any form of financial dependency on the products they were selling. Third world products, they insisted, should solely be seen as means of education and political protest. A couple of months later, this paper was discussed at a general meeting of the AG3WL, where the debate apparently adopted its general line of argument. Certainly the position paper that resulted from the debate repeated its arguments almost word for word. Again, the authors claimed that even in the 'alternative third world trade' the world shops, the import organizations, and the partners in the 'third world' remained trapped in a 'system of exploitation'.[58] As a consequence, the paper argued, 'We cannot build an alternative and just trade without at the same time attacking the current system of the world economy'. In the existing economic context, 'alternative trade can only have a symbolic meaning. It is no real alternative'.[59]

CONCLUSION: MORALIZING CAPITALISM BY MORALIZING CONSUMERS?

As the last paragraphs have shown, the theoretical debates within the Fair Trade movement tended to reach very apodictic conclusions. It is therefore often more interesting to ask how these arguments were taken up in the everyday practices of the world shops. This happened for example when members disputed fiercely whether 'third world shops' were allowed to hire paid sales staff,[60] whether it was legitimate to pay for a professional designer to decorate shop windows,[61] what kind of advertising was appropriate for a world shop,[62] and whether Fair Trade products were allowed to be sold through a mail order catalogue.[63] It is in these practical debates that the tensions and ambivalences of the Fair Trade

[58]'Alter-na(t)iver Handel' (Archive of the AG3WL, AG3WL-Newsletter no. 13, 25–29).

[59]Ibid., 27.

[60]'Arbeitsgruppe: Alternative Ökonomie im 3. Welt-Laden und bei den Produzenten' (Archive of the AG3WL, AG3WL Newsletter no. 16, February 1986, 24–28).

[61]'Schöne Schaufenster' (Archive of the AG3WL, AG3WL Newsletter no. 34, January 1989, 6–7).

[62]'Arbeitsgruppe: Alternative Ökonomie', 25.

[63]'GEPA: Wohin?—Mit wem?' (Archive of the AG3WL, AG3WL Newsletter no. 18, 1986, 6–7).

concept became most obvious. Criticizing consumer societies by means of an alternative consumption model inevitably provoked some internal rifts in the movement, and activists continually debated the problems and pitfalls of the concept. On the one hand, these debates went to the very possibility of establishing a business model that did not follow the economic rationales of the capitalist system—for example, by refraining from the drive to make profits, the logic of competition or the goal of ever-increasing market expansion. On the other hand, though, the proclaimed 'alternative' character of Fair Trade had meanwhile acquired an economic rationale of its own. By the 1980s, 'ethical consumption' had begun to emerge as a consumer market in its own right. In this context, world shops increasingly saw themselves confronted with the expectations of a new group of 'critical consumers' to whom they had to address their products. World shops became in part places of 'anti-capitalist consumption' in which Fair Trade products not only constituted a specific form of development aid in the Global South, but were also supposed to embody the anti-capitalist sentiments of its consumers in the Global North. Some critics have deplored this as a process of 'commodification', in which Fair Trade consumption became a social practice of 'distinction' much along the lines of Bourdieu's analysis of the 'social production of taste'.[64] From a historian's point of view, though, it is more interesting to ask how Fair Trade activists and world shops tried to bridge this tension between a political critique of consumption and the creation of a genuine consumer segment of its own.

This tension can be linked to the question outlined earlier as to whether Fair Trade activists really saw their campaign as an attempt to 'moralize capitalism'. As I have shown, three lines of argument were particularly pertinent in the Fair Trade movement (without being mutually exclusive). Activists interpreted Fair Trade as an alternative to traditional charity and philanthropy approaches. Creating more just relationships between producers and consumers was thus intended as

---

[64] Pierre Bourdieu, *Distinction: A Social Critique of the Judgement of Taste* (Cambridge, MA: Harvard University Press, 1984), first published as *La Distinction: Critique Sociale du Jugement* (Paris: Éditions de Minuit, 1979). On Fair Trade as form of 'distinction' and 'conspicuous consumption', cf. for example, Zick Varul, 'Ethical Consumption: The Case of Fair Trade'. Within a more general framework, see Amihai Glazer and Kai A. Konrad, 'A Signaling Explanation for Charity', *The American Economic Review* 86, no. 4 (1996): 1019–1028.

a way of helping people in developing countries without establishing donor–recipient hierarchies. This idea was particularly important in the early concept papers of the Fair Trade movement. While this approach explicitly referred to the moral significance of individual acts of consumption, it did not necessarily intend a more general critique of economic structures. In opposition to this approach, other activists at the same time argued for a much more political interpretation of the 'third world trade campaign'. For them, selling products from the 'third world' had the primary objective of critiquing political decisions in the Global North and of calling attention to global economic inequalities. It was this approach that led to the cane sugar and Aluschok campaigns in the 1970s and was again emphasized by the activists from the countercultural networks in the 1980s. This approach clearly aimed at a more profound change of economic structures, but it is doubtful whether activists saw it as an attempt to '*moralize* capitalism'. Instead, they predominantly referred to a political and economic critique that in their view went beyond mere references to moral values.

It was the third model, namely the educational dimension of the Fair Trade concept, that can most appropriately be described as an attempt to 'moralize capitalism'. From the outset, Fair Trade activists had claimed that they were mainly concerned with raising awareness for development politics. Even though the same activists were often frustrated by the lack of response to these campaigns, it was this educational dimension that most directly referred to a concept of 'moralization'. But under closer scrutiny, it was not capitalism itself that was the object of 'moralization' but rather the individual consumers who operated within these capitalist structures. In order to change global economic structures, Fair Trade activists claimed, the best approach was to educate Western consumers about their individual contribution to maintaining them. On the one hand this was an empowering discourse because it asserted that everyday consumer practices could contribute to a transformation of the global economy. On the other hand, of course, the opposite was also true: Insisting on the primary importance of individual acts of consumption also meant leaving it to the individual consumer to act as the agent of social change, ignoring the fact that most of the problems that the Fair Trade activists had identified lay to a large extent beyond the power of individual consumer decisions to influence.

It is therefore not surprising that these competing concepts of an 'alternative' model of trade triggered myriad controversies throughout the history of the Fair Trade movement, and still do so today. In the long run, an explicitly political approach lost ground, particularly in the early 1990s when the movement introduced its Fair Trade certificates and entered the mainstream consumer markets. It was in this period that Fair Trade became in public discourse a symbol for new concepts of a 'moralization' of capitalism.[65] It would be easy to criticize this development of the last two decades by arguing that the Fair Trade movement began to capitalize on its own anti-capitalist sentiments; but this narrative of 'commodification' only points to one side of the story and fails to apprehend the movement's ambivalences and ambiguities. Instead, it seems more fascinating to look for the tensions that arose when activists tried to combine their own anti-capitalist agenda with attempts to create a new way of consuming within a capitalist society.

[65] See, for example, Phil Wells and Mandy Jetter, *The Global Consumer: Best Buys to Help the Third World* (London: Gollancz, 1991).

CHAPTER 13

Economic Boom, Workers' Literature, and Morality in the West Germany of the 1960s and Early 1970s

Sibylle Marti

The period of economic boom after the Second World War has gone down in West German historical memory as the 'German economic miracle' (*deutsches Wirtschaftswunder*).[1] Already known as such during this time, the rubric refers to the rapid economic resurgence during the Adenauer/Erhard chancellorships. In the conventional narrative of this 'miracle' as penned in Werner Abelhauser's classic account, economic growth from the early 1950s to the early 1980s precipitated an almost fourfold increase in real per-capita social product, increased individual affluence, led to full employment, dampened social conflicts, contributed

---

[1] On the semantics of the term 'economic miracle', see Martin Wengeler, 'Vom Jedermann-Programm bis zur Vollbeschäftigung. Wirtschaftspolitische Leitvokabeln', in *Politische Leitvokabeln in der Adenauer-Ära. Mit einem Beitrag von Dorothee Dengel*, eds. Karin Böke, Frank Liedtke and Martin Wengeler (Berlin, New York: Walter de Gruyter, 2011), 431–433.

S. Marti (✉)
FernUniversität, Hagen, Germany
e-mail: sibylle.marti@fernuni-hagen.de

S. Berger and A. Przyrembel (eds.), *Moralizing Capitalism*,
Palgrave Studies in the History of Social Movements,
https://doi.org/10.1007/978-3-030-20565-2_13

293

to political stability, and constituted a virtually undisputed set of guiding principles for the society.[2] Due to the 'economic miracle' West Germany underwent what Abelhauser has called a '"deproletarianization" of the labour force' by no later than the 1960s that was reflected particularly in a transformation of the proletarian milieu and associated mentalities.[3] Mark Spoerer and Jochen Streb, too, have emphasized the socioeconomic 'dynamics of the recovery', pointing out that contemporaries ascribed the 'economic miracle' and the rising standard of living more than anything else to industriousness and wage discipline, both incentivized by the regulatory role of the social market economy and the security it provided.[4] Anselm Doering-Manteuffel and Lutz Raphael peg the peak of the boom in West Germany at the 1960s, when its impact became widespread and found expression in the topos of the 'idyll of sweat' (*schwitzendes Idyll*).[5]

Hartmut Kaelble has recently refined these and similar interpretations into the conclusion that, while social inequalities were indeed mitigated as income and wealth disparity declined during the economic boom, little changed for the lowest social stratum in terms of housing, health, educational opportunities and social mobility.[6] Notwithstanding such caveats, 'les trente glorieuses' between 1945 and 1975 in West Germany and other Western European countries rank in both collective memory and historical accounts as *the* period of an emergent affluent consumer society; as noted by Doering-Manteuffel and Raphael, 'Around 1960 the boom reached the little man in all Western European countries.'[7]

Far less well known, and also less present in historical memory, are contemporary narratives that called the success story of the 'German economic miracle' into question. As of the start of the 1960s—thus at the peak of the boom—these perceptions and interpretations functioned

---

[2] Werner Abelshauser, *Deutsche Wirtschaftsgeschichte. Von 1945 bis zur Gegenwart. Zweite, überarbeitete und erweiterte Auflage* (München: C. H. Beck, 2011), 283–284.

[3] Abelshauser, *Deutsche Wirtschaftsgeschichte*, 328–331, quotation 328.

[4] Mark Spoerer and Jochen Streb, *Neue deutsche Wirtschaftsgeschichte des 20. Jahrhunderts* (München: Oldenbourg, 2013), 211, 226, quotation 211.

[5] Anselm Doering-Manteuffel and Lutz Raphael, *Nach dem Boom. Perspektiven auf die Zeitgeschichte seit 1970, 3., ergänzte Auflage* (Göttingen: Vandenhoeck & Ruprecht, 2012), 39, 60–61, quotation 39, 61.

[6] Hartmut Kaelble, *Mehr Reichtum, mehr Armut. Soziale Ungleichheit in Europa vom 20. Jahrhundert bis zur Gegenwart* (Frankfurt am Main, New York: Campus, 2017), 63–101, 171–177.

[7] Doering-Manteuffel and Lutz Raphael, *Nach dem Boom*, 38.

as an early counter-narrative to widespread notions of social advancement and dissolving class antagonisms. This critique crystallized at the height of the economic recovery in the output of Dortmund Group 61 (*Dortmunder Gruppe 61*) and its offshoot the Literature of the Workplace Writers' Group (*Werkkreis Literatur der Arbeitswelt*), which used literary and artistic methods to confront the world of work and its social problems. At the same time, influential actors from politics, business and the press expended significant effort to marginalize these critical voices discursively, attempting in numerous essays, reports and reviews to discredit this new form of workers' literature as strongly exaggerated, literarily inadequate and ideologically suspect.

Underlying both the portrayals of Group 61 and the Workplace Writers' Group and also the arguments of their critics were decidedly moral categories and ideas. Thus, certain forms and conditions of labour viewed as undignified and inhumane constituted the main subject of West German workers' literature, whose narratives fed into the central demand for the humanization of the industrialized world of work. In turn, critics of this workers' literature appealed to morally charged views about the 'economic miracle', the questioning of which was seen as tantamount to violating a taboo. The writings of Group 61 and the Workplace Writers' Group, as well as their reception in the public media, illustrate the strong degree to which discourses and interpretations of the boom were disputed and normatively charged within society.

Following on E. P. Thompson's concept of the moral economy, Stefan Berger and Alexandra Przyrembel have recently called for more significance to be accorded in historical analysis to the moral notions associated with capitalism. They note that capitalism has always been subjected to moral critique, and that a main feature of this critique has been focused on 'the understanding of work'.[8] Thus, perceptions of work and working conditions have been strongly linked to ideas on morality. Picking up on these considerations, I will show that even during the heyday of West Germany's economic growth, 'work' and the 'work regime' were negotiated in moral terms and categories, which at their core involved a disputed understanding of the affluent society's potential for social integration and the repositioning of West Germany under the auspices of the Cold War.

---

[8] Stefan Berger and Alexandra Przyrembel, 'Moral, Kapitalismus und soziale Bewegungen. Kulturhistorische Annäherungen an einen 'alten' Gegenstand', *Historische Anthropologie* 24, no. 1 (2016): 88–107, quotation 89.

Workers' Literature Between Literary Aspirations and Political Practice

Dortmund Group 61 was started in 1961 by the Dortmund library director Fritz Hüser, the mine worker and author Max von der Grün,[9] and the trade unionist Walter Köpping.[10] It primarily brought together authors, journalists, lecturers, critics, scholars, and others whose literary output about the industrial workplace was based either in their interest or occupational experience. Founding member Max von der Grün and journalist Günter Wallraff, who joined Group 61 in 1966, became two of the group's most prominent and widely acclaimed representatives.[11] At the same time, between them they also represented the two formative trends of West German workers' literature of the 1960s and early 1970s. Whereas von der Grün achieved great renown with his industrial novels, which were based on his own experiences as a mine worker, Wallraff elicited a strong public response with his undercover investigative reports on industrial workplaces.

It is no coincidence that Group 61 formed in the Ruhr region. Here the one-sided structural dependence on the coal and steel industry gave rise to crises and structural change earlier than in other regions and economic sectors of West Germany. Abelshauser speaks about the 'contrary trends of "economic miracle" and "mining crisis"',[12]

---

[9]On the life and work of Max von der Grün see Rüdiger Scholz, *Max von der Grün. Politischer Schriftsteller und Humanist. Mit einer Würdigung von Werner Bräunigs 'Rummelplatz'. Anhang: Dokumente und Interviews* (Würzburg: Königshausen & Neumann 2015); *Literatur in Westfalen. Beiträge zur Forschung* 9 (2008); and Gisela Koch, *Zum 70. Festschrift für Max von der Grün* (Dortmund: Stadt-und Landesbibliothek, 1996).

[10]On the history and work of the 'Dortmund Group 61', see Ute Gerhard and Hanneliese Palm, eds., *Schreibarbeiten an den Rändern der Literatur. Die Dortmunder Gruppe 61* (Essen: Klartext, 2012); Gertrude Cepl-Kaufmann and Jasmin Grande, eds., *Schreibwelten—Erschriebene Welten. Zum 50. Geburtstag der Dortmunder Gruppe 61. Herausgegeben im Auftrag des Fritz-Hüser-Instituts* (Essen: Klartext, 2011); and Rainer Noltenius, 'Das Ruhrgebiet—Zentrum der Literatur der industriellen Arbeitswelt seit 1960', in *Die Entdeckung des Ruhrgebiets. Das Ruhrgebiet in Nordrhein-Westfalen 1946–1996*, eds. Jan-Pieter Barbian and Ludger Heid (Essen: Klartext, 1997), 444–457.

[11]On the life and work of Günter Wallraff see Ina Braun, *Günter Wallraff—Leben, Werk, Wirken, Methode* (Würzburg: Königshausen & Neumann, 2007); Jürgen Gottschlich, *Der Mann, der Günter Wallraff ist* (Köln: Kiepenheuer & Witsch, 2007); and Wilfried Kriese, *In meinen Augen Günter Wallraff* (Rottenburg am Neckar: Mauer Verlag, 2004).

[12]Werner Abelshauser, *Der Ruhrkohlenbergbau seit 1945. Wiederaufbau, Krise, Anpassung* (München: C. H. Beck, 1984), 117.

Christoph Nonn about the onset of a 'process of deindustrialization'.[13] From the late 1960s the coal and steel industry would be propped up with state interventions and subsidies. The formative social and mental changes experienced in the Ruhr region in this period have been highlighted by Werner Plumpe. He maintains that as the transformation of the traditional milieu was accompanied by an improvement in material living conditions, in terms of mentality the declining community consciousness—particularly for young people—was linked to greater personal autonomy and individual control over time and consumption. Overall, this had made it possible to break open the 'narrowness of proletarian existence'.[14]

This historical analysis is convincing and accurate in many respects. However, it is worth noting that its narrative, which we see now as emphasizing the opportunities for social advancement and greater individual autonomy, was the very one that the writings of Group 61 called into doubt. Proponents of workers' literature in 1970 summarized the socioeconomic conditions at the time of the group's founding as follows:

> Group 61 arose at a time that today, one decade later, is more clearly recognizable as a time of upheaval in the Federal Republic: the economic reconstruction was essentially completed; it was in the Ruhr region that the 'economic miracle' first became threadbare for many—the spectre of economic crisis, presumed to be dead, entered the eat-in kitchens of the little people along the Ruhr in the form of a coal crisis; the militant anti-Communism of the fifties, which for a long time could persuade the public and workers that the proletariat, the working class, class struggle no longer existed, ... that self-satisfied, hegemonically pious ideology that ... wanted to see nothing but affluence and progress in the FRG, lost its persuasiveness in the face of realities.[15]

---

[13] Christoph Nonn, *Die Ruhrbergbaukrise. Entindustrialisierung und Politik 1958–1969* (Göttingen: Vandenhoeck & Ruprecht, 2001), 9.

[14] Werner Plumpe, 'Das Ende der Koloniezeit. Gedanken zur Sozial- und Wirtschaftsgeschichte des Ruhrgebietes in den 50er und frühen 60er Jahren', in *Die Entdeckung des Ruhrgebiets. Das Ruhrgebiet in Nordrhein-Westfalen 1946–1996*, eds. Jan-Pieter Barbian and Ludger Heid (Essen: Klartext, 1997), 165.

[15] Karl D. Bredthauer, Heinrich Pachl and Erasmus Schöfer, 'Einleitung', in *Ein Baukran stürzt um. Berichte aus der Arbeitswelt*, eds. Bredthauer, Pachl and Schöfer (München: Piper, 1970), 8–9.

Three elements of this counter-narrative should be highlighted: First, it interprets the 1960s not as a boom time but rather as a crucial time of crisis and upheaval; second, it radically calls into question the 'economic miracle' as a guiding concept and the concomitant notion of social advancement; and, third, it rejects the image of an ostensibly classless society.

Despite its broad consensus regarding the social situation of workers, over time conflicts increasingly arose within the group, intensifying towards the end of the 1960s and leading to the formation in 1970 of the Literature of the Workplace Writers' Group, which emerged from an initiative of some Group 61 members but ultimately became independent of the group.[16] The books, brochures and journals of the Workplace Writers' Group subsequently achieved substantial circulation figures. In the Workplace Writers' Group's first decade of existence, 28 volumes appeared in one series alone, published by Fischer Taschenbuch Verlag[17]; and over 350 people were engaged in literary activities in around 25 local writing workshops.[18] The essential lines of conflict between representatives of Group 61 and proponents of the Workplace Writers' Group—which at first included both von der Grün and also Wallraff, but ultimately only the latter—can be traced back to three basic questions: Who writes workers' literature, for which audience, and to what end?

The authors of Group 61—as Fritz Hüser maintained in an anthology the group put out in the mid-1960s—were 'not writing as workers for workers'. Rather, the point was to 'make a contribution to

[16]On the history and work of the 'Working Circle for Literature of the Work World', see Noltenius, 'Das Ruhrgebiet'; Horst Hensel, *Werkkreis oder Die Organisierung politischer Literaturarbeit. Die Entstehung des Werkkreises Literatur der Arbeitswelt als Modell kultureller Emanzipation von Arbeitern* (Köln: Pahl-Rugenstein, 1980); and Peter Fischbach, Horst Hensel and Uwe Naumann, eds., *Ein Baukran stürzt um. Berichte aus der Arbeitswelt* (München: Piper, 1979).

[17]Peter Fischbach, Horst Hensel and Uwe Naumann, eds., 'Wozu dieses Buch?' in *Zehn Jahre Werkkreis Literatur der Arbeitswelt. Dokumente, Analysen, Hintergründe* (Frankfurt am Main: Fischer, 1979), 8.

[18]Peter Fischbach, 'Der "Werkkreis Literatur der Arbeitswelt"', in *Zehn Jahre Werkkreis Literatur der Arbeitswelt. Dokumente, Analysen, Hintergründe*, eds. Fischbach, Horst Hensel and Uwe Naumann (Frankfurt am Main: Fischer, 1979), 13.

the literary configuration of all pressing issues and expressions of our society, dominated as it is by technology and "affluence"'. What mattered here, Hüser further explained, was 'the topic and the ability to represent it artistically'.[19] Thus proponents of Group 61 understood workers' literature, or literature of the working world, not primarily as literature created by workers but rather as literary portrayals of the current topics and issues of industrialized modernity. Accordingly, the group did not have the working class in mind as its target audience but rather the general (educated middle-class) public, which was assumed to read the works for their artistic/aesthetic value as much as anything else.[20]

The members of the Workplace Writers' Group found this constraint on the artistic and literary engagement with the working world highly problematic because the resulting texts abandoned their potential for explosive political force.[21] Political impact and the associated formation of working class consciousness were what proponents of the Workplace Writers' Group were most interested in achieving. In 1973 Erasmus Schöfer, the spokesman of the Workplace Writers' Group, explained: 'Translated into our practice, this means quite simply that we make visible and disseminate the defensive and emancipatory struggles of our class comrades ... with their methods, difficulties, and above all their successes.'[22] These goals were also accompanied by the Workplace Writers' Group's cultivated closeness to the workers' movement and its organization.[23]

In the wake of this program, a new perspective on workers developed at the end of the 1960s as well. Now they were not only considered the target audience for workers' literature but were also supposed to

[19] Fritz Hüser, 'Vorwort', in *Almanach der Gruppe 61 und ihrer Gäste*, eds. Hüser and Max von der Grün in Zusammenarbeit mit Wolfgang Promies (Neuwied, Berlin: Luchterhand, 1966), 26.

[20] Heinz Ludwig Arnold, 'Arbeiterliteratur in der Bundesrepublik', in *Arbeiterliteratur in der Bundesrepublik Deutschland. Gruppe 61 und Werkkreis Literatur der Arbeitswelt*, eds. Ilsabe Dagmar Arnold-Dielewicz and Arnold (Stuttgart: Ernst Klett, 1975), 11–12.

[21] Heinz Ludwig Arnold, 'Vorbemerkung', in *Gruppe 61. Arbeiterliteratur—Literatur der Arbeitswelt?* ed. Arnold (Stuttgart, München, Hannover: Richard Boorberg, 1971), 8.

[22] Erasmus Schöfer quoted in Fischbach, 'Werkkreis Literatur der Arbeitswelt', 12–13.

[23] Arnold, 'Arbeiterliteratur in der Bundesrepublik', 19.

become increasingly active in writing themselves.[24] This new attitude was exemplified in the first reportage contest launched in 1969, which spurred workers to compose their own texts.[25] The writings produced here were not so much supposed to embody a certain aesthetic as attain—according to Günter Wallraff—a 'social truth, something like enlightenment'.[26]

But differences with regard to orientation and goals were not the only reason for the split between the Workplace Writers' Group and Group 61. Another was the fundamental change of the social context towards the end of the 1960s. In particular, the recession of 1966/1967, student unrest, the protests against the emergency laws, and the strike of 1968/1969 contributed to the polarization of sociopolitical topics—and this included debates about 'work'.[27] Against the background of these virulent disputes, it was only logical for the initiators of the Workplace Writers' Group to shift the focus of their efforts from the literary aspirations of workers' literature to associated political practices. Protagonists of the Workplace Writers' Group in 1970 asserted: 'Writing as an activity … is not just a substitute for so-called direct political action; it is also not just a means for creating the preconditions for political action: it is itself political action ….'[28] Writing was deemed to be an explicitly political act to help develop not only workers' self-assurance and consciousness but also their self-empowerment and emancipation.

For all their programmatic differences, Dortmund Group 61 and the Literature of the Workplace Writers' Group jointly played a pioneering role in introducing the topic of 'work' to the West German public and shaping it in a socially critical manner. The next section elucidates the issues addressed by this social criticism, which from the outset was politically perceived and politically disputed.

---

[24] Bredthauer, Pachl and Schöfer, 'Einleitung', 10.

[25] Bredthauer, Pachl and Schöfer, *Ein Baukran stürzt um*.

[26] Interview mit Max von der Grün und Günter Wallraff, aufgenommen in Berlin am 12 December 1970, Gesprächsführung: Hanno Beth, in *Gruppe 61. Arbeiterliteratur— Literatur der Arbeitswelt?* ed. Heinz Ludwig Arnold (Stuttgart, München, Hannover: Richard Boorberg, 1970), 159.

[27] Fischbach, 'Der "Werkkreis Literatur der Arbeitswelt"', 11.

[28] Bredthauer, Pachl and Schöfer, 'Einleitung', 18.

CRITIQUE OF FORDIST WORKING CONDITIONS
AND THE LIMITS OF WHAT COULD BE SAID

Dortmund Group 61 achieved a considerable public response within a relatively short time after being founded. This was reflected not only by numerous discussions and reports in newspapers and (literary) journals but also by many radio features and television broadcasts.[29] I will discuss this development chiefly with reference to the industrial novel *Irrlicht und Feuer* (Will-o'-the-Wisp and Fire) by Max von der Grün and the first investigative reports on industrial workplaces by Günter Wallraff, which both garnered particular attention in the public eye.

First published in 1963, the novel *Irrlicht und Feuer*, which was translated into 14 languages and also made into a movie, brought the mine worker Max von der Grün broad public attention as an author. It is about a pit worker named Jürgen Frohmann who loses his job during the coal crisis of the late 1950s and ultimately finds new work in an automated operation in the electrical industry. Having escaped the arduous labour of mining coal, Frohmann first perceives this job change as a social advancement. But this soon proves to be an illusion, because at the electrical company too the employer and works council are interested not in the needs and concerns of the workers but mainly in increasing performance and profit.[30]

The first investigative reports by Günter Wallraff, for which he went undercover as a worker in various industrial operations for three years, were published in 1966 under the title *Wir brauchen dich* (We Need You) after first appearing in the trade union journal *Metall*. In these reports Wallraff documents work on an automobile factory assembly line and on the scaffolding of a shipyard, piecework with a tube-cutting machine, and work in the sintering plant of a steel mill, creating a portrayal of modern factory work geared towards the ruthless exploitation of human labour and the unfettered pursuit of profit.[31] In 1970

[29] The treatment of the 'Dortmund Group 61' in the public media is extensively documented in the eponymously named holdings in the Archive of the Fritz-Hüser-Institute for Literature and Culture of the Work World in Dortmund. The Archive of the Fritz-Hüser-Institute, which also contains the holdings of the 'Literature of the Workplace Writers' Group', is henceforth referred to as AFHI.

[30] Max von der Grün, *Irrlicht und Feuer* (Recklinghausen: Paulus, 1963).

[31] Günter Wallraff, *Wir brauchen Dich. Als Arbeiter in deutschen Industriebetrieben. Mit einem Nachwort von Christian Geissler* (München: Rütten & Loening, 1966).

Wallraff's reports were republished under the title *Industriereportagen* (Industry Reports).[32]

Forming the central theme in the works by von der Grün and Wallraff are the difficult and/or monotonous working conditions in the mining industry, on production lines and in piecework; the authors describe the work as physically exhausting, hazardous to health and extremely unvaried, with minutely controlled tempos. Like other members of Group 61 and the Workplace Writers' Group, von der Grün and Wallraff thereby tallied the losses of a boom society founded on technological progress and production growth. They reproached the working regime, which they considered exploitative—but without condemning the technological advancement and automation of industrial operations per se.

The top priority was a social critique of the myth of the 'German economic miracle' and particularly the Fordist production system.[33] By the mid-1960s the latter had been established in Western Europe as a model for a stable economic and social order; it was based primarily on the highly standardized production of consumer goods, frequently manufactured in small work steps along assembly lines, and on securing mass demand through wage increases for the working class, achieved by means of involving trade unions in a social partnership.[34]

Around 1965, the degree of industrialization in West Germany reached its peak.[35] Concerning the Fordist working conditions in the Ruhr region's industrial operations, at that time the well-known German sociologist Helmut Schelsky diagnosed feelings of underprivilegedness and embitteredness over a 'distressing discrepancy' (*quälende Diskrepanz*) that were finding expression in workers' literature: While the majority had been freed from heavy labour through technological progress, still today a smaller section of the labour force must physically

---

[32] Günter Wallraff, *Industriereportagen. Als Arbeiter in deutschen Großbetrieben* (Reinbek bei Hamburg: Rowohlt, 1970).

[33] On Fordism as a production regime and period term, see Rüdiger Hachtmann, 'Fordismus', Version: 1.0, *Docupedia-Zeitgeschichte*, 27 October 2011, http://docupedia.de/zg/hachtmann_fordismus_v1_de_2011.

[34] Doering-Manteuffel and Raphael, *Nach dem Boom*, 39.

[35] Ulrich Herbert, *Geschichte Deutschlands im 20. Jahrhundert* (München: C. H. Beck, 2014), 627, 783–784.

toil.[36] This physical burden was no doubt also one of the reasons why, despite often earning higher wages than white-collar employees, workers still enjoyed less social prestige;[37] the 'farewell from drudgery' took longer in the Ruhr region than elsewhere, since particularly in mining physical and often dangerous heavy labour long remained part of daily working life.[38] This challenged the promise of the economic boom, which nourished hopes not only for gains in material affluence but also for improved working conditions.

The social demands raised in the texts and writings of Group 61 and later the Workplace Writers' Group consistently focused on the 'humanization of the work process'[39] and 'democratization and humanization of conditions'.[40] A 1972 review in the *Stuttgarter Zeitung* outlined the needs articulated in workers' literature:

> It is about democratically changing social circumstances, particularly about changing the workplace, and so the demand for co-determination crops up with increasing frequency. It is about workers sharing in the profits. Time and again it is ultimately about creating more humane conditions at the workplace. ... The senselessness of tasks is one of the main motifs in the texts. ... The monotony of always the same hand movement, if possible in piecework, kills mental and physical activity.[41]

The criticism of the prevailing industrial working regime formulated in the workers' literature essentially appealed to certain moral notions of what constituted humane and dignified work. As a result, the social criticism of Dortmund Group 61 and the Literature of the Workplace Writers' Group went beyond questioning the thesis of the levelled affluent society or the image of increasingly differentiated class structures as discussed in contemporary intellectual debates about the emergent

[36] Helmut Schelsky quoted in 'Arbeiterschriftsteller: Umgefallen wie abgesägt', *Der Spiegel*, 7 October 1964, AFHI, 502-12.

[37] Abelshauser, *Deutsche Wirtschaftsgeschichte*, 332.

[38] Wolfgang Hindrichs et al., *Der lange Abschied vom Malocher. Sozialer Umbruch in der Stahlindustrie und die Rolle der Betriebsräte von 1960 bis in die neunziger Jahre* (Essen: Klartext, 2009), in particular 13, 28–29, 31–33.

[39] Wallraff, *Industriereportagen*, preliminaries.

[40] Bredthauer, Pachl and Schöfer, 'Einleitung', 11.

[41] 'Sähen wir die Welt mal kritisch...', *Stuttgarter Zeitung*, 2 September 1972, AFHI, 502-176.

affluent consumer society.[42] This moral indignation took aim primarily at the deprivation of space and sense of human worth that workers suffered in a postwar industrial society shaped by Fordism.

The writings of von der Grün and Wallraff—as well as those by other members of Group 61 and the Workplace Writers' Group—created a huge sensation among the West German public. They commanded attention even from such prominent and powerful personalities as Federal Chancellor Konrad Adenauer.[43] Overall, however, the engagement with workers' literature was extremely ambivalent, ranging from recognition and official appreciation to resolute rejection and attempted censorship.

To be sure, as of the mid-1960s a number of Group 61 members were receiving prestigious prizes for their literary work. Thus Günter Wallraff and another member of the group received North Rhine-Westphalia's sponsorship award for young artists (*Förderpreis des Landes Nordrhein-Westfalen*).[44] But the granting of the award to Wallraff in 1968 provoked critical reactions from both the CDU faction in state parliament and the SPD minister-president, in response to which Wallraff donated his prize money of 6000 German marks to two civic organizations.[45]

The ambivalent reception of the workers' literature was also reflected in reviews by journalists and feature writers. Sympathetic reviewers tried to spare the texts of Group 61 and the Workplace Writers' Group from the fixation on the categories and forms of traditional literary thought

---

[42] On these debates see, for example, Friedrich Kiessling, '"Diktatur des Lebensstandards". Wirtschaftliche Prosperität, Massenkonsum und Demokratiebegründungen in liberalen und konservativen Gesellschaftsdeutungen der alten Bundesrepublik', in *Religion, Moral und liberaler Markt. Politische Ökonomie und Ethikdebatten vom 18. Jahrhundert bis zur Gegenwart*, eds. Michael Hochgeschwender and Bernhard Löffler (Bielefeld: Transcript, 2011), 237–260; Sabine Haustein, 'Zweifel an der Überflussgesellschaft: Die Konsumdebatte der europäischen Intellektuellen nach 1945', in *Selbstverständnis und Gesellschaft der Europäer. Aspekte der sozialen und kulturellen Europäisierung im späten 19. und 20. Jahrhundert*, eds. Hartmut Kaelble and Martin Kirsch (Frankfurt am Main: Peter Lang, 2008), 319–350. More widespread criticism about the consumer society emerged only in the 1970s, see Claudius Torp, *Wachstum, Sicherheit, Moral. Politische Legitimationen des Konsums im 20. Jahrhundert* (Göttingen: Wallstein, 2012), 92–128.

[43] 'Arbeiterschriftsteller: Umgefallen wie abgesägt', *Der Spiegel*, 7 October 1964, AFHI, 502-12.

[44] 'Literaten stellen sich dem Alltag', *NBZ an Rhein und Ruhr*, 5 November 1966, AFHI, 502-44.

[45] Wallraff, *Industriereportagen*, preliminaries.

and instead to acknowledge them as independent socially relevant literary contributions. Thus, for example, the well-known literary critic and author Horst Krüger opined: 'Evidently our literary augurs time and again make the mistake of observing literature only in the display case of literature. As if it had nothing to do with society, with morality and the originary power of the writer, as if it is only language. It is the old bourgeois notion that one can with impunity detach literature from society. One cannot do it.'[46] And in the renowned cultural journal *Merkur* a review argued that workers' literature should not be judged according to purely formal literary criteria, for it is 'something different from a literature of found texts; they appeal not to an aesthetic sensitivity but to a moral one. Basically, the critical reader must ask himself: Where do I stand with regard to the world represented here? The objections will depend on the answer to this question.'[47] Along with such nuanced assessments, reviewers also expressed harsh criticism. Critics sometimes adopted a didactic tone to find fault with the pathos, hyperbole, and/or clichés in these writings. This is exemplified by a discussion in the influential and widely circulating news magazine *Der Spiegel* of the Group 61 anthology of 1966. Among other things, the piece states: 'Reading this anthology strengthens the impression that one is dealing with a literary world of stencil shapes that distorts reality instead of clarifying it.' The *Spiegel* reviewer went on to accuse individual contributions of 'overemphasis' and 'caricature' as well as 'prejudice', 'legend poetry', and 'triteness', ultimately arriving at the devastating verdict that in the anthology 'the stencil shapes are naively written out or stylistically covered with make-up so that the old positions of our literature confront each other unchanged: platitudinous convention and manneristically stylized grimaces.'[48] Such literature reviews sought to dismiss workers' literature on formal grounds and thereby deprive it of any authenticity and connection with reality and thus of any socially critical impulse.

It is hardly surprising that the sympathetic assessments of workers' literature came often (if not exclusively) from left-liberal and church circles.

---

[46]'Die ohnmächtigen Kommissare der Sprache', *Die Welt*, 19 August 1965, AFHI, 502-42.

[47]'Die unbewältigte Arbeit—Zehn Jahre danach', *Merkur*, November 1971, AFHI, 502-83.

[48]Dieter Wellershoff, 'Mal was hinkriegen... Dieter Wellershoff über den "Gruppe 61"-Almanach "Aus der Welt der Arbeit"', *Der Spiegel*, no. 53, 26 December 1966.

Examples of the latter include publications from the Catholic Paulus Verlag, which initially published the works of Group 61. In contrast, members of Group 61 and the Workplace Writers' Group found themselves under sustained fire from not only conservative and right-wing positions but also from members of the far left. It was noted at the time that workers' literature was 'just as suspect to the Communists as to editors of the Springer group and naturally the employer bodies.'[49] Günter Zehm of the conservative Springer press, the features editor and later deputy editor-in-chief of *Die Welt*, stood out as an extremely vociferous critic of Group 61 and the Workplace Writers' Group. He described West German workers' literature as a 'phenomenon on the margins of literature', 'formally and intellectually undemanding' and overall plainly a 'qualitative disaster'. Regarding Max von der Grün's *Irrlicht und Feuer*, Zehm maintained that it was only because of the scandal that triggered a lawsuit against the novel that this book become 'literarily worthy in that fatal sense in which today as never before the incitement of a public scandal seems to be an entry ticket to the Parnassus of professional writing.'[50]

Going far beyond mere literary critique were the efforts of various companies to strike back by legal means against publications of members of the group. Thus one firm filed a suit regarding certain passages from Max von der Grün's *Irrlicht und Feuer* that described the death of a mine worker as the result of a newly introduced coal plough. Although von der Grün won the case after a trial that created quite a stir in the West German press, he was subsequently dismissed by the mine administration and the trade union distanced itself from him as well.[51] A few firms similarly tried to take legal action against certain reports from Günter Wallraff's *Wir brauchen dich* by filing for injunctions, compensatory damages, and lawsuits. Within the affected companies themselves, any solidarity with Wallraff was inhibited with the argument that he

---

[49]'Ich habe Angst. Doch dreh ich mich', *Echo der Zeit*, 31 October 1965, AFHI, 502-42.

[50]'Kann es "Arbeiterdichtung" geben? Notizen zu einer Erscheinung am Rande der Literatur', *Die Welt*, 9 January 1965, AFHI, 502-42. See also 'Nach acht Stunden wird abgeschaltet. Ist die Arbeit in den Fabriken "entfremdet"?—Neue Industriedichtung heute', *Die Welt*, 11 February 1967, AFHI, 502-56.

[51]'Der Kumpel-Autor und die Rache des Ruhrgebiets. Erfahrungen eines Romanschreibers mit ungeschriebenen Gesetzen', *Rheinischer Merkur*, 17 January 1964, AFHI, 502-12; 'Literaten stellen sich dem Alltag', *NBZ an Rhein und Ruhr*, 5 November 1966, AFHI, 502-44.

was disrupting 'workplace harmony' with his texts. On the same basis, Wallraff's opponents successfully persuaded the trade union journal *Metall* to stop printing his reports.[52]

Writings like those penned by Max von der Grün and Günter Wallraff evidently transgressed the limits of what could be said. Prominent figures in politics, business, and the media went to considerable lengths to discursively marginalize the content and views expressed in workers' literature. From today's perspective it comes as a surprise that the writings of Group 61 and the Workplace Writers' Group could trigger such strong reactions and emotions at both the bourgeois and the left-wing ends of the social spectrum. Why was workers' literature, with its demands for the humanizing and democratizing of the workplace, sometimes subjected to such sharp criticism?

'ECONOMIC MIRACLE', THE NAZI PAST, AND THE COLD WAR

The texts of Dortmund Group 61 and the Literature of the Workplace Writers' Group were already formulating a counter-narrative to the story of the 'German economic miracle' during the peak of the economic boom, thus well before the global economic crisis of the 1970s, which was perceived as a seismic shift by contemporaries as well. As shown by the ambivalent reception and sometimes fierce counterattacks, this opposing interpretation was felt as a provocation in broad sectors of the West German public. Central to this were three interrelated arguments through which proponents of workers' literature challenged the dominant 'economic miracle' narrative: They disputed, first, the widespread thesis of the dissolution of class oppositions; second, notions of an affluent society from which all social classes were able to benefit; and third, images of a harmonious social partnership that suggested a democratic involvement of workers at the operational level.

Critical voices in the public media that spoke out against the harsh repudiation of workers' literature did also point out the potential for provocation of these challenges. Thus an author in *Der Spiegel* observed that 'naturally hardly any songs of praise for the fully employed affluent society'[53] are yielded by the group's texts, while the previously

---

[52]Wallraff, *Industriereportagen*, 112–115, quotation 113.

[53]'Arbeiterschriftsteller: Umgefallen wie abgesägt', *Der Spiegel*, 7 October 1964, AFHI, 502-12.

mentioned Horst Krüger elaborated in *Die Welt*: 'How hard have critics strained, how much night-program wisdom was brought to bear already in the fifties, in order to establish why there is no place for committed workers' literature any more: the egalitarian industrial culture, the proletarian as the petty bourgeois of the consumer cooperative—it is all too familiar.'[54] The *Allgemeine unabhängige jüdische Wochenzeitung* (Independent Jewish Weekly) likewise stressed that people are 'not so keen in this country on having their affluent tranquillity upset, and certainly not by so-called workers' poets or writers whose reports, stories, or poems expose the slogan of the "pluralist society" as hypocrisy or concealment tactics or quite simply wishful thinking, and provide sign after sign that we still live in a class society'.[55] In turn, a feature writer for the *Stuttgarter Zeitung* broached the issue of lack of confidence in the social partnership: 'The gulf between top and bottom, between entrepreneur and wage earner, continues to exist and is clearly felt by the workers, despite the higher share of the social product that they earn. ... The workers' mistrust is directed at both the entrepreneur and the unions. ... There is no reason to think that the concept of the proletarian is outdated.'[56] Similarly, the political and cultural journal *Der Monat* discerned a 'taboo sensitivity' on the part of employers and unions that illustrated 'the social necessity of this literature as a contribution to the democratization process'.[57]

The members of Group 61 and the Workplace Writers' Group, too, were aware of the provocative impetus of their writing activities. Thus the author and member of Group 61 Hildegard Wohlgemuth put forward *Do we disturb?—That's our intent* as the latter's motto.[58] The goal was to expose contradictions in the existing social order, that is, between the hegemonic discourse and social reality. The challenge mounted in the workers' literature of the 1960s and early 1970s to notions of improved

[54]'Die ohnmächtigen Kommissare der Sprache', *Die Welt*, 19 August 1965, AFHI, 502-42.

[55]'Hinweise auf eine Klassengesellschaft', *Allgemeine unabhängige jüdische Wochenzeitung*, 21 March 1969, AFHI, 502-103.

[56]'Bergmannsleben ist nun mal so', *Stuttgarter Zeitung*, 20 May 1967, AFHI, 502-60.

[57]'Der Dortmunder Weg', *Der Monat*, November 1965, AFHI, 502-42.

[58]Hildegard Wohlgemuth quoted in Fritz Hüser and Max von der Grün in Zusammenarbeit mit Wolfgang Promies, eds., *Almanach der Gruppe 61 und ihrer Gäste* (Neuwied, Berlin: Luchterhand, 1966), preliminaries.

prosperity and social levelling associated with the 'economic miracle' collided with the topos of a performance-based society balanced by social partnership through which West Germany—with much discipline and hard work—achieved its reconstruction and economic prosperity. This emphasis on one's own achievement was also attractive because it enabled semantic and moral distancing from the Nazi past. Illustrative of such a perspective is the well-known statement by the conservative politician Franz Josef Strauss, who in the late 1960s as the federal finance minister maintained: 'A people that has brought forth these economic achievements has a right to not want to hear anything about Auschwitz anymore!'[59] As well as quite explicitly expressing what many in West Germany at this time no doubt thought (at least secretly), Strauss's statement also illustrates the narrative's highly charged nature in terms of morality and policies regarding Germany's past. In his book *Postwar*, Tony Judt has emphasized the contribution of the Nazi period to the postwar boom, which contemporaries blocked out at the time. For one, according to Judt, West Germany's extraordinary economic recovery benefited significantly from capital investments made during the Nazi period; for another, little of the country's critical infrastructure had been destroyed by the war.[60] The guiding concept of the 'economic miracle' itself served to conceal these continuities with the Nazi dictatorship. Thus, with regard to Germany's politics of the past, challenges to this narrative were hardly welcome.

The reception of workers' literature was also substantially influenced by the period's international political conflicts. Playing a decisive role here against the background of the ongoing Cold War was the close eye that East and West Germany kept on each other and thus the way that West German workers' literature came to be perceived in the GDR and other Eastern Bloc states. In fact, the works of Group 61 were positively received and disseminated in the GDR early on. Walter Ulbricht, the head of the East German state, was said to be an appreciative reader of Max von der Grün's industrial novels. The East German *Berliner Zeitung* serialized von der Grün's *Irrlicht und Feuer* shortly after it appeared in the West, and by 1964 the East Berlin Aufbau Verlag

[59] Franz Josef Strauss quoted in Karl Gerold, 'Strauß—unser aller Risiko', *Frankfurter Rundschau*, no. 212, 13 September 1969.

[60] Tony Judt, *Postwar: A History of Europe since 1945* (New York: The Penguin Press, 2005), 392–393.

published a licensed edition of the novel; the initial print run of 10,000 copies sold out quickly in East Germany.[61] In 1966 *Irrlicht und Feuer* was turned into a movie by the East German film studio DEFA; but not until two years later was the resulting TV movie also broadcast in West Germany.[62] In 1967 Günter Wallraff's industry reports *Wir brauchen dich* were also issued by Aufbau Verlag, only one year after their publication in West Germany.[63] Consequently they generated plenty of interest not only in the GDR but also in Czechoslovakia, the Soviet Union, and Yugoslavia. This resonance in the Eastern Bloc was sufficient in West Germany's anti-Communist political climate of the mid-1960s to register on the radar of political surveillance. Thus shortly after the publication of his industry reports Wallraff was subpoenaed by the political police in Cologne because of a 'suspicion of treasonous relationships'.[64]

The writings of Group 61 initially became known in the GDR primarily through articles that began appearing in the weekly *Sonntag* in 1964. Here its output was presented as a 'qualitative leap in the development of West German literature'.[65] Thus the group received the recognition for its work from the GDR that—at least in its own eyes—it was denied in West Germany.[66] The members of Group 61 also cultivated personal contacts with authors and literary specialists from Eastern Bloc countries. Max von der Grün, for example, became a member of the renowned international authors' association German PEN Centre East and West, headquartered in East Berlin.[67] In the early 1970s the

---

[61]'Arbeiterschriftsteller: Umgefallen wie abgesägt', *Der Spiegel*, 7 October 1964, AFHI, 502-12.

[62]For information on the movie, see http://www.imdb.com/title/tt0233953/?ref_=nv_sr_1.

[63]Günter Wallraff, *'Wir brauchen Dich.' Als Arbeiter in deutschen Industriebetrieben* (Berlin, Weimar: Aufbau-Verlag, 1967).

[64]Wallraff, *Industriereportagen*, 111.

[65]Wolfgang Friedrich, 'Bemerkungen zum literarischen Schaffen der Dortmunder Gruppe 61', in *Almanach der Gruppe 61 und ihrer Gäste*, eds. Fritz Hüser and Max von der Grün in Zusammenarbeit mit Wolfgang Promies (Neuwied, Berlin: Luchterhand, 1966), 315.

[66]Heinz Ludwig Arnold, 'Die Gruppe 61—Versuch einer Präsentation', in *Gruppe 61. Arbeiterliteratur— Literatur der Arbeitswelt?* ed. Arnold (Stuttgart, München, Hannover: Richard Boorberg, 1971), 18.

[67]'Arbeiterschriftsteller: Umgefallen wie abgesägt', *Der Spiegel*, 7 October 1964, AFHI, 502-12.

group twice welcomed visits from the Soviet Union, the first time hosting in Dortmund an author linked with the journal *Soviet Literature*, the second time a professor who worked on contemporary West German literature. In the eyes of the author for the Soviet literary journal, West German workers' literature distinguished itself 'above all through its relentless social criticism', writing that 'in these books the worker rearises, along with his awareness of life in the modern capitalist world. A world that is ostensibly already freed from social conflicts and contradictions.'[68] For his part, the Soviet literature professor found himself enamoured with Group 61 mainly because the focus of its work was 'still the decisive force, the working class'.[69]

Group 61 received a wide and approving response in the GDR and other Eastern Bloc states particularly because, from the perspective of these states, the West German workers' literature seemed to confirm images and ideas of a West German capitalism that exploited the working class. At the same time, the members of the group were very well aware that their writing activity was sometimes instrumentalized and moralized by parties on both sides of the East/West conflict for their own ideological purposes. Accordingly they viewed 'the sweeping condemnation of Springer's *Welt* against an independent workers' literature on the Ruhr as having a causal connection with the preceding sweeping praise that for the purpose of promoting empathy was bestowed by the East Berlin *Sonntag* as Cold War tit-for-tat'.[70] However, the political processes and reprisals, such as those endured by Max von der Grün and Günter Wallraff, show clearly that the suspicion of ideological motivation that members of Group 61 and later the Workplace Writers' Group sometimes came under in West Germany extended well beyond a literary

[68] Irina Mletschina quoted in '"Gruppe 61" wird in der Sowjetunion stark beachtet. Literaturzeitschrift stellt die Autoren vor und analysiert Werk', *Bochumer Rundschau*, 7 January 1971, AFHI, 502-83.

[69] Professor Zatonskij quoted in 'Literaturreise: Von Lenz bis Wallraff. Sowjetischer Professor studiert zeitgenössische BRD-Literatur', *Unsere Zeit*, 24 April 1971, AFHI, 502-170.

[70] 'Neue Grenzen angestrebt. Literatur aus der Arbeitswelt gewinnt an Profil', *Vorwärts*, 7 April 1965, AFHI, 502-42.

critique of what were perceived as traditional (Marxist) analytical categories such as 'alienation',[71] 'exploitation',[72] or 'class struggle'.[73]

Moral ideas and narratives about the 'German economic miracle', which were linked to both political dispositions regarding Germany's past and the competition between the East and West German systems during the Cold War, formed the essential contemporary backdrop against which one should view the sometimes harsh criticism of Dortmund Group 61 and the Literature of the Workplace Writers' Group in the West Germany of the 1960s and early 1970s. Paradoxically, however, these morally charged political contexts also helped the workers' literature achieve greater attention in the public media.

Conclusion

The works of Dortmund Group 61 and the Literature of the Workplace Writers' Group constituted notable contemporary counter-narratives to the 'German economic miracle' that have since been largely forgotten. The social criticism formulated in West German workers' literature in the 1960s and early 1970s focused on the affluent consumer society, which was seen to be failing to fulfil its promise, above all with regard to improving working conditions and humanizing the working regime for the lowest working stratum. It became clear in the workers' literature that the economic resurgence based on the Fordist production system did not do away with the overburdening of working bodies or with monotonous labour. From its perspective, the much-touted levelling of class antagonisms amounted to very little, at least when it came to working conditions and social prestige. Thus the texts of Group 61 and the Workplace Writers' Group were also essentially about immaterial values associated with 'work', that is, about recognition of worth, personal satisfaction, and self-realization, but also about self-determination and democratic involvement. Through this social criticism at the peak of the

---

[71] See, for example, 'Nach acht Stunden wird abgeschaltet. Ist die Arbeit in den Fabriken "entfremdet"?—Neue Industriedichtung heute', *Die Welt*, 11 February 1967, AFHI, 502-56.

[72] See, for example, 'Schwarzbrot für Bürger', *Der Spiegel*, 4 October 1971.

[73] See, for example, 'Worte—Waffen für den Klassenkampf? Bundestreffen des Werkkreises "Literatur der Arbeitswelt" in Frankfurt', *Süddeutsche Zeitung*, 23 May 1972, AFHI, 502-54.

boom, West German workers' literature anticipated two social debates that would increase in urgency during the following decades: those concerning changing values[74] and the precarity of employment.[75]

The members of Group 61 and the Workplace Writers' Group at times found themselves exposed to severe criticism in the public media and to legal and political attack. These conflicts turned chiefly on portrayals and interpretations of the period's boom society. In this respect, for important circles in politics, business and the media the works of Group 61 and the Workplace Writers' Group went beyond the bounds of what could be said because they undermined the hegemonic guiding concept of the 'economic miracle'. The latter was strongly formed as a norm and morally charged because it enabled a dual distancing from both the Nazi past and the socialist path of the GDR (even though the GDR too had achieved remarkable economic growth during the 1950s). The historiography of West Germany's 'trente glorieuses' often emphasizes the great extent to which notions and concepts of the 'economic miracle', commitment, and the social market economy were based on a broad social consensus. In contrast, the conflicts surrounding workers' literature show how these narratives and interpretations were also contested even at the height of the boom.

Both criticism and the emphatic affirmation of the narrative of the 'economic miracle' constitute specific West German forms of 'moralizing capitalism'. On the one hand, the dominant conceptions of an affluent consumer society realized thanks to industriousness, discipline, and performance referred to moralizing imperatives that sought to exclude critical voices. On the other hand, the demands for more humane and more dignified work in the modern industrial and performance-based society also resorted to notions of morality. The workers' literature demanded that the present booming economy safeguard moral principles, thus

[74] See, for example, Bernhard Dietz and Jörg Neuheiser, eds., *Wertewandel in der Wirtschaft und Arbeitswelt. Arbeit, Leistung und Führung in den 1970er und 1980er Jahren in der Bundesrepublik Deutschland* (Berlin, Boston: De Gruyter Oldenbourg, 2017); Bernhard Dietz, Christopher Neumaier and Andreas Rödder, eds., *Gab es den Wertewandel? Neue Forschungen zum gesellschaftlich-kulturellen Wandel seit den 1960er Jahren* (München: Oldenbourg, 2014).

[75] See, for example, Nicole Mayer-Ahuja, 'Die Globalität unsicherer Arbeit als konzeptionelle Provokation. Zum Zusammenhang zwischen Informalität im "Globalen Süden" und Prekarität im "Globalen Norden"', *Geschichte und Gesellschaft* 43, no. 2 (2017): 264–296.

formulating a social criticism that in West German post-war society was perceived as socially disruptive. One can therefore speak about a symmetrical moralization fuelled equally by exponents of workers' literature and its critics. For historiography, this means that the narratives regarding the economic boom have always been and still are morally charged.

Archive

Dortmund, Archive of the Fritz-Hüser-Institute for Literature and Culture of the Work World (Archiv des Fritz-Hüser-Instituts für Literatur und Kultur der Arbeitswelt, AFHI)

Holdings 502 'Dortmund Group 61' ('Dortmunder Gruppe 61')

- 502-12
- 502-42
- 502-44
- 502-56
- 502-60
- 502-83
- 502-103
- 502-170
- 502-176
- 502-254

INDEX

Note The index was compiled by Alessandra Exter.

A

Abelshauser, Werner, 296
Abrams, Frank, 152
Acheson, Dean, 145
Activism, 18, 153, 268, 270–73, 275,
    277, 279f., 282f., 285–88, 290–92
Adenauer, Konrad, 293, 304
Adimon, Charles F., 202
Adler, Mortimer, 137, 147–49, 153,
    157
Africa, v, 164, 171
Agnelli, Giovanni, 160, 176, 179
Aid, 145, 176, 288
    development aid, 22, 279f., 290
    foreign aid, 144, 154
    humanitarian aid, 2
Akerlof, George A., 188f.
Akron, USA, 150
Aktion Dritte Welt Handel (A3WH),
    277, 279, 281
Alberta, Canada, 121
Algeria, 12
Allende, Salvador, 167, 170
Althusserianism, 13

Amerikahaus Berlin, the, 137,
    139–141, 143
Amnesty International, 268
Anderson, Perry, 13
Anti-Semitism, 69f., 73f., 77, 206
Antwerp, William C. van, 189, 194
Appleby, Joyce, 80
Arbeitsgemeinschaft Dritte Welt Läden
    (AG3WL), 277f., 286–89
Argentina, 170
Aristotle, 92
Arizona, USA, 240
Arkansas, USA, 150, 240
Asceticism, 83–87, 92f., 101–103,
    106f.
Asia, v, 136, 146
Astouin, Louis Marius, 217, 223, 226
Athens, Greece, 253, 256f.
Atkinson, Tony, 80
Auschwitz, 309
Australia, 172
Autonomy, viii, 115, 125, 243, 297

Harvard, USA, 98, 154f.
Heald, Henry, 156
Hebrew, 90–92
Heidelberg, Germany, 34, 36
Hennis, Wilhelm, 94, 100
Hermann, Friedrich Benedict Wilhelm
  von, 32
Hilferding, Rudolf, 225
Hilton, Boyd, 49
Hirschmann, Albert, 14
Hitsman, J. Mackay, 132
Homo oeconomicus, 57
Honneth, Axel, 15
Hopkins, John, 43
Howell, James E., 155
Hübner, Otto, 53–56
Hufeland, Gottlieb, 32
Human rights, 3, 18, 182f., 273
Humanism, ix, 15, 138, 149, 154,
  156, 158, 246
  Neo-humanism, 49
Hume, David, 22
Hungary, 177
Hüser, Fritz, 296, 298f.
Hutchins, Robert, 137f., 147–49,
  153, 157
Hymer, Stephen, 178

I

Imperialism, 11f., 17, 154, 157, 164,
  169
India, v, xi, 120, 144, 154
Industrialization, 2, 66, 208, 217,
  225, 302
  Deindustrialization, 171, 297
Industry, 9, 16, 18, 24f., 36, 51, 68,
  80, 85f., 90, 119f., 122, 130f.,
  136–144, 151, 157, 166, 171,
  174, 187, 207f., 210, 218,
  222f., 225f., 280, 294–97, 299,
  301–304, 308–310, 313

Pre-industrial, 80, 90, 105, 254
Inflation, 130, 252, 260
Interventionism, 19, 239
Investment, investor, 6, 46, 50, 87,
  90, 116, 124, 131, 133, 146,
  150, 161, 163, 165, 171f., 176,
  179, 182, 198, 210, 217, 272,
  309
Invisible hand, 48, 175f., 180
Iran, 168
Ireland, 46, 233, 237f.
  Irish Poor Laws, 46
Italy, 40, 155f., 233, 263

J

Jacobin, 256
Jaffé, Edgar, 86
Jamaica, 172, 174
Jefferson, Thomas, 150
Judah Leib, Glikl bas, 75
Judaism. *See religion*
  anti-Jewish, 17, 73
Judt, Tony, 309
Justice, 3, 76, 79, 119, 131, 143, 168,
  171, 174, 180, 224, 242, 246,
  264f.
  economic justice. *See economy*
  distributive justice, 166, 242
  injustice, 60, 62, 80, 242, 282
  social justice, 142, 238f., 243,
  245f., 248

K

Kaelble, Hartmut, 294
Kansas, USA, 240
Kant, Immanuel, 10, 12, 269
Kautsky, Karl, 10
Kautz, Steven J., 16
Kelso, Louis, 148
Kennedy age, 250

Keppler, Rudolph, 187f.
Keynesianism, 163
Khaki election, 132
King, William Lyon Mackenzie, 133
Kissinger, Henry, 176
Knights of Columbus, the, 237
Kocka, Jürgen, xi, 4, 60, 80, 99
Koselleck, Reinhart, 33
Krüger, Horst, 305
Krugman, Paul, 59
Krupp von Bohlen und Halbach,
    Bertha, 67

L
Laboulie, Joseph de, 218, 222f.
Labour, v, vii, 9, 15, 20f., 24, 35–37,
    45, 47, 54–56, 60, 84, 86,
    88–93, 105, 108, 120, 125, 128,
    130, 142, 144, 169f., 172f., 182,
    213, 226, 248, 254, 256f., 260,
    294f., 301–303, 312
  child/children's labour, 60, 239f.,
    244
  division of labour, 45, 55, 84, 86,
    104
  forced labour, 9, 120
  labour movement. *See Movement*
  labour union, 121, 171, 256, 258f.
  manual labour, 36, 90, 92, 103
  wage labour, 21, 88, 104
Laclau, Ernesto, vi, 256, 266
Laissez-faire, 56, 144, 177
Lake Erie, Canada, 115
Lake Huron, Canada, 115
Latin, 91f., 206, 208
Latin America, v, 164, 166f., 178,
    271, 285
Laughlin, James, 146
Laurier, Sir Wilfrid, 119, 128, 131f.
League of Women Voters, the, 151
Leeds, Joseph Ryder of, 102

Lehmann, Hartmut, 95, 102
Lenin, Wladimir Iljitsch, 10
Leo XXIII, 235
Liberalism, 15, 116, 137, 169, 241,
    252, 274
  neo-liberalism, 15, 181, 274
Liberatore, Matteo, 241
Liberty, 139, 141, 148
Liotard-Vogt, Pierre, 176
Little Rock, USA, 150
Livingston, James, 122
London, UK, 14, 42, 66f., 210
    Broun-Ramsay, James Andrew, 1
    Marquess of Dalhousie, 114
Lord Strauss, Anna, 151
Lotz, Johann F.E., 50
Loyer, Eugène-Èmile, 222f.
Lukacs, George, 12
Luther, Martin, 83, 85, 90f., 93, 103
Luxemburg, Rosa, 10
Luxury, 22–24, 45, 68, 72, 84, 86,
    130
Lyon, France, 74

M
MacDonald, Dwight, 149
Macdonald, Sir John Alexander, 115,
    117f., 123, 133
Malthus, Thomas Robert, 35, 37, 39,
    42
Management, Manager, 24, 41, 52,
    101, 103, 108, 129, 137f., 144,
    151–58, 161, 163, 172, 174,
    180, 226, 258
Manchester, UK, 9, 66, 76
Mandeville, Bernard, 29
Manitoba, Canada, 130
Mann, Thomas, 147
Marcet, Jane, 38, 40–46
Market
  capital market, 209, 226

Printed by Printforce, the Netherlands